The Remasculinization of Korean Cinema

ASIA-PACIFIC Editors: Rey Chow, H. D. Harootunian, and Masao Miyoshi

Kyung Hyun Kim   **THE REMASCULINIZATION OF KOREAN CINEMA**

DUKE UNIVERSITY PRESS DURHAM AND LONDON 2004

2nd printing, 2005
© 2004 Duke University Press   All rights reserved
Printed in the United States of America on acid-free paper ∞
Typeset in Minion by Tseng Information Systems, Inc.
Library of Congress Cataloging-in-Publication Data
appear on the last printed page of this book.

For my parents
Byung Kon Kim and Yeon-sup Lee

CONTENTS

ACKNOWLEDGMENTS

The book was first conceived during the mid-1990s—at a time when various South Korean newspaper and magazine articles reported that its unhealthy national film industry might virtually be eliminated in a few years. Such predictions have proven to be capricious. On the contrary, Korean cinema in the early decade of the twenty-first century holds one of the most impressive box-office records among the active national film industries. In an exhibition environment replete with modern multiplex theaters where Hollywood films are known to have beaten every competitor, Korean cinema remains an anomaly. Its local products draw a large number of spectators—much larger than the days when quotas on import films were more restrictive and films relied on one-screen release. Korean cinema reached a historical climax in 2001 when it held all of the top five records in the annual box office. It was the first profitable year in decades for the entire industry, before production costs again rapidly exceeded the income revenue in 2002. The buying, selling, bankrupting, and rumored merging between two distribution giants (Cinema Service and CJ Entertainment) have made up the bulk of headlines in trade magazines since then.

The first two years of the new millennium (2001–2) should be remembered for the rising popularity of crass comedy films and the waning of the New Korean Cinema. Films like *Kick the Moon* (*Silla ŭi tal pam*), *My Wife Is a Gangster* (*Chop'ok manura*), *Hi Dharma* (*Talma ya nolja*), and *Marrying the Mafia* (*Kamun ŭi yŏnggwang*) topped the box-office chart for months and strongly reminded the Korean film industry of a tactless tagline, "the box office is never wrong," while the projects of many Korean directors whose names are synonymous with the New Korean Cinema, Im Kwon-Taek (*Chiwaseon*), Jang Sun-woo (*The Resurrection of the Little Match Girl*), Park Kwang-su (*The Trigger*), and Hong Sang-su (*Turning Gate*), either were aborted at the development stage or failed to show profitable figures to their investors. The prefix "new" that designated the crop of young filmmakers who emerged during the 1980s and the 1990s no longer became applicable. Their films were incapable of impressing the new generation of filmgoers in the era of multiplex theaters.

It is perhaps not a coincidence that this book on the New Korean Cinema is completed at a precise moment when it is finished as a movement. Though Korean cinema enjoys commercial success that is unprecedented in its history, many of its important production decisions are now made by distributors, corporate bigwigs, and talent agents rather than the writers and directors who constitute the very soul of the New Korean Cinema. Commercial priorities make artistic ones useless. The Korean film industry since 1999 has scrupulously followed the path of Hollywood and has shown more interest in making deals and formulaic genres than in innovating and devoting itself to the creation of art. In this book, I am critical of the ways in which the films of the New Korean Cinema have often refashioned the desire for "dominant men" as its most inscriptive trope, but I also duly acknowledge their efforts to create films that have made the historicization of Korean cinema a worthwhile scholarly venture.

Throughout the book, I employ psychoanalytic terms like "fetishism," "lack," and "phallus" not to validate theory but to better elucidate recent Korean films that have increasingly become "Westernized." Contemporary South Korean society is no more Confucian than it is capitalist. There is no doubt in my mind that most people in Korea would agree that the present society demands one to express his/her self, ego, and personal pride even if this means losing the hope of cultivating oneself into a humble Confucian sage. The New Korean Cinema of the last two decades has incessantly pursued themes, characterizations, and narratives that center on a particular notion of subjectivity: the image of an individual modern *man* desperate to free himself from institutional repression, familial responsibilities, and personal anxieties. Mired in the praxis of carving this new image, it can be argued that the cinema of the recent years parallels not the flourishing of its national traditional culture, but its rapid vanishing. In other words, the book aims to narrate the very cultural climate where the meaning of the "native" in the globalizing Korea has become obsolete.

I wish to gratefully acknowledge the help of many individuals and institutions that enabled me to write this book. Korea Foundation provided a valuable grant to assist my six-month research in Seoul in 1999–2000. The Korean Film Commission (KOFIC) and the Korean Film Archive also provided access to archives and films that were essential to this research. Secretary General Kim Hye-jun at KOFIC was especially kind to provide still photographs, which are reprinted in this book. Mr. Kim and his assistant, Ms. Kim Mi-hyun, helped obtain the legal clarification on the reprint use of motion picture stills. The Humanities Center at University of California, Irvine (UCI) and the Northeast Asia Council (NEAC) of the Association for Asian Studies also provided research funds for travel and other miscellaneous expenses. I would also like to thank the dean of my school and the former chair of my department at UCI; Dean Karen Lawrence and Chair Steven D. Carter played vital roles in this project, allowing me more time to concentrate on the arduous yet gratifying task of writing.

A number of friends and colleagues deserve special thanks for their suggestions and counsel. David E. James, Esther E. M. Yau, Henry H. Em, Chris Berry, Jim Fujii, Chungmoo Choi, Roland B. Tolentino, Akira Lippit, Eunsun Cho, Marsha Kinder, Ted Fowler, Kim U-chang, Soyoung Kim, Jinsoo An, and Tony Rayns have read parts of this manuscript from its dissertation stage and gave me encouragements to continue writing it. Kathleen McHugh and Nancy Abelmann also offered me incisive editorial comments that were instrumental in writing chapter 8. I owe a particular debt to Rey Chow, one of the editors of the Asia-Pacific series, for extending her invitation. David Scott Diffrient proofread the entire manuscript and kindly offered many thoughtful insights. The two anonymous readers of my manuscript at the Duke University Press also provided sharp editorial comments. My friends at *Cine 21* and *Kino*, two film journals in Korea, gave me opportunities to publish Korean language film reviews and criticisms. Writing in Korean and communicating my ideas to Korean readers helped me tremendously in the entire process of authoring this book. Kim Young-jin, Chung Sung-Ill, Lee Yeon-ho, Lee Young-jae, Huh Moon-young, and Nam Dong-chul especially deserve credit. *Kino* also helped me secure rare photographs.

Many directors have offered insights and shared with me behind-the-scenes stories. Many of these anecdotes could not be included in this book, but they were useful in painting a colorful backdrop of the South Korean film industry during an occasionally dull, oftentimes tedious process. In particular, directors Park Kwang-su, Im Kwon-Taek, Jang Sun-woo, Park Ki-hyung, Park Ki-yong, Hong Sangsoo (Hong Sang-su), and Lee Chang-dong (Yi Ch'ang-dong) were all great companions. Most films are made over a period of several years. I tried my best to clarify and analyze the work of these talented filmmakers after countless viewings of their films, but all of my discussions, I am sure, will never quite match the rigor and labor in which they were created.

I thank my parents, Byung Kon Kim and Yeon-sup Lee, who have always supported my scholarly pursuit. Lastly, Gina's perceptive power, forbearance, and love all equally contributed in the making of this book. In many ways, she is the coauthor of this book.

Portions of chapter 3 appeared, in different form, as "Is This How the War is Remembered?: Deceptive Sex and the Re-masculinized Nation in *The Taebaek Mountains*" in *Im Kwon-Taek: The Making of a Korean National Cinema*, ed. David E. James and Kyung Hyun Kim (Detroit: Wayne State University Press, 2002), 197–222. An earlier version of chapter 4 appeared as "Post-Trauma and Historical Remembrance in Recent South Korean Cinema: *A Single Spark* (1995) and *A Petal* (1996)" in the *Cinema Journal*, vol. 41, no. 4 (2002): 95–115. Chapter 5 was previously published as "Male Crisis in New Korean Cinema: Reading the Early Films of Park Kwang-su," in *positions: east asia cultures critique*, vol. 9, no. 2 (2001): 369–99. Portions of chapter 9 appeared in Korean language as " 'Namja ran chagi ka sarang hanŭn saram ŭl chuginŭn saram': *Shiri* wa *JSA* ŭi ilt'alja, kukka anbo, pŭlrŏkpŏsŭt'ŏ mihak" ("Each Man Kills the Thing He Loves": Transgressive Agents, National Security, and Blockbuster Aesthetics in *Shiri* [1999] and *Joint Security Area* [2000]), in *JSA*, ed. Paek Mun-im (Seoul, Korea: Saminsa, 2002).

Most libraries and Korean studies scholars in the United States conform to the romanization system that is known as the McCune-Reischauer system. The romanization of Korean terms, titles, and names in this book also follows this rule except for the names that have their own divergent orthography. The preferred names of certain directors whose works have been released in the United States have been retained without using the standard romanization system; they are Jang Sun-woo (Chang Sŏn-u), Park Kwang-su (Pak Kwang-su), and Im Kwon-Taek (Im Kwŏn-t'aek). Korean names are also transliterated in their native standard, with the surname first.

Introduction: Hunting for the Whale

Whale Hunting (*Korae sanyang*, Pae Ch'ang-ho, dir., 1984), one of Korea's biggest box-office films of the 1980s,[1] begins with a fantasy sequence in which the protagonist, Pyŏng-t'ae, dreams that he is standing naked before a laughing public. He is scantily clothed and lined up with bodybuilders whose muscularity accentuates his unattractive, bantamweight physique. The audience in the auditorium hosting this competition bursts into laughter. His oversized eyeglasses, his gap-toothed grin, and his petit stature are laid bare on stage, where he is left alone after the bodybuilders exit. Pyŏng-t'ae slowly regains his confidence and proceeds to strike a few bodybuilding poses, only to fall comically on his back. He is loudly jeered off the stage. Although the film's spectator at first laughs along with the auditorium audience at this surreal scene, it doesn't take long before the scornful laughter turns into sympathy. The scene thus sets the stage for the weak and emasculated Pyŏng-t'ae to make a strong appeal to the audience, who eventually want him to win back his love and, through a heterosexual reunion, regain his manhood. The audience will now root for him as he goes on the road to acquire his social, psychological, and libidinal autonomy.

This dream symptomizes not only the fear and anxiety of Pyŏng-t'ae, an idealistic college student who pledges to find a "whale" after failing to attract the attention of a female schoolmate he fancies, but also the predicament of a postcolonial and rapidly industrializing nation. Made just before the fervor for democracy hit the streets, *Whale Hunting* follows Pyŏng-t'ae as he falls in love with a mute prostitute, Ch'un-ja, and takes her back home to a remote island.

(After being rejected by the student he desires, he had slept with Ch'un-ja at a brothel.[2]) Aided by Wang-ch'o, a wise vagabond with a mysterious past, they journey to the very edge of Korea in bitter cold weather. The trip is Pyŏng-t'ae's quest for a heroic and autonomous identity through the realization of a romantic reunion while overcoming threats of death. Because this is ostensibly a comedy, many explicit symbols of male sexual anxiety are displayed through farcical situations. In one sequence, Pyŏng-t'ae narrowly escapes from a room full of outraged men by turning on a fire extinguisher. The limp hose attached to the red can "ejaculates" its content of white fluid. A couple of scenes later, he falls into a small pond located in a zoo. Cold, wet, and naked, Pyŏng-t'ae's primitive instincts are revived in this act of rebirth. It is here that he declares to Wang-ch'o that he will help Ch'un-ja find her way back home. (Ch'un-ja had been abducted from her hometown and sold into prostitution in the city.) Despite the fact that the three of them are hounded by a gang of muscular pimps equipped with sharp weapons, trendy motorcycles, and leather gear, the woman is returned to her mother. Upon the completion of their journey together, Ch'un-ja regains her voice, which was temporarily lost when she was traumatized in Seoul, and Pyŏng-t'ae regains his virility.

This image of Pyŏng-t'ae as a wandering college student during the 1970s and the 1980s is a popular icon of Korean subculture,[3] one that encapsulates several key themes. First, his transformation from a pathetic, masochistic, and aimless youth to a responsible man who is destined and determined to acquire his adulthood is the linchpin that anchors the narrative movement of not only *Whale Hunting* but also the New Korean Cinema of the 1980s and 1990s. This book traces the trajectory of masculinity as it undergoes this radical transformation, and seeks to explain the socio-political dynamics that underscore such narrative maneuvering.

Second, the remasculinization of Pyŏng-t'ae can only be defined by his relation to the woman and to historical trauma. The two characters who accompany Pyŏng-t'ae on his trip to look for a "whale," the whore and the male vagabond, function as displacements for the "castrated" subject. The predicament of Pyŏng-t'ae, a college student from a privileged background, pales beside that of Ch'un-ja, the wretched whore. The pairing of Pyŏng-t'ae with a woman who is far more disenfranchised than he is helps to disavow his male anxiety.[4] Pyŏng-t'ae's relationship to the vagabond, who is euphemistically called *Wang-ch'o* (Captain), identifies a more profoundly complicated and ruptured sense of history than the relationship between Pyŏng-t'ae and Ch'un-ja. Even though Wang-ch'o is a beggar who makes a living by panhandling for loose change in

An explicit scene of male sexual anxiety. *Whale Hunting* (1984).

Wang-ch'o (left) accompanies Pyŏng-t'ae and Ch'un-ja on their
quest to find a "whale." *Whale Hunting* (1984).

the street, he dispenses an eccentric authority and mysterious wisdom to which
Pyŏng-t'ae immediately submits. "Who exactly are you?" asks Ch'un-ja when
she recovers her voice. Is Wang-ch'o a former student activist who lost his mind
after being tortured by the police? Or is he just a restless youth who left his
bourgeois home in disgust to search for the truth and salvation associated with
a Buddhist way of life? The film does not answer these questions, but what is
clear is that he is a camouflaged man who cannot easily reveal his past, a past
that surely embodies a "trauma," which Slavoj Žižek defines as "an impossible
kernel which resists symbolization, totalization, symbolic integration."[5]

The character of Wang-ch'o resists any specific symbolic representation that
linguistically defines his trauma, and he becomes a repository of the historical
Real or, to use the Freudian "sublime," an experience so intense that it cannot be
properly enunciated. When asked by Ch'un-ja who he really is, Wang-ch'o first
winces painfully and then bursts into a playful dance and sings a *p'umba*, a "beggar's song" that became popular during the 1980s. Wang-ch'o's secret identity
rests within the repetitive "ŏlssigo . . . . chŏlssigo" which he hums, a celebratory
signifier that has no specific meaning. Ch'un-ja has found her home and her
voice and Pyŏng-t'ae has found his whale, but the words that can decode the
mysteries of Wang-ch'o and link his identity to a specific event or to history
remain unspoken; he is left as a floating subject. Only by the decade's end will

his camouflage, madness, and "hidden kernel" be illuminated. This knowledge not coincidentally overlaps the arrival of the New Korean Cinema.

The third theme that the icon of Pyŏng-t'ae embodies is resistance to an absolute, collective identification to project a self that is defined by private and libidinal principles. When Ch'un-ja's home is found, Pyŏng-t'ae has to return to the city alone, and this fact represents a new subjectivity that departs from Confucian ideals or rural identity. Pyŏng-t'ae's character has a modern self-awareness that is bewildered by both the resistance against and the need for social integration. He desires to be a free individual while also trying to struggle against an urban sense of alienation.

The mission of "finding a home" is realized in the rural space where salient families and pastoral views putatively still exist. This helps to accentuate the city as a space of disfiguration where beauty exists only in the imagination. Urban alienation is the theme of many Korean films from the 1980s and the 1990s and sets up the psychic condition that depicts a typical crisis of a modern world where humans are severed from their natural environment. What is not so typical however is that the struggle for lucid interiorities and for the safe recovery of intelligible language from traumatic experiences is exercised in the exclusive domain of men's fantasy. The symptom of dislocation is translated into a metaphor of the "whale" that stands in as an elusive phallus. This battling for an imaginary Whole on one hand underscores the phantasmal nature of modernity, but on the other lays the foundation for Korean cinema's male anxiety. The spectral self-image of the male that perpetually suffers from the fantastic nightmare of deprivation, homelessness, and castration becomes something more desperately real in cinema than the reality itself.

A Bad Guy

The emasculation and alienation of male characters offered strong political, economic, and cultural implications for both the intense industrialization and the harsh rule of military dictators from the 1960s to the 1980s. Throughout the early 1980s, the films that featured the transformation of aimless and anxious men undergoing the process of maturity through violent, introspective searches were ubiquitous. Either physically handicapped or psychologically traumatized (sometimes both), many of the characters emblematized the period's frustration when protest against the military government was disallowed. These men displayed rage, but they were only hapless victims who induced melodramatic viewer identifications. They commonly came from poor urban backgrounds, and they would leave for the countryside, the temples, and ultimately the woman's womb. With significant strides toward political democratization and modernization came new themes that emerged out of the crisis and the loss such radical changes ushered. The quest for the self in this new period hinged upon a specifically gendered position, one that mobilized the question of subjectivity as it relates only to men. While the cinema embraced and yearned for a new historical agent, the negotiation of a post-authoritarian sensibility and value system was structurally rewoven through gendered relations that reinforced masculine subjects. This recuperation of male subjectivity was necessary in order for Korea to cope with its rapid shift into modern, industrial, urban, and global nationhood.

Several representative images drawn from the most well known films of the period illustrate this acute sense of masculine crisis. In *A Fine, Windy Day* (*Param purŏ choŭn nal*, Yi Chang-ho, dir., 1980), Kil-nam, a young man who works in a love motel, is swindled out of his money by a woman he loves. In frustration, he demonstrates his tae kwon do moves while a bulldozer digs a pit at a construction site in the background. His kicks and punches punctuate his rage, but they unthreateningly glide in the air without finding any specific target. Kil-nam's slender body pathetically simulates an act of protest against the dominant power structure that has stripped him of money and love, but his protest draws nothing but silence. This vision of desperate masculinity evinces ineffectiveness and frailty when juxtaposed against the industrial machinery and corrupt urban space. It anticipates other forms of escape or search to redeem the self. In *Mandala* (Im Kwon-Taek, dir., 1981), Pŏb-un, a Buddhist monk, recites religious hymns while his devoted colleague Su-gwan burns his index finger to alleviate his psychological hardship. The practice of burning a part of the body to achieve spiritual sanctification brings out the fear in Pŏb-un, who chose a monastic life to escape memories of a childhood fraught with oedipal anxiety and traumatized by sexual obsessions. Pŏb-un's asylum from his mother, his college girlfriend, and the red-light district in Seoul does not ease his anxieties but instead affirms and aggravates his agony even more.[6]

The absence of the mother is sometimes as crucial to the son as is her presence. That mothers are cast to the periphery in many of these films is hardly surprising given that frenzied postwar urbanization had seriously altered familial relations to a point where "mothers," in their traditionally represented form, gradually disappeared from contemporary-milieu fictions. Yet this absence of the mother had hardly nullified her fascinating and spectral presence, which is structured around the male subject's unconscious desire to return safely to his place of origin. Even though the mothers are not ubiquitously present in *Whale Hunting* and *Mandala*, they are central to the narratives.

Pŏb-un (right) chooses a monastic life to escape his
oedipal anxiety. *Mandala* (1981).

In *Whale Hunting*, Ch'un-ja comes home to her mother while Pyŏng-t'ae
watches their reunion; at the end of *Mandala*, Pŏb-un reunites with his mother.
In the films made during this period often romantic desires and traumatic historical experiences are intertwined to evoke a vivid dream that drives ultimately toward the mother's womb, a part of the female body where both sex
and birth are sublimely conjured. For instance, Park Kwang-su's second feature
film, *Black Republic* (*Kŭdŭl to urich'ŏrŏm*, 1990), which centrally depicts Kim
Ki-yŏng, a blacklisted intellectual hiding in a mining town, unconsciously invokes the mother without physically representing her. In one crucial scene, after
having been interrogated all night at the police station, he murmurs "ŏmŏni"
(mother) while his girlfriend, Yŏng-suk, nurses him. "Ŏmŏni" is not discussed
elsewhere in the film, yet Ki-yŏng's unconscious calling for his mother suggests
that the film has relegated the role of the "mother" to Yŏng-suk, a call girl.
She is now both the "mother" and the lover for the dissident intellectual who
is severed from his family because of his political troubles. Through the dis-
placement of his anxieties onto Yŏng-suk, Ki-yŏng, who is disillusioned by the
self-righteous dogma of the leftists, wishes to be reborn.

The conflation of the iconic whore and mother affirms and complements
the masculine drive to disavow the need to sever the umbilical cord and com-

fortably seek asylum in the woman's womb. It is not coincidental that Yŏng-
suk is physically "contaminated" but has a "heart of gold," taking care of the
man who is in danger.[7] Since the transformation and recuperation of masculinity compose a crucial drive in the films consulted in this book, it is perplexing that the representation of women has made virtually no progress in them.
The images of women remain prefixed on the rigid, bifurcated conventions of
whores and mothers. Although the "whore" is figured in a sexualized body and
the "mother" putatively stands radically apart from it in a desexualized form,
their roles as nurturers of the male subject attest to their resemblance, as far as
their contingencies to men are concerned. Because I recognize that any discussion of masculinity hinges only upon its relationship with femininity, in reading
the films that best represent the South Korean cinema since 1980, I question
how and why the representations of femininity remained strikingly unchanged
while the representation of masculinity underwent various mutations and di-
versifications in configuring itself to mould a modern subjectivity.

The underrepresentation of women not only relegates them to marginal
positions in cinema but also allows for the cinema to underscore themes that
interest men. A misogynistic tendency against women constitutes perhaps the
most visible and disturbing symptom of a cinema that has earned its reputation abroad as consisting primarily of "violent introspective melodramas."[8]
Perhaps nowhere are the violent melodramatic forms of narrative more preva-
lently featured than in the films directed by Kim Ki-dŏk. His films sparked
controversies both in Korea and at international film festivals at the turn of the
century.[9] So explicit is the violence (vivid representations of blood, scalping,
bruises, and mutilated body parts) and so dramatic are the characters (dialogue and acting deliberately depart from realism) that the male subjectivity
constructed by Kim gravitates toward performativity and deviancy. His narrative structure usually involves a wretched man who becomes infatuated and
eventually captivated by the very woman whom he kidnaps and sexually violates. It allegorizes the pathetic men that have long been a fixture of Korean
cinema. Kim Ki-dŏk's characters suffer from lack. But unlike the male protagonists of Hong Sang-su—another contemporary filmmaker with equal distinction—their lack is from both familial and economical deprivation. While
Hong Sang-su's male characters firmly pivot around an intellectual, middle-
class background, Kim's characters often constitute the lowest possible social
stratum of hoodlums, pimps, beggars, and petty thieves. The only assets they
have are their muscular bodies, and in this way Kim Ki-dŏk's characters are
distinguished from such wretched men as Pyŏng-t'ae in *Whale Hunting*. Their
corporeal mastery, however, does not translate into psychic fulfillment. Their

desperate efforts to "reintegrate" into the society that has already rejected them solicit pity, but also horror since the only viable option in their reacquisition of subjectivity is through women. In both *Crocodile* (*Ak-gŏ*, 1996) and *A Bad Guy* (*Nappŭn namja*, 2002), Kim Ki-dŏk uses the same narrative foregrounding: the women are kept captive by the male protagonist because he does not know any other way of loving the opposite sex.

Despite the fact that there are abject qualities in Kim Ki-dŏk films that lead the viewers to often pity the criminals, hoodlums, and other social outcasts, troubling issues linger. My contention rests not on the fact that his films consistently appeal for the abnegation of the men who have committed rape, or that Kim's depictions of sexual violence are too graphic, but rather that *only* men are given performative roles in them. Women function as masochistic and passive objects predicated on the patented image of mother and whore. The male characters shuffle between virtue and irredeemability, between care and violence, and between reality and fantasy while often the women must remain immutable even in these "folktale-like" films. This pattern—so often conjured up in many of the films analyzed in this book—begs a question: Could a story ever be conceived in Korean cinema that focuses on a self-centered woman who is freed from her duties as a mother or a wife, without framing her in the convention of a vamp? Even the best of the Korean directors that are featured in this book—while busy pursuing the male-oriented drive to recuperate their insufficiencies—have never seriously considered vital questions appertaining to women.

Just as Hollywood has used the Vietnam War as a springboard for what Susan Jeffords describes as the "remasculinization of American culture," South Korean cinema renegotiated its traumatic modern history in ways that reaffirm masculinity and the relations of dominance.[10] The word "remasculinization" presumes a condition of threatened masculinity or emasculation. Men are, as Xueping Zhong writes in her study of masculinity in post-Mao literature, "besieged," unable to overcome or transcend their anxieties and miseries.[11] While the notion of emasculation in Korea's popular culture discourse intended to serve as a critique of masculinization ushered in by the postwar military regimes, the tremendous attention paid to emasculated masculine subjectivities did not forgo masculine themes and ideology. Instead, these popular narratives, like the one featuring Pyŏng-t'ae, invoked the need for masculine rejuvenation that ironically ended up affirming the hegemonic political agenda rather than resisting it. The depictions of emasculated and humiliated male subjects set the stage for their remasculinization, and occasioned a revival of images, cultural discourses, and popular fictions that fetishized and imagined dominant men

Agent Yu signals a departure from the traumatized
male character of the 1980s. *Shiri* (1999).

and masculinity. And the longing for an ideal male hero became integrated in
the production of a new symbol for Korea in the era of industrialized, modern,
and global subject formation.

By the late 1990s, the typical representation of Korean men in cinema was no
longer solely composed of self-loathing and pathetic male characters; images of
well-proportioned bodies in sleek suits and professional jobs also began to appear with regularity and unprecedented force. No longer merely the targets of
public embarrassment, many screen males emerged instead as objects of desire.
One of the defining moments of masculine rejuvenation can be found in *Shiri*
(Kang che-gyu, dir., 1999). The film focuses on Yu, a South Korean intelligence
agent, who counterplots against North Korean agents — forces that conspire to
nullify the reconciliatory mood between the two Koreas. Stylistically departing
from the realist convention of the 1980s, the film also tosses together several
formulaic genre codes: a stolen bomb, romantic betrayal, and conspiracy theories. The masculinity of *Shiri*'s protagonist veered away from the Korean male
icons of the 1980s, but it did so by simulating Hollywood action heroes. Alert,
expeditious, and physical, Agent Yu represented a popular cookie-cutter version of blockbuster-type masculinity, one that stretches fanfare and familiarity
across national borders.[12] The recovery of masculinity from Pyŏng-t'ae's flac-
cidity is evinced through the heroic figuration of a government agent who must
defend the security of the nation, and it offers nostalgic references to the local

viewers who had grown up watching anticommunist spy dramas on television in a nation that had not yet moved beyond the cold war era.

Even though *Shiri* demonstrated that the subject of masculine domination has again become fashionable in a once-traumatized nation, the following year's blockbuster, *JSA: Joint Security Area* (*Kongdong kyŏngbi kuyŏk JSA*, Pak Ch'an-uk, dir., 2000), also reminded us that the continuing national crisis of military confrontation between the two Koreas hardly ferments a hegemonic cinematic masculinity completely beyond trauma. In *JSA*, Su-hyŏk, a private who is guarding the South Korean border of the DMZ, is disturbed by the fact that his crossing of the border at night to mingle with his North Korean counterpart has produced a bloody melée, leaving several men — including his friends — dead. This confirms that the war is not a thing of the past but remains the crux of the present crisis. Su-hyŏk's inability to tell the truth to his superiors puts him in a state of shock and schizophrenia. It reminds us of the dysfunctional characters that so haunted South Korean cinema throughout the 1980s and the early 1990s, best represented by a sentiment stammered by Tŏk-pae in *A Fine, Windy Day*: "it is best to remain mute even when you know how to speak." Unable to free himself from psychological guilt and the weight of history that punishes even the slightest gesture of reconciliation between the North and the South, Su-hyŏk takes his own life in the end. The friendship he had fostered with a North Korean soldier transgressed the nation's ban of personal contact with the enemy, a condition that usually prompts narratives of sentimental love and tragic denouements.[13]

These two images of manhood — one of Agent Yu, an exemplary depiction of a self-sufficient and attractive man, and the other of severely traumatized Su-hyŏk, whose life must be claimed at the end — project subjectivities that seem radically distant from each other. Yet they are both crucially bound to the hegemonic values of modern gendered self-awareness, borne of individualism, fantasy, and narcissism. Both are ambitiously articulate and project desires that carve out an identity that can better accommodate the newly shaped modern environment. The last two decades, the 1980s and the 1990s, bracket South Korea's transformation from an insular, authoritarian society to one that is more cosmopolitan, global and post-authoritarian. The dawning of a new modern era is normally punctuated by hope and optimism, but the weight of intense history and its attendant violence loomed so excessively large that it ended up traumatizing, marginalizing, and denaturalizing men. Wrecked and disordered was the male subjectivity after the Korean War, the subsequent division, and the continuing legacy of colonialism through military dictatorship; the metaphor of the "symbolic lack" was astutely installed as one of the primary thematic impulses in the postwar cinemas. The male lack was located in every field imaginable: of the accoutrements of power in sexual potency, paternal authority, communal function, historical legitimacy, and professional worth. The South Korean films of this period sought to reorient the subject back on its track into the Lacanian Symbolic where language could be reacquired, the Name of the Father reissued, and the castration anxiety disavowed. The next section presents a few conceptual strands through which I intend to frame the male subject and its unnatural representations—both splendid and inauspicious—in recent films.

Death and the Modern

> Odysseus is warned by Circe, that divinity of reversion to the animal, whom he resisted and who therefore gives him strength to resist other powers of disintegration. But the allurement of the Sirens remains superior; no one who hears their song can escape. Men had to do fearful things to themselves before the self, the identical, purposive, and *virile nature of man*, was formed, and something of that recurs in every childhood. [my emphasis] The strain of holding the I together adheres to the I in all stages; and the temptation to lose it has always been there with the blind determination to maintain it. The narcotic intoxication which permits the atonement of deathlike sleep for the euphoria in which the self is suspended, is one of the oldest social arrangements which mediate between self-preservation and self-destruction—an attempt of the self to survive itself.—Max Horkheimer and Theodor W. Adorno (1943)[14]

Max Horkheimer and Theodor W. Adorno invoked this famous passage from Homer's story to illustrate, first, that the impending danger of civilization, progress, and modernity could not be detached from the allurement of destruction, death, and fascism; and second, that the obedience of laborers (Odysseus's men) would cause them voluntarily to enslave their bodies and souls to allow their master to indulge in the Siren's songs. The competing temptation between death and pleasure is only compromised when the laborers plug wax in their ears while Odysseus is "bound impotently to the mast."[15] The sexual innuendos raised by the "impotence" to which the "virile" man has bound himself are as equally lurid in the passage above as the references to fascism and the critique of capitalism. This psychic repression to which the man has voluntarily yielded is a perplexing, irresolvable paradox of the modern.

That there is a touch of Freud in the above passage is undeniable. The conflict between "self-preservation" and "self-destruction" that the self must mediate was also a matter of urgency and of tremendous importance in the work of Freud. To him, the death drive was as instinctual to humans as "life instincts" that are composed of self-preservative and sexual instincts. In *Beyond the Pleasure Principle*, Freud initially writes, "[The sexual instincts] are the true life instincts. They operate against the purpose of the other instincts, which leads, by reason of their function, to death."[16] But in what seems to be a swift movement away from the bifurcated system where the two instincts of self-preservation (life) and self-destruction (death) are knotted in fundamental opposition, Freud states later in the same essay that "the drawing of a sharp distinction between the 'ego-instincts' and the sexual instincts, and the view that the former exercises pressure towards death and the latter towards a prolongation of life" is "bound to be unsatisfactory in many respects even to ourselves."[17] The difficulty of separating the ego instinct (which he equated with death) from the sexual instinct (which he equated with life) is attributed to their critical link commonly bound to the libido that is surely sexual, while also "operat[ing] in the ego."[18] This ambivalence created by Freud (who himself was perplexed by "so many bewildering and obscure processes"[19]) drew the life and death instincts closely together rather than in a binary opposition. But also articulated in this framework are the critical workings of libido, repression, and the phallic lack that form the basis of the modern principles of desire—a formula that is rooted in the masculine universe.

It is interesting that the risk of pleasure even at the cost of death is strongly tied to the constitution of a modern subjectivity that acknowledges the miscues and frailties in mapping its autonomous terrain and that overcomes the historical burden that has troubled it. There are many scenes of violence in recent Korean films, but also equally ubiquitous are images of tormented men who end up destroying themselves. From blockbuster films like *JSA* and *Libera Me* (Yang Yun-mo, dir., 2000) to low-budget films directed by auteurs like Hong Sang-su and Kim Ki-dŏk (*The Day a Pig Fell into the Well* [*Tweji ga umul e ppajin nal*, 1996] and *Crocodile*), it is not uncommon to find endings where the protagonists commit suicide. The death drive is intricately tied to the lure—simultaneously libidinal and narcissistic—that seeks to both preserve life and edge closer to death. The compulsion toward death that is a recurrent motif in many films demonstrates that ontological finality is inseparable from the fallible masculinities imagined on screen. The death drive and the reconstitution of the elusive phallus posit an inevitable goal of many narrative movements in the films so far discussed.

Pyŏng-t'ae also struggles against death at the end of *Whale Hunting*. During the climax, he is threatened at the edge of the cliff by three villains—the pimps who have come to claim their eloped woman. The ambition to prove his worth as a man—the film claims—can only be actualized by an earnest sacrifice, one that must offer nothing short of his life. The film casts Pyŏng-t'ae as a hero, not by having him outmuscling or outsmarting the villains to save her, but by pleading to them that he is prepared to sacrifice anything, including his life, to complete his mission. When Pyŏng-t'ae disappears from the frame after being thrown off the cliff by the pimps, viewers are momentarily startled by the possibility of his death. But he soon reemerges from the edge of the cliff— without his glasses and scars on his face—in essence to proclaim the arrival of a new self. The villains are surprised. Showing a glimpse of humanity, they turn their backs and leave for Seoul . . . without the girl. Pyŏng-t'ae emerges victorious; he has found his "whale," a "phallic" metaphor in the film's title that has been referred to as his elusive object. The reclamation of the phallus—to follow Lacan—is desired only in an imagined form because of the very impossibility of attaining it. The choice of the film to end with the reclamation of Pyŏng-t'ae's manhood is then only a male fantasy that seeks to suture the viewers to fetishistic and misogynistic conventions typical in a Hollywood film. But this salvation is only momentary and incomplete, as the film will conclude by placing Pyŏng-t'ae back on the road with Wang-ch'o while singing the beggar's song, p'umba.

The modern subjectivity conceived in the Korean films of the 1980s and the 1990s is both gendered and endangered. Ubiquitously present in many of the characters in the film is a wound, an inerasable scar that atrophies the screen subjects and activates an *objet petit a*, the "Other" in the Lacanian graph of retroactivity and the slippery object of desire that is centrally figured in the question, "What is 'it' that the other wants of me?"[20] So scarred is the castrated subject that the male lack in Korean films is almost a normative function of masculinity. Struggling to accommodate Korea's rapidly changing social and personal relations, men often find themselves to be incompatible with individualism and its values that define the new world. The male subject's pursuit of the mastery of his world (his family, home, work, etc.) and knowledge is repeated ceaselessly, and with it the phallus emerges as a signifier of both desire and destruction, precisely because it is a fetishistic object that lures the castrated male subject as the "it." In all of the films directed by Hong Sang-su, *The Day a Pig Fell into the Well*, *The Power of Kangwon Province* (*Kangwon do ŏi him*, 1998), and *Virgin Stripped Bare by Her Bachelors* (*O, Sujŏng*, 2000), the elusive object of the "it," for which many of his characters are searching, at least on the surface, self-explanatorily articulates itself. "It" functions primarily in the sexual realm, which triggers aromatic pursuit. Suffocating underneath the tightly-sealed social system still dictated by Confucian decorum, the "it" becomes intransigently a symbol of obsession and frustration. Even when sexual unions do materialize through adulterous affairs in dingy, cramped motel rooms, psychic wounds are not healed, but expose further pain. The desire for intimacy and romance in Hong's films is denaturalized, as phrases such as "I would like love you," exchanged between a call girl and a married man on a business trip, enters "a system of exchange: an economy of intimacy governed . . . . by scarcity, threat, and internalized prohibition."[21] The artificiality of the love motels, where the glow of neon lights seeps inside, unfortunately elicits a moral dilemma that intensifies guilt and repression rather than spiritually liberates men. Ultimately, the "it" that manifests the lack of the subject cannot be satiated nor eliminated.

Fictionalizing History in the Era of Military Rule

For a nation that underwent several historical traumas during the twentieth century, emasculation was a normal rather than aberrant condition. Korea was violently ravaged and virtually annihilated during the first half of the twentieth century. It was colonized by Japan from 1910 to 1945, and the subsequent civil war, lasting from 1950 to 1953, totally destroyed any sign of industry, pride, and humanity. What was even more devastating than the direct impact of the war was the denial of a peace process between the two Koreas after the war. The cold war replaced the hot war during the remaining half of the century when both North and South Korea claimed victory. There was thus no chance to come to terms with psychic wounds or war traumas. The rivalry between the two Koreas also necessitated rebuilding an efficient economy that could hurry along postwar industrialization under tightly disciplined political and ideological structures. Regarded as a bulwark against communism by the United States, South Korea was a valuable American ally in the northeast Asian region for its strategic cold war purposes throughout the remainder of the half-century. Under the auspices of the United States, Korea quickly became a model of economic success for developing nations that could not afford to "sentimentalize" its war wounds and simply redirected its painful past into vehement expression of anticommunism and spectacular war heroism. The traumas promulgated by the colonial experience, a destructive war, and repressive military rule explicitly compelled a sense of anguish and misery that demanded attention, but the prerogative given to the rejuvenation of a masculine identity under the era of President Park Chung Hee (1961–79) deterred it from becoming a pivotal element in the dominant fictions of the day.

Any successful fascist regime seeks to blur the boundary between society's reality and the "dominant fiction": the stories of the nation's birth and the heroic accounts of mythological figures burdened with a historical base as if they are no longer mythological. Taking her cues from Jacques Rancière, Louis Althusser, and Ernesto Laclau, Kaja Silverman considers the term "dominant fiction" a "popular-democratic interpellation" that "represents primarily a category for theorizing hegemony."[22] The consensus critical for amassing this hegemony was of course mobilized from images and stories that recounted history from a specific ideological perspective.

Invoking Confucianism and the renewal of masculine nationalism as two founding principles of war-ridden Korea, Park Chung Hee urged the authoring of an "androcentric," militaristic view of history that was transposed to cinema.[23] During the 1970s, strong male agencies began forcefully to appear in Korean cinema. Yi Sun-shin, a wartime hero during Hideyoshi Toyotomi's invasion of Korea (1592–99), was widely disseminated as a cultural model of Korea's nation-narration process.[24] As the leader of the naval fleet that had at its disposal the world's first armor-clad warships called Kŏbuksŏn (Turtle Ships), the maritime admiral Yi was the sacrificial hero who best represented Korea when it sought to reorganize its economy from a spectacular light industry of textile to a heavy industry of steel, shipbuilding, and automobiles. His dramatic death pictured in the middle of a battle was widely disseminated as an official image that best suited the imagination of self-effacing, fascinating, and sacrificial nationhood and masculinity.

Yi Sun-shin was one of the onscreen agencies in the 1970s, a period when the Golden Age of Korean Cinema of the 1960s was woefully dismantled.[25] His iconicity was cinematically reproduced to appease the government, which offered a lucrative license to distribute foreign films only to the companies that made what were certified as "quality films" (usu yŏnghwa).[26] Yi Sun-shin the Hero (Sŏngung Yi Sun-shin, Yi Kyu-ung, dir.) was made in 1971 as a costly venture. Even though this first release was only moderately successful even after a massive public campaign to encourage people to see it, Yi Sun-shin was depicted again in The Diary of the Korean-Japanese War (Nanjung Ilgi, Chang Il-ho, dir., 1977), another expensive epic.[27] As more narratives of nation-saving heroes and their sacrifices dominated screens, people were less inclined to visit movie theaters, extinguishing the postwar fervor for cinema that spurred the Golden Age.[28] There was one crucial reason for the failure of Yi Sun-shin to generate more popular success for ushering an effective "dominant fiction." Even though Yi Sun-shin projected a version of masculinity that vied to sever the tradition of emasculated males that conditioned the popular projections of Korean screen masculinity,[29] it was an icon that offered a good view of total and self-sacrificing belief, not one of modern sensibilities and dilemmas that celebrate nuclear family values and pit social mores against private desires—a key to most film industries' success in the postwar era. The public would have to wait two more decades before a salient manhood could eschew collective imagination and renew the irresistible, combustible, libidinal energy eliminated after the Golden Age. Only after the name of the father was sufficiently processed in a cycle of desecration, disavowal, and re-inscription, I will argue, would the conveyance of a new male subjectivity—persuasive and affable—become possible.

The 1980s was the decade of post-trauma—one that anxiously awaited the replacement of a father-figure of South Korea and the implementation of a social structure alternative to capitalist relations, both of which would not materialize.[30] Two events spurred the crisis that momentarily blacked out public conscience before reawakening it at the end of the decade. First, on October 26, 1979, Park Chung Hee was shot to death after almost twenty years of tyrannical rule.[31] Tightly controlling freedom of expression, labor wages, and market laws, he had been responsible for laying the economic foundation of the so-called "Miracle of the River Han." (The economic infrastructure dependent on the system of *chaebols* [conglomerates], however, eventually produced Korea's bankruptcy in 1997.) So sudden and unexpected was Park's assassination by his right-hand man that the news shocked the nation.[32] Park Chung Hee's legacy has been so strong that he still influences Korean politics even in the twenty-first century, two decades after his death.

The second event to put the nation into an even deeper crisis was a massacre that took place in Kwangju,[33] the regional capital of Chŏlla Province in the southwest, only a few months after Park's death, and startled the nation even more. Representing the region of neglect and underdevelopment for many decades, the city of Kwangju in May 1980 staged an uprising and demanded the removal of Chun Doo Hwan, a general who rose to power in a silent coup. In an effort to restore order, Chun, who would soon declare himself president later that year, ordered the deployment of special forces to Kwangju. Those forces reportedly "bayoneted students, flayed women's breasts, and used flamethrowers on demonstrators" in urban streets.[34] These acts of unspeakable atrocity that claimed the lives of more than two thousand civilians—more violent than the ones remembered when the people's liberation army from North Korea briefly controlled the city during the Korean War—had a lasting impact because they were immediately silenced. Kwangju did not receive as much attention from the international media—unlike the "global" response to China's Tiananmen—because the United States chose to acquiesce and condone the atrocities in Kwangju even though Americans had far more influence on South Korean military matters than the South Koreans themselves. Because of the biased local report announcing the massacre as the roundup of "North Korean spies and leftist infiltrators," as well as the period of terror that continued well after Kwangju (through the silencing and sentencing to death of political leaders, including Kim Dae Jung), the massacre did not immediately summon national rage and grief. But it would continue to serve as Korea's Tiananmen, which for the next two decades became a specter that haunted South Korean politics. The events at Kwangju eventually led to a popular movement for democracy in the latter part of the decade. Ultimately, the two generals (also the two former presidents) responsible for the crime, Chun Doo Hwan and Roh Tae Woo, were found guilty by the court in 1996.

Kwangju split the already partitioned nation in half. The loss of Park Chung Hee loomed large especially in his home province of Kyŏngsang in the southeast, which had reaped the most benefit from his tenure. And the thousands who were killed in Kwangju by the soldiers deployed by Chun Doo Hwan (who like Park was also from the Kyŏngsang Province) left an indelible scar in the psyche of Chŏlla, Korea's southwest. In all of the elections held since then, the vote is split along regional background more than along gender, class, or education.[35]

The 1980s was an anomalous decade that accommodated both leftist insurgence and consumerist excess. Two so-called "Springs of Democracy" took place, one in 1980 and another in 1987, which flowered the streets with an intense yearning for democracy. The authoritarian center was temporarily weakened before its hegemony was restored through political compromises and the inability of the dissident politicians to agree on a united front. It was a period of political inquietude when millions of people marched in the streets protesting the military rule and the complicit role of the United States in sustaining dictatorships in South Korea. It was also complicated by the fact that economic prosperity enabled millions to found their middle-class identities in the boulevards, shopping malls, and high-rise apartment buildings that mushroomed throughout Seoul.[36] The value placed on thrift savings and frugality to foster an export-oriented economic structure during the Park era was thrown out in dramatic fashion, replaced with a consumerist culture of high spending that boosted the domestic economy by the late 1980s.[37] By then, the state had learned the secret recipes of Western-style capitalism, which was built on the fostering of middle-class identity and consumption. With over forty million people (about half of the population concentrated in cosmopolitan areas) and the per capita annual income reaching U.S.$5,000 during the 1980s, South Korean domestic markets attracted the interests of foreign companies. The shift of the social values (developments of suburbia, consumer spending, system of personal credit and loans) and the expansion of the middle class were the key ingredients in fertilizing the major industries of electronics and automobiles during the 1980s that no longer simply relied on exports.[38] Laura C. Nelson writes, "Following the Olympics [in 1988], local markets offered a greatly increased supply of imported consumer goods. These imports entered into the material and imaginative lives of people in Seoul."[39] Chun differed from his predecessor, Park, at least on one account by recognizing the importance of leisure and consumer spending as the crucial engine of capitalism and the comfort pill for the masses to temporarily forget the dispossession of their voting rights.[40] Complementing the time of radical change, a new consumerist culture was made available through special rates for loans on cars, electronic goods, and furniture and in new retail stores, credit cards, and homes, which were in previous decades denied to the middle class. An attempt to curtail and condemn public excesses and foreign imports also appeared.

Peppermint Candy

If the cinema in the 1970s vied to inscribe an unimpaired masculine icon, one that forged a "dominant fiction" out of collective historical memory, the cinema that was touted in the Western film festival circuits during the late 1980s and the 1990s as the New Korean Cinema attained its status, I argue, by demythologizing the name of the national father for the sake of issuing a new modern masculinity. Initially figuring characters who remained candidly fallible and inept without effecting any specific allegiance to the historical traumas throughout the early part of the 1980s, masculinities were shored up to directly confront the male lack and its historical origin by the decade's end. Canvassing a wide range of classes from the alienated intellectual son from a bourgeois family to the traumatized hoodlum wandering in the dilapidated section of the city, the cinematic subjects of the modern era that were rushed onto film were gendered, with the aim of rewriting history from the perspective of the male individual. The films of Park Kwang-su and Jang Sun-woo, who began their careers toward the end of the 1980s, distinguished themselves from the unremarkable cinema of "quota quickies" and "quality films" of the 1970s and the 1980s, as did the works of Im Kwon-Taek that throughout the decade represented Korean cinema in overseas festivals.[41] Park and Jang decoded and interrupted what the official history constituted as the master narrative by engaging public traumas in the private domains. No longer were screen subjects willing to sacrifice their lives for the nation. The New Korean Cinema's contestation was waged not only against the official historiography of South Korea that consistently invoked nationalist agencies but also against the new *minjung* (people's) history that claimed to be the "collective will of the people" while countering the government's version.[42] The films of the New Korean Cinema, which later constituted the films directed by Yi Ch'ang-dong and Hong Sang-su, further invoked pains and injuries that extended far beyond their individual psyche, while standing at odds with what Ernesto Laclau calls a "will to 'totality.' "[43] Instead of offering closure to historical questions, the New Korean Cinema opted for an indeterminate open-endedness; rather than firmly shoring up a historical subjectivity, the films denied easy accessibility to its coherence and salience. These films claimed that the truth was more difficult to expose because of its discursive and subjective condition. In other words, these new Korean films, while allegorizing history, denied the rendering of the immanent subjectivity that is predestined in an absolute hold of, what Fredric Jameson termed, the "Necessity," something that explains "what happened had to happen the way it did."[44]

There were two strands of masculinities that stood out in the New Korean Cinema. The new men were in crises, first in forms of angry young men and second, more specifically, as intellectual writers. The images of angry young men persisted throughout the last two decades of the twentieth-century: a male protagonist working as a barber's assistant slashes to death a loan shark who has been having a secret affair with the woman he loves in *A Fine, Windy Day*; two billboard painters climb to the rooftop of a high-rise building in Seoul to privately demonstrate their pent-up frustrations in *Chilsu and Mansu* (*Ch'ilsu wa Man-su*, Park Kwang-su, dir., 1988); a college student leaves Seoul when two of his best friends kill themselves in a protest against, respectively, the anti-democratic government and Confucian family values in *The Portrait of Youth* (*Chŏlmŭn nal ŭi ch'osang*, Kwak Chi-kyun, dir., 1991); a soldier accidentally shoots and kills a child in Kwangju only to suffer a life-long debacle that eventually leads to his suicide in *Peppermint Candy* (*Pakha sat'ang*, Yi Ch'ang-dong, dir., 1999). These images of despair widely proliferated even as the struggle for democracy intensified during the late 1980s and the early 1990s, and they continued to linger in the latter decade because of the incessant national crisis caused by political uncertainty and economic decline. These epigraphs and the increasing images of angry men and their violence replaced the Korean cinema's tendency to create masochistic and self-loathing characters. Youth violence — sometimes explicit and disturbing — was surely redemptive and cathartic like those pictured in other emergent national cinemas of the West and Japan during the post-World War II era, and the compulsion toward inwardness and self-destruction tendered and imagined a pure form of male subjectivity.

After a period of crisis, that many representative images of the New Korean Cinema picture writers who are anxious over their work should perhaps come as no surprise. As Michel Foucault writes, "[w]riting . . . automatically dictates that we place ourselves in the virtual space of self-representation and reduplication."[45] The birth of a new self was sought through the claim to language that is integral to writing and representation.

Chŏng Chi-yŏng's *White Badge* (*Hayan chŏnjaeng*, 1990), Jang Sun-woo's *To You, from Me* (*Nŏ ege narŭl ponenda*, 1994), Park Kwang-su's *A Single Spark* (*Arŭmdaun ch'ŏngnyŏn Chŏn T'ae-il*, 1996), and Hong Sang-su's *The Day a Pig Fell into the Well* all pivot their narratives around a male writer who in his thirties is undergoing personal crisis, something that is stalling his writing. Han Ki-ju in *White Badge* is a novelist recounting his personal experiences in Vietnam as a Korean mercenary soldier. A couple of months have passed since the death of Park Chung Hee, and he enjoys an unprecedented—albeit brief—freedom in artistic creativity. But his only surviving comrade from the war, Private Pyŏn, appears in his life for the first time since the war and startles him by showing signs of insanity and suicidal tendencies. This—compounded by the fact that his wife has left him—makes his remembrance and narration of the war difficult, if not impossible. In a drama that situates his writer's block as the primary thematic anxiety that needs disentanglement for both narratives' successful resolutions (the novel in the film and the film itself), equally crucial is Han's recovery from sexual impotence that has already cost him a wife.

In *To You, from Me*, the writer also suffers from penile impotence—just when his friend who works as a bank clerk recovers from his own medical impotence—in the middle of the film when he is exposed and humiliated by his girlfriend to be a porn writer in disguise. Unlike Han in *White Badge*, who recovers his writing ability as well as his manhood through a violent ending when he abets the suicide of Private Pyŏn, the writer in Jang Sun-woo's film is never able to liberate himself from his writing block, something that torments him when he pledges to return to the serious writing of novels. In an unconventional move that has patented Jang's work in the last decade, *To You, from Me* disallows the male subject to recuperate from his phallic loss or opt for self-destruction after lamenting his fallibility. He will simply accept—happily—his new role as the assistant/chauffeur of his girlfriend who has become a media star.

The two writers in *A Single Spark* and *The Day a Pig Fell into the Well* (hereafter written as *The Day*) do not suffer from penile dysfunction, but their writings are equally complicated by women in their lives. In *A Single Spark*, Kim Yŏng-su, an underground intellectual who is determined to author a biography of a labor union martyr five years after his self-immolation, is living with his girlfriend. As a worker in a small factory that has no union representation, she tries to organize a union despite the company's violent and treacherous effort to disband it. She is in a perilous situation moreover because she is pregnant with Kim's child, heaping more pressure on him and his work. *The Day* also depicts the banal everyday life of a writer, Kim Hyo-sŏp; his loitering in cafés and restaurants, waiting for his paycheck at the publisher's, and drinking at an evening dinner party are meticulously depicted. His debacle and eventual death are precipitated by his love affairs. He is in love with a married woman who cannot easily leave her husband. Because he is not able to fulfill his desire all the time, Hyo-sŏp keeps a girlfriend, someone lesser than him in social stature, who holds true admiration of him. Rather than spending his day writing, he oscillates between the two women, living in anxieties generated by the male lack and the libidinal economy that is asynchronous with his solemn reality.

The authorial subjectivity and consciousness in the fictional films mentioned above are only secured through either the remembrance of traumatic history (*White Badge* and *A Single Spark*) or the acknowledgment of its impossibility of remembering (*To You, from Me* and *The Day*). In both instances, however, unconsciously raised is the profundity of sexual matter that privatizes the trauma in the phallic function. The impregnation of the woman, the inability of the penis to erect, the illicit adultery, the exposure of the novelist as a soft-porn writer, all point to the male phallus as the elusive yet critical origin where wounds of the day are articulated.

The desire for psychic wholeness and the putative recovery from the male lack continue to be asserted throughout the two decades, perhaps best appropriated in the film that drew the curtain on the period: *Peppermint Candy*. Covering the two decades focused upon in this book, *Peppermint Candy* addresses the male lack and delineates its historical roots. In it, the polyvalence against the linear time is made possible by structuring the film's narrative movement in reverse order, beginning with a prologue in spring 1999 and ending with a segment that takes place twenty years earlier at the same place where the film began. The time progresses backward without the use of flashback, arranging the seven segments to travel in reverse after the prologue, from 1999, 1994, 1987, 1984, 1980, and to 1979.[46]

If "the libidinal investment of patriarchal capitalism," according to Helene Moglen, can be exposed through the "link between materialism and desire,"[47] there is one more theme that *Peppermint Candy* tries to to link to the strains in Korea's postwar industrialization and patriarchy: the *historical trauma* as the origin and also the culprit for its dubious failure. Unveiled is the origin of trauma that was previously concealed in a film like *Whale Hunting*. *Peppermint*

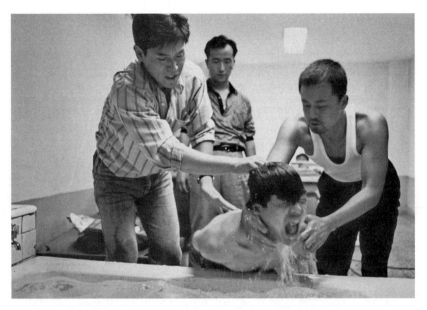

Yŏng-ho (left) joins the police force, which routinely tortures labor activists during the 1980s. *Peppermint Candy* (1999).

Candy reveals that Yŏng-ho's troubles began in May 1980 when he, as a conscripted soldier, was sent to Kwangju to quell the uprising. He was wounded, and while injured he had accidentally shot and killed a local girl. Before his involvement in Kwangju in his early twenties, the film has already chronicled his downward spiral where he had taken part in crisis after crisis. If one takes the narrative in linear time, not in its filmic rearrangement, Yŏng-ho accepts a job in the police force after Kwangju and takes an active role in cracking down on labor and student movements during the 1980s. Just around the time when a civilian president is inaugurated in Korea in 1993 for the first time in thirty years, he quits the force and becomes an owner of a small business. It is here that he gets involved in an adulterous affair with his young staff. After a brief financial success, Yŏng-ho, like the Korean economy that suffered bankruptcy, falls on hard times. In 1999, the year the film begins, his wife, whom he had consistently neglected and brutally beaten, is no longer with him, and he lives isolated in a flimsy shack. He ultimately commits suicide.

There are many metaphors for nostalgic references and masculine anxiety that the film literally renders: a bullet wound in the leg during the Kwangju massacre suffered by the protagonist (like the toothache of Ch'ŏl-ho in *The Stray Bullet*, a 1960 classic) returns as a physical limp at later moments of crisis and punctuates his irredeemable phallic lack; the peppermint candy, symbolizing the sweet love and pure emotions of youth, is first cherished by Yŏng-ho and later rejected when offered by his mistress from work fifteen years later; Yŏng-ho's first torture victim defecates on him and stinks his hands with an odor that won't easily go away, his romanticism forever lost; and finally a view of the railroad tracks from a moving train is framed in every interlude between segments (the sound of the train whistle is also heard in almost every segment) and signals the omnipresence of modernity and its impending killing of Yŏng-ho.

In a film that mobilizes each and every thematic impulse through metaphors, there is perhaps no better symbol that best illustrates Yi Ch'ang-dong's obsession with the trauma and its impossibility of representation than a still camera. Immediately before Yŏng-ho commits suicide, he is summoned by a man who leads him to a hospital. The man had been asked by his dying wife, Sun-im, to find Yŏng-ho with whom she had once fell in love. Yŏng-ho and Sun-im had not seen each other for fifteen years, and when he visits her, she has already become unconscious—her life sustained by a respirator. He leaves her bedside with a camera, a gift for him that she kept for over a decade. Yŏng-ho had once told Sun-im that his dream was to photograph nature including "nameless wildflowers." However, the camera is now useless to Yŏng-ho and he exchanges it at a camera store for petty cash.

The pawned camera symbolizes not only the permanent loss of Yŏng-ho's youth even in the form of a nostalgic photograph, but also his male insufficiency. The failure of Yŏng-ho to photograph "nameless wildflowers" that he so wanted as a young innocent worker recapitulates a motif that is familiar in the films of the 1990s. His inability to photograph beauty after becoming irredeemably corrupt and violent reminds us of *White Badge*'s novelist who cannot continue his novel until Private Pyŏn, a victim of trauma after witnessing a civilian massacre in Vietnam by his Korean comrades, is killed. It is not only the beauty of the world the camera could capture that frightens Yŏng-ho, but also the camera's power of representation that he cannot accept; they impede his growth as a coherent subject. Intimately tied to the process of representation is the discourse of the "other"ing of an object that can help to constitute the self. After suffering from trauma associated with a wounded leg and accidentally shooting an innocent civilian (permanently injuring both the body and the psyche), he is incapable of entering the realm of the Symbolic through representational-linguistic faculties. To be in control of a camera, an instrument that captures and reproduces something desired, means becoming a subject through the very praxis of mimetic objectification. The very thought of image reproduction, however, is categorically unappealing and resisted by the

Rather than facing humiliation, Yŏng-ho decides to die on the
railroad tracks. *Peppermint Candy* (1999).

impaired Yŏng-ho, who is increasingly becoming afraid of his own "ugly" reflection and his putative phallic lack projected in the mirror. I argue in this
book, though *Whale Hunting* (1984) and *Peppermint Candy* (1999) represent
two different periods of Korean film history (one before the new cinema movement and the other afterward) and two different styles of filmmaking (one commercial and the other art) the characters, Pyŏng-t'ae and Yŏng-ho, are almost
identical in their astute refusal to confront and reconcile their mirrored selves,
at the expense of even preferring death.

The projection of melancholia, which laments and fetishizes the lost object
that is stained with impurity, insists that there once was a hope for the pure, the
good, and the beautiful to sublimely emerge in a subject. The nostalgic evocation of Yŏng-ho's romanticized youth before he is enlisted by the army does
not ambivalently obfuscate the boundaries between good and evil, between real
and fiction, but instead affirms them. What can then be problematized is not
just the fact that the violence and the impurity, which is clearly demarcated
from the good and the beautiful, can be abominated, but also that, by so doing,
the hope that the pure, splendid form of beauty lying somehow, somewhere,
is rekindled. This hope treads dangerously toward an essentialist position that
is even more abhorrent than the idea that "life can be ugly." The film literally
asks through Yŏng-ho several times whether or not a "life can be beautiful."

Beneath this lamentation and melancholia lies the blame on the "ugliness" of life that has robbed him of his youth and his romantic ideals, but also a consideration that the phallic lack, the castrated condition that Yŏng-ho has been bound to, is only putatively real. The fall of Yŏng-ho is surely exacerbated by the historical catastrophes, such as Kwangju, the military dictatorship, and the so-called "I.M.F.-crisis" of 1997, but the culprit is also his perceived sense of the lack that is persistently threatening unless its fictiveness is unveiled. Life may not be beautiful, and the belief that a beautiful and splendid subjectivity—free from trauma—can be recuperated is only capable of projecting and lamenting beauty and its loss rather than intimately embracing it.

Even though *Peppermint Candy* re-authors the traumas to mourn the pain that ran askew to the one officially sanctioned by the state,[48] it hardly ferments a vision of postnational imaginary or a nonmasculine universe. What is absent still in a film made almost twenty years after *Whale Hunting* is a female plot, never mind a feminist one. The foreclosure of female agency prematurely ratifies after all that the film's female roles are again relegated to the familiar, contingent, and overlapped inscriptions of mothers and whores. The sense of melancholia that sentimentalizes the loss and heals the pain renders a determined purpose to embrace the lack—not in the feminist sense of the "abject"— but to offer a masculine lamentation of its castration anxiety. The death then prompted at the end of the narrative by Yŏng-ho, a brutal soldier in Kwangju, a violent secret agent, and an adulterous husband, who hustles from one crisis to another and loops himself in a chain of crisis, converts the psychic loss and unspeakable horror into a sense of renewal. But this renewal is possible, the film claims, only through self-destruction. The suicide of Yŏng-ho, where he stands on the railroad track to meet the oncoming train at full speed and yells, "I want to go back!" is haunting. This is an image that is as compelling and desperate as the image that began this chapter and featured the naked Pyŏng-t'ae standing ignominiously onstage, but it is also equally contrived and problematic because *Peppermint Candy* reveals the narcissistic and obsessive tendencies of the male that laments only his loss and failure though the man has enjoyed a privileged representation so far. Turning back the clock is only possible in the fantastic realm of the movies, where *Peppermint Candy* ends with the young Yŏng-ho holding a flower in his hand and wondering about the origin of his "déjà-vu" at the river by the railroad track, the very spot where he will die twenty years later. But the Korean cinema's misogynistic hope of recovering a wholesome maleness and purity from a fantasy, as if it can be transposed to be absolutely real, is, in the final analysis, impossible.

I

GENRES OF POST-TRAUMA

Chapters 1 through 4 trace the social and psychic origins of films that deal with historical trauma and post-traumatic recoveries. This section offers textual readings of the select works that best express the transmutations of historical genres that engage this process of recuperation. Not only are these works representative of Korean cinema's foray into art-house film festivals during the last two decades of the twentieth century, but they are also films that have stimulated local commercial interest. Again, the objective, by way of closely examining the categories of urban dramas, road movies, war films, and finally films of social concerns, is to invoke how even in these representative films of the New Korean Cinema, the narrativization of the society's transformation hinges on the narcissistic recasting of masculine figures. In these films, male sexual desires brush up against historical and social issues that place men in difficult positions. In all of the film categories explored in this section, there is a sight of horror that invokes the traumatic losses of pastoral communities (urban dramas), homes (road movie), faithful wives and asexual mothers (Korean War films), and memory and sanity (social problem films). Men are constantly threatened by the state, by the law, and by the erasure of their origin. Amalgamated, these stories of disfiguration and even self-immolation (in the case of Chŏn T'ae-il in *A Single Spark*) consistently produce inefficacious conditions in which the central protagonists are robbed of their manhood. The post-traumatic recoveries will only be complete once their emasculations are properly reconciled.

The post-traumatic narrative or recovery is intricately tied to the genre conventions of melodrama. All of the films discussed in this section lament the disintegration of the family. Through this loss, which palpably desires some form of reunion at the end of each narrative, the films demonstrate their inability to depart completely from the conventions of genre. "The genre film is a structure," as Thomas Sobchack remarked, "that is opposed to experimentation, novelty, or tampering with the given order of things."[1] The New Korean Cinema, while increasingly edgy about traditional forms, values, and themes, also attests to the difficulty of departing from the restrictions of genre altogether in an industry that had no vital government support. Korean filmmakers had to aim for the creation of art cinema without the aid of public subsidy. The New Korean Cinema was born not because of but in spite of the role of the government, which had blacklisted and censored many of the featured filmmakers such as Park Kwang-su and Jang Sun-woo. All of the films discussed in this book are works that had virtually no financial contribution from sources other than for-profit businesses. Although the Korean government since 1999 has provided subsidies that have led to art film production grants, this is only a recent change. The New Korean Cinema had to strictly play within the commercial rules of an open marketplace (which meant competing with Hollywood films distributed freely across the nation) and could not completely abandon the conventions of popular filmmaking. Either with great subtlety or irony, the films had to negotiate with the codes of genre, heightening the tensions and catharsis of familial fragmentation, loss of homes, and alienation of individual subjects. But while the hope for reclamation of home and recovery of individual persisted in these stories, the endings desperately fell short of reunions, love, and overcoming life's obstacles. The New Korean Cinema engineered a master narrative that engages with trauma—a narrative trajectory where the protagonist is left with a wound so inerasable that even the spectacular and animated endings of melodrama cannot fully recuperate him from his emotional wreckage.

The strong impulse to reclaim home—fragmented because of the violence produced by national history—did not disengage the hegemonic, masculine tradition. The colonial and military occupation by Japan and the United States throughout the twentieth century weakened and besieged both Korean men and women, but, while women are largely left outside the scope of the thematic concerns of films, male trauma emerges as the centerpiece that drives the narratives. The primary motif in all of the ten films highlighted in this section, even in films where the stories pivot on the lives of women (*Sopyonje*, *Silver Stallion*, and *A Petal*), is the frail male whose lack and disenfranchisement must remain as the central concern for both the narratives and the female protagonists. The recovery of the self remains as the objective in these films, but, as argued in each of the chapters, the subjectivity reconstituted or denied in the end is the man's alone.

The birth of a "new" Korean cinema is stretched over two decades. While some of the most significant films were produced from the late 1980s to the early 1990s, the productivity of films with social relevance—despite its decline—continued well into the 1990s. Also, the primary thematic tensions of the New Korean Cinema between masculine agencies and social problems (of class contradiction, rapid urbanization, and military rules) of the postmilitary era could be found in films as early as *A Fine, Windy Day*, which was produced in the spring of 1980, the brief period before the military government resumed its authoritarian rule. While the direct critique of the government through realistic portrayals of the working class in insufferable conditions was categorically censored in feature films during the 1980s, the masochistic men pictured through the characters Tŏk-pae (*A Fine, Windy Day*) and Pyŏng-t'ae (*Whale Hunting*) provided an unconscious sense of urgency through their inability to articulate and their ineffectuality that metaphorically was symptomatic of the terror and trauma ushered by the military regimes. These sardonic characters continued to serve as an anchor for all of the major characters in the first films made by the directors representative of the New Korean Cinema (Park Kwang-su, Jang Sun-woo, and Yi Myŏng-se). It is hardly coincidental that Park Kwang-su's *Chilsu and Mansu* (1988), Jang Sun-woo's *Age of Success* (1988), and Yi Myŏng-se's *Gagman* (1988) all share comic impulses that bind characters who are socially alienated (An Sŏng-gi humorously plays the main characters in all three films). These films—which are now historically significant for signaling Korea's "new" cinema—did not completely break away from the characterization of men previously inscribed as frail and anxious, but instead extended it to parlay aesthetics and themes that were more resonant with the frustrations of the then-young audiences.

What is astounding in this cross section of the films discussed in this volume is that the various forms and transgressions of masculinity canvass a wide-ranging spectrum of men. The projected masculinities are hardly stable as they shift between sadism and masochism, between rationality and insanity, and between morality and unspeakable sin. Focusing on cultivating post-traumatic identities that pivot from masculine sensibilities and perspectives, however, clearly leaves behind attention to women. The New Korean Cinema—in plotting its refiguration of a cinema previously disfigured by state and in following a navigation through Korea's treacherous and conflicting entry into the postmilitary, modern, global era—reconciled with subjects that could potentially legitimate misogyny. This violence ultimately stemmed not only from male narcissism and self-loathing, but also from the neglect of women. In this case, obsessive narcissism of the 1980s already underscores the foundation that lays the basis for sadism, something that becomes more pronounced as Korean cinema becomes more modern, global, and commercially viable.

1

At the Edge of a Metropolis in *A Fine, Windy Day* and *Green Fish*

When the camera cuts to an aerial view of the protagonist Mak-tong's house in *Green Fish* (*Ch'orok mulgogi*, Yi Ch'ang-dong, dir., 1997), the satellite city of Ilsan comes into full view in the background. Mak-tong's under-developed house remains in the foreground as a reminder of the past, in sharp contrast with the countless, slender high-rise apartment buildings that fill the modern skyline of Ilsan. The ceramic *kimchi* jars, the tin slates that unevenly layer the tiled roof, a dusty tractor, a vinyl vegetable house in the yard, an out-door toilet, and a huge willow tree standing next to an electric pole all render a stalled time that has not kept pace with the rest. The concrete house is the kind commonly seen in the farming villages during the intense industrializa-tion drive of the Park Chung Hee era (1961–79). The rickety blue roofing tiles, instead of the thatched hays, display a marker of postwar rural development that was hurried and now threatened with extinction as the metropolis expands itself into the countryside in the 1990s. Like the concrete waste that sits idly against the wall of Mak-tong's house, this home is an unneeded appendix to the new city of Ilsan. It will soon be remodeled into a restaurant, catering to the urbanites who will occasionally use it as a rest area along the unpaved road that runs parallel to the house. At the edge of a metropolis stands the house in *Green Fish*, threatened with disappearance and lurking violence.

The refiguration of the urban space reconstitutes the familial relations that in turn destabilize the premodern values and ethics. Modernity not only impacts the integrity of a family but also threatens its patriarchal order. The frail men

A housewife has her moral virtues questioned. The caption in the
poster asks, "If you were the professor, how would you deal with your
wife who has made a mistake?" *Madame Freedom* (1955).

pictured in these postwar "urban drama" films employ the narrative pattern
that reinscribes a very specific discourse of remasculinization. There are two
issues at disposal when the "urban drama" of the 1980s and the 1990s is considered. First, what had fallen out of the public's favor already by the 1980s was the
genre of family melodrama that for decades had dominated the box office during the Golden Age of Korean Cinema (from the mid-1950s to the early 1970s).
Women's "weepies," which centrally frame a tragic heroine who is betrayed by
men, were no longer popular with audiences. Some of the most memorable
protagonists of the Golden Age were women. Han Hyŏng-mo's *Madame Freedom* (*Chayu puin*, 1956), Shin Sang-ok's *Flower of Hell* (*Chiokhwa*, 1958), Kim
Ki-yŏng's *The Housemaid* (*Hanyŏ*, 1960), and Chŏng So-yŏng's *Bitter, but Once
Again* (*Miwŏdo tasihanbŏn*, 1968) all centrally framed the dilemma of a woman
through whom the changing moral landscape between modern and traditional
values was depicted. The choice between a good woman and a desire-driven
vamp posited the two radically splitting versions of femininity in Korea. The
woman's failure to remain virtuous therefore directly elicited images of a cry-
ing child who is hungry and uncared for (*Madame Freedom*), a brother who
decides to rob a bank to stop his sister from soliciting her clients in the street
(*A Stray Bullet*), and a father who suffers a psychological breakdown after developing an illicit relationship with his housemaid (*The Housemaid*). The domestic melodrama was the genre that swept the box office during the 1960s.
In the 1980s, however, as movie-going audiences dwindled,[1] the conventions
of melodrama became stale and hackneyed even for an audience that had long
tolerated formulaic stories.

Second, the role of men was given much more weight in these contemporary, urban dramas than in those of the Golden Age. In the classic films, the featured heroines fell into traps either of their own misguided trust in men or of the luring circumstances of a pleasurable, consumerist society. The stories centered on *femme fatales* who cannot repress their consumerist desire and/or on victimized women who are injured by patriarchal discourses. Somewhere between the image of women in glittery polka-dot dresses dancing to a jazz rhythm in the U.S. military camps and that of chaste motherhood prescribed by the dominant social mores floundered the postwar female identity. They were forced to splinter into the paths of either *yanggongju* (military prostitutes) or virtuous mothers.[2] The films of the 1980s and the 1990s did very little to divert the characterization of women from these stereotypical roles, despite the intense modernization that made Seoul one of the major centers of global business. As the debacle of domestic melodramas continued in the 1980s, it was the men whose stories demanded attention more than the women's.

The recuperation of masculinity in these urban films hinges *not* on the concealment of male lack through fetishized bodies and excessive virility, but through its exposure. The fermentation of masculine identity is historically precipitated by the dramatically changing urban landscape where territorial control is being violently contested. Violence necessarily engenders trauma when the ownership of land changes hands overnight, when proud farmers become migrant workers in the urban service sector, and when families suffer internal fragmentations. The "dominant fiction," as described by Kaja Silverman, seeks to neutralize the shock of trauma by channeling the individual experience of disruption and disorientation into a collectivized sense of fraternal identity. Silverman, through her analysis of Hollywood films that were released just after World War II, such as *The Best Years of Our Lives* (William Wyler, dir., 1946) and *It's a Wonderful Life* (Frank Capra, dir., 1946), enumerates how the male protagonists in these films strive to normalize the paternal function that had previously failed. She attributes this particular crisis of male subjectivity to the "cataclysmic events of the 1940s,"[3] and explores the narrative pattern that seeks to reaffirm the communal support to reintegrate the male subject back into the "dominant fiction." Likewise, in the Korean cinema the community symbolically functions to supplant the vanishing family and disavow the male protagonists' "lack" as they reestablish their social identities as workers, friends, or cells in gangster organizations. The external danger, in the midst of rapid changes, is at least temporarily subdued. Instead an ego that must compensate for the psychic injury or the phallic lack flares up. However, what is interesting in Korean films is that even after correctly identifying the origin of their troubles, male characters are unable to fully acquire an authorial, post-traumatic subjectivity. In other words, they must learn to live with their "lack." Miserable conditions impose limitations on their dreams, even in cinema, a medium that cannot authenticate reality despite its tireless tries through realism.

The two protagonists in the films featured in this chapter, Tŏk-pae in *A Fine, Windy Day* (*Param purŏ choŭn nal*, Yi Chang-ho, dir., 1980) and Mak-tong in *Green Fish*, exhibit masculinity that is scarred. As argued in the introduction, it is not unusual in Korean films for a man to register his lack, insufficiency, and incompleteness, whereas the women represent the general condition of wholeness and knowledge, albeit one contingent upon the pursuit of masculine recuperation. The men are affable and trustworthy, but their lack of financial autonomy, romantic experience, and physical capability far outweigh their strengths. They are poor, awkward with women, and constantly scarred after brawls. What distinguishes these characters from heroes commonly pictured in Hollywood films is that their male lack is not figured as an unnatural state that must be disavowed through various modes, but as a naturalized symptom of masculinity generated from modernity's violence, which is far and beyond the powers of any individual. The city cannot separate itself from violence that forces these characters to become masochistic heroes who must endure pain. The films use visual and aural metaphors to prominently highlight their lack. In *Green Fish*, the cast that protects the broken fingers of Mak-tong never comes off his hand, and in *A Fine, Windy Day*, Tŏk-pae suffers from a verbal stammer. This is the salient point that must be visually framed to reweave them into the community. From the early 1980s, a period of intense economic growth, late stage urbanization, and political terror, to the late 1990s, one of economic recession, deindustrialization, and postdictatorship, the male position shifts from a passive agent (Tŏk-pae) to an active one (Mak-tong), but each man's lack is still specular for the purposes of insisting on the need for fraternal, communal, and masculine values/ethics to which the society must conform.

A Fine, Windy Day

A Fine, Windy Day marked the return of director Yi Chang-ho from an early "retirement." Yi was banned from making films from 1976 to 1979, and *A Fine, Windy Day* resumed his career after a four-year hiatus.[4] Yi retained his celebrity status, and *A Fine, Windy Day* stirred popular interest. It ranked third at the box office among the Korean films released in 1980. And it was re-released in theaters, in 1988, when the fervor for democracy again hit the streets.[5] Not only was *A Fine, Windy Day* popular with audiences, but it was also a smash with critics. It won several domestic awards and was later voted the best Korean film of the 1980s by the local critics.[6]

The creative rights of the director Yi Chang-ho were restored on December 3, 1979,[7] and the screenplay cleared the censorship board in early 1980. The film was quickly granted a production permit and was released during the summer of 1980, which allowed it to take full advantage of the brief "spring of democracy" in 1980. This optimistic period was made possible when Park Chung Hee was shot to death on October 26, 1979. The reign of terror imposed by the military rule was suspended until the Kwangju Uprising on May 18, 1980, when the civilian demonstrations for democracy were violently quelled by Chun Doo Hwan and his military cronies, who were unofficially in power at the time.[8] (Chun did not officially become president until September 1, 1980.) The film, having been conceived and shot in the early part of 1980—just around Kwangju and before the indictment of the dissident leader Kim Dae Jung and the resignation of the acting president Ch'oe Kyu-ha on August 16, 1980—fully capitalized on the brief interregnum before the military rule resumed in Korea.

After enduring a long period of embarrassment that produced a barrage of unpopular quota quickies and government propaganda, the Korean film industry prepared itself for a brighter future in 1980, a future in which creative freedom would be restored. Confident that democracy would be restored, the film producers' association on January 25, 1980 boldly asked the government to modify its censorship laws by abolishing the preproduction review of movie scripts.[9] (It would actually take more than fifteen years before the court ruled this practice of censorship unconstitutional.) Both hope and the impending anxiety over the future of democracy underscore the making of *A Fine, Windy Day*. Had it been submitted to the censors only a few months later, it would not have been theatrically released.

A Fine, Windy Day features three male protagonists: Tŏk-pae, Ch'un-sik, and Kil-nam. Tŏk-pae is a delivery boy for a small Chinese restaurant, Ch'un-sik an assistant in a barbershop, and Kil-nam an errand boy in a decrepit love motel. If their line of work is any indication, they hardly occupy what is considered to be the dignified roles in Korea's economic development. It is a cold and harsh world that is depicted in *A Fine, Windy Day*, a world in which love and friendship are tested and betrayed. Capitalism and modernity are characterized by sterile bourgeois houses and inhumane businesses, which are hostile to the bucolic and fetid characteristics that best profile the three friends, migrant workers from the countryside.

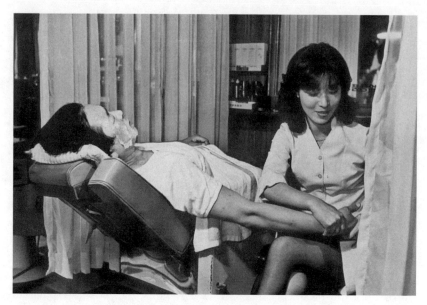

Kim Chong-bae (left), a loan shark, tries to seduce Miss Yu.
A Fine, Windy Day (1980).

The film exploits melodramatic conventions to tell the stories of three friends who separately pursue their dreams and romantic interests. Ch'un-sik admires Miss Yu, a young and ambitious woman working as a masseuse in the same barbershop where he works. Complicating the possibility of their romantic union is Kim Chong-bae, the head of a local real estate company and a loan shark, who has reaped benefits from the rapid development of this section of the city. Kim, though married, fancies Miss Yu and coerces her to sleep with him for the money she needs for her father's hospital fee. Kil-nam, a motel employee, refers call girls for his guests. But the money accumulated through his "side-job" is instantaneously lost when his girlfriend, whom he most trusts, elopes with it in tow. These subplots of betrayal, fraud, and exploitation, common in urban areas where individuals face destitution and minimal healthcare and pension, necessitate the strengthening of friendship and kinship even more.

Threatening the male bondage between three urban squatters is the intervention of a beautiful young woman, Myŏng-hŭi, hailing from the affluent section of the district. She is modern, coquettish, and stylized, but her boredom with her friends from the same class pulls her closer to Tŏk-pae. This is a seductive relationship that pairs a wealthy single woman with a man from a lower stature, which ends up testing his class loyalty. Myŏng-hŭi first meets

Tŏk-pae when her former boyfriend's car accidentally runs him over, while the two race down the narrow alleys of Seoul in separate cars. The accident forces Tŏk-pae to spill his Chinese take-out. Myŏng-hŭi, who has all the time and money she needs, begins to flirt with Tŏk-pae, someone who cannot even look straight at her. The haughty gestures of Myŏng-hŭi radically contrast with Tŏk-pae's demure behaviors. The stylistically excessive decor of Myŏng-hŭi's bourgeois home (which resembles the houses in Kim Ki-yŏng's films), as well as the simple piano sonata soundtrack, also underscore the sense of hysteria that seeps through the crevices of repressed sexual codes and social anxieties.

These are the very traits that made Douglas Sirk's oeuvre such a critical wellspring for the film theorists writing for *Screen* in the 1970s to scrutinize.[10] In *All That Heaven Allows* (1955), for example, the seductive body of Ron (Rock Hudson)—drenched in sweat—immediately catches the attention of a widow, Cary (Jane Wyman), who invites him in for coffee. Hudson's body is spectacular as a male object of desire. But if his spectacular body conceals his putative lack (his economic inferiority), the castration and masochism of the male hero in the Korean film are all-too-clearly visible. The physical timidity and verbal inarticulacy of An Sŏng-gi's Tŏk-pae when he is matched against the modern woman, Myŏng-hŭi (played by Yu Chi-in), threaten his manhood.[11] If stars indeed have a utility outside the institution of cinema, what is the protruding sign when the male star solicits pity, not desire? Instead of an articulate and immaculate masculinity, Tŏk-pae, like Pyŏng-t'ae in *Whale Hunting*, represents a frail antihero who remains overwhelmed by the realist constraints at the time, failing to inscribe the Name of the Father. Constantly ridiculed by Myŏng-hŭi, who literally "takes him for a ride," Tŏk-pae patents the humiliated, wounded character who ubiquitously appeared in the Korean films throughout the 1980s.

The anomaly of Korean cinema throughout the early to mid-1980s as characterized by these masochistic heroes is that it is ambivalently positioned between the conventional pleasure of a melodramatic narrative and the resistance against spectatorial desire. Both Pyŏng-tae and Tŏk-pae, though constituting a wide-spectrum of social classes, fall into the same category of pitiable men who are stripped of talent, glamour, and charisma, which are traits that a male hero usually possesses in Western narrative cinema, either in Hollywood or in European art films. In the working class dramas that made postwar British cinema hallmarks of "kitchen sink" realism, Albert Finney, Tom Courtenay, and Richard Harris emerged as "angry young men" stars because their defiance and psychic complications of the working class masculinity appealed to audiences. The French New Wave was also equally inundated with strong images of sexually appealing heroes such as Jean-Pierre Leaud and Jean-Paul Belmondo. If mass culture, as Roland Barthes once stated, "is a machine for showing desire,"[12] stars are critical ingredients in narrative films of any capitalist enterprise. Surprisingly, in Korean films from this period, the male protagonists are excessive only through their frailty, insufficiency, and impotence, registering only laughter and pity even in romantic situations.

The severity of the masculine lack overwhelms even the impulses and trajectory of a melodramatic plot that is foundational on realizing the heterosexual union of a couple chafed by class differences. For this boundary to be transgressed, the male working class hero must be proud, charismatic, and glamorous, qualities that are denied to Tŏk-pae. Not even the fact that he is a fictive character who only exists in a melodramatic story on a movie screen helps him to acquire a fetishistic value that functions beyond reality. For instance, on a windy day, Myŏng-hŭi cajoles Tŏk-pae to go on a picnic with her underneath a tree by a riverside. After a long bath in a public sauna, a haircut, and a shave, he is wearing his best casual outfit to get ready for the date. But Tŏk-pae is nevertheless nervous as he has never been out with a woman before. He stammers, "What do you intend to do with me?" Myŏng-hŭi does not bother answering this question and instead asks, "Have you ever had a girlfriend?" After Tŏk-pae nervously replies that he hasn't, she moves closer to him and puckers her lips. She asks, "Then have you ever been kissed? Do you want me to teach you?" Even with this invitation of seduction, the class gap between the two remains immutable. Tŏk-pae is incapable of physically engaging with Myŏng-hŭi as she playfully pulls away. Myŏng-hŭi has only tested his temptation and desire, ensuring that she — along with her haughty class identity — is irresistible to Tŏk-pae.

The axiom of class intersects the filmic text as an insuperable force that a true romance cannot possibly overcome. The pedagogical gesture first rendered by Myŏng-hŭi, a member of the upper class, to "teach the act of kissing" to a young man whose class identity is considerably lower signifies her expertise in the realm of sexuality, a sense of pleasure that is categorically denied to Tŏk-pae. Myŏng-hŭi's knowledge of sex (an identity that accentuates decadence in her aristocratic background) further emasculates Tŏk-pae since he is both economically and sexually vulnerable. The fairytale narrative components, which were part of the Korean cinema of a previous era when the love of a gangster hoodlum (Sin Sŏng-il) for an opera-attending daughter of a political dignitary (Ŏm Aeng-ran) was requited in Barefoot Youth (Maenbal ŭi ch'ŏngch'ŭn, Kim Ki-dŏk, dir., 1964), is structurally impossible in A Fine, Windy Day. So, when Myŏng-hŭi pulls herself away laughing, Tŏk-pae can only murmur in disappointment, "I knew it," to illustrate that he already understood that his sexual

"Have you ever been kissed?" taunts the rich girl to Tŏk-pae
on a windy day. *A Fine, Windy Day* (1980).

desire was so excessive in its class transgression that it had no chance of ma-
terializing. Myŏng-hŭi's facile attempt to seduce him and her later rescindment
of the offer to teach him how to kiss emasculate Tŏk-pae both as a man and
as a worker. He can liberate himself neither from the repressed male sexuality
nor from the economically depressing condition. After being taunted, he suffers further from verbal insult and physical abuse. He is beaten by the friends
of Myŏng-hŭi's jealous ex-lover.

For a male character to possess anger is also to hold pride and unwavering
subjectivity. To excessively masochistic characters in Korean films of the 1980s,
anger is an invisible trait, though their goals and heterosexual unions are constantly frustrated. In *A Fine, Windy Day*, Tŏk-pae remains gutless and pitiable.
The class division affirmed in a newly realigned space of Seoul only leaves a
brutal scar in his psyche. His only favorable characteristic is his honesty, invoking his relatively happy upbringing in the harmonious countryside. But the
countryside is no longer a functional space as it is mostly absent from the screen.
(The countryside is featured only in the opening shots of the film showing an
old man and a child gazing at a train passing.) The ever-expanding city has
now subsumed and ruptured his rural origin, further obfuscating his subjectivity. The film suggests that the city itself is directly responsible for his verbal
handicap. Noting that his impaired speech patterns are not inborn but circum-

stantially developed while living in Seoul, Chungmoo Choi notes, "[Tŏk-pae] stammers that in order to survive, he must pretend not to see, not to hear, and not to speak up. The alienating life in the city has silenced this man and disrupted what remains of his language."[13]

The disruption of language and the migrant worker's verbal inarticulacy signify that the collapsing boundary between the city and the countryside has produced a trauma that has yet to convey the man beyond the stage of initial shock. Characterizing Tŏk-pae and his everyday reality is the very incorporation of the trauma into the psyche that has produced an undeniable gap in the center of his Symbolic Order and ruptured his linguistic faculty. The lack is both self-regulated by Tŏk-pae as he chooses to "pretend not to see, not to hear, and not to speak up," and violently policed by the external world that refuses to integrate Tŏk-pae into a stable linguistic world and a salient manhood. Because his castrated identity is partly self-imposed, Tŏk-pae is incapable of publicly venting his frustration and anger.

A primordial scene of trauma is literally captured in the film when Tŏk-pae's teenage coworker who works as a busboy in the Chinese restaurant witnesses the wife of the restaurant owner illicitly seducing the manager late at night. In the middle of the night, a woman's groans seep out into the hallway, prompting the teenaged worker to peep through the hole. He catches a glimpse of his female boss copulating with her manager. In a state of terror, he screams, "You dirty bastards, I know what's going on in there. Get outta there now!" His vocal excitation wakes Tŏk-pae. Alertly, Tŏk-pae throws the boy back into the room they share and calms him down by telling him that the affair is not their business. The boy replies, "That is how my mother left me." Therein the witnessing of this sexual scene between the woman who reminds the boy of his mother and the restaurant manager who to him is an authority figure lies the boundaries of relations that ambivalently shuffle between symbolic — therefore legal — identifications of a father-mother-me triad and the prohibition imposed by its illicitness (both the historical one between the boy's mother and her boyfriend, and the present one between the owner's wife and the manager) that repels such identification. The boy recognizes that there is a father who sleeps with his mother, but this realization does not allow him to come to terms with his identity — subjectivity beyond the imaginary realm. He knows the origin and the cause of his trauma, yet he cannot break free from his shock and paranoia. The boy later informs the ailing owner, who is in the hospital, of his wife's betrayal. The owner's return to work however only exacerbates his illness, and he promptly dies of a natural cause. When the boy leaves the restaurant, he tells Tŏk-pae, who to him has been like a brother, "I too will stammer like you."

Rather than externalizing his anger, he has learned from the experience that the specular image of the "imposter" father copulating with the "imaginary" mother must be internalized through the very praxis of rupturing language. The subject, who is stuck at the edge of a postcolonial metropolis, must voluntarily refuse a fixed, unified, or natural identity, and nullify its capacity to know the world, the world beyond his own image and corporeality.

Tŏk-pae belongs to a community where male fraternity and friendship keep them together, despite the woman's taunting and betrayal, and the authorities' threat. In a period when the government planned its urban renewal programs in close collaboration with private companies, which led to the sharp increase of land prices in Seoul and minimized the chances for families with meager incomes to purchase their own homes, *A Fine, Windy Day* criticizes the social contradictions of the day. It is difficult to empathize with Kim Chong-bae's character who takes Miss Yu away from Ch'un-sik even when he is later killed. Kim is one of the major benefactors of the urban redevelopment programs, reaping huge benefits from land speculation activities, which were rampant in the 1970s and the 1980s.[14] He profits from dismantling other people's lives and also their dreams. Not only does he break apart Ch'un-sik's hope of one day marrying Miss Yu, but he also runs his business without mercy. During an opening ceremony for a newly built commercial building, an old man disrupts the festivities by attacking Kim. Calling Kim a bastard and a thief, the old man desperately yells, "Give me back my land. . . . Give me back my land you stole from me." This scene suggests not only the underhanded nature of the real estate business, but also the violence that framed Seoul in the late 1970s and the early 1980s, when the vast region formerly in the outskirts of the city changed hands of ownership primarily from individual farmers to corporate businesses. Hastily undergoing rapid industrialization, many rural areas faced razing and bulldozing. The district occupied in the film by the migrant population will also soon be developed to make room for the new middle-class residents. Such "creative destruction"[15] that accompanied the hurried modernization campaign of Park Chung Hee cannot generate much passion in the migrant community since it will soon be forced to leave the sector once the construction noise dies down. The workers are then subjugated to humiliating positions, and the forms of urban masculinity available to them split into two extreme poles: anger (Ch'un-sik, who decides to execute justice with his own hands by slashing Kim Chong-bae to death), on one hand, leads to imprisonment; and passive male subjectivity (Tŏk-pae), on the other hand, remains the only alternative. Both appear to occupy two extremes, but they are flip sides of the same coin, an identity that is ruptured by the complications of modernity.

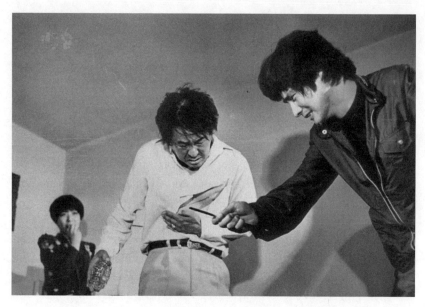

Ch'un-sik slashes Kim Chong-bae for stealing Miss Yu away from him.
A Fine, Windy Day (1980).

Tŏk-pae, the pivot from which the triadic masculinity of the three friends is formed, is the only one who is left unaffected at the end of the film. In the epilogue, Tŏk-pae, who has lost both of his friends (Ch'un-sik to jail for his murder of Kim Chong-bae, and Kil-nam to the army to serve his compulsory military duty), tries a new career in boxing. In an otherwise somber story, the film chooses to end on an optimistic note as Tŏk-pae trains as a boxer. In the closing sequence, he is comically matched in the ring against a muscular, skilled boxer twice his size. Soon, Tŏk-pae's face is drenched in blood, and his body dangerously staggers to the ground before it finally falls aimlessly on the canvas. But, not to be outdone, the last image of the film frames from behind Tŏk-pae running, as his shadow grows under the rays of a morning sun.

Desiring a fantasmatic corporeality through Tŏk-pae's gazing at the boxing poster at the end of *A Fine, Windy Day* aims to relieve the masculine insufficiency that he so painfully acknowledges. An imaginary identification with a masculine corporal image, Kaja Silverman argues, brings with it "values capable of shifting the ideological significance of the fantasmatic, and so of altering its relation to power."[16] The shift that takes place in Korean films, unlike Rainer Werner Fassbinder's films that exemplify the term "aesthetics of pessimism,"[17] is one that moves from "a will to live with the lack" to "a will to destroy the self," which harbors sadism. By the late 1990s, this transition was quite evident. This identification with the muscular, athletic body by a masochistic character who is otherwise ineffective in his social-linguistic world will not only later be recycled in a blockbuster film, *Foul King* (*Panch'ikwang*, Kim Chi-un, dir., 2000), but also presages the narcissistic impulse that destroys Mak-tong in *Green Fish*, a character who cannot forego his scarred reflection in the mirror that confines his lack within his reflected specularity.

Green Fish

By the late 1990s, it was not uncommon to find the representation of the male working class subject, virtually absent during the 1970s and the early 1980s, in mainstream feature films. The films of Park Kwang-su that were largely responsible for anchoring the new wave of Korean films, such as *Chilsu and Mansu* (1988) and *A Single Spark* (1996), had focused on realistic portrayals of masculinity that were not of the upper or middle class.[18] Park's male characters confronted personal crises, which are precipitated by historical traumas, and departed from the masculine conventions by becoming active agents in reconstituting their "lack" through linguistic means. This portrayal of masculinity differed from the masochistic tendencies of antiheroes that the male characters onscreen exhibited throughout the 1980s and the early part of 1990s.

The frail masculinity that characterized the Korean cinema in the early 1980s through such characters as Tŏk-pae and Pyŏng-t'ae continually persisted as a formulaic form that defined male characters. *Gagman* (*Kegŭmaen*, Yi Myŏng-se, dir., 1988), *Lovers in Woomuk-Baemi* (*Umukpaemi ŭi sarang*, Jang Sun-woo, dir., 1989), *My Love, My Bride* (*Na ŭi sarang, na ŭi shinbu*, 1990), *Marriage Story* (*Kyŏlhon yiyagi*, Kim Ŭi-sŏk, dir., 1992), and *How to Top My Wife* (*Manura chukigi*, Kang U-sŏk, dir., 1994) were exemplary films that had comically rendered male characters who were suffering from castration complexes in urban milieus. The rise of Pak Chung-hun, a comic actor, as the most visible star of the 1990s (and also a star in several of the titles mentioned above) affirmed the status of Korean screen masculinity that had cultivated its prime star persona through his material inefficiency and sexual insufficiency. That a star persona had been carved without either charisma or romantic prowess but through his patented comic excesses that yield only pitiable laughter even in the decade of 1990s is significant. In the mass-driven Korean films, this was an image of masculinity that was most palatable and familiar to the audiences.

While Park Kwang-su attempted to distinguish his work from such comic images of masculinity (though he had cast Pak Chung-hun in his first feature, *Chilsu and Mansu*, in a comic role and had been responsible for jump-

Pak Chung-hun (center) defined his screen persona through his
masculine insufficiency. *Lovers in Woomuk-Baemi* (1989).

starting Pak's career in comedy) by pivoting around ostracized intellectuals,
Yi Ch'ang-dong's heroes hardly resembled intellectual subjects. They are, in
a sense, outcasts, but they do not easily fit into the social categories of gangsters (*p'ongryŏkpae*), hoodlums (*gŏndal*), or workers (*nodongja*) because they
occupy the position at the fringe of an organization. Whether a crime syn-
dicate to which Mak-tong in *Green Fish* belongs or a special police force to
which Yŏng-ho in *Peppermint Candy* belongs, their memberships in these violent, inhumane organizations have corrupted them. Like Park Kwang-su's protagonists, they are also detached from the communities and organizations to
which they subscribe, but they lack the means of seeing the world past their self-
interests. Without college degrees and lacking marketable skills and personal
ideals, Yi's protagonists had no choice but to follow the paths of many other
youths who also shared their own class background. They are not disillusioned
by the fact that their decisions always have to be framed in the best interests
of the mafia boss or the state until a particular piece of trauma pushes them
toward death. Once realizing that their lives have been corrupted beyond repair,
they seek to turn the clock backwards, a feat that is impossible to accomplish.
Both Mak-tong and Yŏng-ho are at first narcissistic, but their obsession with
the self is negated after they enroll in an organization. But once they confront

traumas (like the task of killing a man or filing bankruptcy), they are unable to look past their wounded souls. Only death awaits them at the end of both narratives, in a state of longing for a hetero-normative masculine identity that had been denied to them. Gendered masculinity is not a "masquerade" for Yi that can easily be put on and taken off, as Murray Pomerance argued,[19] nor is it a dramaturgical and corporeal performativity, as Judith Butler stated.[20] In Yi's films they are ideal and pure, something beyond the reach of perhaps any individual.

Green Fish is one of the rare films released in the late 1990s that did not exploit the conventions of comedy or action.[21] The fraternal community that is so central in sustaining a masculine space on the fringe of a metropolitan area in *A Fine, Windy Day* is redeployed as a world of gangsters in *Green Fish*. Erased is the vision of a bustling city commonly seen in comedy films; Seoul is instead pictured as a set of run-down, dilapidated buildings, rusty trains and empty stations, and third-rate nightclubs. In the opening scenes of *Green Fish*, Mak-tong (played by Han Sŏk-kyu) returns from his military duties (compulsory for men in Korea for twenty-six months) to his home in Ilsan. Ilsan, a rural community when he left for the army, is now a satellite city of Seoul. Where his family farm once stood, wide asphalt roads, high-rise buildings, and modern subway stations are present. Dropped off at a spotless yet empty subway station, he finds himself disoriented. When he returns home (the house by the willow tree), he realizes that the expansion of Seoul has transformed the lives of all of his family members. The mother, a widower, now works as a maid in the city. An

Mak-tong returns home after serving his military duty. *Green Fish* (1997).

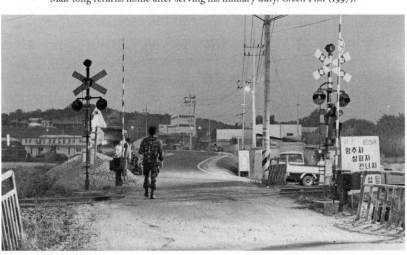

older brother, a policeman in the city who left home long ago, has fallen prey to alcoholism to the point where he is drunk even when on duty. Another brother drives a truck through the neighborhood, selling eggs at wholesale prices. His younger sister lies to the family that she is working in the factory when in fact she offers her services as a hostess in a rundown coffee shop. The only family member who remains unaffected by the rapid urbanization of their environment is the oldest brother, who is permanently handicapped by epilepsy.

Verbal and physical disabilities burden Mak-tong, who sojourns into manhood. Bragging to the mother that the family no longer needs to worry about money once he starts working, Mak-tong also decides to pursue his dream in Seoul. Yet, in the city, every dream has a hefty price tag. He is immediately recruited as a chauffeur in a gangster organization that is structured around loyalty, hierarchy, and use of force. The only way Mak-tong, who has neither skill nor talent, can "make it" is through the mob connections he has established through Mi-ae (Shim Hye-jin), a disgruntled club singer. Mak-tong is solicited as a chauffeur of Mi-ae's boyfriend Pae T'ae-gon (Mun Sŏng-gŭn), a leader of a crime organization. Young Mak-tong immediately builds a strong bond with Pae, to whom he is adopted as a brother. Pae fills the patriarchic center which had been left void by Mak-tong's absent father and his dysfunctional brothers. Mak-tong rapidly moves up the hierarchical order in the gangster organization, only to find himself in an all too familiar situation. His loyalty both to the organization and to its head (Pae) is tested when Mi-ae romantically tempts Mak-tong.

Mi-ae is positioned as both a victim and an agent in the process of respatializing Seoul where the slum district Yŏngdŭngp'o, the commercial and industrial center of the past, is selected for a redevelopment project by Pae's organization. In the film, Pae has the dream of remodeling a run-down business complex in the district where he grew up as a juvenile delinquent. To realize his dream, however, he must fully exploit all of his resources. Pae not only has to eliminate his rival triad, which may be in his immediate control, but also needs to persuade the authorities far beyond his influences. Exploiting the people who are close to him, Pae orders Mak-tong to create a scam in order to blackmail a lawmaker and forces Mi-ae to perform sexual favors for the district attorney who has the power to grant him the construction permit. Increasingly frustrated by her situation, Mi-ae constantly rebels against Pae and momentarily considers running away with Mak-tong, who crucially figures in her plan, on a night train. Yet given the choice of staying with the organization or eloping together with the woman of his dreams, Mak-tong chooses to "go back to the big brother (Pae)." Mi-ae recognizes that there is neither a partner to accom-

Mi-ae, the boss's mistress, lures Mak-tong to bed. *Green Fish* (1997).

pany her nor a pastoral past to which she can return. She feels that her body has already been wrecked beyond repair, and her real family, which is given no direct mention in the film, is replaced by the gangster organization.

The relationship between Mi-ae and Mak-tong is based more on the desperation with which the two are pulled together, rather than on any shared feeling of intimacy. They are also bound by both their disdain toward the organization and the inability to leave it. As Pae points out, she can never leave the organization. Mi-ae's character is shaped by a desire, but one that remains inarticulate beyond the domain of power, which is enforced by masculine authority and violence. (She constantly recites a chant when desperate or in trouble, a quasi-religious prayer that is indecipherable to others.) Her role is not insignificant, but she is subjected to a narrative description that is made all the more explicit as the relationship between Mak-tong and Pae intensifies. Mi-ae, first seen riding on a train and wearing a red dress, is beautiful and enigmatic. She is a performer in the nightclub and also the boss's muse, who is thereby capable of possessing the gaze of the male looker and also of punishing them, for she already has a lover who is a violent, jealous mafia king. Like Myŏng-hŭi in *A Fine, Windy Day*, who remains complicit within the confines of bourgeois sphere, Mi-ae poses a threat to the male subjectivity that falls outside the circuit of power. When Mi-ae and Mak-tong again meet outside the nightclub after their initial, brief encounter on the train, she—like Myŏng-hŭi who had taunted nervous Tŏk-pae—is playful toward him. She teases him, when he is unable to quickly respond to Pae T'ae-gon who asks Mak-tong what special skill he has, by saying, "There is one thing that you are good at. That is running." This painfully reminds Mak-tong of the day they met, when he wasn't able to outrun a group of hoodlums. She too teaches him how to kiss, using her mastery of the art of seduction to establish power over naïve Mak-tong.

Like Jocasta in *Oedipus Rex*, Mi-ae is a dirty mother who lures her son to bed, providing the source of mimetic violence and hence creating the institution of incestual prohibition. She seduces him and is later pregnant with a child whose father could either be Mak-tong or Pae T'ae-gon. When the rival gang offsets the hegemonic sway Pae exerts in Yŏngdŭngp'o, he orders Mak-tong to kill the rival gang leader. Fearing that the authorities will trail his link to Mak-tong, Pae at the end of the film then kills the person who had been most loyal to him. At the site of Pae's murder of Mak-tong—which reverses the patricidal act in *Oedipus* since it is a father killing his adopted son—Mi-ae, though the actual killing of Mak-tong is veiled to her, is also present. As Mak-tong, with blood running from his stomach and his mouth, powerlessly falls onto the car windshield, she hysterically recites her magic chant from the passenger seat, but otherwise remains complicit with the slaughter.

The erasure of the "rural" is lamented in the film, and its vanishing is figured as the film's primary trope that affects all of the major characters. As a nostalgic reference point, the train becomes a visual metaphor that signifies both the anomie of the urban as Mi-ae goes out for nocturnal joyrides and the futility of modernity that seemingly has offered no salient destination. The critical significance of the train, which has been a symbol of suffering in the colonial context of Korea as the migration of the people signified familial separation, war conscription, and migrant labor, has now been refigured.[22] The train also is neither a sign of modernity (as the case may be in Vertov's *The Man with the Movie Camera* and Walter Ruttmann's *Berlin*) nor the prime means of transportation between the countryside and the city (as the case was in Yi Ch'ang-ho's *A Fine, Windy Day*). Like the night train ride that the two illicit lovers share in *Lovers in Woomuk-Baemi* (Chang Sŏn-u, dir., 1989), which can only temporarily relieve their fears and insecurities, Mi-ae's random train ride offers her only a momentary lapse from her confinement in Seoul; it fails to permanently remove the tyranny of the city from her. Her pager constantly rings while she's on the train, reminding her of the impossibility of severing her ties to the gangster boss. Like her past that is erased from the film, the panoramic view of the pastoral space is denied to her from the window of the moving train because of the darkness. The unlimited expansion of the urban that has previously consumed

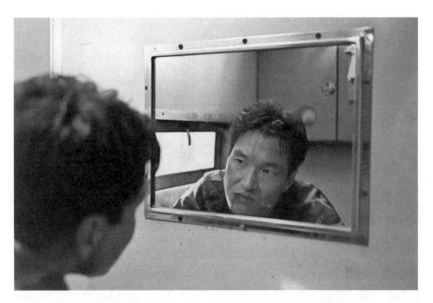

Bruised, Mak-tong gazes at himself in the mirror. *Green Fish* (1997).

Mak-tong's rural community has similarly removed the rural space from even an imaginary realm that can fantasmatically liberate the two from the terrors of Pae T'ae-gon.

The extremity of Mak-tong's determination to sacrifice seals his destiny as self-abnegation and eventual death. Mak-tong's castration is self-inflicted, but it requires strength to literally impair and destroy a part of his body. Han Sŏk-kyu, like Jack Nicholson whose nose is awkwardly bandaged in *Chinatown*, performs Mak-tong with his hand bandaged, visually reminding the viewers of his symbolic lack. His physical handicap—two broken fingers that never heal until the end of the film—is a self-inflicted injury.[23] Earlier in the film, Mak-tong is given the task of coercing a politician who opposes Pae's redevelopment plan to change his vote. In a plan to blackmail him, Mak-tong chooses to break two of his fingers before deliberately picking a fight with the official in a bar. The politician is drunk and Mak-tong must act as if he is responsible for causing the injury. Right before Mak-tong hassles the drunk lawmaker, he enters the bathroom. After taking a long look at his own reflection in the mirror, he slams the door of a stall on his own hand. Repeating the same action of slamming several times, Mak-tong ensures that the index and middle fingers are broken before heading out purposely to wreak havoc. This slamming action is dramatic and violent and it is not a behavior that solicits pity from the audience. Mak-tong is too determined and proud of his identity—unlike Tŏk-pae—to be in a posi-

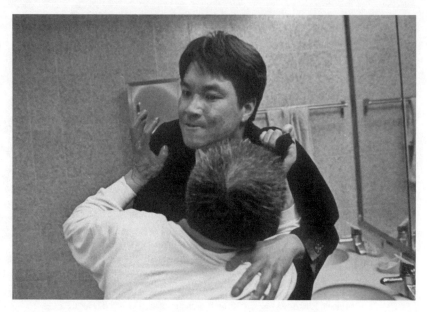

Mak-tong's determination leads him to murder. *Green Fish* (1997).

tion that demands the audiences' pity. (Han Sŏk-kyu, who is cast in the role of Mak-tong, was afterward able to play serious parts in thrillers and blockbuster action films like *Shiri* and *Tell Me Something* [*T'elmi sŏmssing*, Chang Yun-hyŏn, dir., 1999], roles that were rarely available for An Sŏng-gi, whose star persona was defined by his comic gags throughout the 1980s.)[24] Rather than diffusing power, Mak-tong, ironically through the impairment of his body, reacquires his charisma and reconstitutes his power.

The mastery over his corporeality is exercised through the will to exert violence and accept bodily pain, even if it requires a self-imposed castration. But this charisma dangerously encroaches upon the ideals of bodily sacrifice, intense narcissism, and unwavering loyalty to the organization. Mak-tong's staging of breaking his own fingers ironically shatters the masochism of suffering and disavowal that so long patented Korean cinematic masculinity, and rechannels it into the making of a splendid form of subjectivity where the frail ego wilts under the pressure of the superego, which dominates all the rest of psychic functioning. The aggression toward the rival gang and the killing almost take a ritualistic form where the "sacrifice" bathed in blood christens him as a full-grown man. But his maturity also terrifies Pae, who is constantly fearful that his insufficiency will be exposed. The reconstituted masculinity of Mak-tong, in other words, signals a return of a subject that must be slain, by none

other than the figure who to him had been like a father. The remasculinization of Korean cinema takes a circuitous route in addressing the phallic lack as
an unnatural state of masculinity that nevertheless becomes accepted through
violent means. For now, at least, it remains a self-inflicted wound, but he will
soon assume a sadistic, misogynistic subjectivity where the denial of the uto-
pian vision of an elsewhere will unleash violence against women.

2

Nowhere to Run: Disenfranchised Men on the Road in *The Man with Three Coffins, Sopyonje,* and *Out to the World*

Let's get outta here! Let's get outta here!
—from *The Stray Bullet* (1960)

Made seven years after the cease-fire of the Korean War (1950–53), *The Stray Bullet* (*Obalt'an*, Yu Hyŏn-mok, dir., 1960), one of the most celebrated films in Korean history, features a desperate family that cannot make ends meet. One of the most frantic moments in the film is captured by the senile chant of the old mother who lies in a corner of the barren house: "Let's get outta here!" This horribly dark yell from a dying woman is repeated several times in the film and reminds us of the grim and suffocating enclave the family is forced to occupy. The house is no more than a shack, with a bunk bed placed in the middle of a hall. The senile mother, who is seen lying on the *maru* (open wooden floor) cannot be segregated from the rest of the family. There are only two small rooms for a family of eight (with one more due), forcing them to crowd the hall, a space that is nothing more than a patch of backyard with a flimsy roof. Located in *Haebangch'on* (the Liberation Village), this is a community where the refugees from the north have temporarily squatted in the mountainous outskirts of war-wrecked Seoul. The home—unlike the one in *The Housemaid* (*Hanyŏ*, Kim Ki-yŏng, 1960) that was made at the same time—is uninhabitable even before any outside threat is invited in. Through the mother's hopeless desire to be relocated elsewhere, the film's historical background prominently emerges. History—rather than being effaced—is strongly evoked through this simple phrase, "Let's get outta here" (in

Korean, this mother's line is enunciated with only the two-syllable word, *kaja*), registering the horrors of the war even after the cease-fire armistice has been signed. Home is here in the south and, at the same time, somewhere else. The partition of Korea into the communist North and the capitalist South prevents the simplest desire of an old exile who wants to return home.

The choice of the scene from *The Stray Bullet* as a departure point for the discussion of the road movie genre may seem ironic. The image of an immobile, fragile, and senile old woman hardly conjures up the conventions of the road movie genre familiar to Western audiences. In Korean culture, words like *kohyang* (homeland), *p'inan* (evacuation), and *silhyang* (loss of home) all carry significations that strike heartbreaking emotional chords because of the violent modern history that forcibly separated family members for more than a generation after the war. The loss of homes or the fragmentation of families suffered by many then amplifies the meaning of the road as a site of neither transit nor freedom. It is where people suffer: traumatized beyond recuperation, disenfranchised without a place to return, and the prospects of leaving behind the road unrealizable. The road is only a temporary place, but, given the distant prospect of national reunification and the violent intervention of modernization, it is also a permanent site for many thousands of refugees who have lost their homes and families. This image of an old woman lying in her deathbed desperately repeating "Let's get outta here!" best illustrates the symptom of Korea's road movies: she fears that her *kohyang* might have been lost forever the moment she fled to the south. What must be particularly emphasized is that the road in Korean movies is linked to the home in a number of implicit ways. The home and the family do not appear in many of these road movies, but their absences do not suggest their complete erasure. On the contrary, they are constantly re-imagined and fetishized. In response to the painful and brutal history fraught with colonialism, war, and modernization Korea's emasculated and traumatic men pour out onto the road. The characters are visually encased with overwhelming landscapes and victimized by historical pathos, which refigure their constant wanderings. Unlike many Hollywood road movies, such as *Easy Rider* (Dennis Hopper, dir., 1968) and *Thelma and Louise* (Ridley Scott, dir., 1990) in which the characters are running away from home, Korean films feature men and women searching for their lost homes in a vain effort to relocate their families and the past.

From *Home Is Where the Heart Is* (*Maŭm ŭi kohyang*, Han Hyŏng-mo, dir., 1948), one of the earliest films to survive the pre–civil war period, to the more recently produced *Sopyonje* (*Sŏp'yŏnje*, Im Kwon-Taek, dir., 1993), home remains an elusive site in Korean films. In many of the acclaimed works produced in the cinemas of both North and South Korea during the post–Korean War period, the desire to reclaim a home—a harmonious and communal social space that cleanses the contaminated and tired bodies from historical pains—is strongly displayed.[1] Yet the impossibility of locating a stable home, not unlike the itinerant musicians in *Sopyonje* who are forever peregrinating on the road, activates the road as a space where the search for home, and by proxy a salient national identity, is pursued incessantly. Throughout the 1980s and the 1990s, the popularity of road movies was immeasurable. *Sopyonje*, a film discussed in this chapter, shattered the box-office record when it first came out in 1993. *Whale Hunting* (*Korae sanyang*, Pae Ch'ang-ho, dir., 1984), one of the biggest box-office hits of the 1980s, was also a road movie that featured Pyŏng-t'ae's journey to maturity.[2] Many other comedy films such as *The Declaration of Fools* (*Pabo sŏnŏn*, Yi Chang-ho, dir., 1984) and *Gagman* (*Kegŭmaen*, Yi Myŏng-se, dir., 1988) also take place on the road, the site where traumatic protagonists attempt to recover their sanity and seek salvation. I argue in this chapter that the sufferings of the characters laid bare on the road inscribe the pain of familial unbelonging, oedipal anxiety, and post-traumatic shock.

These exemplary road movies determine not only the condition of historical discourses embedded in the memories of the colonial past, the war, and the subsequent division, but also the present dilemma that continues to frustrate the effort to give birth to a new cinema that veers from the masculine discourse. As in all road movies, the reclamation of the self is the objective in these films, but the subjectivity reconstituted in the end is the men's alone. The strong impulse to reclaim home—broken up because of the violence produced by national history—does not disengage the hegemonic narrative conventions even in the road movies.[3] The colonial and military occupation by Japan and the United States throughout the twentieth century has weakened and besieged both Korean men and women, but, while women are largely left outside the scope of the film's thematic concerns, male trauma emerges as the centerpiece that drives the narratives of many of these road movies. In all three road movies focused on in this chapter, *The Man with Three Coffins*, *Sopyonje*, and *Out to the World* (*Sesang pakkŭro*, Yŏ kyun-dong, 1994), losses of wives are depicted either through death (in *The Man with Three Coffins* and *Sopyonje*) or foreign immigration (*Out to the World*) and are suffered by all of the male protagonists. With the actual death or disappearance occurring very early in the film or before the diegesis even begins, the lack or the absence of the woman de-centers the masculine identity, throwing it into disarray. All of the masculine characters wander the snowy roads of the hilly Korean landscape to replace and recuperate this loss or this home, not to detach themselves from suburban conformity typically presented in American road movies. But, in the process of recuperation, these Korean films gravitate toward a negotiation of two male characters, rather than between a man and a woman. Eventually, the wife is replaced by a younger woman (in the case of *Sopyonje*, by the daughter), yet the woman remains contingent to the drama, unable to usher a narrative of her own and remaining a prized object of male rivalry. Through these tensions, generated by oedipal forces, a recharged masculinity emerges, seeking to overcome the personal trauma.

The Man with Three Coffins

The Man with Three Coffins (hereafter *The Man*) is centered on a traveler, Sunsŏk. A middle-aged salaried-man, he is on his way to bury the ashes of his dead wife. On the road, he meets a nurse accompanying a dying old man who wishes to visit his hometown, now located "either just north of the DMZ (the Demilitarized Zone) or somewhere this side (south) of the DMZ." They travel through the most frigid region of South Korea in winter; the snow-covered road, frozen river, and barren trees make the mountainous landscape of Korea appear even more desolate. Their companionship only lasts a couple of days because the old man is caught by men sent by his son, who wishes his father be brought back to Seoul. There are many parallels between the old man in *The Man* and the mother in *The Stray Bullet*; they are both from North Korea and are immobile, making it impossible to carry out their wishes by themselves. But the old man's demand is at least partially met by his nurse, who attempts to take him closer to his hometown. Only the wealth of this retired company chairman with a twenty-four hour nurse (hired to perform "special treatments") permits him to travel, distinguishing him from the wretched mother in *The Stray Bullet*, who is ignored by her working-class family.

   The Man often refuses to stay within its linear trajectory as it shuffles between Sun-sŏk's personal loss of his wife to illness and the old man's loss of his home because of national partition. The purpose of the journey is surely "returning home," one of the primary motifs in many road movies. Yet, this simple desire becomes a complicated and unrealizable mission when Wŏlsan is revealed as both the hometown of the old man and of Sun-sŏk's wife. Wŏlson is now enveloped in the DMZ, the border-region between North Korea and South Korea. The border—unlike other national partitions that are becoming increasingly amorphous and ambivalent—is immutable, physically denying any transgressions. There are three forces that halt the upward movement of the old man to the North: the uniformed guards who represent the *military*, his son who rep-

Sun-sŏk travels to the north to bury the ashes of his deceased wife.
The Man with Three Coffins (1987).

resents *capitalistic greed*, and the black sedan driven by the men sent by the son, which represents *technology*. These come into conflict with the national desire to reunify and the shamanistic destiny that together drive the fate of the nation.

The two narrative trajectories that involve Sun-sŏk and the old man overlap not only because of the geographical proximity of their final destination, but also because Sun-sŏk and the nurse are fatally attracted to each other.[4] The film relies on various strands of religious themes, one of which is shamanism, echoed by the repetitive voice-over of a fortune-teller who reminds the nurse that she will meet the husband of her past life by a riverbank. The rendezvous between the nurse and Sun-sŏk not only fatalistically reunites the wife and the husband, but also couples the two primary thematic tenets of the film: national reunification and Buddhist reincarnation. The shaman's description of the nurse's husband as a man carrying three coffins fits Sun-sŏk's profile. The three coffins are ironic yet symbolic since Sun-sŏk carries only one small box containing his wife's ashes. Yet, in this trip, he had experienced two other deaths when two prostitutes he slept with on the road died: one from a heart failure and the other from a car accident. The deaths of these two prostitutes along with his wife's death make him the bearer of three coffins. The deaths of the two prostitutes inevitably provoke the memories of his deceased wife as she had also suffered from cardiovascular disease and had died later in a car accident.

On the road, Sun-sŏk meets a nurse who reminds him of his dead wife.
The Man with Three Coffins (1987).

Interweaving these two plotlines—one that highlights the grief of national division, and the other the belief of reincarnation—the film deliberately attempts to engage the issue of division through the religious framework of Buddhist karma. The nurse's body functions critically to mediate these two themes. While attempting to fulfill the old man's dream of returning home both by complying sexually and accompanying the old man physically to the North, the nurse also embodies the soul of Sun-sŏk's wife, who has been dead for years. The visual and aural symbols of the shamanistic rituals—close-up images of the shaman's body and sounds of the traditional bell—continue to disrupt the film's narrative, forecasting the eventual fate that reunifies Sun-sŏk and his wife. The wife is now reincarnated through the body of the nurse who has, through the sexual intercourse, physically consumed the old man's desire to return home. They happily discuss the possibility of finding a home back in Seoul. Yet, this sanguine reunion between the two can only be brief.[5] They are forced to go their separate ways when a shamanistic ritual of a funeral, *gut*, attracts the nurse just before Sun-sŏk hops on a boat leaving for Seoul. The nurse, mesmerized by this ritual, enters a stage of spiritual trance and is unable to accompany Sun-sŏk. The ending finalizes the physical separation of the two, but also leaves an ambivalent opening that suggests their spiritual reunion. The boat leaves with only the man aboard, and the film crosscuts between him on the boat and the nurse who is now spiritually possessed onshore. She begins her dance movement, performing her initiation as a shaman. The closing shot collages a close-up of the nurse's open hand displaying a peculiar palm line (acknowledged earlier in the film) over a shot of Sun-sŏk's desperate face. The shot creates an unorthodox moment where a close-up of an open palm that covers the entire frame unambiguously retrieves not only a shamanistic twist of fate but also a sense of denial deeply registered in the division of Korea. This ending elevates the personal separation of the two lovers into the realm of national unconscious, linking the psychic and the social, the mythic and the real, and life and death.

If even the two people who are destined to be reunited fail to sustain their relationship within the system of national division, it should come as no surprise that the old man's reunion with his home in the North is a project verging toward the impossible. The old man's son has political aspirations and is aware that the old man's illicit relationship with the nurse and his ties to the communist North could potentially jeopardize his public career. The son tries to preempt the family scandal by immediately sending his company men for the elopers. Sun-sŏk makes a genuine attempt to aid the nurse and her patient, the old man, trek northward, but the men hired by the son move too quickly in a private sedan. When the pursuers find them, the old man realizes that his forcible return to Seoul is imminent and his dream to smuggle himself out of his dysfunctional family in the South and into his imaginary family in the North will remain unfulfilled. For the old man who has already lost his speaking abilities, memory is articulated only through a faded black-and-white photograph featuring the lost members of his family. Held onto obsessively by the retired entrepreneur, this photograph remains as an image that best approximates the old man's vision of his home.[6] The reproduced image not only activates past memories of reunion and harmony, but also reminds us of the fractured discordance within the old man's current family in the South, and the present political reality that disallows him from returning home. Despite the wealth he has accumulated from his successful business in the capitalist region, the boundary that separates the old man from the communist North cannot be transgressed.

Unlike the nostalgia evoked in the ahistorical postmodern framework of time, memories in *The Man* clearly provide a means to reconstruct the present. The contemporaneous time is rendered visible through images that hauntingly invoke history while still speaking in the present tense. The tragic terms of present reality—where the memory of the war has yet to fade—produce a "hauntology" that sharply critiques the present political circumstances that have not been severed from the violence of the past. Several shots of the film directly invoke the painful memories of the war. Documentary footage of the war features a crowd of people quickly evacuating the regions that have been heavily damaged by the bombing. At one point, the film also presents a Godardian tracking shot of the road that displays a bridge post without the physical bridge, a long stretch of barbed-wire fence, and public bulletins of anticommunist slogans. The film demonstrates that the road and the division are inseparable as much as the war is remembered by the migration and dislocation of the people. The various people Sun-sŏk meets on the road who speak many diverse forms of regional accents—from the northern dialects to the southern vernacular—also remind us of the dislocated figuration of Korea.[7]

One of the most significant motifs is the aforementioned faded photograph kept by the old man. It is later separated from him when it becomes clear that his hope of returning home will remain unfulfilled. As the company men forcibly carry him to the car headed back to Seoul where his greedy son awaits, the image of his past drops from his hand. The photograph is recovered by the nurse, but she later tears the picture up and throws it into a nearby river, as if to suggest that even this visual reminder of a nostalgic past is pointless when irrecoverable in the present moment. Like the prospect of reunification that politically dominates Korea still as only a distant aspiration, the dying man's dream of returning home can never be fulfilled. However, this dream, as the film points out, is provoked neither from a nonpolitical idiom nor from an imagination that has no reclaimable past. It is a union that can only be remembered historically, yet cannot be consummated realistically in the present, much like the national discourse of the two Koreas that, only grudgingly, and at a snail's pace, edge toward reconciliation.

The challenge of reading this kind of discursive film text, which destabilizes and collapses the interlocutory relationship between the *personal* and the *national*, becomes further complicated when we ask through whom the dilemma of the nation is visualized. It is undoubtedly the female body of the nurse through which we witness not only the reincarnation of the wife, separated from Sun-sŏk for years, but also the idealization of the old man's dream—both sexually and psychically. The faded memory of Sun-sŏk's wife—like the blurred photo treasured by the old man—provides a nodal point from which the past of the old man can be fantasized and reconstructed. It comes as no surprise that the old man's dream to return to his home in the North cannot be approved by the son, who aspires to run for public office. The son's disapproval allegorizes South Korean state politics at a time that sought to condemn and prohibit even the slightest gestures and hopes for national reunification.[8] However, what is intriguing about the film is that the woman's body functions fetishistically as a site where the symbolic act of "returning home" is both psychically and physically performed. This structure bifurcates the gender roles so that women's utility is relegated to the "point of access" through which men's material and historical desires are processed. Together, the two men and the woman travel through the time and space of the partitioned land, and are denied return to their respective homes and spouses. Yet, it is the woman who remains a wanderer, eternally exteriorized from the material history and space, and interwoven through time only as a spiritual shaman. Such conventional use of gender roles sets up a systematic pattern of masculine orientation that continues to plague Korean road movies.

Sopyonje

When the longing for a home does not materialize, the fetishistic desire to replace the home creates violence on the road. *Sopyonje* is a film that portrays the threat to the nation and the home through an obsessive itinerant musician who is driven to perfect his aesthetics, despite the trying times. Yu-bong, in the film, leads a family troupe of traveling musicians who continue to perform *p'ansori*, the traditional vocal music accompanied only by drums. Although it spectacularly recites some of the most popular folktales,[9] the public's interest toward local music is quickly dwindling at the time of rapid modernization. The Western tune, "Belsame Mucho," amplified in the streets through the loud speakers, demoralizes Yu-bong and his family, who have neither the money nor the resources to technologically "upgrade" their art. Further marginalizing Yu-bong are the loss of his wife, which occurs minutes into the film, and his recalcitrant refusal to return to Seoul even when his peers invite him. *Sopyonje* spans thirty intense and volatile years, from the Japanese colonial period of the early 1940s to the intense industrialization period of 1970s. But the deterritorialization of Yu-bong had already taken root in the period prior to the film's temporal setting, in his confrontation with his master. Revealed in a barroom discussion between him and his old friends, Yu-bong had been purged by his teacher of p'ansori after he had fallen in love with the master's mistress, a victim of forbidden love who later committed suicide. Yu-bong is unwilling to either compromise his music or eroticize it through permitting his young daughter, Song-hwa, to be a *kisaeng* (courtesan).

Sopyonje was an unlikely hit that dominated the box office in 1993.[10] Released at a time where the invasion of Hollywood films peaked in the Korean film market, *Sopyonje* became the nation's riposte to foreign imports.[11] The characters' struggle to resist foreign cultural invasion and to secure p'ansori's spot in the pantheon of national aesthetics resembled the Korean film industry's uphill

A scene from the surprise hit film of the 1990s. *Sopyonje* (1993).

battle against the Hollywood onslaught. The box office success of *Sopyonje* was remarkable given the fact that the film avoided using Hollywood-type action and comic codes. The story is primarily conveyed through long takes and long shots, with restricted use of close-ups. Also, the use of p'ansori music throughout the film's soundtrack disorients audiences' expectations of a melodrama that is normally structured on Western classical overtures. Most of the positive remarks on the film overwhelmingly issued by both critics and the public singled out its effective presentation of the repressed sentiment of *han* through a tranquil and still camera.

What is interesting about *Sopyonje* is that it shuffles two narratives that run parallel to each other (like *The Man*, which also pairs together the lives of two men from different generations). The tragic story of Yu-bong who died without ever realizing his dream is accounted through his adopted son, Tong-ho. Tong-ho searches for a trace of his family throughout Korea's countryside in the 1970s. The son, who never had much musical talent, had rebelled against his staunch father and the hardships he exacted. Working now as a salaried employee of a pharmaceutical company, he begins coming to terms with his own past. But the past is not easily recoverable after decades have passed. Through the numerous encounters with people who know of Yu-bong and Song-hwa, Tong-ho learns that his father has long been dead and his sister — also separately adopted — is now blind. Yu-bong's dedication toward cultivating and continu-

Genres of Post-Trauma 61

ing the tradition of vocal art (*sori*) through Song-hwa has not only segregated him from the rest of the society, but also led him to commit a crime against Song-hwa, robbing her of her vision (believing that it would make her a better singer).

The narrative structure that frames Yu-bong's destruction of his family through the viewpoint of his mature son (who now seeks to reconcile with his past) places Tong-ho and Song-hwa in the same shot at the film's climax. After a long search, they finally meet in a small tavern and, without exchanging much dialogue or acknowledging each other as long-lost siblings, perform music together. Tong-ho accompanies his sister on drums. The performance scene where the two intensely recite the *Tale of Sim Ch'ŏng* throughout the night — sweat dripping from their faces filled with joy toward the end — is more compulsive and erotic than any of the sex scenes in Im Kwon-Taek's other films. Their rhythmic movement is sensitively captured on camera and edited in a way far removed from Im's signature long-takes. The sequence eventually adopts close-ups as the two reach a climactic outburst and quasi-orgasmic denouement. (The owner of the tavern later tells Song-hwa that they were making music "as if making love.")

Juxtaposed against the beautiful and exquisite shots of the road, which sometimes overwhelm the hardship suffered by the family pennilessly wandering around the countryside, this scene of Song-hwa's and Tong-ho's performance is pictured unglamorously. Yet, the emotions produced by the underlit scene release all of the tensions that have been slowly escalating throughout the film, and the musical "lovemaking" between brother and sister both celebrates and mourns the death of the father who had previously been suppressing their reunion. In this crucial climax, the film's protagonist Yu-bong becomes conspicuous through his absence — his terror remembered and forgiven when a smile appears on Tong-ho's face. Once the morning arrives, however, the two must go their separate ways. Tong-ho hops on the bus that stops on the dirt road where Park Chung Hee's New Village Movement industrialization has yet to pave its way. And blind Song-hwa — led by her small daughter — returns to the road where snow flurries begin to fall.

The discursive mechanisms that textually ferment the film are indeed the national sentiment of han and its musical medium through which the film rearticulates its fetish. Here, I focus on the intricate connection between the *fetish* and *han* as both are rendered meaningful through internal repression. Han is conventionally understood as the sentiment that sublimates the suffering and sorrow that have tested the endurance of Koreans throughout the twentieth century. Usually positioned as one of the most actively mobilized referential idioms in Im Kwon-Taek's films, the significance of han is intensified in *Sopyonje* as Yu-bong and his family are pushed to society's periphery without the recognition of their talents and determination to preserve national aesthetics. The film underscores han through the melodramatic configurations of *melos* (music) and drama. In other words, the convention of melodrama reorders the excessive filmic tragedies—Yu-bong's social marginalization and his wife's death, Song-hwa's loss of vision and her beloved brother, and Tong-ho's oedipal struggle and his later futile search for his family members—into a dramatic structure that is familiar to the popular audience. Yet the exquisite p'ansori and the beautiful landscape are unfamiliar to most young, urban audiences and position them in a highly ambivalent viewing position.[12] In this convention, the beautiful music performed by Song-hwa and the glorious Korean landscape stand in as fetish objects compensating for the loss perceived by audiences who believe they have been deprived of national beauty and aesthetics and for the emasculation (or phallic lack) imagined by Yu-bong. If one were to follow this interpretation, *Sopyonje* is a regressive film that seeks to delimit and contain "a potentially transgressive feminine sexuality,"[13] where the father is reconstituted as the center of the family. As Chungmoo Choi has elsewhere argued, Yu-bong's violent act against Song-hwa is irreparable since concealed beneath the façade of national(ist) aesthetics is Yu-bong's sexual desire, which sought to make Song-hwa exclusively his even at the expense of her physical mutilation.[14] For Choi, *Sopyonje* mobilizes a nationalist discourse through the incubation of masculine desire that promulgates irrevocable violence against women, the only domain and body where a fully repressed and marginalized man like Yu-bong can unleash his power.[15]

There are, however, two impulses within the diegesis of *Sopyonje* that ruffle and strain Choi's feminist critique. First, even though *Sopyonje* embodies many of the codes and the conventions of family melodrama, it is extremely difficult to label the film as a hallmark of a melodrama due to the failure of the family to withdraw from its peregrination and settle down in one place. Even when Yu-bong and Song-hwa find an abandoned shack to wait out the bitter cold days of winter toward the end of the film, Yu-bong's patriarchal power falls short of rehabilitating his family. Yu-bong, now old and decrepit, is too frail to maintain control of his immediate surroundings. In one instance, after having stolen a chicken to feed Song-hwa, Yu-bong is severely beaten by the neighbor. From the vantage point of patriarchal discourse, Yu-bong's power—despite the terror he has committed against Song-hwa—cannot be absolute as long as he lacks

Yu-bong, old and decrepit, is too frail to exercise his
masculine power. *Sopyonje* (1993).

command of his spatial domain. Even the private space of a home cannot be
secured for these traveling musicians. Knowing all too well that on the road —
which is ultimately their home — his authority has its limits, Yu-bong attempts
to territorialize and inscribe his supremacy onto the body of a woman, the only
object that allows his fetishistic compunction to materialize once he no longer
has the young voice to prolong p'ansori's aesthetic tradition himself. But the
absence of a safe haven denies Yu-bong his potential to masculinize, compro-
mising his authority. He suffers a pitiful death at the end without really fulfilling
his dream, inviting viewers to empathize and finally forgive his violence. This
sense of unbelonging plagues and even extends after Yu-bong's death. Tong-
ho, Song-hwa, and her daughter are all seen back on the road by the end of the
film after their brief reunion. Tong-ho is last sighted on the bus taking him back
to Seoul, while Song-hwa and her daughter continue their peregrination in the
rural countryside. The home to them is no longer elusive because the road is
where the home is.

Not only does the figuration of the road as "home" de-center the hegemonic
masculinity in *Sopyonje*; the narrative structure of the film that frames Yu-
bong's story as a remembrance of his grown-up son also derails the oedipal
rivalry that promulgated his rebellion against the father. Tong-ho, who is him-

self now a father, instead reinscribes a new masculine identity that operates on characteristics that make him different from his bitter and stubborn father. This renewal of masculinity is predicated on the recovery of his childhood memories and the reconciliation of history. In my mind, Tong-ho—rather than Yu-bong—is the crucial character, the central subjectivity of the film. By figuring Tong-ho as the main subject through which the audience accesses memory and history, the film accomplishes two things. First, by assuming the viewpoint of a young son who recollects the memory of the dead father, Tong-ho emerges as the abused child who is now capable of reconnecting the family that had been disfigured by the father. This allows the viewer to concentrate on the viewpoint of the underdog victim, the key in establishing a melodramatic formula that challenges the codes of domination and exploitation of any given society, that ushers what Thomas Elsaesser recognized as the radical and subversive function in melodrama.[16]

Despite its subversive element, it would be difficult to argue that *Sopyonje* loops out of the hetero-lineal genealogy that moves from the father Yu-bong to the son Tong-ho. Choi is correct in pointing out that *Sopyonje*'s narrative focus from the perspective of Tong-ho, rather than of Yu-bong, does not completely derail the film's masculine orientation and instead may affirm it.[17] The film begins with Tong-ho's arrival at Sorije, a hill named after his father's sori (voice), and ends with his departure after finding his sister. Tong-ho emerges as the hero of the film because he has endured history, and now, as a father, he reaches out to reconcile his painful past, relieving the men from the burden of historical guilt. Park Kwang-su's *To the Starry Island* (*Kŭ sŏm e kago sipta*, 1993), released in the same year as *Sopyonje*, also uses a similar narrative strategy by employing a middle-aged intellectual who recollects his forty-year-old past after visiting his hometown to bury the body of his friend's father.[18] In Park's film, because the deceased father is responsible for a massacre that killed many innocent villagers of the island during the war, the film negotiates the violent history and the guilty father's legacy through both personal memory of the child and the collective remembrance of the village. To reconcile is not simply to forget a traumatic past and remain lost in the dark, but to awaken and relive the moment— the frozen slice of time when the world came tumbling down—and to heal the pain, overcome trauma, and transcend the suffering or the han. Yet even the attempt of a post-traumatic film such as *Sopyonje* to reconcile the past remains a struggle that is exercised only in the domain of men. Song-hwa, who is undoubtedly the victim of both violent history and her father's violence, remains outside the ideological fulcrum around which the narrative authority pivots. Her frustration and suffering remain only indirectly articulated, contingent to

A middle-aged intellectual is trying to come to terms with his past.
To the Starry Island (1993).

the single organizing narrative principle that relies on a patrilineal legacy inherited by Tong-ho. Song-hwa still remains on the road even after Tong-ho
returns home.

Out to the World

Out to the World radically departs from the convention of Korean road movies
produced earlier and engages more with American films such as *Butch Cassidy
and the Sundance Kid* (George Roy Hill, dir., 1969) and *Bonnie and Clyde*
(Arthur Penn, dir., 1967).[19] The film does follow the structure of two Korean
road movies, *The Road to Sampo* and *Whale Hunting*, which both featured a
random meeting between a prostitute and two male travelers.[20] But the film's
frank depiction of sexuality and profanity previously unpermitted on screen
opens a space for the crude representation of anti-heroes that defy and criticize
social norms. *Out to the World* also reverses the gender roles from the previous
Korean counterparts where the two men aided a prostitute in her escape from
the whorehouse, by figuring the two men as escapees from prison. In the film,
two fugitives, Sŏng-gŭn (convicted for involuntary manslaughter) and Kyŏng-
yŏng (for petty robbery) reluctantly acquire freedom from prison when several
other inmates lead a jailbreak.[21] When several of their attempts to turn them-

Two prisoners are reluctantly freed. *Out to the World* (1994).

selves in to the police fail, they continue their trek northward toward the DMZ, where they are eventually shot by the military soldiers guarding the barbed wire shoreline. Although the film generically participates in South Korea's long tradition of "road movies," it also features previously unseen car chases, humorous puns and situations, a rock 'n' roll soundtrack, and even parodies of famous scenes from *Butch Cassidy and the Sundance Kid*. Like many other Korean road movies that usually take place in bitter cold weather, *Out to the World* pictures leafless tree branches, barren rice fields, and snowflakes. Yet, the film acknowledges Korea's changing landscape in a newly aligned global, postmodern era. There are glittering supermarkets, vending machines with the latest fashionable drinks, and fancy sport-utility vehicles alongside the rural landscape. The primary mode of travel — unlike that in *The Man* and *Sopyonje* — is not on foot, but in automobiles and trains. On several occasions when they are forced to go on foot, they awkwardly run, prompting Hye-jin to yell, "Don't run! I hated running even when I was little." Set mostly in rural spaces, the film exposes the slogan of *segyehwa* (globalization), rendered officially by the then-president Kim Young-sam, as an empty signifier.[22] The film pictures a desolate space (which is rare in a densely populated nation like Korea where even the rural roads are often heavily congested), a perfect site for their masculinities to disintegrate.

If *The Man* and *Sopyonje* prefigure male trauma from the onset and mobilize narratives that attempt to recuperate their loss and troubles, by the film's end *Out to the World* tells a story of tragic demise, an eventual disfiguration of masculinity. The two prisoners, Sŏng-gŭn and Kyŏng-yŏng, are freed from their cells when their transfer bus is taken over by the revolting prisoners. Unwilling to accompany other prisoners, who are primarily responsible for the mutiny, Sŏng-gŭn and Kyŏng-yŏng begin their own journey, joined by a grumpy call girl, Hye-jin. As they move, the film poses a question as to whether or not Korea has achieved a postcolonial, postindustrial, and post-authoritarian status. On their way from Mokp'o—a city famous for being the home of the former president, Kim Dae Jung (then a dissident political leader)—to Seoul, they encounter a diverse body of characters that represent fragments of Korea. They first run into an old woman in a white *hanbok* (traditional Korean dress) who misrecognizes them as people who have come to help her return to her hometown in North Korea. Yet, unlike Sun-sŏk in *The Man* who is drawn to the wish of the old man, Sŏng-gŭn and Kyŏng-yŏng are fugitives from the law and are hardly in a position to help an old woman who wishes to travel three hundred miles north. Yet, this misrecognition of the fugitives as the "people from the north" early in the film becomes significant in the end since Sŏng-gŭn and Kyŏng-yŏng may be just as homeless in the South as North Koreans are. Sŏng-gŭn's home has vanished while he was in jail, something he realizes when his call home does not go through, and later he finds out that his wife had emigrated to Japan. Neither Kyŏng-yŏng nor Hye-jin discuss their families, and they thus depend on one another just as if they are family members. The signposts that verify the various social contradictions such as national division, modernization, and the U.S. military occupation continue to provide visual metaphors of the road from which they cannot easily escape. They also meet a reckless bunch of male teenagers from the nouveau-riche class in a sporty jeep who race down the freeway, almost crashing into their sedan. Their presence produces discord in a society that still has poor farmers protesting out on the road against the impending opening of the market. Also ubiquitously featured in their trip are the impatient warden who constantly yells at them through the cell phone, a gas station owner who habitually lies, and the tyrannical yet cowardly local policemen. Even though Sŏng-gŭn and Kyŏng-yŏng are the ones segregated from society for being "cancerous elements," one can hardly tell whether they deserve punishment and "correctional treatment" anymore than the people outside prison.

Such ambivalent articulations of morality cannot properly distinguish real criminals from the rest, and they critique the society that purges and punishes small-time crooks while the most serious offenders of law remain immunized

A winter scene. *Out to the World* (1994).

from the law.[23] The title of the film, *Out to the World*, which in Korean has a meaning other than the one suggested in English, "out *of* the world," imbues the film with a sense of confinement and ineffectualness even when the prisoners are freed from their cells. Even after their release from prison, there is simply no place for Sŏng-gŭn and Kyŏng-yŏng to hide as the voice of their warden on television or through Hye-jin's cell phone constantly undermines their effort to run away. It is only a matter of time before they are caught or killed. And unlike in *Butch Cassidy and the Sundance Kid*, there is no "Latin America" — a land of fantasy that is conjured as a space putatively unaffected by the law — across the border from Korea. South Korea, a peninsula, shares its border only with North Korea along the 38th Parallel, the most heavily militarized zone in the world. Even on the road, freedom is simply unavailable. The protagonists are followed, and every move they make is scrutinized before they are violently shot, one after another, as if it is an event of spectacle.[24]

Contrasted radically against the state that controls the surveillance circuit and signals that travel through the airwaves of radio, television, and cellular phone is the protagonist Sŏng-gŭn's unfamiliarity with any of the machines around him. The state does not necessarily have to physically shadow the fugitives as long as it is in control of the signals that detect them. Unlike Hollywood's typical outlaw protagonist whose mastery of pyrotechnics subverts authority, Sŏng-gŭn feels like an idiot when it comes to machines and simple, everyday utilities. The identification of Sŏng-gŭn as Sundance Kid, the fastest gunman in the West, is only a fantasy imagined inside the head of Hye-jin. Having been put away awhile, it is difficult for Sŏng-gŭn to recuperate his masculine identity as he relies on Hye-jin even for simple routine procedures, unlike the men of previous Korean films where they helped the prostitutes escape from their pimps. Early in the film, he refuses to carry the gun stolen from the prison guard during the revolt, deliberately rejecting the phallic symbol as his own. His incompetence with technology becomes even more desperate when he reveals that he does not know how to use a cellular phone. Complicating matters even more, Sŏng-gŭn cannot take over the steering wheel since he does not know how to drive, despite the fact that Hye-jin is only a novice driver. In a crucial scene at a gas station, his frustrating inability to work the machines around him finally erupts into rage.

Shortly after their meeting, the three stop at a gas station for a coffee break. Sŏng-gŭn, who has already displayed his discomfort toward technology by refusing both the pistol and the steering wheel of the car, continues to have trouble with machines. The cellular phone he borrows from Hye-jin fails to connect him to his wife. The coffee vending machine does not work even after coins have been properly fed. When the owner of the gas station refuses to reimburse Sŏng-gŭn, he can no longer control his temper. He attacks the coffee machine with a nearby hammer and breaks open the cash register of the gas station. (He takes only the exact change he has lost.) When Sŏng-gŭn and Kyŏng-yŏng return triumphantly from the gas station with their 500 won (50 cents) reimbursed, Hye-jin slips into a brief mind screen, an interiorized scene where the male characters are repeating the same action—this time wearing campy cowboy costumes and holding rifles. With the use of yellow-filtered lens and the "Raindrops Are Falling on My Head" soundtrack blazing in the background, the film parodies *Butch Cassidy and the Sundance Kid*. Carefully mediated by the narrative structure, Sŏng-gŭn's assault against the machine is an act that is diegetically legitimized. The act of violence serves a multiple metonymic function where it becomes both a retaliation against the system of social injustice symbolized by the greedy owner of a gas station, and an expression that seeks to compensate for his own ineffectual manhood. This provides a rare moment for Korean cinema, which by this time has become regulated. Sŏng-gŭn's violent attack at the gas station forecasts the primary trope of a later hit film, *Attack the Gas Station* (*Chuyuso sŭpkyŏk sagŏn*, 1999). While Kim Sangjin's comedy, *Attack the Gas Station*, deliberately attempts to remove any trace of social malaise behind the disgruntled youth's inexplicable conquest of a gas station, *Out to the World* seeks to reclaim masculinity and emancipate it from the social oppression created by humanity's appendage to modern technology such as cell phones, automated services, and vending machines. This becomes a metonymic act that deliberately talks back to both the Korean film industry's emasculating tendencies before its turn to blockbuster-type films in the late 1990s and Hollywood's techno-masculinizing impulses.

Out to the World, like other films of the New Korean Cinema of the late 1980s and the early 1990s, is positioned at a cross-section of the traffic between pitiable men of the early 1980s (such as *Whale Hunting*) and the superman-like characters of the late 1990s blockbuster films (*Shiri*). Juxtaposing Sŏng-gŭn and Kyŏng-yŏng, two misfits, against two of the most memorable gunmen in the American cinema results in a humbling of their masculine potencies even more. In many ways, these characters are closer to the self-agonizing characters like Pyŏng-t'ae (of *Whale Hunting*) and Tŏk-pae (of *A Fine, Windy Day*) than No Mark who leads the youth gang in *Attack the Gas Station* and who is seemingly freed from any mark of anxiety or trauma. The breakup of the linear narrative movement with a scene fantasized by Hye-jin, the female protagonist, provides the interlude that also humorizes the masculine lack depicted elsewhere in the film. The insertion of the comical allusion to *Butch Cassidy and the Sundance Kid* recasts Korea's masculinity as well as its relationship to women. As much as the real romance in *Butch Cassidy* is between two male protagonists played by Robert Redford and Paul Newman, *Out to the World* colors the relationship between Sŏng-gŭn and Kyŏng-yŏng with homoerotic tones.[25]

The two characters both have "masked" roles, their pasts remaining largely unveiled. Here, I use the word "masked," following the title of Steven Cohan's book, *Masked Men*, where he characterizes the Hollywood representation of masculinity during the 1950s to be highly conflicting, unstable, and incoherent beneath the societal presumption that American men are capable and normative.[26] In *Out to the World*, the male masquerade is quite evident as the two fugitives are at times dressed up in riotous costumes in order to evade the vigilant eyes of the authorities. This masquerade, albeit comical, is deeply engrained in the psychic loss and the social disenfranchisement of all three characters. Further disorienting Sŏng-gŭn's ego is his wife's runaway to Japan while he is in prison. His absence from the "world," with his body literally confined in prison, is both a symptom of a cinema that did not have much identifiable masculinity available in public other than a few self-loathing characters patented by the actor, An Sŏng-gi, in the 1980s and a withdrawal of the moviegoers who instead preferred to find it in Hollywood cinema at the time. *Out to the World* does seek to replace the erotic impulses created void by the disappearance of Sŏng-gŭn's wife. If Sŏng-gŭn is positioned in the center of the narrative and it's his lack that the film tries to replenish, Kyŏng-yŏng—the younger prisoner with a charming face—complements him at his side. Kyŏng-yŏng is like a child suffering from separation anxiety, and, despite the insults levied against him by Sŏng-gŭn, he refuses to part from him. Unlike Sŏng-gŭn, who is reticent and only talks about things that are credible, Kyŏng-yŏng is a chatterbox. Very little truth resides beneath all of his embellishments and exaggerations. He is also volatile, danger-ously threatening even to Sŏng-gŭn, and dares to pull the trigger against him at point blank. His overzealous confidence and putative toughness convince the bunch to rob a high-security bank smack in the middle of downtown Seoul.

Acknowledged in the marketing catch phrases of the film as a gay charac-ter, Kyŏng-yŏng is one of the few nonstraight characters depicted in a Korean film who is not villainous.[27] His unstable identity is immediately made clear not only through his volatility that shifts from emotional outbursts to flirtatious, playful manners, but also through his relationships with Sŏng-gŭn and Hye-jin. Kyŏng-yŏng at one point bashfully calls Sŏng-gŭn "hyŏng" (older brother) to deflect an awkward moment. When Sŏng-gŭn remains stern, Kyŏng-yŏng calls him "oppa," the same designation used only by women when calling their older brothers. Also, he calls Hye-jin a *mich'innyŏn* (crazy bitch), which ami-ably forges their lowbrow "feminine" alliance. At this juncture, the relationship between the two men becomes inscribed as "butch-femme" relations and af-firms the film's strategy to masculinize Sŏng-gŭn and to feminize Kyŏng-yŏng. Although the film figures a triangular relationship that could potentially cre-ate a rivalry between the two male characters, because of Kyŏng-yŏng's "flam-ingly" gay characteristics, no romantic tension or violent conflict arises be-tween the two. Also remarkable about Kyŏng-yŏng are his resiliency when things go wrong and his inherent optimism. Contrasted against Sŏng-gŭn, who is constantly anxious of the police, Kyŏng-yŏng has a fearless determination that keeps them moving upward, eventually headed to North Korea. He is able to endure humiliation and insults, and retranslate them into something useful.

Kyŏng-yŏng's masochism naturally resists the symbolic castration endowed in heterosexual impulses. According to Rey Chow, "[Deleuze] suggests that while sadism is, in accordance with Freud's Oedipus complex, oriented toward dominating and controlling the other under the father's law, the origin of mas-ochism lies in the preoedipal phase of infancy, where the goal is fusion with the mother and the mother alone."[28] What Rey Chow explains is Deleuze's re-interpretation of masochism that stands radically apart from Freudian sadism and its dominating tendencies. Violence is indeed muted or suspended in this moment of masochism where suffering becomes emotionally heightened. One of the strengths of *Out to the World* is that the relationships among the three

Hye-jin (center) with two men. *Out to the World* (1994).

characters, unlike in *Sopyonje*, are hardly perverse or violent. The relationships among the three are "naturalized" because the film does not conceal the desire of the masochistic male to unite with his "mother" character. If, in Freud, the fear of castration functioned to prohibit incest, Deleuze argues that the masochist has liberated himself from such fears by welcoming the possibility of sexually engaging with the mother and thereby erasing the father and his patriarchic power. Yet the drive to relocate the mother also continues to condition the symptom of male weakness, the very crisis the New Korean Cinema putatively conceives.

The search for the absent mother is compromised by designating Hye-jin—the whore—in the role of the surrogate mother to help the two men to pull themselves out of the crisis. Interesting in the film is that the profiling of Hye-jin as the mother realizes two objectives: she nurtures Sŏng-gŭn and Kyŏng-yŏng while shrinking the possibility of homoerotic union between the two. Much like the American buddy movie genre represented by movies such as *Butch Cassidy*, *Out to the World* diffuses the homophilic impulses between Sŏng-gŭn and Kyŏng-yŏng by strategically positioning the female character literally between the two male bodies. Toward the end, when the three characters bathe and sleep together in a motel, Hye-jin occupies the center position. The overlapping of the "contaminated" female body with the two men fits Hye-jin into the double role of whore and mother. As much as the film is about the demise of two men who cannot conform to social norms, the film documents Hye-jin's transformation from a prostitute to a mother. When Hye-jin enters the film for the first time, she is wearing bright-colored eye shadow and lipstick, pink stockings, and a yellow dress. Her subjectivity is firmly holed in a traditional profile of Korean women that radically shifts between a virtuous mother and a dirty whore. This is one among the five films Shim Hye-jin starred in in the 1990s, where she played virtually the same character, a call girl or a prostitute: *Black Republic* (*Kŭdŭl do uri ch'ŏrŏm*, Park Kwang-su, dir., 1990), *White Badge* (*Hayan chŏnjaeng*, Chŏng Chi-yŏng, dir., 1991), and *Green Fish* (*Ch'orok mulgogi*, Yi Ch'ang-dong, dir., 1996) among them. In *Out to the World*, Hye-jin is first introduced as a caricatured whore in an exaggerated tacky sexual outfit; she is later transformed into a "real" woman, becoming a mother to the two bewildered men. Throughout the story, she has all the reason to be a victim since she is, after all, kidnapped and held captive by dangerous, emotionally unstable, and armed fugitives. Yet, she never once allows herself to be victimized like the characters portrayed by Victoria Abril in *Atame!* (Pedro Almodovar, dir., 1989) and Christina Ricci in *Buffalo '66* (Vincent Gallo, dir., 1998), women who are kidnapped by men who have just been released from state institutions and who end up falling in love with their abductors. Hye-jin has no reason to be afraid, because once she is positioned as a mother to the two men, her sexuality becomes stripped, making her sexually unappealing to them. Her subjectivity indeed mutates. Sitting among the empty cargo of a train, she embraces first Sŏng-gŭn and then Kyŏng-yŏng. As if to confirm that she is an erotic mother to these men who are undergoing a preoedipal rite of passage on the road, she allows Sŏng-gŭn to stroke her breasts, eventually holding his head gently against her chest. No sex scene follows between the two, and the subsequent scene that takes place at a countryside inn frames the relationship among the three characters in a nonsexual frame. Hye-jin is no longer the mich'innyŏn (crazy bitch) referred to by the foul-mouth Kyŏng-yŏng when she settles comfortably in a maternal role that strips the vulgar sexuality that initially characterized her. The masochistic impulse of the men who desire to unite with the mother is satisfyingly unleashed, but whether they can fully assert themselves beyond the oedipal still remains a question unanswered.

Hye-jin's romanticization of the film *Butch Cassidy* and her continuous misidentification of the film with Audrey Hepburn are elements that humorously complicate her local, gendered identity. Her performative role offers a rare glimpse of contemporary Korean film that directly confronts the deprived image of women that are reduced to whores and mothers. Hye-jin thinks that it was Hepburn who played the female lead in *Butch Cassidy*. For Hye-jin, the identification with Hepburn, her favorite Hollywood star, rather than the lesser-known Katherine Ross (who actually played the female lead in *Butch Cassidy*) allows her to fully participate in a fantasy that she always dreamed of. Hye-jin is enchanted by Hepburn's screen persona as a "glamour girl" or a "peasant girl" who later dramatically transforms into a high-society woman, popularly projected in such films as *Sabrina* (Billy Wilder, dir., 1954), *Funny Face* (Stanley Donen, dir., 1957), *Breakfast at Tiffany's* (Blake Edwards, dir., 1961), and *My Fair Lady* (George Cukor, dir., 1964). Hye-jin can now pursue the freedom featured in *Butch Cassidy* while purchasing Hepburn's dream. Yet, unlike Hepburn's dream, Hye-jin's remains unrealized in the end. Her relationship with "*Butch Cassidy* featuring Hepburn" on one level symbolizes her individual obsession with freedom, and on the another level connotes the ambivalence of Korea as a nation that has an ex–Third World status but will never be allowed to join the ranks of the First World.[29] Hye-jin's fantasy of sharing the experience of being in the Western cultural space and stripping her "real" social identity as a prostitute for the rich is not distant from Korea's dream of "catching up with Japan" and terminating its subservient role to the First World nations. The ambiguity of Korea's status is further parodied in a collective dream during which the main characters gather in the famous Millet painting of peaceful harvest, *The Gleaners*. But the film is quick to point out that this can only be a dream—like the film's possible ambition to be elevated to the revered status of *Butch Cassidy*—that can never be fulfilled.

Despite the brief scene where they were happily pictured for the first time under a roof, the film's finale is sealed in death, which was forecasted earlier in their discussion of the ending of *Butch Cassidy and the Sundance Kid*. The Korean film's ending, where Sŏng-gŭn and Kyŏng-yŏng are shot by soldiers near the DMZ, provokes the painful memory of the acts of self-immolation that were popularized during the late 1980s and the early 1990s, an intense era for democracy. However, unlike the underground political films where such acts of self-immolation were documented as spectacular heroic instances, the death motif present in this film and other films from the New Korean Cinema, notably the ones made by Park Kwang-su, poses questions that cannot easily be answered.[30] One must decide whether the ending is a disintegration or a recuperation of masculinity. Unlike the other two films discussed in this chapter, *Out to the World* cannot fully recuperate the masculinities of the two outlaws. Is it the weight of historical trauma that still splits Korea into two ideological halves? Or could it be that the masculine complex really has no answer to castration anxiety, even though the repression against the reunion with the mother has been lifted? It is not coincidental that their violent deaths occur on the beach—

their dead bodies falling into the ocean rather than on earth. Through this ending, their death drive meets the ultimate form of resistance against castration anxiety by their bodies reentering the mother's womb, affirming their failure to sever their umbilical cords. After a long road trip that has taken them as far as they can go in the peninsula, they return—in some sense—to their origin, one that also happens to be their grave.

3

"Is This How the War Is Remembered?": Violent Sex and the
Korean War in *Silver Stallion*, *Spring in My Hometown*,
and *The Taebaek Mountains*

In *Land of Exile* (*Yuhyŭng ŭi ttang*), a short story by Cho Chŏng-nae published
in 1981, Mansŏk, the protagonist, has a secret he has been keeping for thirty
years. This fragment of his past contains images that juxtapose passionate sex
and bloody violence. Just the thought of these images, so haunting and still
vivid, freezes him. He has drifted from one construction site to another for decades, and his memories are no longer reliable, but he still recalls the smell of
prohibited sex that intoxicated and infuriated him when he stood as a voyeur of
a scene of sexual intercourse between his wife and an initially unidentified man.

> Mansŏk almost cried out. He couldn't identify the man, whose buried face
> was turned away. But the one on her back, moaning, eyes tightly closed,
> mouth half open, was his very own Chŏmnye. . . . Arms crossed over her
> breasts, blanching with fear, she waddled to a corner of the room. Mansŏk,
> eyes blazing and teeth clenched, stepping closer to her. Cornered, unable
> to retreat further, the woman trembled, her nude body shriveling before
> his eyes.[1]

Mansŏk's fear quickly translates into uncontrollable rage when he recognizes
the man as his commander in the North Korea's People's Army into which he
had been recruited. He empties the bullet chamber of a machine gun into the
couple. When he is through, the room has become "a sea of blood where two
sprawled corpses spewed forth their intestines." But in killing the pair he has
lost both the woman he loves and a man he admires. Fearing a court martial,
he immediately leaves his hometown in Chŏlla Province.[2] Even after the war is

over and the People's Army has long since retreated, Mansŏk does not dare to return home. As a former soldier of the communist party, he was responsible for ordering the executions of landlords. With the sons of the landlords now back in power, he would surely face decapitation. Deprived of home and ideology, both lost forever at the moment of irretrievable violence, Mansŏk now spends his life on the road where there is only hardship. Because of this incident, Mansŏk also lost his masculinity: he has become a victim, never able to reclaim either his home or a salient fatherhood from this point forward.[3] For Mansŏk, this is how the war is remembered. The Korean War is here reduced to a series of voyeuristic images, irrevocably articulated in sexual terms.

This intricate webbing of sex and violence is a prominent phenomenon in contemporary films about the Korean War. In two of the films discussed in this chapter, *Silver Stallion* (*Ŭnma nŭn oji annŭnda*, Chang Kil-su, dir., 1991) and *Spring in My Hometown* (*Arŭmdaun sijŏl*, Yi Kwang-mo, dir., 1998), the prostitution of a mother to an American soldier instigates the violent revenge of the son through whom the story is told. Im Kwon-Taek's *The Taebaek Mountains* (*T'aebaek sanmaek*, 1994) is a film about the Korean War that also frames sex as a destructive and deceptive element that induces broken homes, intensifies rivalries between brothers, and reframes masculinity. Every sexual impulse in the film ignites guilt and shame. The guilt is borne by the women, however, not men, and subsequently the matching of deceptive sex and senseless violence affirms the phallocentric discourse. By amplifying the horror of sex and denying pervasive desires, the film protests the contaminating process of women and the dislocation of families. In other words, by focusing on abhorrent, illicit, and transgressive sexual encounters, the film's crisis becomes the men's crisis, justifying the restoration of "tradition" and order under a recharged masculine ethos. In *Dangerous Women* (1998), Chungmoo Choi writes that by disdaining the local women who have become sexualized, the "Korean male is complicit with the colonizer."[4] The stark naked body of Chŏmnye, along with numerous representations of "shameful" women copulating with men other than their husbands, strikes an ignominious image that is so shameful only the women's deaths can mend the damage and protect the honor of men and of the nation.[5]

During the 1980s, cinematic depictions of the Korean War were scarce. Among the films that received critical and/or popular attention during the 1980s, only two feature scenes from the war: *So Warm Was That Winter* (*Kŭ hae kyŏul ŭn ttattŭthaenne*, Pae Ch'ang-ho, dir., 1984) and *Gilsottum* (Im Kwon-Taek, dir., 1986). And even these films had to package the war as only memories, in flashbacks that pivotally dramatize the melodramatic tension in the featured families; there is no attempt to engage it ideologically. Of course, the vigilant censorship board then known as the Public Performance Ethics Committee discouraged any depiction of war that failed to carry messages of anticommunism. *Seven Female Prisoners* (*7 in ŭi yŏp'oro*, Yi Man-hŭi, dir., 1965), a Korean War film that for the first time attempted to depict soldiers of the People's Army humanely, was found to be violating the then-terrifying anticommunist law.[6] The arrest of its director, Yi Man-hŭi, one of the most popular filmmakers at the time, and the severe excising of the film ordered by the censorship committee made any future engagement with the Korean War outside the formulaic ideological circuit of anticommunism impossible, despite the eventual release of Yi.[7]

In the 1990s, as the political mood began to shift toward liberalization, the Korean War became once again one of the most popular historical events on screen. *The Southern Army* (*Nambugun*, Chŏng Chi-yŏng, dir.), released in 1990, opened the floodgate of films that critically retraced Korea's modern history. If there was one element that distinguished the new Korean War films from the ones that dominated theaters in the 1960s, it was the erasure of North Koreans as enemies. Dichotomous depictions of the war that simplistically characterized all North Korean communists as villains and all South Korean nationalists as virtuous victors had long since become unfashionable. The New Korean Cinema reengaged the Korean War by focusing on the previously taboo subject of underground partisan guerrillas in the South. Chŏlla Province, a mountainous region known for intense local guerrilla activities during the Korean War, had been neglected in the popular culture for most of the postwar decades, but it became the primary setting for *The Southern Army*, *To the Starry Island* (*Kŏ sŏm e kagosipta*, Park Kwang-su, dir., 1994), and *The Taebaek Mountains*.[8] This directed attention away from the spectacular war images and introspectively toward the internal conflict within a community or a family, allowing the gender question to resurface in cinema. The films produced during the Golden Age of Korean cinema in the 1960s desperately sought to reconstruct Korea's masculinity that was devitalized when Korea's military sovereignty (along with cultural subjectivity) was relinquished to the United States upon the outbreak of the Korean War in 1950.[9] In the early 1990s, the Korean War became one of the most popular settings of Korean cinema, but there was one crucial change that distinguished the New Korean Cinema from that of the Golden Age. The stylistic insistence on realism in the New Korean Cinema ended up proliferating representations of men who had lost their virility and authority during the war.

The films of the 1990s distinguished themselves by demythologizing the heroes. Nothing could better embody the image of an emasculated man than the Korean War films from this period. Consider, for instance, the final image of *The Southern Army* of Yi T'ae (played by An Sŏng-gi), a socialist guerilla ostracized by his platoon. Standing outdoors in the bitter cold weather, he holds a rifle to his chin, contemplating suicide. The humbled image of Old Hwang in *Silver Stallion*, a feudal aristocrat who is embarrassed not only by American soldiers, but also by local prostitutes who dare to use vulgar profanities against him, is also a remarkable imprint of the war. As male authority dissipates, women too are consistently victimized, brutalized, and betrayed.

I argue in this chapter that even as these new Korean War films display gender identities that are more complicated and less auspicious than the ones from the films of the 1960s, they still project a nationalist agenda that imagines a salient form of masculine identity. *The Taebaek Mountains*, for instance, is no exception. Here its director, Im Kwon-Taek, holds firm to the hope that the nation will overcome the chaos of the war, which has contaminated the Korean landscape with artillery pockmarks and Korean women with scars of sexual rape in the process of achieving a patched-up patriarchal system. By featuring lurid bodies of naked women as well as the patricidal and sadistic actions of violent men, Im Kwon-Taek—along with other directors of Korean War films—proposes that the father's absence and/or futility has allowed the woman's transgressions. Like his other films that so brilliantly dramatize the perverted narrative of the nation by depicting a repressed and dysfunctional family (one need look no further than *Sopyonje*), *The Taebaek Mountains* effectively reinscribes and legitimizes the need for the restoration of patriarchal authority.

Not only do the Korean War films of the 1990s—*The Southern Army*, *Silver Stallion*, *To the Starry Island*, *The Taebaek Mountains*, and *Spring in My Hometown*—represent the nation's crisis through the characterization of traumatic males, but they also revise the dominant historiography of the Korean War by focusing on the internal conflicts. The overriding official view in South Korea placed a strong emphasis on June 25, 1950 as the penultimate date of the war's origin—the day North Korea staged a surprise attack along the 38th Parallel, thus violating the international treaty then acceded to. By contrast, these films emphasize the tensions among the local populace in South Korea. As Kim Pŏm-u, the protagonist of *The Taebaek Mountains*, asserts, the concentration of land ownership in the hands of a few landlords who collaborated with the Japanese was one of the principle causes of the war. Representations of the North Korean People's Army are generally absent from these films. Instead the focus shifts to the southern region, where the dramatic tension is promulgated between a feudal patriarch and a subaltern woman (*Silver Stallion*), between a nationalist army camouflaged as communists and innocent villagers who are branded as

Yanggongjus challenge the local patriarch. *Sliver Stallion* (1991).

"commie-sympathizers" (*To the Starry Island*), or between two brothers with competing ideological persuasions (*The Taebaek Mountains*). Also absent are familiar images of the war: the arms of a marine reaching desperately out from a trench to rescue his wounded comrade, handsome faces of South Korean pilots in red scarves who risk their lives to carry out dangerous missions across the enemy zone, and vicious and raw expressions of the North Korean soldiers who are motivated by nothing more than killer instincts. Indeed, in *To the Starry Island*, when soldiers who represent themselves as communists are unmasked, they prove to be South Korean soldiers who deceived the naïve southern villagers in order to induce them to voluntarily identify themselves as communists before they were massacred. Such films inscribe a new meaning to the war, blurring distinctions between the "enemy" — merciless communist soldiers — and "us" — South Korean men of distinguished valor. Korean cinema had finally accepted that the list of blame for the war was indeed — as Bruce Cumings puts it — "multiple" and "long," and that it included Japanese, Americans, Soviets, and the Koreans themselves.[10]

Silver Stallion

Nowhere is the nightmarish fantasy where the "mother" is a "whore" for the *bengkos* (a derogatory term for American servicemen that literally means "big nose") more literally articulated than in *Silver Stallion*, one of the first films that signaled the public's return to the Korean War. In the film, the dyadic relationship between mother and child is rudely intervened not by the presence of the phallic father, who establishes the social norm and represses the child's desire, but by the intrusion of an uninvited outsider whose very penetration into the mother's sacred body violates the rules and the principles of the communities. With the scene of the mother having sex with bengkos positioned as the very object of "looked-at-ness," both the social norm and the psychological world of the child are threatened. Upon learning that it is not his father who has denied the oedipal dream of sexually bonding with the mother, but a foreigner who intercedes and institutionalizes himself as the Name of the Father, the oedipal taboo is differently imposed. The child's desire for the mother becomes much more accentuated, leaving the child caged in the oedipal stage.

In *Silver Stallion*, Ŏllye is the mother who becomes a victim when she is raped by American soldiers and then becomes a *yanggongju*, a local prostitute for the U.S. soldiers. Initially a poor peasant widow in a rural village, her life is dramatically transformed after the U.S. soldiers arrive in her community in order to "assist" the South to diffuse the communist aggression, and then is later spurned by the villagers for contaminating herself. Unable to garner support even from Hwang, the aging patriarch of the village who before was like a father to her, she seeks her means of survival outside the village by working as a prostitute near the military barracks. Ŏllye learns from the yanggongjus, who are shunned by the local villagers and embraced by the foreigners, not only English but also self-esteem, something that the feudal patriarch denied her. This enables her to reject her peasant status and to rebel against traditional patriarchy represented by Hwang. But she cannot completely escape from her wretched identity as her little son, Mansik, continues to make Ŏllye feel ashamed. Narrated mostly from his young perspective, *Silver Stallion* rewrites a national allegory of Korea that is positioned as an innocent victim fallen prey to the aggression of the colonizers. When the American soldiers retreat and Ŏllye is forced to make a decision whether to leave with the yanggongjus to whom she has become attached or to stay with her son, she finds it impossible to leave her maternal responsibilities.[11] At the end of the film, the warrior mounted on the silver stallion conjured up in a local legend as a savior of the village is demythologized against the violent pains of historical reality as he fails to arrive.

In *Silver Stallion*, the primary conflict is not between the foreign troops and the local village led by the aging patriarch Hwang, but between the two locals, Ŏllye and Hwang. When Ŏllye contests the authority of Hwang, she is challenging the local patriarchy, which for centuries has controlled the town. The

Ŏllye is recruited by the women. *Silver Stallion* (1991).

film criticizes Hwang's incapability of protecting Ŏllye's body from becoming "damaged" and "violated" by the foreign troops. But the criticism of Hwang is doubly complicated by the fact that it is the U.S. soldiers, foreign aggressors, who have discharged Hwang from his authority, humiliating him and ignoring his power. This triangular relationship pits the foreign soldiers against Hwang, with Ŏllye positioned as the prize between the two. Exacerbated by the insults from the Dragon Lady (Yong-nyŏ), a migrant yanggongju, Hwang's power quickly disintegrates. The patriarchic power represented by Hwang is already dismembered and decrepit before Ŏllye even decides to challenge him, a situation that requires a desperate substitution.

Through the crevice left open by the loss of Hwang's power however emerges not a feminist voice or foreign masculinity, but yet another local male, who quickly reconstitutes the patriarchic authority. Ŏllye's son, Mansik, despite his schoolboy age, vies to replace the now powerless Hwang. Hwang's tenure as the local patriarch continues its downward spiral when he is constantly humiliated by the American soldiers, by the Camptown prostitutes, and even by his surrogate daughter, Ŏllye. Hwang is insulted by Ŏllye in one of the most crucial scenes in the film when she refuses to accept an ultimatum presented by Hwang. Faced with the choice of leaving either her profession of yanggongju or her hometown, Ŏllye declares to Hwang that she will no longer accept his terms. This explosion of anger staged by a prostitute directly against an aristocratic patriarch must be remembered as one of the rare moments in Korean cinema that has historically been reluctant to challenge patriarchic authority. But even after she proudly expresses to Hwang her willingness to protect both her "sacred" home and her "dirty" profession, the terms of mutual exclusion between these two categories remain unchanged when she is speechless to her son, Mansik. Mansik's question that asks Ŏllye whether she really is a "Yankee prostitute" goes unanswered. The pride established from the moment Ŏllye declares her "independence" from Hwang quickly dissipates, and it translates into guilt and shame when she becomes the object of her own boy's suspicious gaze. At one point in the film, Ŏllye confesses to the Dragon Lady that she is considering leaving home because the gazes of both the village and her son suffocate her. Ŏllye accepts her role as a "good mother" at the end of the film, even though she has rejected the presupposed notions of filial daughter. Once she agrees with her boy, the authorial power in the family bypasses Ŏllye and it is transferred from Hwang to Mansik, establishing once again a patriarchal lineage.

Relying on the perspective of the young innocent boy as the primary viewpoint allows the film to play with the trauma of the loss and the fetishistic desire to substitute for that which is lost. The infantilization of the male characters through whom the narrative authority in both *Silver Stallion* and *Spring in My Hometown* is mobilized accomplishes two things. First, the young age of the boys in these films further highlights the diegetic absence of the father who needs quick replacement and the dyadic relationship the single widowed mother forms with the adolescent boy. The boy must be rushed into the Symbolic, but the removal of the father does not automatically convey him into adulthood. Complicating the process of the oedipal trajectory is the presence of the foreign army who substitutes for the absent father and sexually seduces the mother. The Name of the Father, which is foundational in the establishment of the Symbolic Order, is replaced by the violent projection of the foreign aggressor who proves to be far more powerful and competent than the local patriarch or the invisible father. The threatened and frustrated masculinities prominent in these Korean War narratives therefore enter the familiar cycle of disavowal, acknowledgement, and substitution before realizing the impossibility of fulfilling their desires, the desire to fully recover from the loss of home, mother, and ultimately phallus (metaphorically visualized, for instance, by the loss of Mansik's index finger in *Silver Stallion*). No way can his growth as a unified subject be verbally engendered, communicated, or acknowledged by his superego or the foreign aggressor; the situation leaves him constantly shifting.

Second, this constant shift of the infantile boy impacts not only the libidinal

Ŏllye threatens the local patriarchal order. *Silver Stallion* (1991).

economy of the mother-son bond, but also the maternal subjectivity that vies to manifest itself through her earnings as a prostitute for the U.S. soldiers. Insisting the need for care as a child in the treacherous environment of war-ridden Korea, motherhood is not forgotten but remembered as the most significant function for women in these films. Already having lost his father, the boy is unwilling to accept his mother's transformation into a whore for the bengkos. It is Mansik then whose gaze turns into one of authorial surveillance, a phallic gaze that disallows Ŏllye from becoming a "shameful" mother. In other words, Mansik now holds power—power no longer possessed by Hwang—which allows him to demand that Ŏllye choose between being a mother and a whore. The masculine power bestowed on a young child's gaze in *Silver Stallion* reminds us also of a Chinese film, *Judou* (Zhang Yi-mou, dir., 1990), where the transfer of authority is made breathtakingly from the uncle/owner of the mill to Judou's son, Tienbei, bypassing Judou. It is Tienbei's suspicious gaze that formulates the patriarchic power at the end of the film, condemning the sexual passion consummated between Tienqing and Judou, and killing them for violating the code of family honor. In *Silver Stallion*, the male gaze closely surveys the female body, her sexual passion and ultimately power, denying still the possibility of a woman formulating her own autonomous subjectivity.

The terms of gender in Korea, according to Chungmoo Choi, cannot be separated from the question of nationalism as Korean men have always been "complicit with the colonizer in disdaining Korean women."[12] She argues that women who have come into close contact with the U.S. servicemen are perceived to be threatening to the national integrity of Korea not because of the "danger of real rape [by foreign colonizers] but because of the suspicion of conspiracy against the already disempowered Korean men."[13] The raped women are assigned a position that is not simply misfortunate, but shameful and "dangerous" to the national discourse determined by local men. The image of the "conspiring women" visualized by their sons also superimposes the oedipal desire with the fear of miscegenation. This promulgates and dispatches contradictory versions of manhood that both dreams of and abhors the fantasies of forbidden love. By featuring the suspicious gazes of a male child who looks at his mother having sex with Yankee soldiers, the film profoundly figures the crisis of castration anxiety within the codes of xenophobic fear and racial tension. Here, the strategy engaged is *not* to free the women from the pains of the colonization and the war, but to develop a crisis that is astutely masculine, a crisis that discourages a (male) child from entering the Symbolic.[14]

Mansik not only protests against his mother's "dirty" work, but also disallows his friends from peeping into the window of the brothel where Ŏllye works. The children's gaze into the rooms of the whorehouse, often shot from their visual perspective, is "pleasurable" because of the gratuitous visual offerings of women engaged in transgressive sexual behavior underscored by upbeat jazz music and of the spectators' surreptitious positioning. The gaze is also discomforting because our, the spectators', consciousness cannot escape from the fact that the object of the desire (more often than not, the sexual acts engaged between Mansik's mother and U.S. soldiers are physically painful for her) is none other than *our* mother. In identifying with the young hero, the male spectator becomes complicit with the production of prohibited pleasure and anxiety in an oedipal drama. With the viewpoint of the camera assuming a subjective perspective of the children, between our identity and those of the children, the difference is blurred. Instead of participating in the children's game of peepshow, Mansik attempts to patrol the window, barring his friends from transforming his mother's workplace into an exhibition hall; but they ignore his warning. Once his masculine dignity is betrayed by their penetrating gazes, which expose his mother as a whore, Mansik, not unlike Mansŏk in *Land of Exile*, violently reacts. He pulls a gun, made from the metal scraps and fire powder left in the American military garbage, on his friends. But the shabby gun hurts Mansik rather than them, causing him to lose his index finger. This accident signifies the fragile, traumatic child who can neither accept fetishistic representation of the mother nor satisfyingly replace the absent phallus (with an American soldier already sexually replacing his father). Mansik's anxiety in an era of American military occupation ends up metonymically castrating the boy. Ironically, it is this loss that convinces Ŏllye to stay with her family and not follow the prostitutes who move with the fleeing U.S. army. The absence of the father then forces Mansik to remain in the Imaginary where he cannot acknowledge his misrecognition of the desired object, the mother. The final scene of *Silver Stallion* captures the whole village that is now in a collective evacuation when the war closes in. This scene of collective migration, which makes the whole community now needing refuge a metaphor, declares the psychological instability that remains unresolved. The film blames this dislocation on the contamination that has already taken place, and more so on the failure to effectively replace the patriarchic authority.[15]

Spring in My Hometown

The psychoanalytic crisis found in the oedipal drama that turns a mother into a whore again underscores the tension in another Korean War film made later in the decade, *Spring in My Hometown*. This film directed by Yi Kwang-mo returns the Korean War to the screen for the first time since *The Taebaek Mountains*'s lukewarm response from both general audiences and the critics in 1994. *Spring in My Hometown* was greeted with critical praises and easily won the best picture prize at the 1999 Grand Bell Awards (Korea's equivalent of the Academy Awards).[16] The avoidance of historical films from the mid- to late 1990s was particularly poignant since no historical film, with the notable exceptions of Park Kwang-su's *A Single Spark* and Jang Sun-woo's *A Petal* (*Kkotnip*, 1996), received much critical or popular attention after 1994.[17] With its uncharacteristically realist style that frequently features one-shot sequences, *Spring in My Hometown* was one of the films that stood out in a period where Korean cinema vied to survive through popular genre films featuring gangsters or comic romances.

Taking place during the late stage of the Korean War, a span of one-year before the signing of the armistice in 1953, the film tells the story of two friends, Ch'ang-hŭi and Sŏng-min. By depicting the families of these two whose fortunes go radically separate ways, the film figures the nascent stage of a new class tension during the postwar period. When Ch'ang-hŭi's father fails to return home from the prison camp, his family enters an economic downward spiral requiring the mother to sell her clothes and seek menial jobs. Meanwhile, Sŏng-min's family, which has migrated from North Korea, celebrates newfound material comfort when the father finds a job on the American military base. However, even as they enjoy steak dinners in an area and an era desperate for food, Sŏng-min's prosperity comes not without unpleasant moments of grief as they mourn the loss of their eldest son and other family members who were left behind in the North.

All this is too difficult to understand for the innocent schoolboy, Sŏng-min. His favorite after-school activity is peeping through an abandoned hut where clandestine sexual encounters are held between American soldiers and local women, with his best friend, Ch'ang-hŭi. One day, they both witness a completely unexpected event as familiar faces appear in the hut. Ch'ang-hŭi's mother greets an American soldier while Sŏng-min's father, Mr. Ch'oe, stands guard as her pimp. As his mother seduces the American soldier, all Ch'ang-hŭi can do is dejectedly look away. But later, on another occasion, determined to seek revenge, he sets fire to the hut after locking it up, burning an American soldier and another local woman to death. Ch'ang-hŭi's father returns from prison after the United States signs a cease-fire armistice with North Korea on July 27, 1953, but Ch'ang-hŭi is nowhere to be found. When the rotten body of a child is found in the village pond, rumors spread in the village that he was killed by American soldiers.

Sŏng-min's gaze often provides the visual frame and the thematic perspective of *Spring in My Hometown*, where the immorality, violence, and ultimately horrors of the adults are prominently featured. The world of grown-ups during a volatile time—particularly highlighted against the relative innocence of the young boys—is hardly serene; it includes brutality regularly exercised against the "commie" families and the prostitution of unfortunate village women to the American soldiers. Even the father of Sŏng-min and the mother of Ch'ang-hŭi cannot escape the violence and shame that web and implicate the whole community. Like his son who steals from the American soldiers a lighter and a pair of binoculars, Mr. Ch'oe uses his position in the American military camp to smuggle metal scraps and also to make sexual arrangements for the American soldiers. Not only did he encourage Ch'ang-hŭi's mother to sexually seduce American soldiers, but he even condones his daughter's romantic affair with an American officer and her subsequent pregnancy to attain his own advancement.

The Ch'oe family cannot shake loose the historical contradiction of a Korea that, having fallen into an economic abyss, can only dig through the pile of dump left by the Americans. In order to "suck the American teat for all it was worth," to use the words of Bruce Cumings, Korea also had to leave its own teat exposed.[18] Of course, there is a radical difference between the two nations mutually "sucking each other's teat": while the United States was allowed to suck Korea's teat with arrogance and conceit, Korea had to suck the American teat while enduring the fear and anxiety of being caught. The "rusty tin bucket" that contains the garbage and scraps left by the Americans, which appears in *White Badge*, the original novel by Ahn Jung-hyo, could only surreptitiously be smuggled out at night.[19] The conclusion of the film features the Ch'oe family, fearing the American military force's retribution, forced to pack their belongings throughout the night and to take to the road. The beautiful mansion purchased at the midway point through the narrative by the Ch'oe family, a symbol of the nouveau riche, must also be abandoned, leaving it in the care of the uncle, a staunch anticommunist. The family, which initially migrated from North Korea to this farming community in Kyŏng-gi Province, must again abandon their home and relocate in yet another uncertain environment. No longer can their home be considered a safe haven while the threat from the outside—exemplified by the hanging laundry of the dark uniforms of the American soldiers that overwhelms the pristine local scenery—persists.

Spring in My Hometown delineates the process of a family that first uses the chaotic situation of the Korean War to its advantage, becoming the prime beneficiary in the war, before the very reason for its success ends up destroying its foundation. If the focal relationship in *Silver Stallion* was formulated between a mother and a son, here the one between father and son pivotally anchors the film. A critical moment in the film takes place in the scene where the father, Mr. Ch'oe, demands to know where Sŏng-min found an American lighter. When Ch'oe realizes that the lighter had been stolen, he takes his son into the master bedroom and beats him with a stick. His anger toward his son's theft of an American good later proves to underscore the contradictions of Ch'oe. Like his son, he is a thief. At the end of the film, the audience finds out that the Ch'oe household's rapid economic ascension was only made possible through the father's illegal smuggling activities while working for the U.S. military. When the father returns home—released from his job—with red paint poured all over him by the American soldiers after being caught, the son follows his humiliated father through the village alley. The positions are now reversed between the father and the child. It is Sŏng-min's sympathetic gaze in this scene that has replaced his father's eyes, which earlier followed the son's hobbling path off screen. This look of the boy that follows his corrupt father exculpates the father's crimes and cowardice. The boy effectively replaces the authorial position his father exhibited during the lighter incident, without leaving the masculine authority in the film vacuous. This sympathetic look at the humiliated father starkly contrasts with Ch'ang-hŭi's angry and unforgiving gaze toward his dirty mother when he first sees her in the sacrilegious hut.[20] These differ-

ent gazes—one that easily forgives the father's duplicitous and complicit behaviors and the other that permanently remembers the mother's unfortunate
transgressions—underscore Korea's contradictory gender bias.

The sexual desires, rape, victimization of the woman, and the masculine orientation coupled with American military superiority all enunciate the ideological idioms that are now all too familiar in Korean War films. Many of the motifs
that are highlighted in *Spring in My Hometown*—from the choice of the child
narrator to the binary mother/whore structure—also laid the foundation of
Ŏllye's victimization in *Silver Stallion*. Yet, there is a radical difference between
the two films and the mode of varying representation of masculinity. *Spring
in My Hometown* refashions the function of masculine nationalism by portraying the patriarch not as a protector of women's chastity, but as an abettor or
an active agent that commodifies the women's body. The conflict of interest
between masculine nationalism and contaminated yanggongju that mobilized
the thematic tension in *Silver Stallion* is replaced in *Spring in My Hometown*
by the complicit patriarch and the women who are *encouraged* by native men
to sexually seduce the American soldiers. The patriarch no longer protests his
daughters sleeping with the colonizers or attempts to protect their chastity. Instead, he collaborates with the foreigners, taking an active role in the process
of "contaminating" his own daughter and his community in order for his personal gain and selfish accumulation of wealth. No native man had encouraged
the contamination of Ŏllye, leaving the role of the pimp in the hands of other
local prostitutes.

The nationalist formula that equates good women with sexual purity and
"cleanliness" is sabotaged and frustrated by the native men themselves. This is
made clear at the very beginning of the film when a woman is seen outside an
abandoned barn in the village frequented by the American soldiers as a temporary brothel. Moments after an American soldier comes out thanking a native
man guarding the barn, a young local woman in plain traditional clothing exits.
The elderly man who has been guarding the post pays her and tells her that no
daughter more virtuous than the woman who just had sex with an American
soldier can be found elsewhere. She has sacrificed her "body" to pay for the
medical bills of her ailing father. No longer can the patriarchic nationalism and
the contaminated female body secure domains mutually exclusive from each
other, once the term "virtuous daughter" is designated by the native men who
play an active role in the lecherous business with foreign troops.

Though *Spring in My Hometown* reframes the question of chastity and the
historical role of patriarchy, implicating the fathers' complicit function in the
process of national victimization, the question still remains whether this is

An abandoned hut used by American soldiers as a temporary brothel.
Spring in My Hometown (1998).

a counter-hegemonic film. The film does offer a vision that falls outside the phallocentric gaze. For instance, in the crucial scene where the sexual meeting between Ch'ang-hŭi's mother and an American soldier takes place, the camera, unlike the one used in *Silver Stallion* or *The Taebaek Mountains*, refuses to offer scopophilic pleasures to the audiences. The sequence is hardly erotic and the characters remain even unidentifiable, until Mr. Ch'oe addresses the woman as Ch'ang-hŭi's mother. The primary shot of the scene is actually a lengthy medium shot of Ch'ang-hŭi whose face dramatically turns from curiosity to utter gloom, and then to fury. When the shot cuts to the scene of action for the first time, the couple is already dressed and the voyeuristic gaze onto the vision of sex denied. Despite the fact that the film's overarching theme services to remember the Korean War from a phallocentric perspective, this particular sequence self-consciously disrupts the hegemonic operation of the gaze. The spectator's line of gaze is not one of exteriorized identification with the naked female body, but an interiorized one with the troubled youth who cannot believe what he has seen: the naked body of his mother copulating a black American soldier.

The film closes with the director's remark: "I dedicate this film to my grandfather and my father who never lost the spark of hope even during the period of hardship and despair." Despite moments in the film that yield alternative viewing perspectives, this dedication reaffirms the film's masculine position that conveniently forgets our grandmothers and mothers whose bodies had been violated not only by the colonizers but also by our fathers and our grand-fathers. Why should there be a need to sympathize with the father if he had conspired to expose Korea's teat to be sucked by the Americans, to whom he had remained ideologically loyal, if not materially so? The film establishes the patriarchic lineage through the gaze of Sŏng-min, whose innocence continues to be irreclaimable. It is also frustrating that the story of his sister Yŏng-suk, who must endure the pains of childrearing and of raising her biracial child out-side wedlock, remains obfuscated throughout the film.[21] Again, it is the film's refusal to depart from a male perspective that demands the viewer to forgive our fathers who had putatively forsaken their dignities in order to survive, while the "misdeeds" of the mothers remain unforgotten. What is left unstated is the fact that the women were "sold" not only for survival but also for men's capital-istic profit and greed. The home is contaminated to a point where it has become uninhabitable, yet the phallocentric perspective must desperately be restored, if not by Ch'oe, then by his son Sŏng-min.

If the issue of gender perspective troubles us, the trope of class in the film is further problematic. Class division between landlords and peasants, the center-piece of social tension at the time and the primary cause for the war, is virtually erased in the film. The unmarking of class—other than the growing economic disparity between Sŏng-min's household and Chang-hŭi's, which is renting a room in Sŏng-min's house—allows the film to achieve its postcard impression of the past that has its historical depth blotted out. Even as the political slogans of "anticommunism" and red-hunts are repeatedly displayed in the film, the camera remains distant from the sequence of action and drama. The frequent long takes and long shots where movement of the camera is minimized seeks on one hand to establish the tableau effect of a faded photograph similar to that found in the family picture albums, but on the other to remove the hor-ror and violence historically unleashed by class contradiction. The anticommu-nist dogma constantly amplified in schoolyard gatherings—filled with people but devoid of enthusiasm; the riverbank filled with hanging laundry of dark American soldiers' uniforms; and the interior of the barn frequented by the American soldiers shot through the peeping gaze of the children are all con-tained in lengthy long shots where historical reality *competes* with the aesthetic beauty rendered in each shot. Then, the history that is enunciated in all of these shots—all of them registering horrible memories from the violent past— is translated into the mythological, unidentifiable, and indecipherable mur-muring that can easily be consumed by the West as picturesque images from the non-West. The memories of an inauspicious past where collaborations with the enemy, class contradictions, and domestic violence mobilize painful history

U.S. military laundry hanging out to dry. *Spring in My Hometown* (1998).

ironically framed in pristine, placid, and exquisite tableaus offer possibilities for the West unfortunately to appropriate these images as decorative pieces.[22]

The Taebaek Mountains

Im Kwon-Taek's *The Taebaek Mountains* attempts to locate the origins of the war in the 1948 Yŏsu-Sunch'ŏn Rebellion, staged two years before the war's full outbreak.[23] Born and raised in a leftist family in Chŏlla Province himself, Im finally had a chance in the mid-1990s to create a more detailed picture of the liberation period (1945–50), a time marked by intense ideological struggles. Im wanted to make this film immediately after the novel on which it is based became a bestseller in the late 1980s, but he had to wait until the inauguration of a postmilitary government before beginning work on this project.[24] No film director was in a better position than Im to adapt Cho Chŏng-nae's bestselling epic novel. Aside from having grown up in Chŏlla, Im was capable of raising the enormous production budget required for an epic, and he also shared the nationalist and humanist vision Cho proffers in the novel. Moreover, by the 1990s, he was the only active director who had lived through the war years. Although some of Im's earlier efforts—*The Hidden Hero* (*Kitbal ŏmnŏn kisu,* 1979), *Pursuit of Death* (*Tchakk'o,* 1980), and *Gilsottum* (1986), for example—focused on the everlasting impact of ideological conflict, *The Taebaek Mountains* is the film that allowed him to rethink the origins of a war that haunted him for decades. After the enormous box-office success of *Sopyonje* the year be-

Im Kwon-Taek (bottom) on the set of *The Taebaek Mountains* (1994)
with his longtime cinematographer, Chŏng Il-sŏng.
Courtesy of Im Kwon-Taek.

fore, he had a greater measure of financial freedom than he had ever had. His budget to recreate this historical epic represented, at the time, the most money spent on a Korean film.[25] Although times had changed, Im's central themes had not. Once again he placed much emphasis on the difficulties of maintaining liberal humanism and searching for a corresponding national identity.

The Taebaek Mountains undoubtedly represents Korean cinema's renewed interest in questioning the past, but perhaps its most salient feature is its stylistic reprisal of the hackneyed convention of melodrama to motivate the story.[26] The film's principle characters find themselves caught up in personal, internal, and ideological conflicts in the period from 1948 to 1950 — the three critical years that preceded the full-blown war. While Yŏm Sang-jin is a highly educated guerilla commander in the communist "partisan" army encamped in the mountains, his younger brother Sang-gu is a vulgar right-wing leader of the local Anticommunist Youth League in the small southwestern town of Pŏlgyo, collaborating with the police to quell the local socialist insurgency. Not uncommon for the time, the seeds of family conflict have already been sowed.[27] Sang-gu is repressively brutal, and by unleashing violence against communist families he intends to emerge from the shadow cast by his older and more intelligent brother. This surely exploits a familiar genre convention in which the younger brother — the bad son — becomes irrationally violent in his attempts to dispel the pressures imposed by the specter of an older brother who excels in every aspect of life. Usually in this melodramatic narrative structure, the immoral or useless son is ultimately redeemed or eliminated. Yet, unlike, for example, the Robert Stack character in *Written on the Wind* (Douglas Sirk, dir., 1956), who is accidentally killed by the character played by Rock Hudson — a friend who is like a brother to him — Sang-gu remains alive, though Sang-jin confronts him with a pistol at the end of the film and would be justified in killing him, for he is a violent rapist and a murderer. Instead, the two brothers fight, allegorizing the present-day divided Korea where antagonists quarrel with each other without actually pulling the trigger.[28]

Despite their ideological differences, the brothers share a measure of common ground through their nationalist friend, Kim Pŏm-u. Kim is the son of a landlord, but he is also an intellectual, and he maintains his moderate ideological position in the face of terrorist and coercive tactics designed to induce him to join either the rightists or the leftists. At the end of the film, the two brothers are forced to leave Pŏlgyo, but Kim remains firmly tied to his homeland. The stories of these three characters are deftly woven into Korea's turbulent history. Ideological impulses, in the form of communism, nationalism, and reactionary terror, break down the harmony of this small town. Distrust and inhumanity

Kim Pŏm-u occupies the ideological center, while Sang-jin and Sang-gu
stand to his left and right, respectively.
The Taebaek Mountains (1994).

are all that survive in this lifeless place, where the only public gatherings are guilt-ridden, anticommunist marches. Traditional divisions between the peasantry and the landowners, between male and female, and between domestic space and the public domain are continually in flux, instilling fear and anxiety in the town.

Im accentuated the perception of fear by shooting many scenes at night. Night and day are visually juxtaposed as radically different from each other, yet they are also inseparable. The significance of nighttime dramatically changes the temporal order of the farming community that normally functions only in daylight. Night has become so transgressive and disorderly that a curfew is declared, prohibiting people from going outside after sunset. Yet both socialist guerrillas and right-wing terrorists defy this ban. Although ideologically disparate, their daily schedules are similar, for their clandestine activities are most effective at night. Civilians are rounded up by the rightist youth guards at night, tortured in darkness, and killed. When the terrorists are not at "work," they either drink or play cards in their dark quarters. Taking advantage of the rightists' enjoyment of their nocturnal leisure, the partisan guerrillas make surprise attacks, rob villages, and establish espionage contacts when the night falls. In one sequence, the radical shift between day and night is profoundly articulated. Sang-jin's army takes over a village near Pŏlgyo each night, but when the nationalist army retakes control of the village after sunrise, the people who collaborated the previous evening are rounded up and punished. And the villagers who terrorized people by randomly sending some of them off to their deaths during the day are killed as soon as the day has ended and the socialists return. The village, eventually decimated to only women, children, and the elderly, is burned down, forcing the villagers to leave. This constant exchange of power—Pŏlgyo itself is taken over by socialists twice in the film—disrupts order and ethics, endangers people's lives, and fragments homes. Nighttime activity not only produces indiscriminate killing; it also promulgates multiple instances of disorderly sex that crucially underpin the central themes of the film.

As I mentioned briefly above, by foregrounding the two brothers in direct conflict with each other, *The Taebaek Mountains* institutionalizes its thematic foundation on classic sibling animosity. The acrimony between the two is precipitated by the older brother's success and by the younger brother's jealousy and patricidal urges. Sang-gu feels that his older brother consumed all of their mother's love and then ignored him. (Even Sang-jin acknowledges, when his brother is appointed to an important right-wing post, that he seriously underestimated Sang-gu's abilities.) Sang-gu, on the day he receives word of his appointment as the new captain of the local youth league, comes home drunk.

He proudly brags to his mother that he is no longer inferior even to his high-ranking brother on the other side of the conflict. Seeing Sang-gu in a good mood, the mother requests his permission to send some rice to Sang-jin's starving family. The mood changes abruptly. Sang-gu flatly refuses his mother's plea, and, in a rage, he reveals the real reason for his hatred of socialism: Sang-gu, who constantly refers to his brother only as *ppalgaengi* (commie) or *kaejasik* (son of a bitch), announces to his mother that had his brother been a right-wing, he himself would have become a ppalgaengi. This clearly demonstrates that his engagement with anticommunism is motivated not by his firm belief in right-wing causes but by deep-rooted contempt for his brother. Sang-gu laments the fact that the family was able to finance only one son's formal education throughout college, forcing him to drop out of elementary school. In effect, both his right-wing cause and his brother's leftist sympathies spring from the same source: their family's poverty.

The loss of homes and migration promulgated by the war is translated into not only ideological warfare, but also sexual transgressions. The war, in other words, induces sex that is dangerous and violent, something that reweaves the narrative desire for a unified male subject. After the Yŏsu-Sunch'ŏn Rebellion is quelled, a new "sheriff" arrives in Pŏlgyo to put down the communist insurgency. Lim—the captain of the military forces newly dispatched to the region to minimize the impact of the communist guerrillas and reinstitute social order after the rebellion—is dissatisfied with the efforts of the local police. The red-baiting search begins once again; the community is terrorized, and communist sympathizers are executed without benefit of trial. Lim declares that "all the villagers who stayed in town [during the brief socialist takeover] are communists." He goes on to demand that reluctant local officials "gather all the residents at the schoolyard" after sunset. Lim's intrusiveness is heavily accentuated. He speaks clearly in an "extra-territorial" tongue, a northern Korean dialect that is particularly distinctive in this southern village. As we later find out, he had also been personally victimized: his house in North Korea was destroyed, and his landlord parents were executed after the communists found them guilty of treason. His *official* disdain for the left-wing, which is firmly rooted in his *personal* vendetta against communism, further implodes the boundary between public and private in the village—a boundary that was already imperiled even before Lim's arrival there. The outside threat to Pŏlgyo not only radically widens the rift between the left and right, it also creates tension within the nationalist camp—among politicians, landlords, military officers, and police.[29]

The anger and anxiety induced by Lim's loss of his parents affect the lives of people in Pŏlgyo. Though its origin is hundreds of miles away, Lim carries

the trace of "unbelonging," which sexually works its way into Pŏlgyo throughout the next three sequences. After Lim's official orders are disseminated, many
villagers are rounded up into the schoolyard. In the darkness, a flashlight in-
discriminately surveys the crowd, rehearsing the "finger-pointing" schema to
find out who is to live and who is to die. The selection of the communist sympathizers here clearly has no legal or rational grounds. The desperate outbursts
of a woman whose voice rings out in the dark — "It's her. She is the one who in-
formed on my husband. . . . My husband was killed because of you" — becomes
a sufficient reason to claim yet another victim. By contrast, Sang-gu allows
Oesŏdaek to live because he finds her attractive — despite the fact that since her
husband Kang Tong-gi is a socialist leader, it would have been justifiable to have
her shot.

The shift between public and private continues in each subsequent scene,
where the sadistic pleasures of sex and violence underpin the tensions of the
film. In the next episode, which takes place in an interrogation room at the
police headquarters, Chuksandaek, the wife of socialist Sang-jin, answers Lim's
questions. Lim does not seem to be concerned with the whereabouts of Sang-
jin (he knows that the guerrillas are in the mountains); instead he focuses on
accusing Chuksandaek of being a "commie sympathizer." When Lim suggests
that she should have discouraged her husband from engaging in socialist activities and encouraged him to focus on feeding the family, she boldly cor-
rects the fearsome captain. "Let's get this straight," she asserts. "It is because
of hunger that people become communists, not because they are communists
that people go hungry." Lim physically attacks Chuksandaek, and she retaliates
by biting his ear.[30] Here the film concedes that Korea's national historiography
of underdevelopment and poverty during the colonial and postcolonial phase
has inevitably found an ally in socialist politics. But one must also note that
Chuksandaek's resistance is motivated not by a desire to defend her communist agenda but by her courageous protection of her husband's public ideology
and her private body against Lim's threat. Her stance ensures that her sexuality
is unexposed, allowing her to achieve honorable purity and thereby immunity
from criticism. By comparison, as we will see, Oesŏdaek's "failure" to ward off
Sang-gu can be rectified only through her suicide.

The Taebaek Moutains depicts a period — the late 1940s — when sex was rig-
idly circumscribed, yet in the film, ideology intervenes and makes sex pervasive and excessive. There are three crucial scenes of sexual intercourse, and all
of them — even when they are physical expressions of love and desire — lead to
violence and death. One rape scene quickly follows the interrogation scene.
Oesŏdaek, asleep at home, is rudely awakened by Sang-gu, who insists that she

repay him now for her freedom. At nighttime, violent rape takes place, and the external threat of the community, which surfaced in the village with the arrival of Lim, now continues its circuitous "intercourse," invading the female body. In the scar tissue of Sang-gu's poverty and inferiority complex, Lim's political disenfranchisement finds vulnerable and penetrable host. Sang-gu's patricidal feelings toward his older brother are transferred into misogynistic violence directed against women whose husbands are absent. He rapes and tortures women of leftist affiliation in order to fulfill his job description as a rightwing youth guard.

Ideological instability, oedipal anxiety, and sadistic violence all undergird the troubles of the nation where homes are psychologically and ideologically fractured. Sang-jin's family and Sang-gu's family are already split into two houses—unusual given that the nuclear families were not yet standard—and only their mother can cross the ideological boundaries between the two houses. (Since the father is dead, it is the mother, the affectionate and benevolent one, who delivers food from one house to another and hides Sang-gu when Sang-jin returns from the mountains after the socialist takeover.) Confucian unity or harmony is now gravely threatened. Because "home" can no longer be conceived of as a coherent whole, Sang-gu seeks other means of self-fulfillment. He literally invades another broken home, which is already suffering from the absence of the father. By raping Oesŏdaek—whose husband Kang Tong-gi has joined Sang-jin in the mountains—and forcibly taking her on as his mistress, Sang-gu accomplishes two things. First, when he assumes the role of surrogate husband in a socialist home, he gets the revenge on his brother and tries to sexually compensate for the phallic absence created by both Kang and Sang-jin. Second, he transfers his anger and frustration to another household already tormented by a family's separation.[31] We remember that this all began with Lim's intrusion and his order to gather up all the villagers. The psychological anxiety that frustrates Kang's masculinity (a condition that also afflicts Sang-gu) compounds the external ideological factor, exacerbating the village's instability.

Oesŏdaek's "contaminated" body is now incompatible with her "pure" spirit, and in the end, her only alternative is death. Later, when rumors of Oesŏdaek's "sleeping with the enemy" has spread to the mountains, Kang forsakes his duty while briefly in Pŏlgyo and visits his home. There he finds the naked Sang-gu, who has usurped his position next to his wife, and Kang fires at him—a clear violation of the code of undercover guerrillas, who must remain anonymous and silent. Once again, transgressive sex and the deceptive gaze—not unlike the predicament of Mansŏk discussed at the beginning of this chapter—lead to violence and death, though Sang-gu escapes with only a leg injury. But once the

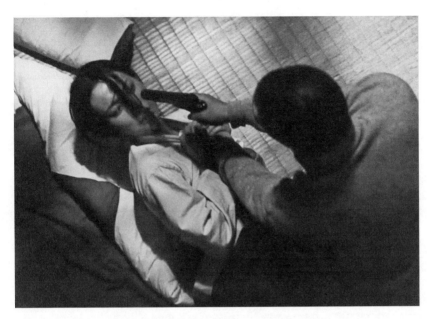

Oesŏdaek (left) is raped by Sang-gu at gunpoint.
The Taebaek Mountains (1994).

vision of her illicit sex is exposed to her husband, Oesŏdaek can no longer live. Later, when the People's Army occupies the village and the return of her socialist husband from the mountains becomes immanent, she commits suicide. Sex cannot be confined to the private realm. It has translated into discourses of power, primarily enacted and inscribed on a woman's body—once again the ventriloquist site of fiercely contested ideological warfare.

Im's handling of sex is nothing less than extraordinary. Sex is central to the narrative, for it moves the plot, complicates relationships among characters, and heightens ideological tension. Another sexually explicit scene involves Ha Tae-ch'i, a loyal leftist soldier and also a former resident of Pŏlgyo. His house, ironically situated next to Kang's, has already been ravaged by Youth League terrorists. In a scene where Sang-gu rapes Oesŏdaek once again, we hear a woman screaming from outside, and there are loud noises of household items being broken. Next door, Sang-gu's subordinates are destroying Ha's house, wife, and children. Both Oesŏdaek and Ha's wife pay heavy prices for their husbands' ideology; their bodies are punished and their homes "unhomed."

Now it is Ha's turn to find vulnerable homes suffering from familial disintegration and to politically and sexually exploit them. Camouflaged as a merchant selling wood, he travels to a commercial town, where he initiates contact with a widowed tavern-keeper, Market Lady, who welcomes him. Ha is following an official order from his guerrilla army to use the woman as a spy to get medicine needed by his comrades, and the Market Lady seeks the phallic replacement of her absent husband. Their different agendas complicate their sexual relations. In this sexually explicit sequence, Ha's loyalty to the party is perversely projected as his entire body repeatedly moves up and down, in perfect rhythm with the woman's pleasurable moan from below. Afterward, exhausted from his "labor," Ha finds blood dripping from his nose. The Market Lady tells him: "You are now responsible for lighting me up. Never will I let you go."

Several significant issues can be raised here. First, the newly established romantic relationship between Ha and the Market Lady replaces Ha's real family in Pŏlgyo that has already been ravaged and exiled. Second, women, not men, shoulder the guilt for sexual transgression. A comparison of this relationship with the one forcibly forged between Sang-gu and Oesŏdaek illuminates this point. Although Oesŏdaek has no choice but to sleep with the brutal right-wing leader, she feels such guilt and pain that she must kill herself. By contrast, even though his wife's misfortunes are directly caused by his socialism, Ha displays no guilt when he begins his new romantic relationship with the Market Lady. Ironically, the Market Lady shows more sympathy toward Ha's family than he does; at one point she tells him that she has tried to find Oesŏdaek and give her some money. Third, transgressive sex and desire always produce a female victim. Even the Market Lady pays a price for seeking sexual pleasure and replacing her absent husband. The police arrest her, and she is only freed when she agrees to become a double agent, collaborating with the police and betraying Ha and the socialists. There is neither "a white man" nor "a brown man"—Gayatri Chakravorty Spivak's sarcastic description of people who compete to save "brown women"—to rescue the Market Lady.[32] She is a *femme fatale*—promiscuous and dangerous—who cannot be left alive in this phallocentric universe. After the town is liberated by the socialists, she is seized as a spy—and shot to death by none other than Ha Tae-ch'i himself. Ha offers her a brief apology, but he doesn't hesitate to pull the trigger, punishing her for a crime that originated with her first embrace of him. *The Taebaek Moutains* demonstrates that ideology intrudes into people's homes, showing the erosion of the boundaries between public and private spaces, and the division of the village into at least two distinct ideological terrains inseparable from each other.

A different kind of relationship than those discussed above is the one that exists between Ha-sŏp, an intellectual and an undercover agent for the guerrillas, and So-hwa, a shaman's daughter who is sympathetic to socialism. Unlike the other sexual relationships, the one between Ha-sŏp and So-hwa is genuinely romantic. Yet it is also clandestine. The pair cannot take a stroll together, and Ha-sŏp can only visit So-hwa surreptitiously, in the course of "official" business trips in which he engages her to deliver messages to his wealthy parents. So-hwa, born without a father and thus a marginal figure in the village, has long been a secret admirer of Ha-sŏp. He surely exploits her love and trust to advance his own ends, but he is also a socialist, free from class biases, and he sincerely loves her. They have widely divergent views of shamanism, however, and this leads to protracted debates between them. Ha-sŏp claims that it is hocus-pocus; indeed, he tells her that as the future wife of a socialist cadre member she should abandon "poisonous" religious myth. As if to confirm that her beliefs are well founded and that there is a world beyond rigid Marxist historical determinism, she becomes unexpectedly pregnant with Ha-sŏp's child.

Yet two people forestall the relationship between them from becoming a "productive" one: Sang-gu and Ha-sŏp's mother. Right-wing violence—exercised by Sang-gu—literally aborts the child carried by So-hwa. The feudal order of rigid class distinction insisted upon by Ha-sŏp's mother blocks any possibility of a marriage between Ha-sŏp and So-hwa and the birth of their baby. Suspicious of So-hwa's frequent visits to Hasŏp's parents, Sang-gu tortures her, extracting evidence of espionage and collaboration—that is, serving as an agent for the transferal of funds from Ha-sŏp's parents to the socialist cause. When Sang-gu kicks So-hwa's gut as he tortures her, So-hwa miscarries. While she is hospitalized following the miscarriage, So-hwa receives a visit from Ha-sŏp's mother. Though initially sympathetic, the mother finally tells So-hwa, "I heard that you were pregnant with Ha-sŏp's child. Not many people know what has happened. . . . Ha-sŏp must also never know. . . . As you know very well, you could never marry him. That could never happen. So, you must forget about him. I am sorry for what has happened, but do not blame me for it." As Ha-sŏp's mother makes these unabashed statements, the camera lingers on So-hwa's face in a medium close-up. She never opens her mouth, but through her silence we understand her pain as a subaltern woman who is unsure whether her miscarriage is a relief (at the loss of a child who was destined to be a bastard and thus alienated like herself) or a reason for grief. This particular loss serves fair warning that right-wing terrorists will root out any "impregnation" by socialism. And the mother's demand that she stay silent about the child of course signifies that feudal power will ensure that such a "mistake" between a *yangban* (aristocrat) son and a *ch'ŏnmin* (low-class) shaman will not be whispered in public. All the sexual transactions explicitly visualized in the film—the one between Oesŏdaek and Sang-gu, the one between Ha and the Market Lady, and the one between So-hwa and Ha-sŏp—produce death; they demonstrate the impossibility of climbing out from under the weight of ideological loyalty, rigid class structure, and political terror.

How does the feudal patriarch respond to sex that is becoming more dangerous and rampant? One community leader in *The Taebaek Mountains*, Kim Pŏm-u's landlord father, like Old Hwang in *Silver Stallion*, no longer possesses the authority he once had, for tenant farmers are increasingly challenging traditional ethics and systems. However, in a departure from the structure of *Silver Stallion*, *The Taebaek Moutains* develops and strengthens the role of the landlord's son; Kim Pŏm-u emerges as a young man who insists on wielding power himself. As both a liberal, intellectual nationalist and a landowner, Kim Pŏm-u refuses to be drawn into the crisis that threatens the nation's phallic presence. No melodramatic tension erupts in Kim Pŏm-u's house; he is a filial son, willing to negotiate between the rioting tenants and his sick father. He quickly fills the power vacuum created by his father's illness. Through this episode, Im Kwon-Taek cautions that oedipal anxieties and precipitous challenges to the feudal patriarchal order produce only senseless violence. And he demonstrates that national order must be restored by people like Kim Pŏm-u, the young liberal son of a nationalist landlord, and a man who is neither rebellious nor anxious.

Im dramatizes two versions of family in *The Taebaek Mountains*: one that suffers from the absence of the father and the other that benefits from stable patrilineal heritage. A reverse image of the house of Sang-gu and Sang-jin, which lacks a father and is dependent on the mother, Kim Pŏm-u's house is without a matriarch. While Sang-gu's patricidal feelings toward Sang-jin, his surrogate father-figure—at one point in the film, Sang-gu mentions that he will be much better off when his brother is dead—unleash right-wing terrorism and sadistic rape in a fractured home, Kim Pŏm-u's house produces hope for the nation's future. In the opening scenes of the film, when the guerrillas taking part in the Yŏsu-Sunch'ŏn Rebellion briefly control Pŏlgyo, Kim Pŏm-u's father is tried in the people's court on charges of being a landlord. He is threatened with execution, but Sang-jin spares his life by recalling that he was a patriotic landlord who was fair to his tenants. The elder Kim's life may be saved, but as Kim Pŏm-u later acknowledges, the humiliating proceedings killed his spirit. From this point on, the elder Kim is bedridden, and he becomes increasingly decrepit and voiceless. His son develops as a leader, negotiating with the tenants, attending business meetings with other community overseers, and making crucial decisions about land distribution. Even though he comes from the landowner class, Kim Pŏm-u refuses to support right-wing causes, nor does his friendship with Sang-jin lead him to become a left-wing subscriber. The film depicts a period in which people were forced to choose between two radical politics, yet

So-hwa performs *gut*, not for the dead but for the living.
The Taebaek Mountains (1994).

Kim Pŏm-u offers an alternative. The two households frame two dramatically different pictures, not so much along the axis of ideology, but rather along the lines of family stability. Kim Pŏm-u's choice of liberal nationalism makes him a tempting target for political repression by both rightists and leftists, yet he remains above the psychological traumas that torment and fragment Sang-jin's house. Maintaining a filial relationship with his ailing father also reaffirms Kim Pŏm-u's position as the *de facto* leader of the village, even though he possesses neither Sang-jin's military authority nor Sang-gu's terrorist power. He knows that eventually history will be on his side, as long as he can hold firm to the tenets of humanism and nationalism. Im's portrait of Kim confirms once again the agenda of the nation that must remasculinize under the ideologies of liberal democracy, while avoiding self-destruction.

The Taebaek Mountains imagines a nation guided by phallocentric liberalism, where the harmonious, traditional universe of the prewar period can be restored. The film ends with Kim Pŏm-u and So-hwa talking to each other, for the first time since her miscarriage, in the midst of mayhem as the communists retreat from Pŏlgyo once more—this time from the Americans, who have entered the war. The destruction cannot be contained, even by Sang-jin, whose specific orders not to harm civilians are ignored. As buildings burn, people are massacred, and women are ravaged, Kim Pŏm-u and So-hwa fall outside the film's critique. They are "nonideological" characters; they are also the only ones who are still able to talk, for everyone else's hands are stained with blood and their voices have lost legitimacy. Their humanitarian and "pure" intentions draft a sacred identity of *minjok* (nation), proposing the present-day hope for a new Korea in its search for an uncontaminated past. What is interesting here is that minjok is synonymous with the kind of liberalism that must set itself free from socialist agency. So-hwa performs a *gut* (shamanistic ritual) at the end, comforting the souls of the newly deceased Oesŏdaek and her husband Kang, who had requested her service despite the socialists' ban on gut. So-hwa's ritual also reminds us of her grief over her aborted child. By mourning death, life will be remembered and celebrated. Yet unfortunately life privileges the "pre-ideological" past where, the film has conveniently forgotten, landlords ruled and tenants suffered, and men talked and women were silenced.

Together So-hwa and Kim Pŏm-u provide the final image unlike the proto-typical endings of other Korean War films such as *Silver Stallion* and *Spring in My Hometown*, which depict the forced migration of their principal characters. Kim Pŏm-u and So-hwa have no reason to migrate or deterritorialize. As everyone else rushes madly through the fiery streets of the village, Kim Pŏm-u admits to So-hwa, who has just finished an all-night performance of gut, that he was impressed by her performance of the ritual. But he asks how she can "spend so much energy on dead people when so many people alive are suffering?" So-hwa replies that the gut is for the living and for their han. With his ultimate focus on the two characters of nationalist and native heritages instead of on Sang-jin and Sang-gu, Im implies optimism. The "unbelonging" conjured up throughout history, as also noted in the last chapter, may not be completely re-solved even through ritualistic practice, but there remains hope for life as long as humans are not completely annihilated. What is important here is that life is valued and celebrated through the remembrance of the dead. Recall that one of the deaths So-hwa mourns is that of Oesŏdaek, a victim left unprotected by her socialist husband and then ravaged by a disturbed right-wing brother. Having slept with both a leftist and a rightist, she suffers a fate not unlike her nation's, which has fallen prey to two ideologies. Ironically, only self-destruction can salvage her life. Her fate parallels that of her country, which, having "slept" with both America and Russia, underwent a devastating civil war that produced mass self-destruction. Like Ŏllye and Ch'ang-hŭi's mother, she remains guilty of having transgressed their sexual boundaries, but she is pivotal in the ratifi-cation process of the (infantile) male subjectivity borne out of violence, anger, and deception.

4

Post-Trauma and Historical Remembrance in
A Single Spark and *A Petal*

Park Kwang-su's *A Single Spark* (*Arŏmdaun ch'ŏngnyŏn Chŏn T'ae-il*) was
released in November 1995, and *A Petal* (*Kkotnip*), directed by Jang Sun-
woo (Chang Sŏn-u), followed in April 1996.[1] By dealing with sensitive postwar historical issues at a time when most films released in South Korea were
reprising old genre formats (gangster stories, screwball comedies, and melodramas), these two films stand out. *A Single Spark* concerns the life and death
of labor union martyr Chŏn T'ae-il (1948–70), while *A Petal* depicts the 1980
Kwangju uprising, in which two thousand civilians are believed to have been
massacred.

Narratively and stylistically structured in ways that departed from normal
conventions, the cinematic figurations of the violent deaths of the labor union
leader and of the thousands in Kwangju highlighted the tragic, not-so-distant
past. However, these subjects were already familiar to the public. The uprising
had already been depicted in a popular television miniseries, *Hourglass* (*Morae
Sigye*), which aired in the early months of 1995, and was one of the focal
issues of the trial in which former South Korean presidents Chun Doo Hwan
and Roh Tae Woo were found guilty of treason and embezzlement of political
funds.[2] During the period between the arrests of Chun and Roh, in November-
December 1995, and their verdicts in April 1997, Kwangju was frequently the
subject of lead stories in the popular media. Likewise, Chŏn T'ae-il was a respected and sacred symbol of the labor and civil rights movements in Korea
long before *A Single Spark* was conceived. In particular, the Korean movement
for democracy, in which images of Chŏn and of Kwangju represented dissenting

voices for collective reckoning and historical remembrance, had already been exploited as a nostalgic reference point in the 1990s.

This chapter investigates how a new historical subjectivity becomes formulated in cinema and how these two films reveal the threats to and the eventual recuperation of that subjectivity. I am particularly interested in cinematic depictions of traumas and crises that dismantle a conventional worldview before rendering a new subjectivity. The cinema's fascination with psychological trauma is hardly new. Personal amnesia is a prominent motif, for instance, in Alfred Hitchcock films that spur obsessive drives by the victims' lovers. Dr. Constance Petersen (Ingrid Bergman) in *Spellbound* (1945) and Mark Rutland (Sean Connery) in *Marnie* (1964) risk their careers and lives to help their lovers recover traumatic childhood memories. On a larger scale, a similar dilemma is often articulated in national cinemas in countries trying to come to terms with their own humiliating pasts by confronting the task of self-reflexively engaging a history that resists both remembrance and representation.

In any new national cinema that has long endured political terror, a "posttraumatic" identity often emerges whose mission is to help viewers remember what is too painful to recuperate.[3] This is eerily similar to the mission of psychoanalysis — that is, "to reestablish the broken network of communication by allowing the patient to verbalize the meaning of his symptom: through this verbalization, the symptom is automatically dissolved."[4] As early as 1980, Thomas Elsaesser began looking at German cinema to investigate how specific national subjects were historically constructed. The films directed by Rainer Werner Fassbinder received special attention. For Elsaesser, the fading of subjectivity in Fassbinder's films demonstrated not only the deconstructive techniques in German cinema that dislodge voyeurism and fascination as the primary viewing impulses but also the critique of German fascism that so brilliantly radiated from these films' historical focus. What Elsaesser found common in Fassbinder's films is that cinema transforms from "a machinery of surveillance" into an "occasion for self-display" and exhibitionism.[5] For instance, everything falls apart in the opening of *The Marriage of Maria Braun* (1979); visual metaphors for the phallus, the nation, and modernity are in a state of ruin. Yet, even as the city hall is being bombed, the marriage of Maria Braun and Herman is pronounced by a city hall official. The ironic display of this birth of a new family juxtaposed with the hysteria and the crisis on the national scene challenges viewers to question the nation's identity.[6]

As Susan Hayward reminds us, the relationship between cinema and the nation necessarily invokes a narcissistic process whereby an individual watching his or her national cinema undergoes an identification that "implies both the individuation of the subject (within the state) and the sacrifice of the self (to the state)."[7] In other words, the viewing subject simultaneously both constructs and deconstructs him- or herself.

German filmmakers were allowed to experiment with unconventional narrative structures, as cinema was "produced outside box-office returns," giving filmmakers the status of "self-employed entrepreneurs."[8] In contrast, South Korean cinema was governed strictly by box-office considerations. Although *A Single Spark* and *A Petal* targeted primarily foreign audiences at international film festivals, the films had to recuperate a good part of their budgets for the directors' next film projects to be viable. South Korea had no equivalent source of public funds like the German Film Subsidy Board or the Australian Film Finance Commission until 1998, and the limited exposure of "art films" on domestic television shortchanged filmmakers who tried to construct a cinema that was not completely tethered to the box office. Not only were public funds denied for Korean films, but so also were bank loans, forcing filmmakers to seek alternative financial resources and credit.[9] Chaebŏls (conglomerates), including Samsung, Daewoo, and SKC, made significant investments in film projects during the 1990s, sustaining the domestic industry through this decade, but their shortsighted vision only raised actors' fees and genre film production budgets.[10] After 1997, when an economic crisis hit Korea like a monstrous tidal wave, no Korean filmmaker could neglect the box office.

A Single Spark and *A Petal* were expensive films to produce. They were made because the producers believed that the films could find audiences and also because filmmakers Park and Jang had gained international reputations that afforded them prestige and respectability with the companies investing in the productions. Not unlike Fassbinder, Werner Herzog, and Wim Wenders, Park and Jang were capable of marketing themselves and their projects as auteurs.[11]

There was probably no nation in East Asia in the 1990s that was more insecure about its national identity than Korea, given the country's history of having its sovereignty and subjectivity threatened and invalidated by the violence of both Japanese and American colonialism. If anybody could help Korea recuperate its history through cinema, it was Park and Jang. The recognizability of Park as a public figure as well as the well-known subject matter of his film helped him raise about $100,000 for his production from more than seven thousand individuals in a public campaign. This covered only about one-tenth his costs, but it became one of the key ingredients in the film's box-office success.[12] By contrast, Jang's reputation was as a political director whose films had frank sexual content. This helped him raise money for *A Petal*, which was marketed as a political film with erotic substance.

Although Park's and Jang's approaches to filmmaking differed radically, their career paths often converged. They were both from the same post–Korean War generation that grew up during the intense period of industrialization. Born during the years immediately after the war (1952 for Jang and 1955 for Park), they witnessed the renaissance of Korean cinema, which peaked in the late 1960s and the early 1970s, as well as the mass distribution of television in the 1970s. Park and Jang were still in college, at Seoul National University, when the Kwangju Uprising (Korea's Tiananmen Square massacre) occurred. Park was studying art, and Jang was majoring in anthropology and active in a theater group.

After the brief spring of democracy, ushered in by the sudden death of dictator Park Chung Hee in 1979, was crushed by a military coup, Park and Jang both pursued film as the cultural medium through which to express social discontent. Both worked briefly together in the Seoul Film Collective (Seoul Yŏnghwa Chiptan), which was devoted to alternative filmmaking and to making short political films.[13] In 1988, one year after mass protests generated democratic reforms, they both made their feature-film directorial debuts.[14]

Park's films focused on the problematics of Korea's repressive history and present reality by featuring male characters. This distinguished his work from the cinema of the Chinese Fifth Generation, which was notable for deploying female characters as allegories of the nation. By making serious social dramas, Park helped lead Korean cinema out of the 1980s, when quasi-pornographic films and melodramas featuring dysfunctional males proliferated.[15] With *A Single Spark*, Park further recuperated young masculine men who were confident, rational, and expedient. Equally important, this new cinema aligned political intellectuals with the *minjung* (people).

While Park attempted to reidentify modern Korea by presenting a new vision of men as stable and articulate, Jang's projects veered into the terrain of psychological repression.[16] Featuring dysfunctional, violent, and hysterical characters, Jang's catalog is replete with films that explore the root of not only a particular form of political terror but also an instinctual human tendency toward violence. His iconoclastic and confrontational filmmaking style has already drawn comparisons to that of Japanese director Oshima Nagisa.[17] Although Jang experimented with different styles, the underlying constant was deviant sexual impulses, making the state censors nervous every time a film of his was submitted to the ratings board. All of his last four feature films — *To You, from Me* (*Nŏ ege narŭl ponena*, 1994); *A Petal*; *Timeless, Bottomless Bad Movie* (*Nappŭn yŏnghwa*, 1997); and most recently, *Lies* (*Kŏjinmal*, 1999) — faced difficulties with the censors while generating fierce cultural debates.

Thus, despite their many similarities, Park and Jang in *A Single Spark* and *A Petal* constructed divergent historical subjects. By creating a young, masculine, working-class hero in *A Single Spark*, Park contends that the male crisis so often projected in his early films has been virtually invalidated. No longer does the protagonist, Chŏn T'ae-il, have to mask his working-class identity, as the leading men do in *Chilsu and Mansu*, who at one point disguise themselves as a college student and an artist in France. Instead, Chŏn champions his identity and fights for his rights, never once allowing the humiliation and insults he confronts for being a worker to overwhelm him. The tragic endings that seal the fates of both Ch'il-su and Man-su do not elude Chŏn, who cannot escape death either. However, the cause of his death is not ambivalent, unlike those Man-su and Maria Braun suffer.[18] Ambiguity does not promise a new beginning, only melancholy and depression. Chŏn chooses death voluntarily in order to awaken collective consciousness, giving birth to a new political agency.

In *A Petal*, Jang radically departs from Park's approach to the constitution of a firm historical subject by focusing on private sadistic impulses: cruelty, brutality, and anxiety. In addressing the question "Why were thousands of civilians killed in the Kwangju massacre?" he takes an unconventional path, looking at a romantic relationship between a handicapped worker and a hysterical young girl who is orphaned during the uprising.[19] Here, the violence so often emphasized in Jang's work corresponds to psychological fear and repression, making *A Petal* a critique of narcissism and even fascism. The film seems to suggest that the recuperation of any new political subject only fuels the masculine center and can leave the subjective empty, schizophrenic, and incoherent. Jang's protagonist in *A Petal*, Mr. Chang (undoubtedly an alter ego of Jang himself), is a repressed rapist who is humanized before finally becoming hysterical like the girl with whom he has a relationship. Released around the time of the trial of the presidents who commanded the soldiers to "restore order" in Kwangju, *A Petal* recontextualizes the event by deconstructing its historical agency.

Both *A Single Spark* and *A Petal* were released in the mid-1990s, a few years before Korea's monumental financial crisis and a few years after the inauguration of Korea's first civilian president since the early 1960s. But neither the impact of the national struggle for democracy during the late 1980s and the early 1990s nor the humiliating reality behind Korea's so-called economic miracle (exposed during the financial crisis of 1997) was clear at the time. Rather, in the mid-1990s, the prevailing cultural attitudes were defined by terms like nihilism, disillusionment, and ennui. Although the people elected President Kim Young-sam, who was inaugurated in 1993, it was uncertain whether this government was the one for which people had literally given their lives only a few years earlier.[20] With close alliances between big corporations and the Korean government maintained, the exploitation of the minjung continued. It was thus extremely difficult for the masses to generate resistance against the newly formed hegemonic power.[21]

Commonplace has been the claim that class relations are concealed or reified in capitalist relations of production, which deny the working class the means to properly represent itself.[22] The process in which a worker emerges as a true subject is a necessary if a difficult one, requiring, as Marx wrote, according to Georg Lukács, that the proletariat destroy "the conditions of its own life."[23] The crisis, then, which rests between the masses' need and desire to represent itself and the difficulty of attaining this without self-destructing, produces not only a narcissistic tendency but also hysteria. In other words, the conflict and tension between the need to represent and the impossibility of doing so unless accompanied by dramatic measures are likely to generate psychic states of trauma and hysteria. According to Kaja Silverman, "historical trauma" is "a historically precipitated but psychoanalytically specific disruption, with ramifications extending far beyond the individual psyche."[24] Externally, this symptom is communicated through violence and rage, two of the characteristics of social revolution. It is interesting that the critical moments of historical crisis have often been cinematically depicted through the characters who suffer from hysterical conditions.

Neither *A Single Spark* nor *A Petal* presents revolutionary agendas or—at their opposite end—nostalgic pastiche. Rather, like Alain Resnais's *Hiroshima Mon Amour* (1959), they are *post-traumatic* films that explore a violent public history through personal memories that evoke trauma and pain. Without gentrifying the trauma or patently resolving it, these films refuse to be integrated into prevailing ideology. Yet, as any cynic knows, the mere representation of historical misery in a commercial enterprise immediately inscribes the work in an exploitative praxis. As Ken Loach—a director known for his sensitive treatment of working-class subjects—recently admitted, when making a "film about people who are victimized and exploited, there is always the charge that you are just wallowing in their poverty and hardship."[25] Because the dominant convention of cinema is the melodramatic impulses that motivate a victim to triumph against the odds, Park and Jang must have been sorely tempted to adopt sentimental plot lines, especially given the pressure to recover the production costs of making *A Single Spark* and *A Petal*. Yet both films self-consciously resist pat dramatic endings.

A Single Spark

Death, violence, and trauma are all crucial elements of *A Single Spark*, the pinnacle of Park's career so far. The film focuses on Chŏn-T'ae-il, who immolated himself in 1970, at the age of 22. Chŏn's life is represented from the perspective of Kim Yŏng-su, a dissident activist who is trying to author Chŏn's biography five years after his death.[26] The film moves back and forth between black-and-white sequences that frame Chŏn and scenes shot in color of Kim. However, the stark visual contrast between the two time periods does not signify any change in the political mood. The sweltering and claustrophobic sweatshops lined with rows of adolescent girls laboring in front of sewing machines and their putrid bath stalls had yet to improve by 1975. Also familiar are the tactics of terrorism and coercion companies used to prevent workers from organizing and associating with labor unions. Furthermore, the state has yet to enforce workers' rights, guaranteed by the constitution, by bringing legal action against companies violating standard labor practices. Instead, the state casts a suspicious gaze on Kim, whose activities it deems subversive.

Having divided the film into two parts so that Kim's underground activities are depicted as important as the life of Chŏn (Kim has never met Chŏn and his life has to be constructed from interviews), Park demystifies the heroic representation of the political martyr. The passion that consumed Chŏn inspired many workers and intellectuals to pursue underground activities in the period when political suppression was most severe, much as, seven years earlier, the self-immolation of a Buddhist priest in Saigon did so much to bring down the Diem regime.[27] Kim Yŏng-su's biography of Chŏn's life would surely spread further his famous, desperate cry, "do not waste my death," when it's in print.

But what about the film? Its objective is neither to awaken workers' political consciousness nor to frame a haunting history as pleasurable nostalgia. Instead, the film tracks and interrogates the emergence of Chŏn as a mythical figure. The film asks, How did Chŏn come to be celebrated posthumously as a national icon? What were the conditions that precipitated his rise to legendary status, and why must Kim, a writer of fiction, resurrect Chŏn after his death? A shot of Chŏn gasping his last breaths while waving the book of labor standard law in his hand is a recurring one in the film, not because it is the image that most accurately represents Chŏn's death but because it is a powerful image of martyrdom Kim has constructed. Kim must commemorate Chŏn and reinspire the democratization movement so that conditions will be better in the future for his child, whom we are visibly reminded, will be born soon.

Rows of adolescent girls are crammed into a sweatshop.
A Single Spark (1996).

Chŏn's death is narratively juxtaposed against Kim's yet unborn baby, whose parents come from vastly different backgrounds: Kim is an intellectual and his girlfriend is a member of the working class. This is a relationship newly aligned by Park, who in previous films displayed skepticism about the possibility of a successful union between an intellectual and a worker. In a crucial moment in the film, while he is writing the conclusion to Chŏn's biography, Kim asks his father to see his pregnant girlfriend from a distance. (He cannot openly meet her in person because authorities are tailing her.) Both Chŏn's death and the baby's birth structure the two narrative strands in the film. Korean viewers, who are aware of Chŏn's inevitable self-sacrifice, await not only his death but also the safe delivery of Kim's baby, who is at risk because of the physical and psychological harassment his mother is being subjected to by the company where she works. By refusing to show the birth of the baby and using only minimal melodramatic codes when showing Chŏn's death, the film becomes somewhat anticlimactic. Yet we are aware that the baby is born at about the same cinematic time as Chŏn dies — or when Kim describes his death. Thus, there is a glimmer of hope that in the future workers will be conscious of their contradictory condition.

In Park's first four feature films, familial tension, especially intergenerational, is a crucial motif. Neither the oedipal tension that structured his previous work nor the melodramatic impulses derived from it are conspicuous in *A Single Spark*. For example, although Chŏn's efforts to mobilize a labor movement generate only lukewarm responses from his coworkers and hostility from company and state bureaucrats, his family remains supportive. In fact, neither Chŏn's nor Kim's family features prominently in the film. Chŏn's father speaks only once, while the family is eating dinner, when he says, "All of those bastards who violate the labor standard laws should be arrested." The father's endorsement of Chŏn T'ae-il's political commitment encourages Chŏn to study labor laws later on and to protest company policy on legal grounds. The father is no longer the target of youth rebellion and anxiety as he is in previous Park films,[28] in which he sexually molested his child (*Berlin Report*), betrayed his child's mother for another woman (*The Black Republic*), and blackmailed an entire village, precipitating its massacre (*To the Starry Island*). Even more supportive of Chŏn is his mother, Yi So-sŏn, who in her real life did emerge as a spiritual leader of the labor union movement throughout the 1970s and the 1980s.

His family's support and love form the foundation for Chŏn's dedication and strength so that he can adopt the role of leader, although he is only a teenager. This is not unlike the situation in Zhang Yi-mou's *Not One Less* (1999), in which Wei Minzhi, a thirteen-year-old, becomes a schoolteacher. In this Chinese film, Wei Minzhi temporarily replaces an older teacher who is attending to his ailing mother. At first, she declines to accept her new responsibilities, but later she understands that her students in the poor remote school where she teaches need her. Both Chŏn and Wei Minzhi become leaders under conditions that are both financially difficult and socially unacceptable. They are stubborn and intent, endlessly waiting for government bureaucrats who are uncooperative, ineffective, and imprudent. In both films, it is the media—television in *Not One Less* and print journalism in *A Single Spark*—that offer a glimpse of hope of change. Yet neither film presents a romanticized picture of modern Asia. Nor are there Asian beauties, such as Gong Li or Kang Su-yŏn (who became an international star for her roles in Im Kwon-Taek's Korean period pieces), who eroticize East Asia and invite a seductive foreign gaze. Yet, despite their many similarities, *Not One Less* and *A Single Spark* differ in crucial ways. While the young schoolteacher is a hero, it is her foolhardiness that allows her to emerge as a media star. *A Single Spark* is a lot more ambitious in that it tries to reposition Chŏn as a young masculine figure who represents a new beginning for Korea. Whereas the schoolteacher solicits public curiosity through her silence, Chŏn is verbally eloquent and driven to raise public awareness about the workers' miserable condition.

Chŏn's masculinity is a striking departure from the prototypical male persona that dominated in the Korean cinema of the 1980s and early 1990s. No longer is he a "masked" character who is ashamed of his class background.[29] What is fascinating is *not* that Chŏn T'ae-il is a departure from Park's previous male characters but how he differs from other working-class heroes of that period. A notable character who deserves comparison is Hansu, the protagonist in *The Night before the Strike* (*P'aŏp chŏnya*, 1990), a 16mm film that was produced underground when most dissident films were declared illegal by the state.[30] In this sensational social realist hit, which sold an estimated 300,000 tickets in underground screenings, mostly on college campuses and in small theaters, Hansu is a worker who is transformed from a cowardly scab into a labor hero. The film presents Hansu's initial dastardly betrayal of his friends and coworkers as a not uncommon action taken by poor young men who had to weigh the risk of layoff for participating in "illegal" union activities. Ambivalent about joining the struggle to form a union, Hansu masquerades as a counterrevolutionary, a role the management of his company offers him, until he awakens during the film's climax. Clearly, such conflicts are not major concerns in *A Single Spark*, where Chŏn's masculinity is unwavering and confident.

This new form of masculinity is confirmed not only through the conspicu-

Chŏn T'ae-il tries to persuade his coworkers to join the
labor movement. *A Single Spark* (1996).

ous absence of familial conflict but also in the representation of women as only
marginal characters. In *The Night before the Strike*, it is Hansu's girlfriend, a coworker and an active participant in the union movement, who tries to awaken
his working-class identity and threatens to leave him if he crosses the picket
line. The problem is that in Park's film women are regressively repositioned
as recipients of power and knowledge but are not producers of them. Chŏn is
the only developed character in *A Single Spark* and also always the "giver" in
any power relationships in his workplace. He allows his female assistants to go
home early, buys them lunch, and takes care of them when they are sick. In portraying Chŏn in this way, *A Single Spark* responds to the masculine subjectivity
that was in constant danger of dissolution throughout the 1980s. Chŏn is never
unsure of his subjectivity; however, he seems more like a regimented soldier
or a faithful worshipper than an ordinary human with internal conflicts and
moral ambiguities. As such, Chŏn becomes mythologized in an almost spiritual fantasy. For Kim, Chŏn's death is inexplicable outside a system of belief,
prompting him to mutter at one point that the death was like a "religious sacrifice." In Kim's mind, Chŏn, who as he dies yells "Do not waste my life!" in
slow motion with his hands held high, resembles Jesus Christ carrying a cross
to save others.

Chŏn T'ae-il immolates himself while holding the book of labor
standard law. *A Single Spark* (1996).

As a worker, Kim misrepresents Chŏn, a common problem when an intellectual tries to construct a working-class hero. But how does *A Single Spark* — the film — also fictionalize Chŏn? Is it sufficiently self-reflexive of its own contradictions that it too can only reconstruct history? The opening shows documentary images of a peaceful Labor Day parade in Korea in the 1990s when thousands of workers marched in organized rows as authorities stood by. But how does the film conclude? Have the masses finally acquired a revolutionary ideology, inspired by Chŏn's death? In other words, does the film successfully render the birth of a working-class subjectivity through the protagonist's martyrdom, and thereby expose the arbitrary and indeterminate capitalist conditions that deny the working class from acquiring power? These are extremely difficult questions, not because *A Single Spark* is insincere about working-class consciousness but because the very function of narrative cinema is to reify and fetishize images. Viewers are surprised in the end, not because they see Chŏn die — virtually all South Koreans are well aware of his tragic fate — but because his death is framed so anticlimatically.

In the last sequence, every effort is made not to romanticize Chŏn's death. On the day of his self-immolation, Chŏn meets a woman he knows on his way to work. Framed in long shot, the neighbor, who is barely visible or audible, says her customary "Come back safely!" to Chŏn. Chŏn's response is conspicuous in its silence. He turns around as if to say something but says nothing. The camera remains distant from its subject, who knows he will never see the woman again.

After finding out that his coworkers are reluctant to join the lunch rally against the company because their boss has threatened to fire any participants, Chŏn immolates himself. He lights the book of labor law and allows the flames to spread to his clothes, already drenched in gasoline. His motions are slow and deliberate, but the movements of the flames are swift. Soon Chŏn's entire body is covered in flames. Chŏn runs a few steps toward a small crowd before collapsing. Shot mostly from behind Chŏn, this whole sequence is quickly executed, making it difficult to see his facial expressions. After this sequence, in black-and-white, we see Kim's representation of Chŏn's death. Chŏn's body is once again in flames, but his face is now clearly seen, in color and in focus, as he holds his arms high and faces the camera.

In the differences between Chŏn's "actual death" and Kim's rewriting of it lie the issues of representation and remembrance that A Single Spark questions. While the film casts doubt on the authority of its narrator, who romanticizes Chŏn's death and dramatizes its significance, the problem remains that the actual death is also a fictional representation, by Park Kwang-su. Needless to say, both scenes are dramatic, and for spectators they are difficult to distinguish, not because viewers are untutored, but because all images of death—especially those of self-sacrifice—are shocking, regardless of the perspective.

A Petal

If A Single Spark proposes that the sacrificial virtues we see in Chŏn T'ae-il are not common, A Petal claims that there resides in everyone a cruel monster that must be tamed. A Petal insists that violence is exercised not only by the state but also by common individuals, who are often asked to repress their instincts. Even though he was aware that the public expected A Petal to indict the state for its past injustices, Jang Sun-Woo manages to steer clear of moral issues. By redirecting the political focus to a "private" relationship between a physically handicapped man and a psychologically disturbed girl, the film dramatizes a site of horror that is perhaps as shocking as the story of Oedipus. I propose an oedipal reading of A Petal, even though the protagonist's father is conspicuous in his absence—something never explained in the diegesis.

Jang is no different from other directors of the New Korean Cinema—Im Kwon-Tack and Park Kwang-su, for example—who have dealt with feudal fathers by focusing on their dysfunctions or absences.[31] However, Jang does not seek to replace the absent father with a salient form of masculinity. Instead, he cautions us against longing for the reconstitution of nation, home, family, and masculinity since they all point to a distinct and dangerous movement toward fascism, one of the tropes that is consistently negotiated with the oedipal impulses in his films.

Although *A Petal* was moderately successful at the box office, its critical reception was, at best, mixed.[32] As the two best-known feminist critics in Korea, Kim So-yŏng (Soyoung Kim) and Yu Chin-a, pointed out, the film's use of sexual violence as the primary mode of retelling history is trite and gratuitous. Kim So-yŏng questioned the need continually to use "the metaphor of rape," while Yu Chin-a asked on similar grounds: "Why must sexual violence again be used to properly represent Kwangju?"[33]

As is true of countless other national cinemas, one of the dominant tendencies of Korean cinema is to provide allegories of the nation through the figurations of tragic women. From *The Cruel History of Women in Chosŏn Dynasty* (*Yijo Yŏin Chanhoksa*, Shin Sang-ok, dir., 1969) to *Ticket* (*T'ik'et*, Im Kwon-Taek, dir., 1986), some of the best-known Korean films feature female protagonists who are the victims of society's sexism, and end up suffering tragic fates: sexual violence, suicide, and insanity.[34] Is it necessary to frame South Korean history using such trite metaphors? This is an impossible question to answer, not necessarily because it is difficult but because the question itself is woefully misdirected. In *A Petal*, Jang Sun-Woo deliberately used Kwangju as an occasion to explore human nature and not the other way around. In fact, reading *A Petal* as national allegory produces futile and frustrating results, despite the temptations the film presents.

In trying to explain what precipitated Kwangju, the director refuses to delimit the answer to that of a historian. Instead, Jang approaches the uprising from a psychological perspective: What causes amnesia, hysteria, and schizophrenia and how are they remedied? The answer is rather simple. The victim must remember the source of the trauma and recognize that he or she is a victim. Unfortunately, *A Petal* seems to say that the memory of history or recovery from trauma—especially one that involves thousands of deaths—is never satisfying or complete. In so doing, the film rejects the conventional strategy used in films by Hitchcock or, more recently, in *Forrest Gump* (Robert Zemeckis, dir., 1994), in which contested elements of history are neatly disentangled. *A Petal* is an oedipal horror story that illuminates the profound crisis of masculinity and fascism still prevalent in Korean society even now that former generals have been found guilty of their crimes.

Adapted from the story *Chŏgi sori opsi han chŏm kkopnip i chigo* (*Over There Silently Wilts a Petal*), by Ch'oe Yun, a prominent woman writer who emerged in the 1990s, the film is discursively structured, resisting a tidy linear progression. Like the novella, the film is divided into three segments. The first is the story of a wretched worker, Mr. Chang, who meets a homeless teenaged girl on his way home. Even after he rapes and stones her to prevent her from following him, she refuses to leave him. The second part focuses on four college students who wander around the country looking for their friend's younger sister, who was orphaned earlier that year. The third segment tracks the flashback memories of the same girl, who witnesses Kwangju. Although the girl is the only one in the film who can accurately answer the question fiercely debated by Chang's coworkers—did it happen or did it not?[35]—the experience is too traumatic for her to recount. Thus, instead of solving the riddle, in the fashion of Oedipus, she cannot translate the images inside her head into meaningful language. In other words, she cannot stop the tyranny that torments the people of Korea.

Perhaps no other myth in Western society is more profoundly haunting than the one about Oedipus, Jocasta, and Laius, because, as Sigmund Freud argued, men dream of their dead fathers and of having sexual relations with their mothers. The cultural and social prohibition against this desire for death and sex induces psychic repression, which resurfaces through guilt, anxieties, and traumas. In A Petal, Jang reverses this structure, shifting the gender roles of the principal characters while retaining the foundations of the crisis that articulate the instincts of parricide and incest. Indeed, the mother's death engenders the girl's guilt, and Mr. Chang, whom she calls "oppa" (older brother), sexually abuses her. The incest suggested here substitutes metaphorically for desire and eradicates the distinction between the child and her origin, the mother's womb.[36]

The girl's mother is killed during the Kwangju massacre, and her older brother is killed earlier while in the military, after being forcibly conscripted for participating in dissident activities.[37] The girl is completely abandoned, and she aimlessly wanders the dirt roads of Korea's countryside. The search for her by the four student activists—the friends of her dead brother—constitutes the director's wish to allegorize the Korean intellectuals' pursuit of the truth about Kwangju that was covered up by the state. The girl wears the red dress previously worn during the march for democracy. She seems to embody the spirit and collective memory of Kwangju, a site of democratic passion that became the target of unspeakable violence. The nation's attempt to restore order has produced the girl's mental disorder. Her inability to speak except for occasional mumblings and her failure to regain her memory reflect the contested historiography of Kwangju.

The students who comb the nation for the girl are only successful in finding

The four student activists follow the trail of a missing girl.
A Petal (1996).

a couple of men who have seen her. From them they learn that she was raped and harassed on the road. Meanwhile, the girl becomes sexually involved with Mr. Chang, who continuously rapes and beats her. Slowly, though, Chang begins to transform as he takes care of the girl. Buying her clothes, bathing her, and feeding her, he finally feels he needs to take her home. When the students find Mr. Chang's shack, however, she is no longer there. Instead, they find only Chang, who has lost his command of language. The girl has disappeared, and we are left only with her trace in the worker's unconscious. As Chang mimics the girl, the question arises, Did she ever really exist?

The presence of a ghost, whom the girl sees on a train, reinforces the film's nonlinear depictions of time and mortality. The ghost torments the girl, telling her that she is responsible for her mother's death. The evocation of horror through a specter temporally disrupts the boundaries of time—the past, the present, and the future—and refigures the identity of the girl as someone who exists halfway between reality and fantasy.[38] By opting for an indeterminate denouement, in which a meeting between the girl and the students is denied, *A Petal* leaves viewers to flirt with the idea of Kwangju as a phantasm, a specter that resides on street corners and in everyday life. Kwangju, like the fervor for democratization it embodies, is a magnetic field that pulls at Koreans with immense force. Yet, it also suffocates them with its mythological ambiguities.

In a film that features many scenes that are visually intense and haunting, there is one that is particularly worth noting. Nothing really happens in it, yet much is subconsciously revealed. Mr. Chang stops by the market after work and browses through women's clothing. Although all he wants is simply to pick out a new item for the girl, he is visibly nervous and runs away after realizing that he is unsure of her dress size. As he awkwardly retreats, the salesman murmurs, "Idiot, how can you not even know your own daughter's age?" This scene operates on many different levels. It shows Chang's motivation to change his attitude toward the girl, whom he had perceived of as only a sexual object but who is now more like a daughter to him. However, there is one issue that complicates their father-daughter relationship: they sleep together, and he has raped her several times. Viewers continue to feel uncomfortable even when Chang's primordial violence is tamed. In fact, the more custodial and fatherly he becomes, the more the relationship is seen as taboo. Chang runs away from the salesman in the marketplace not only because he does not know the girl's age but also because he is unsure how to answer the salesman's question: "Who is it for? Your wife . . . or your daughter?" He is unable to respond because the horrifying truth is that she is something caught in between.

A Petal succeeds in creating a male protagonist who is unbelievably familiar yet distant. Unlike the volatile girl, Chang is spiritless. (Even when he is violent, he displays hardly any emotion.) When he is outside, he is nervous and repressed, unable to engage in small talk with his coworkers. But when he is home, he violently shifts from being a violent rapist to a caring father.[39]

Why does the girl remain attached to this man who continues to brutalize her? Why did the director choose to use the metaphors not only of the loss of a mother but also of the girl's misrecognized sense of guilt to represent the trauma on such a monumental national scale?[40] It is important to remember that the girl initially thought Chang was her elder brother. This is a crucial knot, in that she seeks to displace and replace the absence of her mother with a father figure and refuses to come to terms with her own individual ego. Stuck in this mirror stage where she must relearn the social environment, her development is suspended indefinitely until she can acknowledge her mother's death.[41] She remembers only fragments about the monumental day when thousands were killed. The girl had followed her mother to the demonstration, against the mother's wishes, and then had fallen in the street as the paratroopers marched toward them. While trying to save her daughter, the mother was shot. Now the girl remembers the face of her mother (in white traditional clothes) turning back just before her death. This image is inserted as a brief mind-screen flashback when Chang rapes the girl for the third time. This rape sequence is particularly disturbing as the girl rubs her body hard with a rock when Chang forces her to take her clothes off. The girl's pubescent body streaked with blood, the screeching sounds, and the man's terrified reaction all create a site of horror that is possibly more gut wrenching than the shooting spree itself. Once the girl settles down and her fear subsides, Chang continues to sexually violate her even though she has yet to regain consciousness. The black-and-white image of her mother turning back to aid her fallen daughter returns. Here, we ask the question: Why does the film weave together the man's sadistic impulses, the mother's death, and the girl's self-torture?

The girl's masochistic tendency is a good place to begin. By not presenting sexual intercourse between the girl and Mr. Chang as a pleasurable exchange, the film rejects the famous Freudian phrase "I am being beaten by my father" that functions as a mechanism for latent pleasurable desires.[42] Yet how do we interpret the girl's endurance of pain while evoking the memory of her dying mother? Following Gilles Deleuze's study of masochism, which argued for a reevaluation of the Freudian conception of sadism and masochism, Gaylyn Studlar emphasized that what initially placed the two perversions as inseparable was that masochism makes the "mother the primary determinant."[43] Studlar claims: "Rooted in the fear of being abandoned by the mother, masochism obsessively recreates the movement between concealment and revelation, disappearance and appearance, seduction and rejection. Posited as 'lacking nothing,' the mother is allied with the child in the disavowal of the destruction of the superego."[44]

By "lacking nothing," there is not a thing that can instill fear in the girl. A Petal recognizes that the terror of the state will not cease simply by resisting it. Instead, by accepting and enduring torture, pain, and rape, the girl becomes more saintly. In the process, she emerges as a subject who disavows the fear of death. The girl is indeed a survivor of a holocaust, yet she has been left with only traces of knowledge of the clash at Kwangju, including that between her mother and the guns. Although she is really a hero who has survived the slaughter, others see her as mad.

Unlike A Single Spark, in which men emerge as agents of history and women are merely its recipients, A Petal attempts to deconstruct and empty out every salient subjectivity it drafts, and it replaces each with an incoherent subject like the girl. Not only is recuperation of the family ultimately denied but so also are the girl's recovery and her reunion with the students.

The complex workings of memory and history are further made discursive when language recedes from the girl's control. She regresses, ironically, to the oral stage, when the child fears separation from the mother's breasts (both instinctual and erotic), explaining in part her reluctance to detach herself physically from Chang even though he beats her.[45] Her phantasmatic subject, which

124

functions between appearance and disappearance, between real and imaginary, reminds us also of the unstable presymbolic identity in the Lacanian schema. In this stage, the mother is even more sorely missed, as the child, through the reflection of himself or herself with the mother in the mirror, recognizes selfhood. The girl's mother, however, has "a hole drilled in her stomach," and the impossibility of her return intensifies the sense of crisis and guilt the girl experiences. The temporary relief she feels when she believes Chang is her lost brother is gone when she realizes that he isn't. Soon after she departs, looking for her brother again. However, she leaves not to find agony and pain, since that would undermine the film's thematic foundation of antiauthoritarianism and antiviolence. On the contrary, she leaves because Chang—the multilayered metatrope for the complicit common man, the father, the brother, and the state—needs time to repent for his sins.

When Chang stops by the market after work for the second time, he is surprised to see the girl. Her mission is still to find her lost brother. Soon after, she places a flower on a grave and takes a seat in front of it. We hear the girl's voice: "Oppa, it's me. Do you recognize me? Tell me that you do. I have so much to say to you." And thus she begins to tell him the story of that fateful day in Kwangju, which is depicted in black-and-white. Her account of Kwangju is finally available for the viewers. But when the story ends, the girl collapses, retreating again into mental disorder.

Like Marnie Edgar or John Ballantine, two of the victims in Hitchcock films (*Marnie* and *Spellbound*), the girl must remember and articulate the past. Yet there is no Mark Rutland or Constance Petersen, believers in the value of psychoanalytic treatment, next to her, willing to risk their lives to cure her. Also, the student activists—the only ones in a position to help—never find her. (Similarly, in *A Single Spark*, Kim also finds Chŏn only after his death.) The worker, even after understanding that she needs help, has no material resources or medical knowledge to cure her. If language, according to Lacan, is the crucial means for the child to free him or herself from the preoedipal crisis, then the girl's identity will forever be impaired without the return of language. She remains hysterical: narration is ruptured, and her ability to recount history and to translate scattered images into verbal discourse is denied.

Not only is the girl unseen at the end of the film, but Chang's sanity is also gone. How are we to cope with an ending in which the girl is lost despite the meeting between Chang and the students? Furthermore, what are we to make of Chang, who has fallen under the girl's mimetic spell, reversing the process Freud described whereby *the child* pursues mimetic identification with *the father*?[46] Why has Chang also lost command of language? Have the thickness

Could the girl be a phantom of Kwangju? *A Petal* (1996).

of Kwangju and the phantasm of the girl made others forget as well? The film depicts the trajectory of Chang's transformation from a beastly rapist into a responsible and humane father. But, given that he now resembles the hysterical girl, we can only assume that the weight of *both* Chang's crime *and* the massacre in Kwangju, which are inseparable from each other, has led Chang to lose his sanity and language. The sin of stoning and raping her earlier in the film cannot easily be expiated.

Like *Hiroshima Mon Amour*, which helps viewers remember the humiliating history of France's collaboration with fascists through a woman's traumatic experience, so too *A Petal* effects a link between fascist history and psychological trauma.[47] Although this is not an uncommon theme in films directed by Pier Paolo Pasolini, early Bernardo Bertolucci, Oshima, and Fassbinder, it had not yet been popularized in Korea. Of course, Korea never experienced fascism the way Italy, Japan, and Germany did. However, the term "fascism" does not necessarily have to be framed within these particular national experiences. The term can also be deployed to describe a state of mind. It was Wilhelm Reich who wrote that "fascism" is a "structure that is confined neither to certain races or nations nor to certain parties, but is general and international," and it is the "basic emotional attitude of the average man of our authoritarian machine civilization and its mechanistic-mystical conception of life."[48] Fascism can be visualized as an ordinary man who is sexually repressed, tracing its origins to any authoritarian order and structure. Foucault also explained that fascism is "in us all, in our heads and in our everyday behavior, the fascism that causes us to love power, to desire the very thing that dominates and exploits us."[49]

A Petal holds not only the former presidents of Korea who gave the orders to shoot in Kwangju accountable for the girl's loss of sanity, but also ordinary people who passionately championed reactionary politics. Mr. Chang, a minjung, is capable of becoming a fascist, a beastly man who envies power and unleashes violence upon a powerless girl.

The link between the crimes that occurred at Kwangju and the men who rape the girl creates a powerful theme that goes beyond a single massacre. What is even more haunting is that she is raped by other men and stoned by women and children she randomly meets on the road. Before she settles down at Chang's shack, she is sexually assaulted by a group of men in a rural town. Instead of feeling ashamed for the vicious crime the town has collectively committed against the girl, the women of the village accuse the girl — orphaned and demented — of "soliciting" adulterous sex and cast stones at her through her hospital window. The film again discloses the severity and endless cycle of violence that can hardly be contained in a single historical epoch, in a single city, or in a single massacre. Despite the witch-hunting, Mr. Kim — the only person in the town who has a conscience — cares for the girl because she reminds him of when he fell in love with a teenaged girl. Later in the film, the four student activists listen to his story night after night. Singing a popular song that is repeated several times in the film, *The Woman outside the Window* (*Ch'ang pak ŭi yŏja*), about suicide after failed love, Kim affirms his masochistic tendency. It is no coincidence that the two men the girl meets on the road are either perversely sadistic (Chang) or hopelessly masochistic (Kim).

No one in the film can be absolutely free from the circuit of sin, and everyone must bear the responsibility for the girl's pain, not just the paratroopers who shot her mother or the state that ordered the soldiers to shoot. What *A Petal* painfully reminds us is that Kwangju does not — and cannot — simply fade away once the politicians and the soldiers who are responsible are punished by the law. This admission that fascism inhabits our unconscious is a truth we cannot easily shake loose. To admit that we — like Chang — embody the psychic primordial impulses that can potentially unleash destruction and sexual violence is not a pill that is easy to swallow. As the film makes painfully clear, fascism is not a term that is trapped in history, completely deleted and irrecoverable. When this is forgotten, the image of the phantom — symbolized by the brutalized young girl wearing a red dress — will return and haunt us even more.

Readers who are familiar with European art cinema might quickly conclude that the questioning of subject-hood, psychological angst, and modernist film language in *A Single Spark* and *A Petal* attest to Korean cinema's belated experimentation with what the First World pursued many decades earlier. Rey Chow, dealing with a similar issue in the context of new Chinese cinema, explains that the similar histories of post–Cultural Revolution China and post–World War II Europe—both ending with mass destruction and loss of confidence—have allowed contemporary directors like Chen Kaige to draw comparisons with European modernist writers in the ranks of Samuel Beckett and Eugene Ionesco. Yet she argues that, because of the absence of material and inspirational resources and the "full development of capitalism" in China, such comparisons are "quickly unuseful."[50] According to Chow, one of the crucial differences between Western modernist art and a film like Chen Kaige's *Yellow Earth* (1984) is that the Chinese film's process of deconstruction is not within the vocabulary of Western modernist discourse but within a "Daoist principle of nonpresence."[51] Yet even she seems to concede later in her analysis of *Yellow Earth* that the boundary between Daoist "emptiness" and Western modern philosophy has become obfuscated, fused in terms like "lack" and "aphanisis," which she defines as the "fading of the subject," after Lacan.[52] The truth is that any realist film set during the period of intense economic development and explicit social contradiction must self-reflexively question the validity of the self.

Tracing the origins of *juch'esŏng* (subjectivity) and *cha-a* (self) in Korean films and exploring the exact social conditions in which they are perceived and dislodged is almost impossible, if not futile. Not only has Korea undergone intense and compressed capitalist development, but it also experienced a severe crisis of national identity during the Japanese colonial occupation (1910–45) and the subsequent American military occupation (1945 to the present). Several films from the early to the mid-1990s self-consciously articulate the trauma collectively experienced by Koreans throughout the recent history. But this movement, as it turned out, was ephemeral—leaving the crisis largely unresolved like the indecipherable and screeching rants of a thirteen-year-old girl in *A Petal*.

I insist on the dialectical conception of subjectivity, acknowledged in Marxist thought that must first deconstruct itself in order to acquire the means to represent itself properly. It would be difficult simply to argue that the death of Chŏn T'ae-il and the disappearance of the girl are necessary preconditions for a subaltern minjung to resurface as a viable political agency. Would this not be the very abstraction of historical determinism that Marx warned us against?

Instead, I would like to propose that in these desperate images—Chŏn running while engulfed in flames and the girl laying on the ground pleading for help—reside a glimmer of hope that the fires will someday be extinguished and a helping hand will be extended. Until then, history will remain unseen and the trauma unrecovered.

II

NEW KOREAN CINEMA AUTEURS

This section profiles and extensively engages the texts of the three best-known directors of the New Korean Cinema: Park Kwang-su, Jang Sun-woo, and Hong Sang-su. All of them born within ten years of the Korean War's outbreak,[1] they are of the generation (Park and Chang slightly ahead of Hong) that grew up during the period of political acquiescence and rapid economic development. Having spent the maddening 1980s as college students and young filmmakers in their early careers, the period has had conflicting yet inerasable impact on their work. The social tension of the 1980s, a period of both political activism and economic prosperity, constitutes the major tension of their work. From the late 1980s (with the exception of Hong whose career began in the mid-1990s) to the early 2000s, they made films that were perhaps most relevant to a society that bore both the fruit and the waste of rapid industrialization and condensed modernization through the punctuation of many different levels of crises that ranged from the political to the personal.

This section, comprised of chapters devoted exclusively to the work of these three directors, does not attempt to reclaim auteur criticism as a required mode of studying cinema. It acknowledges that their films are fraught with many contradictions—both internal and external—that deny their underpinning as sole creativities uniformly marking individual signatures. But the fact that there is a pattern, structure, and regularity to styles and themes that remain common to their respective work is undeniable. After all, they at least share the writing responsibilities of their own films (Jang Sun-woo being an exception in a couple of projects), develop their original conceptualization, and are responsible for overseeing the entire project from beginning to end, extending the auteur film-making tradition in Korea that first began when Na Un-gyu wrote and directed films of monumental importance during the Japanese colonial period.[2] Also, perhaps most importantly, their works continue to feature male protagonists who embody the anxieties of intellectuals at a time of social change, and they are based on their personal encounters and experiences.

Involvement of directors in their own creative projects as producers — often without credit — during this period of dizzily paced changeover of the industry was often not a voluntary choice, but a necessary one. This environment of filmmaking in the mid-1980s when Park Kwang-su and Jang Sun-woo began their careers in Ch'ungmuro, the district in Seoul known for its concentration of movie studios, was dismal. At the time, the Korean film industry was almost dismantled, its "Golden Age," which peaked during the late 1960s and the early 1970s, long forgotten.[3] Unlike the beginning of the twenty-first century when two Korean companies, Cinema Service and CJ Entertainment, emerged as major movie companies that encompassed production and distribution that reached global markets, almost all Korean film companies then were understaffed with aging personnel hovering from the glorious days of the 1960s, housed in nondescript offices with no network beyond the local market, and incapable of producing films that either appealed to the public or were socially relevant of the day. Most Korean moviegoers grew wary of Korean movies in the 1980s. Throughout that decade and most of the 1990s — until the commercial renaissance of the Korean cinema at the turn of the century — Korean cinema only comprised about 20 percent of the domestic market share, while Hollywood films cashed in an overwhelming majority of the box-office receipts.

Korean cinema could not match the technology or the star system that Hollywood extended into its domestic market. The diminishing glamour of Korean cinema and the collapse of its star system, especially male stars, were conveniently replenished with Hollywood action heroes. Against Rocky, Rambo, and Robocop that swept the Korean movie theaters after the relaxation of import restrictions, the Korean film industry countered with the naked bodies of local women in erotic films.[4] Without half-naked female bodies sexually posing for the filmgoers on posters, Korean cinema could not be produced or marketed. During this period, even films like Im Kwon-Taek's Mandala (1981), a Buddhist film with limited sexual content, had to offer obligatory, formulaic sex scenes to guarantee its distribution.

The emergence of the New Korean Cinema through its identification with a few names of film directors must be contextualized within this inauspicious milieu. The Korean film industry had to revalorize itself to the media, to the

audiences, and to the society at large that it was producing films that were intel-
lectually engaging in order to diffuse the criticism that it was only catering to
an audience seeking gratuitous images of sex. This need for Korean cinema to
earn the respectability that it duly lost throughout the early to mid-1980s co-
incided with the new cultural and creative impulse that was fused by the social
insurgencies of the time, opening doors to many young filmmakers vying to
make films that would distinguish themselves from the conventional crop of
cheap erotic films. The local media and critics who championed the early success of these filmmakers, Park, Jang, and Hong, played pivotal roles in defining
the practice of auteur as a particular agency that was often translated into commercial value in promoting a film. The system of "auteurism" would however
soon run out of steam. Following Hollywood's infamous model of *Heaven's
Gate* (1980) and the subsequent bashing of its director Michael Cimino, the
two high-profile and over-the-budget film projects, Park Kwang-su's *The Uprising* (*Yi Chae-su ŭi nan*, 1999) and Jang Sun-woo's *The Resurrection of the
Little Match Girl* (*Sŏngnyang p'ali sonyŏ ŭi chaerim*, 2002) suffered disastrous
commercial results and ended up bankrupting their respective investors. The
results made the industry question the use of "auteurism" as a brand to make
and market films.

That all of the highlighted directors have made works that foreground male
intellectual characters and their impotence (both literal and figurative) is significant. The crisis of gender — particularly of masculinity — was the foremost
concern for the New Korean Cinema. The first five films Park directed — *Chilsu
and Mansu* (*Ch'il-su wa Man-su*, 1988), *Black Republic* (*Kŭ dŭl do uri ch'ŏrŏm*,
1990), *Berlin Report* (*Perŭlrin rip'ot'ŏ*, 1991), *To the Starry Island* (*Kŭ sŏm e kagosipta*, 1993) and *A Single Spark* (*Arŭmdaun ch'ŏngnyŏn Chŏn T'ae-il*, 1996) —
all hinge upon male intellectuals. By casting only two actors, An Sŏng-gi and
Mun Sŏng-gŭn, in the roles of intellectuals, Park's films helped shift the landscape of Korean cinematic masculinity, ushering the Korean cinema out of the
1980s during which the most popular productions were quasi-pornographic.
Jang Sun-woo and Hong Sang-su also developed a reliance on astutely male
perspectives.

All of the featured directors articulate sometimes similar, at other times radically different, values and themes. If Park Kwang-su's films vied to reawaken the
role of male intellectuals from their dysfunctions, the works of Jang Sun-woo
and Hong Sang-su reaffirm that masculinity — irrelevant of class background —
suffer crises that make the process of (phallic) recovery necessary and yet impossible. The male protagonists in *The Road to Racetrack* (*Kyŏngmajang kanŭn
kil*, Jang Sun-woo, dir., 1991), *To You, from Me* (*Nŏ ege narŭl ponenda*, Jang Sun-

woo, dir., 1994), and *Turning Gate* (*Saenghwal ŭi palgyŏn*, Hong Sang-su, dir., 2002), just to cite a few, are from intellectual backgrounds and are dismayed by their penile impotence. What undeniably surfaces even in the midst of the narratives of masculine reconstitution are the humiliating and candid scenes where their unimpressive sexual capability is repeatedly exposed.

Despite these differences, what is equally striking in the works of the three filmmakers is the uniform manner in which autonomous subjectivities and consciousness are desired from personal perspectives. The gender identities are constructed through the tensions with a discourse in which values, ethics, and psyche are defined by the parameters of historical forces. But embraced are *not* simply memories that become repositories of collective and absolute signifiers such as minjung (people) or minjok (nation), which were heavily used during the period of intense political upheavals, but the recuperating and reauthoring of them from the overwhelming categories of traditions, giving way to a modern subjecthood.

Park Kwang-su's films reclaim a subjectivity mired in state violence and contradiction, often relegating the father to complicit roles. Jang Sun-woo's films take a cynical attitude that recasts the question of subjectivity in a frame that resists coherence and goodwill. In them, the entry into the Lacanian Symbolic by his subjects becomes vehemently denied as they are permanently and irreparably injured by the contradictions of the modern society. On the other hand, history in Hong Sang-su's films, unlike the works of Park and Jang, becomes conspicuous through its absence. Desires that ceaselessly promulgate then do not proffer links to specific sights of horror in history. Yet both history and personal trauma are unconscious sources for many repressed subjects, spatializing virtually every corner of Korea into a spectrum of sexual libido. History ironically resurfaces through its deconstruction in Hong Sang-su's film where the viewers are asked to choose between equally possible yet mutually contradicting stories. The Truth that lies somewhere between historical remembrance and personal forgetfulness becomes ambiguous and almost irrelevant.

Among the many directors who were omitted from the list of film directors I have amassed, one particularly stands out. Kim Ki-dŏk has developed a string of films especially since 2000 that are perhaps the most relevant materials to the discourses focused in this book. *The Isle* (*Sŏm*, 2000), *Address Unknown* (*Such'wiin pulmyŏng*, 2001), and *A Bad Guy* (*Nappŭn namja*, 2002) all lay bare the monstrous contradiction of a Korean screen masculinity that is torn between external aggression and internal self-hate. Had the design of this book's content been defined a little later than the actual date, Kim Ki-dŏk's work would have comprised a discussion worthy of a separate chapter. There has never been a film director in the history of Korean cinema whose body of work has been as controversial as that of Kim Ki-dŏk. Though consistently selected for competition in prestigious film festivals in Europe (Venice, Berlin, and Locarno), his films have irked many local feminist critics for producing narratives that terrorize women. How deeply affective and symptomatic his films are of the standards of Korean masculinity through the reproduction of the male unconscious that harbors sadistic impulses is often neglected in these critiques, which have mostly concentrated on denigrating the films' deliberately ominous content. Kim Ki-dŏk's films are no more mysogynistic than the Korean society itself that has adopted its masculine hegemonic values by fusing neo-Confucian ethics and military rule and structure that stem from decades—if not centuries—of foreign occupation and martial violence. The most critical issue that must be underscored in reading the films of Kim Ki-dŏk is not his representation of men who are violent, but the explicit nature in which this violence is depicted and the portrayal of women who remain uniformly masochistic, without their subjectivities being declared independently from the men's. These are symptoms engendered by not only Kim Ki-dŏk; they are recurrent in most of the films discussed in this book.

Stating that all of the films discussed in this book explicitly and implicitly embody the limitations of men's perspective is perhaps just another way of saying that no work by a woman director is featured. During the period of a little more than two decades that received attention in this book (1980–2000), no woman has directed more than one feature film that has caught critical or commercial attention. (Both Yi Chŏng-hyang's *Way Home* [*Chip ŭro . . .*, 2002] and Im Sun-rye's *Waikiki Brothers* [2001] were only their second feature films and were released only after the first draft of the book had been submitted to the press.) The omission of women in the industry is glaring, a pattern that will hopefully change by the time the next volume on contemporary Korean cinema is written.

5

Male Crisis in the Early Films of Park Kwang-su

Park Kwang-su's film *Chilsu and Mansu* [*Ch'il-su wa Man-su*] (1988) depicts the lives of two working-class billboard painters in Seoul. At the beginning of the film, Ch'il-su has a date with Chi-na, a college-educated woman he has been pursuing outside his economic class. His attempts to woo her have already cost Ch'il-su one job after he arrived late for work. Ch'il-su cajoles Chi-na into going to see *Rocky IV*. In the movie-within-a-movie, Rocky displays the super-masculine gestures of the last-minute cold war showdown with a Soviet boxer. Before this boxing match, James Brown — the counterculture African-American icon from the 1960s — sings "Living in America," blessing Rocky's triumph. This scene, evidently inserted into *Rocky IV* to flaunt U.S. patriotism and celebrate the Reagan-era façade of the multicultural alliance (between Italian American and African-American), is deliberately appropriated by Park for two reasons. First, the scene, with its crass Las Vegas–type setting, produces a visual fantasy that enacts Ch'il-su's desires. Second, through the activation of the spectatorial desire of a character in the movie, it also reminds *Chilsu and Mansu*'s viewers of Ch'il-su's reality where his potency and masculinity have been constantly undermined. By specularizing Rocky, Ch'il-su's emasculation is exposed. He has been lying to Chi-na, who is looking for her prospective husband, that he attends a prestigious art school and his departure to the United States is imminent. Ch'il-su identifies with Rocky, but it is an identification that operates on masochistic impulses that both fetishize the white man's splendid body and punish his ego through guilt and shame as an unemployed working-class man who has camouflaged his identity even to his girlfriend. He tries to overcome his vulnerability and anxiety by overcompensating for his frail masculinity. He takes advantage of the dark movie theater and tries to get intimate with Chi-na. While James Brown sings in his glittery red-white-and-blue suit, Ch'il-su awkwardly reaches out to hold Chi-na's hand. Yet, his advance is thwarted when she pinches him. The denial of his desire further humiliates Ch'il-su. It reminds him of his miserable reality rather than making him forget his lies, his mask, and his real identity.

What is most intriguing is that this discursive web of discourses reaches its pinnacle inside a theater where Ch'il-su activates the scopophilic desire of the male spectator to achieve an "imagined unity" or "sutured coherence." The suture is more than simply a standard viewing praxis in a conventional Hollywood film critiqued by feminist film scholarship to problematize the fetishistic identification of the female body as an object of the male gaze.[1] It is, in Rey Chow's words, "the process of subjective activation and reactivation through complex transaction between symbolic and imaginary significations, transactions that give rise to an illusory sense of unity with the field of the other and the coherence in narrative meaning."[2] In this passage, Chow illustrates that the suturing of a look requires engagement with both of the Lacanian fields, a movement that shuffles between the identifications of both the imaginary and the symbolic. The image of powerful Rocky creates narcissistic fantasies for Ch'il-su as if the object on screen were his own reflection. But for this to be fetishized, Ch'il-su also must simultaneously recognize and disavow his identity, which is fraught with personal traumas. In other words, Rocky, standing in as the object of fetish, must be prompted by a desire that pivots on Ch'il-su's identity crisis. His mimicry of Sylvester Stallone's Rocky as well as other Hollywood male stars is pitiful because these images only further inscribe the anxiety of a colonized, emasculated, working-class man without a family.

This scene in the movie theater and Ch'il-su's imitations of his other heroes such as Marlon Brando and James Dean punctuate the crisis of masculinity, a master trope Park constantly weaves throughout his films. In *Chilsu and Mansu* and his next film, *Black Republic* (*Kŭ dŭl do uri ch'ŏrŏm*, 1990), sexual, economic, and political oppressions leave the filmic subjectivity in a void. Overdetermined by both textual and extratextual matters that navigate the historical crisis through personal traumas and injuries, these films focus on characters whose identities remain masked and fragmented because of the dire sociopolitical situation. The political contradiction in modern Korean history leaves its legacy in these male characters whose inability to properly communicate ostracizes them from a larger social linguistic network. The masculinities depicted by Park are consequently unstable; traumas suffered in a violent political past are as common as dysfunctional families. The four protagonists in his first two films, Ch'il-su and Man-su and Ki-yŏng and Sŏng-ch'ŏl in *Black Republic*, have trouble articulating themselves. Words are repressed, and even when they are not, they often mask the truth. Ch'il-su is talkative and often uses English words to elevate his cultural status, but he is a habitual liar. His partner, Man-su, is mostly reticent. When he drinks, he often has to resort to violence in order to communicate his frustrations. Their inability to explain the intentions behind their actions later results in Man-su's death and Ch'il-su's arrest. The discord between their intention and the public's misperception builds up a narrative crescendo until the film ends in tragedy. In Park's next film, *Black Republic*, "Kim Ki-yŏng" is a name borrowed from another worker because the protagonist is a blacklisted intellectual. Unable to assert any political influence or speak of his past to the people around him, Ki-yŏng remains, like Man-su, mostly wordless. His boss, Sŏng-ch'ŏl, also has difficulty saying what he really feels. Unlike Ki-yŏng, who is in trouble because of political oppression, Sŏng-ch'ŏl's anxiety is personal. He has been betrayed by his father, who left his mother for another woman, and he is also traumatized by his mother's death. He communicates primarily through sex and violence, which temporarily relieve him of his fears. Although they give him instantaneous sadistic pleasure, his anxiety will continue to haunt him until his death.

These young men in a troubled period are not only repressed, they are also besieged by their social relations and their rattled and dismantled lives. They are scarred by psychic and political problems, and thus their symbolic order is already discursivized, with the enunciation of a signifier so multiply textualized. In reading these films, I pay attention to the Lacanian theory of the Imaginary and the Symbolic. The Symbolic distinguishes itself from the Imaginary order, a world heavily dependent on the visual field and specular relations, by emphasizing the primacy of language as a means of establishing social network. If in the Imaginary order the child enters an early form of social life by redefining itself separately from the mother by looking in the mirror, in the Symbolic phase, the child inscribes itself as an agent or a subject capable of relating to a larger linguistic community. The problem is that there is constantly a circular movement between Symbolic and Imaginary identifications, at which point the phallus interweaves the two, becoming the slippery object that is desired but never attainable. That the phallus is an empty signifier without its signified complicates the subjectivization through language. Not to be confused with the real penis, the phallus is symbolic, only represented as a signifier, not as a signified. The phallus, in other words, exists as, in Slavoj Žižek's words, "a signifier of castration."[3] So, however much the subject incessantly desires it, the phallus will remain forever out of reach.

This Lacanian model is particularly useful in interpreting Park Kwang-su's films. So many of them display the very crisis in subjectivity that remains caught somewhere between the fields of the Imaginary and the Symbolic, with the Name of the Father remaining critical even after the ailing patriarch's loss of power. What is intriguing about Park is his figuration of the problematics of repressive history and reality through his male characters. Through his figuration he distinguishes himself not only from the cinema of Chinese fifth-generation filmmakers that exhibited the agency of history and the allegory of nation through female characters (most notably played by Gong Li), but also from the most prototypical and prolific director in Korean cinema during the 1980s and the 1990s, Im Kwon-Taek, who thematized the Korean national crisis through the innumerable wrecked female bodies.[4] The four films Park has made since *Chilsu and Mansu — Black Republic, Berlin Report (Perŭlrin rip'ot'ŭ,* 1991), *To the Starry Island (Kŭ sŏm e kagosipta,* 1993), and *A Single Spark (Arŭmdaun ch'ŏngnyŏn Chŏn T'ae-il,* 1996) — all center around male intellectual figures, which had been underrepresented in previous Korean films. This focus on intellectuals realigns the paradigm of realist films that, as depicted in chapter 1, previously concentrated on characterizing the urban poor as their agencies.

The new cinematic masculinity vies to figure a new political intellectual aligned with minjung (the subaltern class), but Park's films also demonstrate the realistic difficulty of coupling the two. Here is the triadic relation between ostracized intellectuals, young frustrated workers, and ineffective patriarchs that so often renders the primary character figurations in Park's films. They all are in desperate need of each other, but their linguistic handicap and social dysfunction keep them apart. Missing from this trinity is, of course, the woman, who remains contingent to Park's narrative imagination, and relegated to only insignificant roles such as surrogate mother whose maternity is sought by the ostracized male protagonist who wishes to be nurtured. On the other hand, the male intellectual characters in the films *Black Republic, Berlin Report, To the Starry Island,* and *A Single Spark* all hold crucial roles that must unveil the public discourse of past injustice that has derailed into present-day personal traumas among the people around him. Yet, the knotting of the historical violence, usually symbolized by the complicit and ailing fathers (in *Chilsu and Mansu, Berlin Report,* and *To the Starry Island*), with the present-day crisis is a task that cannot be easily assumed by the intellectual who is severed from the community. He, like the frustrated worker or the youth, remains incommunicado

Park Kwang-su (right) directs actor Yi Chŏng-jae
on the set of *Uprising* (1999).

from the rest of the society. The inability of the intellectual to present himself as an agent or represent others as historical subjects allows the personal crisis to linger, eventually producing another round of violence and death. Most of his male characters in *Chilsu and Mansu* and *Black Republic* displace their rage and troubles by masquerading in identities other than their own and eventually end up in jail or dead.

After a couple of years as assistant to Yi Chang-ho, one of the very few successful filmmakers in the 1980s' box office, Park directed his first feature, *Chilsu and Mansu*, in 1988, the year the Olympics were held in Korea.[5] Park was among the first wave of film directors who had crafted his trade during his student days, working on Super 8 and 16mm films and participating in an alternative film collective, the first of its kind in the early 1980s.[6] *Chilsu and Mansu* signaled a new wave in the mainstream film culture, bringing back "social critique" in movies after its long hiatus during the Chun Doo Hwan regime (1980–88). Loosely adapted from a short story, "Two Signpainters," by the Taiwanese dissident writer Huang Ch'un-ming,[7] the film exhibited a cautiously orchestrated, symbiotic mixture of the popular genre codes of comedy and melodrama with psychological and political themes, vying to reach for the potential of cinema that can enmesh entertainment, art, and politics. For Park, a feature film required an astronomical budget, so he could not completely abandon the popular conventions favored by the producers who financed his films. The formula of male bonding that ties the narrative knot in *Chilsu and Mansu* was proven box-office material as even Park's former mentor, Yi Chang-ho, had successfully demonstrated in his hit films, *A Fine, Windy Day* (*Param purŏ choŏn nal*, 1980) and *The Declaration of Fools* (*Papo sŏnŏn*, 1983). Also, Pae Ch'ang-ho's immensely popular *Whale Hunting* (*Korae sanyang*, 1984) that combines a college dropout who is in search of his "whale" with an itinerant beggar, proved to the producers that audiences respond favorably to male bonding on the screen. In these films, male crisis is depicted, yet their social origins are hardly defined. What separated *Chilsu and Mansu* from the rest was its determination to investigate politically the traumas of male characters that had never before been shown to a general audience. The public manifestations rendered in these films declared the constitution of a nascent, yet provocative, element that announced the arrival of the New Korean Cinema.

What distinguishes Park's work from the previous films is his realistic representation of his subject. Park not only resists melodramatic temptations to have the male protagonist's crisis resolved by heroics that reintegrate him into the society,[8] he also moves the social problematics toward the individual and private realm. In his films, the personal crisis that pivotally moves the narrative normally remains unresolved in spite of the exposure of its link with the historical. Once this is disclosed, the state, by invoking the Name of the (dead) Father, intervenes, putting an end to the crisis by destroying the subject. The very placement of political and historical imperatives of the U.S. military occupation, ideological conflict, and bourgeois crisis in the familial cultural landscape, which eventually creates a tension across generations that seeps into the desire and the repression of masculine youth, renders textual circumstances in which the use of psychoanalysis is not only favorable, but also necessary.

In a pioneering essay that introduced Zhang Yi-mou's *Red Sorghum* to Western scholarship, Yuejin Wang argues that Chinese men suffer from a femininity complex that forms the "unconscious in the Chinese psyche."[9] For Wang, the emasculation of Chinese men is symptomized by their "lack," which allows them to fit more comfortably into a space traditionally designated for women. Therefore, he can claim that through the articulation of autonomous female subjectivity peeks the repressed desire expressed in *Red Sorghum*, which eventually "rewrites the maternal discourses of Chinese textuality."[10] Even though Wang's elucidation of the Chinese text as the sexual figuration of the maternal is informative, his presumption of the "lack" as a biological essence that belongs to women because they have no penis fails to consider the Lacanian theory that men suffer from the phallic lack just as women do.[11] This Lacanian position — despite the debates among feminists whether even this model frees women from phallocentrism — has transformed the concepts of penis envy and lack so central to Freud in distinguishing the psyche of women from that of men using more degenderized models.[12] This allows a critique that treats phallocentrism not as an overvaluation of the male sex organ and a gendered domain, but rather as an interlocking system of language and subjectivity susceptible to the domination of rational speaking subjects.

But perhaps the most conspicuous problem of Park's films is that only the male intellectual characters are taken as being credible, as the only ones who have something important to say. There is no doubt that in his films, language emerges as the primary site of filmic contestation, and the crisis centers on the politics of representation. Even though all of his protagonists are frustrated by the difficulty of finding the appropriate linguistic channel to talk back to the state, which exercises political repression that would overwhelm anyone, the crisis is for the men to bear because language is their domain.

Unlike the films of Yi Chang-dong and Kim Ki-dŏk who have later focused on the mastery of corporeality as one of the preconditions of the subjecthood of their male protagonists, the crisis in Park Kwang-su's films can only be resolved in linguistic terms. The acquisition and command of language so primal to the constitution of a subject is an unrequited dream conceptualized elsewhere in other "new" national cinemas, typically cast in any post-traumatic cinemas that come out of periods of intense political repression. The cinematic construction of a national crisis through the paradigm of familial and gender tensions is found in many national cinemas including the post-Mao Chinese cinema, the post-Franco Spanish cinema, and the post–World War II German cinema.[13] Park's themes and motifs immediately welcomed by the European art-house festival circuits and hailed by the Western film critics as de facto the most representative works of the New Korean Cinema attest to this familiarity. To the question, "Can the real man and his ego ideal be constituted?" his films have continuously responded negatively, despite their incessant desire to usher in a subject beyond the crisis and the dysfunction that haunted the Korean cinema during the 1970s and the 1980s. Instead of resolving the crisis, the traumatic subject is unable to undo the knot that ties him to the colonial identity, fetishized images, familial dysfunction, and even the dogma of radical politics, which continues to conjure up the question of self-representation, allowing the state to destroy the subject at the very last instance.

Ch'il-su tries to cajole the girl of his dreams out on a date.
Chilsu and Mansu (1988).

Chilsu and Mansu

Not only inside the movie theater can Ch'il-su assume identities other than his own. In Seoul, already a postmodern city dependent on visual signs, Ch'il-su is like a child who is placed in front of a magic mirror, where images from movie billboards, street signs, arcade games, discotheque lights, and movie posters offer multiple identities for him to fantasize about. Even though his fantasy will only be that—something that is conditioned by its very impossibility—young Ch'il-su spends his leisure time playing arcade games that feature American coastal highways, loitering in a Burger King, and imitating American movie stars pinned up in his room. Ch'il-su sits as voyeur and consumer of these images to forget his anxieties about living as an underprivileged worker, but his masculinity remains pathetic because there is no remedy for his identity crisis. His identification with American movie heroes of the 1950s is significant. James Dean's rebellion against Eisenhower-era conformity and family oppression means even a privilege to Ch'il-su who has no salient family around him to protest. By showing Ch'il-su's desire to place himself inside the American imaginary scenery (the film at one point constructs a fantasy sequence of Ch'il-su driving a convertible along the coastal highway with Chi-na in his arm), the film amplifies Ch'il-su's displaced familial crisis: his father (a retired "houseboy" for the American soldiers) is an alcoholic, and his sister (a surrogate of his dead mother) has been "sold" to the Americans as a "GI bride."

Ch'il-su also lacks the material wealth that can fetishistically substitute for his familial instability. Though Chi-na thinks he is an art student, Ch'il-su is in fact a billboard painter laboring in hazardous conditions. He is also a compulsive liar who must fabricate his past, present, and even future to conceal his working-class identity and miserable life. Not only has he bumped up his status from billboard painter to art student, but he also lies about emigrating to Miami Beach, which he knows only from arcade games and street paintings. His obsession with anything American is soon revealed. He grew up a motherless child in Tongduch'ŏn, one of the red-light districts famous for courting U.S. soldiers. His father worked there as a pimp in a brothel. Ch'il-su desperately waits for an invitation to join his sister who has moved to the United States. Behind the comic gestures of Ch'il-su in front of the mirror imitating Brando lurks a narcissistic impulse and a sense of crisis that remind us of his tragic past and inferiority complex.

Only through a romantic reunion with an upper-class woman can Ch'il-su have a glimpse of hope, albeit temporarily, to compensate for his diminished masculinity. This pursuit of course is handicapped by his social status. When he accidentally sees Chi-na with her mother in a department store, he slips into a fantasy in which he is proudly introduced to Chi-na's family. In this brief sequence, Ch'il-su is in a "respectable" suit, further removing him from his working reality where he wears overalls drenched in paint. Yet, when the film repositions him in reality, his hope cannot be materialized because he realizes that appearing in his work clothes would repulse Chi-na's mother and reveal his true identity to Chi-na. Ch'il-su is painfully reminded of his mother's absence when he keenly observes Chi-na's intimacy with her mother. His fantasy is interrupted when a department store manager interrogates Ch'il-su, who looks out of place. Instead of arguing that even people like him can shop in department stores, Ch'il-su runs away as if he had committed a petty crime. Chi-na later breaks off their relationship by announcing that she has found an eligible bachelor, presumably from a class and family background similar to her own.

By pitting Ch'il-su against Man-su, another worker, the film nets their psychic anxieties in a web of class configuration as the two alienated workers learn that their common experiences bind them. Man-su is undoubtedly the only person Ch'il-su feels close to and safe with. Coming from a fragmented family where the father has been absent for twenty-seven years, Man-su has learned basic survival tactics and, except when he is drunk, is never as whimsical as Ch'il-su. Older than Ch'il-su, he camouflages his identity not merely to get dates, but to survive financially in the competitive world. Because his work is not steady, he occasionally must make phone calls to look for other jobs. In each call he makes, he fakes different regional accents, presumably to impress the other person. But different accents do not necessarily constitute the law of language that would place him in a stable social relation; instead it destabilizes him and uproots his identity and origin. Man-su does not even share the "American dream" of Ch'il-su that would allow him to escape from his everyday rigors and familial fragmentation. Both Ch'il-su and Man-su must assume different identities because only disadvantage has been offered by society once their real family identities are revealed to others.[14]

The relationship between Man-su and his father is complicated by the political reality that has rendered the father invisible, an absence that has yet to entail a complete loss of his patriarchy that legitimates Man-su's replacement of him as a grown-up son. Man-su's familial identity is finally exposed, and his dilemma clarified, when he briefly visits his home in the countryside. Sitting on the *maru*, the open wooden floor, that directly overlooks the exterior of the rural house, Man-su's homecoming is hardly an occasion of celebration for the family. When his younger sister proposes a public petition campaign to free their father, a prisoner of conscience, Man-su tells her that it would be "useless." Man-su does not believe that the time is changing, nor does he appreciate his father who spent his life in jail making the lives of other family members intolerable. In a flashback, the film had earlier explained that his leftist family background had barred him from leaving Korea to seek a fortune in the Middle Eastern construction industry, a fact that prevented him from having a middle-class life upon his return.[15] His "unfortunate" family history is thereafter constantly invoked whenever his personal record is checked by the state. The permanent record that continues to repress him materially can hardly erase the "threat" that is conjectured through both the physical invisibility of the father and his psychic omnipresence. Unable to confront him, Man-su can only play out his patricidal hatred and reconciliation in his mind. Stability for Man-su cannot be found as he moves from one job to another amid the construction boom in Seoul, even though his associates claim he is "one of the most talented painters in the industry."

Man-su's psychological pain from his decision not to forgive his father, who chose political honor over familial responsibility, leaves him psychically atrophied and politically indifferent. Here, the amnesia of history—both personal and political—defines a subjectivity that impedes the development of both his class agency and salient masculine identity. It is crucial that *Chilsu and Mansu* was filmed in 1988, one year after presidential election fever and the passion for democracy swept Korea.[16] Man-su is seen near the crowd gathered in a political street rally and in a bar with a television set that shows political candidates making speeches. Yet he remains intentionally distant and isolated, carefully detaching himself from the frantic situation. *Chilsu and Mansu* might seem mystifying because it is a political film that refuses to fully visualize the spectacular scenes generically available through television reports when the intensity and dynamism of social protest reached virtually every street corner of Korea. However, the aesthetic decision to divert the camera from the scenes of demonstrations and rallies demonstrates the film's determination to avoid cinematic spectacle. Instead, it focuses on an individual who is tormented by his hatred for his leftist father whom he can neither desecrate nor honor in the face of everyday political protest.

Neither father of Man-su and Ch'il-su symbolizes power and authority, but their legacies are left imprinted on the two painters' realities. Unlike Man-su who opposes meeting his father, Ch'il-su confronts his father on his return to Tongduch'ŏn, his home district. In this neighborhood where the U.S. troops and English-language shop signs (New House Club and Miss Oh Shop) are still ubiquitous, Ch'il-su slips into a fantasy—in which he, as a child in a school uniform, remembers his father push his older sister, throw her suitcase out the door, and tell her "never to return home." When the scene returns to the present, the adult Ch'il-su is immediately recognized by a middle-aged woman living in the house. She tells Ch'il-su that his father is at a local tavern where he spends his day drinking. The meeting of the two, despite the time lapsed, generates no affection or an exchange of greetings. Ch'il-su had run away when he was younger and never had the courage to return until now. The aged father—now haggard and ailing—glares at Ch'il-su and tells him cynically, "You are still alive. I was worried that you might have died of hunger." As if to shake loose his fears and anxieties, Ch'il-su asks if he may order a drink. His father replies, "Go ahead. Who would stop you from drinking when you can pay for your own?" The brief exchange suggests that the father no longer has the authority to control his son and is willing to celebrate the return of his son only because he can pay for drinks. The father has yet to hear from his daughter, and Ch'il-su's hope of receiving her invitation to the United States is crushed. The sound of the father's cough signals his fall into wretchedness and makes Ch'il-su withdraw his patricidal instincts. As he departs, Ch'il-su tells the tavern owner to "take good care of him" and leaves her a few bank notes.

This scene and the physical absence of Man-su's father determines the frailness of both fathers who remain economically, politically, and ideologically ineffective. However, they are still powerful signifiers that are invoked by the state to keep Man-su from a steady job and that drive Ch'il-su's desire to leave Korea for the United States. Slavoj Žižek, in his humorous elucidation of Lacan's Name of the Father (evidenced by his mocking chapter title, "You Only Die Twice"), states that "everyone (including the father) must die twice."[17] Žižek argues that actual deaths are rarely—if ever—accompanied by symbolic deaths and cites as example the apparition of Hamlet's father who had to settle his account before disappearing from Hamlet's unconscious.[18] Caught somewhere between the two deaths of the father, the young men's crises deepen. The title of the film refers to only the given names of the protagonists, deliberately erasing their family names, which came from their fathers (the Name of the Father). It is no coincidence that their surnames are revealed only when the state speaks in the film. The first time we hear Man-su's full name is during a flashback, when he is officially hailed by the construction company agent who informs "Mr. Pak Man-su" that his passport application has been denied. And we learn Ch'il-su's family name from the police. When the government agent later asks "Mr. Pak Man-su and Mr. Chang Ch'il-su" to follow his orders, he is not simply requesting them to follow the procedure. He is also confirming that the state is aware of their identities that extend far beyond "Ch'il-su" and "Man-su" into their pasts, their families, and their fathers. The fathers have yet to suffer their symbolic deaths, and the Name of the Father still demands their attention.

Complementing the serious thematic mood is the film's visualization of the urban space of Seoul, which hardly generates images of the bustling economy and the spectacular postmodern cultural standards achieved during the 1980s. Cultural centers such as art galleries and discos are instead depicted as anxious spaces where the masked identities of Ch'il-su as a college student and Man-su—cajoled by Ch'il-su to dress as a French artist—must be tightly concealed. Only through such performative identities can these troubled youths be guaranteed entries to the halls and associations with women in them. The highrise buildings and the colorful billboard frames that now define Seoul's status as a global metropolitan center only translate into a dreadful and dangerous workplace for the two billboard painters. The image signifies both fetishistic fantasy and hard labor for Ch'il-su, capturing him in the field of Imaginary during both leisure and work. Even labor unions that proliferated during the late 1980s and gave workers political representation do not have any impact on the two workers.[19] Unlike many workers who are on strike at the time, Ch'il-su and Man-su climb up the concrete buildings on shaky scaffolding or skimpy ropes and paint corporate logos. The irony is that without their participation, the stake of this capitalist expansion, which now depends on signs and simulacrum, is threatened.[20] Yet, their labor hardly returns even a basic subsistence as Ch'il-su and Man-su are forced to share a small room in a shanty warehouse, with only instant ramen noodles to eat.

In what turns out to be their final job, they must paint a huge billboard that is on the top of a building in a remodeled section of Seoul. The visual places the metropolitan globally, but it moves farther away from their reach.[21] They have been hired by an advertisement agency headed by an entrepreneur who speaks Korean colored by a conspicuously Japanese tongue. He demands that the billboard, an advertisement for liquor, be as sexual as possible and emphasize the large breasts of a white model in a bikini on a sun-drenched beach. Ch'il-su and Man-su spend their days painting the Western woman against a blue background (so blue that it pales the "real" skyline in the shot). Constantly employing long shots that juxtapose Ch'il-su and Man-su with a gigantic white Western female, the film—by visualizing the commercial irresistibility and the historical impossibility of the reunion between the "colonized male" and the "colonial female"—amplifies the wretched identity of both the national and the masculine. The almost-nude body invites the desire of the colonized male gaze and further detracts the two painters from their realities. The film suggests that the spectacular vision of economic prosperity in the nouveau riche section of Korea can be manifested only by the skills and labor of the working class. Yet, such a sight further disintegrates their already threatened subjectivity. The city has now erected a commercial sign that is heavily endowed with both post-colonial masculine fantasy and postmodern late capitalist visuality. Yet, the two men, whose labor visualizes these ideals, are ironically disallowed to participate even in this dream. For them, familiar with the taste of only *soju* (a cheap Korean liquor), sharing a glass of whiskey with a white woman on a beach is not even remotely within their reality. The sign is as close to Miami Beach that Ch'il-su will ever get. This anomaly—generated from their working-class identity in a nouveau-riche environment and Ch'il-su's aborted pursuit of Chi-na, a woman of higher class—is further dramatized in the ending when Man-su chooses death and Ch'il-su is taken away by the authorities because they have been mistaken for militant labor protesters.

In this final sequence, by breaking their silence, their repressed personal memories are restored, and their political indifferences forgotten. Once their remembrance enables them to reclaim their language, Ch'il-su and Man-su stand confidently, without fear, released from the image of the gigantic white woman that represented the fetish of their American dream and their working-class oppression. Sitting on the top of the billboard after work, Ch'il-su confesses to Man-su that his life is so far a lie and a disaster. Drinking *soju*, he reveals that the invitation to the United States never arrived and his relationship with

Man-su (left) and Ch'il-su are signpainters who stand on
top of Seoul. *Chilsu and Mansu* (1988).

Chi-na is over. On hearing this confession, Man-su faces his own frustration, having just heard that his "righteous" father has refused a three-day parole to celebrate his sixtieth birthday with his family. Although in prison, his father still exercises his moral authority beyond the reach of Man-su. In a blinding rage, Man-su stands up and shouts, "Every bastard occupying high positions with education, talent, and money! Everyone in the world, listen up! Let me speak. I've nothing to say, yet many things to say. Who have you been fooling?" (At this juncture, the sentimental trumpet music that had been underscoring the dialogue between the two stops as if to state that the film has ceased to function as a melodrama.) Ch'il-su stands and joins his chant, and together they yell obscenities, trying to release their frustration.

The final scene literally spectacularizes their *personal* lives located in the society's periphery and thrusts them into a *public* event. When a crowd gathers below, Ch'il-su and Man-su are branded as protesting subversive workers. Their bottle of liquor is mistaken for a Molotov cocktail and their gestures are taken as being suicidal and destructive. The playful act that lays bare the rage of both Ch'il-su and Man-su in an open public unfortunately cannot remain unrecognized by the vigilant authorities. The military police steps in to quell the potential riot in a busy commercial district. At such a historic time many political activists, including workers and students, staged public suicides by jumping off buildings, and so the extreme reaction of the authorities is not far from reality. This is a pivotal moment where the film tries to release the two repressed males—marginalized and trampled by society—who protest their crises by taking off their masks and telling the truth. But the minute they do this, the state, represented by a platoon of uniformed national guards, mobilizes to thwart them.

Thwart them from what? Why must Ch'il-su and Man-su be stopped? What do they demand that is so feared by the state? To whom are they speaking? For their masculinities—once reconstituted—to pose a threat, somebody in the diegesis should be able to hear them. They have finally found their voices, but they are still so far removed from the society—high above ground—that no one can hear what they have to say. The people gathered below are simply curious. But it does not matter what Ch'il-su and Man-su desire or to whom they are talking because the state has already defined this for them. Having scanned the personal files of the "protesters," a government chief warns Man-su that his anger—as a frustrated son of a long-term political prisoner—is understandable but unacceptable. He tells Man-su, "We already know everything about you. But you must think that you are a person different from your father. What is the point of becoming a person cancerous to the society [like him]?" The chief addresses Man-su as "Mr. Pak Man-su," invoking the name of his father. The state does not distinguish him from his father and does not think of him as separate from his father, even though Man-su has never supported his father's politics. The authorities repeatedly ask, "What do you want?" or "What is *it* that you want?" The paradox here replicates the riddle first conceptualized by Lacan's Che vuoi?, which means "What do you want?" or, more precisely, "What does the Other want of me?"[22] The "it" in the question is an empty signifier, the phallus or its lack. Neither Ch'il-su nor Man-su have a demand that qualifies as "it," and so the question asked by the state returns unanswered. Instead, it only prompts another question, "Am I what you are telling me that I am because you have already represented for me?" This is no different from the question Žižek poses in his analysis of Alfred Hitchcock's *North by Northwest* in order to shed light on Lacan's Che vuoi? of the Other that so eludes fixity, precisely because there is no agent, George Kaplan: the invention of the CIA that exists only as a signifier.[23] This madness that shuffles between misrecognition and false accusation can be stopped only by "accepting his being as *non-justified by the big Other*"[24] (Žižek's emphasis), which, in our case, happens to be the state.

Once caught, Man-su realizes he will join his father in jail but without having the political conviction of his father. And it would be inconsequential to the big Other what his demand is, since "it" has already been identified. Man-su instead jumps off the building just as the paratroopers reach him. The playful act, or *jouissance*, is now beyond Man-su, who has arrived at the final stage, one that involves death, once the Law is about to grasp him. The last image of the film is a freeze-frame of Ch'il-su in handcuffs in the police car, looking back at Chi-na in the crowd. She is more distant than ever. The exhibition and the utterance of social discontent is quickly and violently terminated without even reaching the receiver. The moment they begin to verbalize their frustration, in their effort to reconstitute their masculinity, they are found guilty by the state, subject to arrests and even death for a crime no one—including the state—knows exactly how to identify.

Black Republic

In *Black Republic*, Ki-yŏng, a disillusioned dissident intellectual,[25] strolls into a remote mining town, which is experiencing labor trouble caused by the cheaper coal imported from Russia.[26] By 1990, Korea had a new president, Roh Tae Woo, the first to be elected by popular vote in two decades. He was an ex-general who pushed globalization policies without any consideration for the declining local economy. The "rational" economic policy pursued by Roh made Korea dependent on foreign imports, and industries such as mining consequently suffered. In this declining environment, in which an aging patriarch, a factory owner who also loans money to villagers, has enormous power, Ki-yŏng is immediately identified as a suspicious character. He has the intellectual resources to represent the community in its negotiations with the management, but he remains ostracized from the workers because he cannot reveal that he is a blacklisted intellectual. His name, "Kim Ki-yŏng," is borrowed from another worker (the real Kim Ki-yŏng remains outside the diegesis), and he must remain silent in self-imposed exile from the underground political movement in Seoul, which has become, in his own words, "too self-righteous." He no longer knows what he wants. Ki-yŏng's crisis is that he is neither a worker nor an intellectual who wants to represent the labor insurgency. So, he remains distant from the masses, unable to make any meaningful impact. His inability to change the ill-fated town echoes the plot of an often-referenced Chinese film, *King of the Children* (*Haizi Wang*, Chen Kaige, dir., 1987),[27] in which an educated youth (*zhiqing*), Lao Gan, must question his authority so his students can learn in a mountain village during the Cultural Revolution.[28] By the film's end, if there is anyone who has changed, it is not the masses, but Lao Gan himself.

As Rey Chow explains, the subjectivity that emerges from *King of the Children* "takes us in the direction of a determinate and determinable form of hope,"[29] when Lao Gan, the intellectual, through his collaborative experience with the children (masses), begins to understand who he is. The mission to teach the children to read and write punctuates the symbolic signification of written words that can mediate the hope for a historical subject to move beyond the presymbolic infantile stage. Yet, not even in the form of hope can this be raised in the Korean film that displays the inability of the intellectual to communicate with the minjung. Park's film departs from Chen's film because the intellectual in the Korean film remains isolated from the masses, with the exception of a teenage worker who has replaced his father, a convicted union leader, as a breadwinner. With the teenage worker's subjectivity in question, representing the masses is a task that cannot be fulfilled. This community where the shift of power dynamics is symbolized through the aging capitalist and his tyrannical son, Sŏng-ch'ŏl, is an obscure place where Ki-yŏng must not only locate the other but through this other redefine who he really is. As he explores introspectively the relation between his life and the collective struggle in the community, the alliance between him and the minjung becomes more unlikely. Ki-yŏng, as a passive observer, becomes the very intellectual he has criticized, unable to break out of his masked identity or to become "Kim Ki-yŏng," the worker.

Like the double masculinity projected in *Chilsu and Mansu*, the two male

Inspectors are suspicious of a man (right) who has drifted into
a dilapidated mining town. *Black Republic* (1990).

characters, Ki-yŏng and Sŏng-ch'ŏl, have had traumatic experiences that are
both historically and privately manifested. From the opening sequence we realize that the two characters are bound by troubles: one because of political reasons, the other because of psychological ones. The first image of the film frames
Ki-yŏng, about thirty, in a medium close-up on a bus. He is dropped off in a
mountainous town where only a few children—playing war games—are in the
street. The opening grimly frames a gray town where soot, metal helmets, and
dark blue jackets are common. Mine labor, so idealized and romanticized by
leftist intellectuals, has its life deflated in this declining town with dirt roads
leading to dark caves where lives were lost. Ki-yŏng looks for a job as a miner,
but a suspicious police inspector in the office turns him away. After examining his ID card, the inspector calls out "Mr. Kim Ki-yŏng" to test his response.
Ki-yŏng momentarily freezes at this hail, but then responds immediately and
is released. As soon as his khaki pants, woolen sweater, and tweed jacket are
replaced with working clothes, he gets a job in a company that manufactures
coal briquettes.

Sŏng-ch'ŏl, vice president of this company, wears a black leather jacket and
rides a high-speed motorcycle, reminiscent of Marlon Brando in *The Wild One*.
Sŏng-ch'ŏl is a rogue who terrorizes the town. He is first seen in a motel room
sleeping, while his girlfriend, Yŏng-suk, is getting dressed. Yŏng-suk is a call

The violent son of a local tycoon. *Black Republic* (1990).

girl. Her leather miniskirt, polka dot blouse, red coat, bright lipstick, and dark mascara announce her profession. Her colors signify sexuality and promiscuity in a town that is unaware of colors symbolic beyond work. When she walks away from the screen after fixing her makeup in the mirror, Sŏng-ch'ŏl is exposed for the first time. It is through a mirror his awakening is framed. As if he has not yet recovered from the last night's party, he murmurs, "Bitch, [she left] without saying goodbye." He moves into the frame, and makes a phone call to the front and asks for some soup and a bottle of soju.

Even though Sŏng-ch'ŏl is played by Pak Chung-hun, who also played Ch'il-su, no longer does the intense image in this mirror remind us of Ch'il-su's humorous imitations of Brando.[30] Even the line we first hear manifests Sŏng-ch'ŏl's psychological problems: he is incapable of respecting others, and, as a consequence, he is not respected. His fear of abandonment and separation detected also in this line further punctuates the self-obsession that exposes his narcissistic self-hatred. To be a narcissist is not to simply develop self-love. As Xueping Zhong argues in her study of Chinese masculinity in post-Mao Chinese literature, there is nothing incompatible between self-love and "just the opposite—self-loathing."[31] The dark representation of Sŏng-ch'ŏl is Park's attempt to demonstrate just how bereft of normative subjectivity Korea is within this particular historic moment of sociopolitical crisis, and to show the need for remasculinization. To Sŏng-ch'ŏl, whose mother was deserted by his father for another woman, Yŏng-suk must not only play the role of whore but also that of the mother. Only booze makes him forget his fears, and when it is gone, he will descend further into misery. The community fears Sŏng-ch'ŏl because he articulates only the language of violence when he collects loans from the people who owe his father. Sŏng-ch'ŏl's shame and intense dissatisfaction with himself make him look outside himself for a positive image and draw him inexplicably closer to Ki-yŏng, who appears ethical and just.

The hysteria, which is subconsciously manifested in this claustrophobic environment where the tycoon's son depends on alcohol and violence to mask his anxiety over the loss of his mother and of his masculinity, is familiar to us from the Hollywood melodrama of the 1950s in which the male oedipal crisis exposed the contradictions in seemingly placid bourgeois homes.[32] Like Kyle Hadley (Robert Stack) in *Written on the Wind* (Douglas Sirk, dir., 1956), whose manic-depressive symptoms and alcoholism are traced to his trauma over the absence of his mother and the fear of disappointing his authoritarian father, Sŏng-ch'ŏl overcompensates for his weaknesses and grows more violent each day. His self-pity and repression lead him, as Yŏng-suk reminds him, to become more miserable, violent, and irresponsible than the person he loathes: his father. Sŏng-ch'ŏl's problem has no hope of resolution because he has neither a reliable friend nor a loving wife.[33] Even Yŏng-suk, who provided psychological stability to the unappreciative Sŏng-ch'ŏl, drifts away from him and falls in love with Ki-yŏng. When she departs, Sŏng-ch'ŏl's depression deepens because he has been severed from the only people he trusts: Yŏng-suk and Ki-yŏng.

In spite of the similarities between the two films, *Black Republic* of course must be contrasted aesthetically with *Written on the Wind*. The everyday details of Park's characters remove the material and psychological excesses that had figured Sirk's characters. Also, Park's preference for realist shots that minimize the use of close-ups contrasts with the dramatic and skewed mise-en-scène that patently reproduced the fractured pathos of Sirk's films. Yet, the pairing of the two polar masculinities in *Black Republic* is reminiscent of the narrative strategies of Sirk's classic film in which Kile Hadley and his ethical friend, Mitch (Rock Hudson), form the psychic dyad of troubled ego and authoritative super-ego. Eventually, the morally inferior Kile is killed by his promiscuous sister, allowing Mitch to unite with his wife, Lucy (Lauren Bacall). The narrative aim in *Black Republic* is not dissimilar, as the oedipal crisis requires a complete revamping of masculinity until Sŏng-ch'ŏl must detach and destroy himself in order to reconstitute a salient form of masculine subject. In other words, Sŏng-ch'ŏl cannot be salvaged, and it has to be Yŏng-suk, the female protagonist, with traits of both mother and whore, who must execute the evil half to save the virtuous other half, Ki-yŏng. Through this radical ending, the film vies for a new subject that leaves behind narcissistic obsession and imaginary captivation of the self in the mirror.

Yŏng-suk plays a contingent, yet crucial role in the film that mediates the relationship between Ki-yŏng and Sŏng-ch'ŏl. The projection of Yŏng-suk's identity as both sexual object and historical subject who is exploited and humiliated by Sŏng-ch'ŏl and the society confuses Ki-yŏng. Initially, he cannot distinguish between the two because he only recognizes the "contaminated" image of Yŏng-suk and not the crisis that she must live with. At the recommendation of Sŏng-ch'ŏl, who "offers his girl," Ki-yŏng is forced into the hotel room with Yŏng-suk. Park shows the room from outside the window in a long shot as the television that faces away from the camera airs a report about the formation of a new national labor union coalition. Protests of the workers can be heard in the background as the broadcaster reads the official position of the government confirming the illegality of these protests. Ki-yŏng, reclining in an armchair, watches silently. Although much of the news footage is blocked from the spectator's view, the scene is not without a spectacle. Yŏng-suk, uninterested in the news, begins to take off her clothes, as if this is her routine. This is framed in a detailed mise-en-scène. The television is in the lower part of the frame with the bed on the left side and Ki-yŏng on the right. At the top of the frame, Yŏng-suk's naked body is screened through a wide yellow-tinted window of the bathroom. The audience hears the news report on labor strife, while watching a young woman take off her clothes. It is not clear whether the intention here is to eroticize politics or politicize the erotic impulses. Ki-yŏng, however, is disinterested in conflating sexuality with politics. He ignores the live spectacle in front of him and instead watches the one on television. He cannot tie the knot between Yŏng-suk's *private* labor as a downtrodden worker forced to sexually please her sugar daddy's friend and the *public* protest of the workers in the broadcast. Unable to shake loose the contradiction between the two and determined to identify what precisely the contradiction here means, Ki-yŏng leaves the motel. No other image in Korean cinema has evoked as powerfully as this scene the tension between minjung as an abstract image and a live subject literally stripped bare that traumatizes the intellectual. But the paradox remains because this scene illustrates the inability of Ki-yŏng, who is unable to lift himself from the crisis, to represent for her. On the contrary, it is he who needs Yŏng-suk as his other to reidentify himself and move beyond his crisis.

In spite of the condition of radical otherness that frames the two male characters, Ki-yŏng and Sŏng-ch'ŏl have much in common. They are both lonely,

Miners protest labor conditions. *Black Republic* (1990).

homeless, and wounded. Sŏng-ch'ŏl is lonely because he was abandoned by his mother, and Ki-yŏng is wounded by political defeat and disillusionment with the dissident political movement. The relationship between the two also becomes more firmly bound because they both chase the same woman. Ki-yŏng is trapped in a town that desperately needs an effective social agenda, but without a bridge between intellectuals and the people, there simply is no hope.[34] Labor negotiations in a coffee shop—with Ki-yŏng eavesdropping—heat up after the manager argues with the labor representative. But there is not much Ki-yŏng can do. He does not know what he wants, and this uncertainty eventually allows him to have an affair with Yŏng-suk, through whom he hopes he can recover his real self. *Black Republic* questions whether Ki-yŏng can ever realize his love for the minjung when they pop out of the ideological literature and conceptual abstraction as real people.[35] Here, we realize that the class differences that distinguish the two characters, Ki-yŏng the intellectual and Yŏng-suk the prostitute, are affirmed rather than erased when Yŏng-suk represents even to Ki-yŏng his muse and his mother. In one crucial moment, she runs ahead of Ki-yŏng into a dark alley. Standing a few yards in front of him, she hollers, "Do you see me well?" Ki-yŏng shakes his head while she steps closer to him until her face is illuminated by a street light. She tells him her real name is Yi Kŭm-ran. Yŏng-suk, renamed as Yi Kŭm-ran, is significant. Kŭm-ran is commonly read in Korea as the quintessential name for a migrant woman working in a factory

Ki-yŏng realizes that his love for the *minjung* is real.
Black Republic (1990).

under hazardous conditions. Also, she is just like him, hiding behind a masked identity. The moment Ki-yŏng recognizes her, both visually and figuratively, he gives a nod of approval. They consummate their love, and both the subject of Ki-yŏng's history and the object of his desire overlap in Yŏng-suk.

However, although the male crisis is played out, the woman does not move beyond her fixed position as the prize for the two protagonists or as the other positioned to rearticulate Ki-yŏng's identity and desire. Even if she were to be properly represented by the intellectual, can she ever claim faculties to represent herself?[36] Can female subjectivity be separately constituted in this ostensibly masculine universe? Toward the end of the film, Ki-yŏng returns from the police station after days and nights of interrogation. He had been accused of stealing after a physical altercation with a drunk Sŏng-ch'ŏl. Yŏng-suk, no longer dressed in revealing clothes, nurses Ki-yŏng, who is unconscious in bed. She cleans his feet with a warm towel. When he shouts in his sleep, "I don't know," Yŏng-suk gently holds his head. With his body relaxed in her arms, he murmurs "ŏmŏni" (mother). This utterance signals the conclusion of Ki-yŏng's pursuit and the film's narrative objective of curing the male trauma. The phallic lack is disavowed as he romantically embraces Yŏng-suk. He has found his home, his mother, and his womb, resolving the trauma that tormented both him and his alter ego, Sŏng-ch'ŏl. But there is far greater resistance from the law than they can muster before he is able to fully reestablish his subjectivity. Even as they promise to run away together, Ki-yŏng's recuperation of masculinity remains frustrated. The state catches up with him after he is identified by his fingerprints as a subversive leftist wanted by Korean intelligence.

The film that initially began with two ambivalent masculinities now completes its circuitous tour, presenting a more stable self that will have to cut off its violent and sexually unstable element as the police inches closer to Ki-yŏng's real identity. Left alone, the fractured Sŏng-ch'ŏl must end his life, leaving Ki-yŏng to receive a full blessing from Yŏng-suk (the mother), who takes up the knife at the dare of Sŏng-ch'ŏl. Half-suicide and half-murder, Sŏng-ch'ŏl dies at the hands of Yŏng-suk. It is the political Ki-yŏng rather than the narcissistic Sŏng-ch'ŏl to whom the mother will attend. Once she is repositioned firmly as a "mother," Yŏng-suk's virtues are redeemed, and her "sin" of being a contaminated woman is forgiven. But only through a sacrifice will her rebirth be further confirmed. In the violent ending Yŏng-suk kills Sŏng-ch'ŏl and helps Ki-yŏng escape from the authorities, which affirms the film's imbalanced gender representation. Yŏng-suk's predicament at the end is like the one Mildred Pierce faces when she finds out that her beloved daughter has killed Mildred's husband. In *Mildred Pierce* (Michael Curtiz, dir., 1945), Mildred must choose between her maternal instinct to take the blame for her daughter's crime and allowing the state to punish her daughter. The difference between Yŏng-suk and Mildred Pierce is that Yŏng-suk has committed the murder herself. She automatically becomes a sacrificial mother once she assumes the role of murderer. While Ki-yŏng is allowed to escape, Yŏng-suk is literally and figuratively arrested after killing the rogue son. Her desire to escape from the claustrophobic environment is once again denied, and the symptoms of her hysteria inevitably remain incurable.

Who can claim responsibility for the death that so often concludes Park's films? We find a link between authoritarian violence and male crisis because the state has interceded in the relationship between Yŏng-suk and Ki-yŏng. Like *Chilsu and Mansu*'s ending when the state intervenes at the final instance, in *Black Republic*, the police inspector reserves his most crucial function until the end when he reveals that Kim Ki-yŏng is really Han T'ae-yun, the dissident intellectual. By matching the dangerous name "Han T'ae-yun" with Ki-yŏng, who had borrowed his name from someone else, the puzzle for the police inspector is solved because he had always wondered why an intelligent man like Ki-yŏng would work in such a run-down town. Once he exposed Ki-yŏng's real identity, the inspector exclaims, "I knew it." Here, the "it" let out by the representative of the state is an obscure object that on the one hand is at once subversive because the state has already declared Han T'ae-yun a dangerous intellectual intending to overthrow the government, and on the other hand has its signified deflated because there is nothing Ki-yŏng did in that town that is worthy of state prosecution or condemnation. But the "it" is sufficiently threatening, though all Ki-yŏng ever wanted to do was to build a new home with Yŏng-suk, to the state for it to generate violence, a violence that is deferred to Yŏng-suk. The question, "What is it that Ki-yŏng wants in the film?" as in the case of Man-su, depends on the response to Žižek's aforementioned question, "Why am I (Ki-yŏng) what you (the state) are saying that I am?"[37] The obscure, surplus-object "it" has rendered the subjectivization of the "I" — Ki-yŏng/Kim Ki-yŏng/Han T'ae-yun — impossible. With the crisis of self-representation prolonged, Ki-yŏng's power to represent others and to put an end to state violence is aborted. The film determines the operation of the state violence that is heavily dependent on naming the subversive and conveying him through a chain of symbolic signifiers, where the irresolvable riddle has rendered the crisis interminable.

Is He Dead Yet?

The never-ending crisis returns us to its origin where the corruption and abandonment (Sŏng-ch'ŏl's father), foreign collaboration (Ch'il-su's father), and even leftist ideology (Man-su's father) radiate in the father who remains undead. It is only in Park's fourth feature, *To the Starry Island*, in which the father finally suffers his second and symbolic death, positing hope of a new subjectivity that at some point might be reclaimed. In this film, a male protagonist living in the present returns home to a southern island for his father's funeral, only to find that the local villagers oppose the burial. The rest of the film anticipates whether or not his dead father can be properly buried because of the island's tragic memories of the war. Through flashbacks, we learn that his father had been responsible for a "commie" witch-hunt that prompted the nationalist army to finally massacre the villagers during the height of the Korean War. (The state again having intervened only in the last instance.) Even though decades have passed and most of the principal victims and witnesses have died, the past still haunts the present. For the past to be successfully resolved, the notorious father must again die.[38] At the end of the film, all the characters fantastically appear in a festive dance superimposed across the star-lit sky. Immediately after the dance, the ship that contains the body of the father is burned by one of the angry villagers whose father had been killed during the melee. The red flames envelop the ship that contains the man who was forced to live his entire life in exile after the massacre. The father burns, along with his legacy of domestic violence, adultery, and communist hunting and collaboration. By destroying the father's body, neither the son who wanted to bury his father nor the islanders who resisted his burial emerges as the victor. Could this be an occasion in which, according to Freud, the totemic rules prohibit the killing of the father, but, once he is killed, his death prompts a celebration?[39] The flames that engulf the dead father inspire both a celebration and a mourning of the old and the new. This gesture of ambivalent reconciliation between history and the present, at least for now, signals the completion of a tumultuous period that anticipated the birth of a new male subject, yet was unable to acquire a name for him other than the name of his dead father.

6

Jang Sun-woo's Three "F" Words: Familism,
Fetishism, and Fascism

So there was peace. More, more, peace, peace . . .
— *To You, from Me* (1994)

In one scene that illuminates the central theme of Jang Sun-woo's *To You, from Me* (*Nŏ ege narŭl ponenda*, 1994), the male protagonist licks the feet of the woman who has just threatened to leave him. In a tightly framed shot, the writer cleans her feet with his tongue, demonstrating his willingness to do whatever pleases her. Situated below the woman, Paji rŭl ipŭn yŏja (literally meaning a woman who wears pants),[1] he proceeds to move his mouth toward her vagina and then, complying with her demand that he might as well "lick her dirty spot," to her anus. Because he dares not to lose her, he will do anything to please her. What makes the scene even more visually provocative is the writer's face, bruised from a beating by a corporate executive for whom he had been ghostwriting. His status as a "fallen man" is made conspicuous by the black-and-blue marks covering his face, the scattered papers of his yet-to-be-published porn novel, and his sexual submission to the woman, his first and so far only love. Despite the fact that he has reached quite possibly the lowest point in his life, he does not seem as pathetic as the person we might imagine — someone thoroughly humiliated and castigated. On the contrary, the writer rests peacefully, for he has accepted his role as a masochist. (This act of kissing a woman's feet invokes an unforgettable image in the opening sequence of Luis Bunuel's *El* (*This Strange Passion*, 1952) when a priest kneels down to kiss the feet of a peasant — a saintly moment which is immediately undercut to reveal

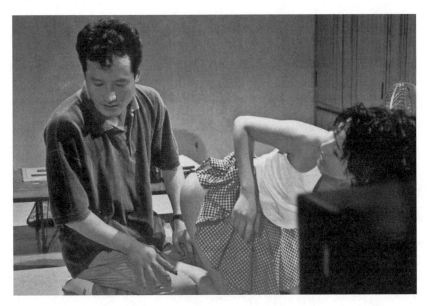

A writer releases his guilt, while a woman bids farewell to shame.
To You, from Me (1994).

the perverse sexuality and lust of Don Francisco, the protagonist.) The writer in *To You, from Me* is relieved from his ego, guilt, and shame during the moment of this sexual act. Paji orders the writer during cunnilingus to throw out the agreement with his publisher to write five porn novels and concentrate on his true literary calling. Initially reluctant, because of his fear of the illegitimate publishing company—an underground enterprise that releases pornographic books under the disguise of subversive North Korean communist manifestos (both porn pictures and communist manifestos are fetishized materials in Korea, for they are both banned)—that may seek violent retribution, he eventually agrees to return to "real" writing.

The writer's withdrawal from the commercial contract between him and his employer does not completely set him free. In lieu of the underground publishing company, Paji will now be his twenty-four-hour guardian under whose supervision new writing must be produced—novels that would place him at a much greater literary height. He will become her slave, and, in so doing, Paji will help the writer to sever his ties to the corrupt and deceitful institution that has extracted his labor and to restore to his own creative world. Guilt is transformed into triumph when the man enters into a masochistic relationship. This is precisely the relation Gilles Deleuze envisioned when he insisted on the difference between de Sade's libertines and Sacher-Masoch's subjects. The mission of the sadian hero is to subvert the law, but, as Deleuze points out, "the masochist aims not to mitigate the law but on the contrary to emphasize its extreme severity."[2] The only way the writer can relieve himself from the condition of exploitation is to demonstrate self-discipline and self-restraint. Also by positioning the woman as the "master and torturer" who is cruel, cold, yet sympathetic, Deleuze argues that the patriarchal system in which the "woman typically figures as an object" is reversed in the masochistic contract.[3] Paji is now the enforcer of a new contract accepted by the writer, and becoming both a "mother" and a lover to him, she symbolically removes the obstacle of incest prohibition. But, in what is probably one of the most ironic points in the film, once this repression is lifted, the writer who had previously been sexually desperate becomes impotent. Despite Paji's help, the writer who for too long had engaged in erotic writing cannot come up with anything serious. His writing block not only disables him from his profession but also deflates his sexual potency. Paji soon leaves him to pursue a modeling career and will instantaneously become a pop icon. The writer, in need of new employment, finds her and becomes her chauffeur. Even though, at the end of the film, Paji urges him to resume his original work and tells him that she is willing to release him on a paid leave, the writer refuses to accept her offer and tells her that he is happy just to be her assistant.

Using masochism as a point of entry, this essay explores the films of Jang Sun-woo that have generated far more controversy than works by any other director of the New Korean Cinema. If the last twenty years of Korean film history has indeed ushered in a train of masculinity that moves from an image of frailty, incapability, and contradiction to one that is mature, sexual, and professionally viable, there is perhaps no director who makes more explicit claims to tensions between these two polar images of masculinity than Jang Sun-woo. Ubiquitous in his films are *male* characters who are imperfectly volatile, constantly shifting from penile impotence to sexual virility. From his first feature, *The Age of Success* (*Sŏnggong shidae*, 1988), to the more recent, *Lies* (*Kŏjinmal*, 1999), he has continuously explored characters who remain outside the film genre orientation that conjures up the hegemonic image of a professional managerial class of the industry successfully resolving romantic and business dilemmas. In his films, images that endorse capitalism are quite unlikely; instead he explores men who remain on the margin of these circuits of capitalism.

Jang Sun-woo's masculinities emblematize a model of manhood in New Korean Cinema for they are characterized by shame, ineptitude, and mourning, which cannot be erased even at the end of the diegesis. Many of his characters are sexually repressed and physically violent, creating a wide-ranging spectrum of overdetermined and contradictory masculinities that remain permanently injured. For Jang, these frail masculinities are reflective of the unresolved social crisis in South Korea that began with the elimination of the political dictatorship, when the longtime president was abruptly assassinated in 1979, and the ensuing period of political unrest. His films continually depict the spontaneity and fluidity that arise from the absence or the negation of subjectivity. Men do not possess the phallus any more than the women do, and they vie for power that is often elusive in a humorous and satirical vein. Images of rape scenes, where men wield violence against women that disturb, and even torment his audiences, are ubiquitous in his films. But such are the moments when his films are most affective, for these rapes escape realism and allegorize the very function of frail masculinity that the film exposes. By questioning the unity presumed of any given subject, especially that of the protagonist, Jang's films dispel the fascination and identification the spectator makes with the character on screen. They often mingle violence with desire and sexuality, breaking apart one of the taboos in the cinema of a nation that has witnessed much violence in modern history and repressed its representation in popular culture.

Familism, Fetishism, and Fascism

I have chosen the three terms *familism*, *fetishism*, and *fascism* to structure this essay because each of them parlays modes of repression that are central in Jang Sun-woo's films. Jang's films derail from collective identities that so critically figured the national characteristics of Korea, a country that historically relied on neo-Confucianism as the ideological principle of its authoritarian politics.[4] Here, what seems to be at stake is Jang's nearly compulsive and instinctive slide away from the belief that people are inherently virtuous. Instead, his characters are depicted as incomplete and frail, and in order to mask and disavow their anxieties, they become sexual fetishists, violent fascists, and irresponsible sons and fathers. All of the three terms listed above, familism, fetishism, and fascism, are both a source of and a triangulated response to the social repression that fragment the self, which is repeatedly humiliated and expiated in Jang's films. The intricate relation masochism strikes with all of these terms will be thoroughly investigated in this essay.

These terms are inseparable from power since they anchor varying forms of repression in order to sustain themselves. What also binds them is their common opposition to reason, which simply does not yield easily to family-oriented values, fascist ideology, and fetishistic desires. To enumerate, no justifiable reason beyond kinship can be offered when two members of the family who had been enemies all their lives dramatically resolve their differences in a melodramatic ending; no reason beyond desire can be conceived to subjugate when people from specific ethnic or regional background are targeted for mass slaughter; and there is nothing but fetishism to explain the activation of an irrepressible sexual desire generated by the simple gaze at a pair of shoes, as is common in Bunuel's films.[5] Even though the kinship, the desire to subjugate, and the fetish-compulsion do not constitute the most rational principles in modernizing foundations, Jang is the first Korean filmmaker since Kim Ki-yŏng, director of *The Housemaid* (1960), to have understood their significant roles in Korea's modernity.[6] What his works embody is the careful reordering of these dangerous, yet affective and primitive, senses that mobilize many of the powerful themes they exert. Jang's films are controversial because he is confident that these are the emotions that not only structure a violent fascist regime, but also affect ordinary people who have remained complicit with the principles of such a regime. To envision the nation as a network of kinship, to mobilize an ideology built on elitism, self-sacrifice, and success, and to fantasize the moment when repressed egos are imagined to be free are structurally important to rebuild the nation through principles of kinship and family values. These are of course only shortsighted solutions to fundamental problems in the system of unequal distribution of power, but they are appealing to many who would rather choose to spectacularize history and one's place in it.[7] Jang Sun-woo's dysfunctional, irrational, and violent characters are threatening not because they are dramatic, but because they so closely frame many people's ordinary reality and common fears. Masochism for Jang Sun-woo, as elucidated throughout this chapter, is the alternative model that proposes to leap beyond the structure of repression that bifurcates the moral and the immoral, as well as domination and submission. Jang follows the condition prescribed by Deleuze, who so fervently advocated masochism as a mode that effectively protests violence and domination by accepting and indulging pain. This is the only attempt that can transcend the law, a system that "enables the tyrant to exist, form the essence of his thinking."[8] In its opposite pole, as noted in *To You, from Me*, "there is more peace" when the man accepts his punishment and redefines himself as a masochist.[9]

Any meaningful discussion of masochism must begin with the investigation of familial tension and dysfunction. Freud's study on masochism began when he realized that many of his patients who were being treated for hysteria or obsessional neurosis had "indulged in the phantasy: 'A child is being beaten.'"[10] This particular obsession with childhood is triggered by the memory of the father who is beating another child, most often a brother or a sister. What Freud argues is that the child observing the sight of beating senses relief because he is not the one who is being punished, but the very memory of "a child being beaten" testifies that guilt and shame had been closely associated with this pleasure. A desire to subjugate or be subjugated is closely bound by the fantasies of being beaten by the father that ultimately becomes a site where fascism could be imagined. Taking his cue from Jean-François Lyotard, Fredric Jameson argues that the concept of "libidinal apparatus," which resists the idea that private fantasy or psyche has a life of its own, is completely severed from the material and historical dynamics. Though "produced by the *accidents* of a certain history" (my emphasis), the private fantasy-structure is "reinvested with new and unexpected content, and adapted to unsuspected ideological functions which return upon the older psychic material to re- or overdetermine it in its turn as a kind of retroactive effect."[11] Jang's webbing of the guilt repression, the punishment, and the father in a triumvirate of libidinal apparatus is also a rewriting of history where both internal limits of history and ideological permutations of fantasies materialize the dynamics of social and psychic repressions that underscore the paradox of the Korean society.[12]

Fathers are often absent in Jang Sun-woo films, and even when they are present, they are too disfigured and frail to exercise much power beyond the symbolic. But identification with an idealized other and an unquestionable authority can simply be perceived without it being physically present. The father is conspicuous through his absence, yet he is still capable of generating guilt to shame the protagonist. The concealment of families in Jang Sun-woo's films displays the director's own resistance against the tendency of commercial cinema to motivate or even simulate a melodramatic plot. By removing the traces of family, he is also repressing history, a traumatic site where premodernization poverty, violent war, and massacres are constantly reinvoked. Jang's avoidance of family is notorious, as his recent film, *Lies*, attests. In the original novel, *Na ege kŏjinmal ŭl haebwa* (*I Dare You to Tell Me Lies*) by Chang Chŏng-il, the father of female protagonist Y is a former military man whose sadistic violence sparked his daughter's sexual perversions. But neither the father nor the family of Y is depicted in Jang's adaptation.[13] Also, in *Timeless, Bottomless Bad Movie* (hereafter *Bad Movie*, 1997), none of the parents of the runaway youth are given much attention, and the tension between them and the group of young punks is only orally recited by the interviews of the kids.

Nevertheless, guilt and shame, despite the absence of the family and the repressive space it engenders, are crucially generated by familio-ethical conventions in these films, as the stories of fathers punishing their children are narrated through flashbacks and other authoritarian figures who stand in as surrogate parents. Jang's characters constantly desire; they desire power, love, sex, home, and freedom. But never do these incessant obsessions materialize, for they exist only as a form of fetish. Deleuze explains that fetishism "as defined by the process of disavowal and suspension of belief belongs essentially to masochism."[14] Rather than placing fetishism in the category of sadism, Deleuze argues that the occurrence of fetishism is far more primary in the case of masochism since through the fetish Masoch, the writer whose work gave birth to the term "masochism," was not simply idealizing nor destroying a world of dreams, but disavowing and suspending it. Because the fetish is a manifestation of something that has been deeply repressed, the metaphoric usages of money in *The Age of Success*, the miniskirt in *To You, from Me*, and the wooden bat used in the sadomasochistic tussle in *Lies* all are integral components in the fetishistic desires of the films' main characters. However, since the lack that is desired to be masked through these fetishes is perceptual rather than real, despite the incessant struggle to compensate for their loss or absence, the films acknowledge that it can never be fulfilled.

The "male lack," as stated in the Introduction, is what constitutes the very symptom of the New Korean Cinema. What distinguishes Jang Sun-woo's work from others is his insistent claim that the "search for the elusive phallus" can only be materialized through the fetish that is more essential than the real. Jang Sun-woo is also aware that the "desire to be led," which structures the principle of masochism, can also easily be gobbled up by fascism. The awareness of the "lack" of the real, of the salient subjectivity, of the breakdown in any meaningful social network and communication, also renders a longing that transforms masochism to sadism. The boundary between fascism and fetishism is ambivalent, yet firm. Rey Chow writes that, like fetishism, fascism is "an expression of *our own repression* — our oppression of ourselves — and . . . as an inner or internalized violence from which we need to be 'liberated'" (her emphasis).[15] If fetishism is a masochistic mode that articulates and masks one's frailty and repression, fascism expresses sadistic, aggressive, and violent tendencies that both acknowledge and disavow internal anxiety.[16] The temptation here to assume a fascist outlet to anxiety rather than masochistic engagement is the primary thematic tension in virtually all of Jang Sun-woo's films. Jang, to borrow the words of Slavoj Žižek, accepts "a certain delusion as a condition of our historical activity," agreeing that there is nothing unnatural about the delusional state of the people who radically shift between pacifism and violence, and between sadism and masochism. In this acknowledgment of history where its dynamics of process is one without a "telos or a subject,"[17] Jang resists the ordering of history by the officials in the Korean governments of the twentieth century (the proto-fascist governments during the Japanese colonial rule and the Park Chung Hee regime that have always insisted that one must accept individual sacrifices for the prosperous and harmonious future where Asia or Korea will be unified into one) who have constituted the subject of the present through the objectification of an ideal future.

Style and Authorship

The disintegration of the self in Jang Sun-woo's films is expressed in a complex mode that rearticulates modernist and postmodernist film language. Though initially not an experimental filmmaker, Jang Sun-woo continually reinvents himself, engaging self-reflexive filmic modes that expose his struggle with the question of postauteurian subjecthood that previously enchanted many European art filmmakers. The issue of authorship is indeed hardly resolved in Jang Sun-woo's films as his masochist characters reveal the director's moral dilemma of cinematic representation. The attention devoted to the extradiegetic matters — for instance, the documentary footage of the massacre in *A Petal*, the mutiny of his film crew in *Bad Movie*, the insertion of footage shot from an alternative camera that lay bare the production process in *Lies* — not only exposes the contrivance and the artificiality of the drama, but also draws his audiences closer to its realness. I use the word "real" with extreme caution but also with firm assurance, because Jang's attempt to deduce deceit from his films is what precisely irks many audiences, critics, and censorship boards. Although he is perhaps one of the most recognizable and successful filmmakers in Korea, all of the films he made during the 1990s have been placed in the eye of a controversial storm.[18] Contrary to the popular perception that the irritation engendered by his films is caused by the depiction of lewd sex, it is the *frank* depiction of sex perceivably unchained from erotic grounds through self-reflexive mechanisms that rankles many viewers. Sex scenes are ubiquitous in these films, yet they are hardly erotic. They are instead disturbing, preventing the audience from engaging it from a scopophilic viewpoint. The reflexive camera that calls attention to the filming process both spurs ethical question whether violent scenes of rape performed by the amateur actors should be filmed and exposes the viewer who conventionally wishes to remain discreetly anonymous in the theater.

What is often remarkable is that Jang Sun-woo does not simply exculpate an individual's penchant for sexual freedom. His films, during his experimental phase of the late 1990s, indicate that he has not yet completely abandoned ethical questions that derive from age-old traditional values and family conventions in Korea. The question of authorship and matters of representation intervene in this paradigm where moral restraint and sexual desires compete against each other. One of the questions frequently conjured up in his films is, "Am I doing the right thing by filming this scene or depicting a character with questionable morals without punishing him?" It is precisely this uncertainty or ambivalence that places the audience on unfamiliar ground. The startled audience becomes self-conscious and finds themselves uprooted from the anonymous scopophilic position that is standard in watching a narrative film. The self-reflexive camera constantly reminds the viewers that the sex scene is in fact being photographed, and it is the acknowledgment of the camera that also reveals the viewing point of the audience as peeping toms. The discomfort wreathed while watching Jang Sun-woo's films derives from an unfamiliar viewing position because the dominant conventions of Hollywood — despite the post-Mulveyian attempt by feminist scholars such as Gaylyn Studlar to realign the spectatorial position with masochism[19] — are still heavily dependent on a scopophilic and domineering gaze that wishes the phallic woman either dead or fetishized, something that is categorically subverted by Jang Sun-woo.[20]

In this chapter, three of his films spanning the first ten years of his career will be discussed. *The Age of Success* (*Sŏnggong shidae*, 1988), his first feature film with full directorial control (he shared the director's credit with Sŏn-u Wan in *Seoul Jesus*, a 1986 film), *To You, from Me*, and *Bad Movie* are all monumental contributions, ushering a new mode of historical disfiguration that was only reworked through radical and complex psychoanalytic insights and intense passion to refigure cinematic language. I will draw attention to both the psychic impulses that drive the masochistic and dysfunctional characters and narratives and the pointed aesthetic style that redefined Korean cinema. In other words, how questions of sex and authorship are complexly intertwined in Jang Sun-woo films will be critically examined. The transformation of style and characterization of masculinities over these three films will also be given utmost attention. What must not be overlooked is that sex, desire, and the libidinal economy are only tools that visually and psychically deploy the uneven power dynamics that mediate the narrative drives in Jang Sun-woo's films. These sexual impulses are closely associated with the political upheaval in South Korea during the late 1980s and the early 1990s. I do not intend to suggest that sex is a palimpsest allegory that metaphorizes the catastrophic 1980s where social protest and labor unrest placed the nation in an uproarious mood. On the contrary, sex is perhaps the only expression through which the Chun Doo Hwan regime's perverse strategy to rule can be critiqued. Perhaps the most unpopular leader in postwar Korean history,[21] Chun tried to compensate his low popular support by retaining the draconian censorship on political matters but offering clemency on erotic representations in publications and in cinema.[22]

If the sexual impetus in the works of Japanese new wave filmmaker Nagisa Oshima corresponds largely to the Japanese militarist culture during the post-Meiji period, and if Luis Bunuel's career is inseparable from his Spanish Catholic roots and the military reign of Franco, Jang Sun-woo's films must be contextualized within the 1970s and 1980s of Korea where the two dictators, Park Chung Hee and his crony Chun Doo Hwan, terrorized and repressed the nation. Jang Sun-woo's protest of authoritarian politics aims to explore the frailty of subjectivity that is at the core of authoritarian political rule, but also the public that remains complicit in their "desire to be led." Instead of dramatizing the historical past, when a common man emerges a hero by overcoming the systematic tactics of oppression or stripping it to a nostalgic point for the effect of pastiche, Jang cultivates the libidinal impulses of sadomasochism, fetishism, rape, and even incest that activate violence in a private realm and elevates them as matters worthy of anchoring an extraordinary historical subjectivity. The sexual deviance depicted here closely excavates a definite linkage with historical contradiction where the issues of social prohibition and taboo even in their intimate forms are explored and critiqued as an endorsement of power. The various forms of psychological deviance and anxiety expressed in his films redefine the severity of political repression throughout the postwar history in Korea.

The Age of Success

Jang Sun-woo's reluctance to depict a heroic figure who victoriously emerges against the system of oppression is laid bare in his first feature, *The Age of Success*. Made at the height of the minjung movement, the film departs from heroically representing the working class, and instead focuses on a young white-collar worker in the sales department who is driven to succeed.[23] The film begins with the job interview of Kim P'an-ch'ok (Marketing Kim) at Mack Gang (Mighty) Corporation. Standing alone in front of several corporate executives seated behind a long table in an otherwise large barren meeting hall, Kim P'an-ch'ok is asked to persuade the company executives to buy whatever product he wishes to sell. All of the previous interviewees have failed to impress the executives. Unwavering and firm, P'an-ch'ok holds out his hand yet refuses to expose what he is holding in his clenched fist until he sees money placed on the table. Curious to see what he is so confident about, the corporate executives participate in his ploy by offering him all of their cash and even credit cards. Once P'an-ch'ok is confident that all of their money has been dispensed, he unclenches and reveals that there is nothing in his hand. The level of curiosity that had been elevated soon deflates, engulfing the old executives in rage, but P'an-ch'ok argues that the product they have bought is his *sangsul*, "business talent," the best product one can possibly find. At least one executive is impressed with P'an-ch'ok's daring move, and he is soon hired in a critical position in the marketing department of the food and chemical division that concentrates on artificially flavored spice (MSG) products.

There is a difference between P'an-ch'ok and the other interviewees who have failed to solicit the interests of the executives: P'an-ch'ok has not told them lies, but has successfully manipulated them to believe that what he holds is perceptually valuable. He holds nothing, yet this "nothing" has gained fetishistic and phantasmatic value through P'an-ch'ok's confident poise. Not only is the real "value" of the concealed product determined by his ploy, but the marketing itself already assumes a value, exposing the discreet function in capitalism of the exchange value that congeals the use value of labor. What is intriguing even from the first sequence of his film is that Jang Sun-woo is conscious of the very crucial term on which capitalism is dependent: the commodity fetishism that is far more significant than the commodity itself.

Instead of tracing the Lacanian notion of subjectivity solely in Freud, Slavoj Žižek focuses on Marx to address the question of how the "symptom" was invented. The "hidden kernel of commodity" or money that so often appears in Marx's work, writes Žižek, is the very place where desire is stimulated, precisely because of its latent and sublime quality "like the corpse of the Sadian victim which endures all torments and survives with its beauty immaculate."[24] It is indestructible, because there is simply nothing real or material that is susceptible to destruction, once labor or the means of production has been congealed or has become invisible in the market of capitalistic exchange.

Having begun exposing the fetishistic nature of capitalism, *The Age of Success* comically draws the rise and fall of P'anch'ok, whose simple desire to succeed carries him to the top of the corporate ladder before the ladder is pulled from underneath, literally throwing him flat on the ground. The secret of P'anch'ok's success is to expose and steal the rival company's marketing strategy before the competing products go on sale. Competition in the market is a war, and only the strong few who produce the power to possess information will win. Immediately after P'an-ch'ok begins his first day in the office, he and his coworkers are briefed about the marketing plan of their product. The film then quickly moves onto a theatrical sequence where the struggle for customers be-

P'an-ch'ok (center) enjoys his rise to the top of the corporate ladder.
Director Yŏ Kyun-dong (far left) appears in a minor role.
Age of Success (1988).

tween P'an-ch'ok's peers and their competitors eventually erupts into a yakuza-style brawl. Shot without dialogue, this theatrical sequence obliquely represents that there is nothing more important than intensive marketing for a product to succeed in the system of late capitalism. This scene — like the overarching visual characteristics of the film that deliberately opt for a flat and artificial cinematic surface — demonstrates Jang Sun-woo's insistence not only to borrow the theatrical conventions from *madang gŭk* (mask dance theater) he had been exposed to in his precinema days, but also to remain experimental in his initial approach to filmmaking. Having neither undergone formal filmmaking education nor practiced apprenticeship under an established filmmaker,[25] his involvement in film was quite differently conditioned than that of other filmmakers representative of the so-called New Korean Cinema (such as Im Kwon-Taek and Park Kwang-su, who had served time as assistants to important directors of Korean cinema).[26] While Im and Park also aimed to explore historical issues and their violent repercussions in their films through realist film language and aesthetics, Jang has — from the very beginning of his career — opted to use contemporary settings through an astutely modernist aesthetical approach. Only through formal innovation could his provocative social themes prove to properly address the impossibility of recuperating a coherent subjectivity.

The day after the grueling marketing day, P'an-ch'ok returns to his office with a scar of honor drawn from a fight with his competitors. He is determined to use other means and resources in the battle of advertising to secure the market for his product. The manipulation of the media, the aggressive gathering of information, and the exploitation of sex in advertising will soon be Pan-ch'ok's way of business. He will explore heretofore only "civilized" strategies such as coercing the press to write articles that raise health concerns about abundant use of MSG in daily diet to strike against the leading brand, bribing the female owner of the bar frequented by his rival company executives to act as an agent for him, and mobilizing an ad campaign that maximizes the sex appeal of his company product. The use of sex—as in Park Kwang-su's *Chilsu and Mansu*—underscores a protest against President Chun Doo Hwan's perverse politics that had compensated for the lack of political freedom with the liberalization on popular representation of eroticism. Sex is dangerous, yet alluring. P'an-ch'ok draws on his "poetic" talent, confident personality, and charming looks to seduce Sŏng Sobi (which literally means "sexual consumption"), the owner of the bar, and use her as an infiltrator of the competing company. In order to maintain the flow of information, however, P'an-ch'ok needs to satisfy Sobi sexually. The increase in the sale of the new MSG product, *K'ŏmp'yu-mi* (Compu-taste), marketed by P'anch'ok as diagramed on a graph, is visually juxtaposed against the image of P'an-ch'ok having steamy sex with Sobi. Money, sex, and success are literally conflated in this scene, and without the others any one of these elements cannot fully be operative.

Gender representation produces disjuncture with the prevailing characteristics of women and corresponds to the narrative trajectory that recuperates the rich textual matters of Jang Sun-woo. Jang Sun-woo relies on the multilayered representation of women, which at first sight draws on its stereotypical conventions by shaping women as masochists. Women are simply victims of the society, unable to address and articulate their suffering, imagining and indulging only fantasies of rape. In one fantasy scene that loops out of the narrative plot, a plain female receptionist in the office slips into a dream where she is stripped naked by P'an-ch'ok, who violently tears her clothes off in the bathroom. Her dream of being raped is a disturbing portrayal of an underdeveloped character that reinscribes the director's phallocentric impulses.

Indeed, in every Jang Sun-woo's film at least one scene of rape or forced sex can be found, sometimes functioning pivotally within each narrative. He flirts with controversy and potential public fury because rape, as Maureen Turim writes, is "a basic violation of the woman's physical and psychological integrity as subject, and no event within a narrative is more highly ideologically

P'an-ch'ok (right) builds a powerful alliance with Sobi.
Age of Success (1988).

charged than the depiction of rape."[27] But he veers from the standard praxis of misogyny in cinema by using the rapes, much as Oshima did, as tropes of psychological allegory and not of realism. They are inserted to explore sometimes dark and mystifying forces of desire and repression that structure the patriarchal elements of the family that Jang wishes, self-reflexively, to critique. Also important is Jang's determination to retain a voice for his female protagonist, who is responsible for P'an-ch'ok's demise but is exculpated in the end. Despite the fact that Sobi has all the elements of a *femme fatale* or a vamp (for she is a double agent), she is not condemned even after concocting a plot that humiliates P'an-ch'ok and indirectly causes his death. P'an-ch'ok's crisis is staged at the very moment he is being rewarded by the company chairman with financial bonuses and gifts (including a new car, chauffeur, apartment keys, private office, and credit card). Sobi chooses this moment to upset his victory over his competitor, who is rumored to be bankrupt—to unmask P'an-ch'ok's utility that had only been dependent on stealing information through her. On the day of his promotion, the news agency announces that the competitor— rumored to be filing for bankruptcy—is planning a comeback with a new product. Once Sobi begins to feed him false information about the competing company's financial crisis, P'an-ch'ok loses his grip on power and reverts to his roots, which is the "nothing" that he is. He is quickly replaced by a man who holds an M.B.A. degree from an American university, someone who is formally trained to run a modern marketing campaign. P'an-ch'ok instead is relocated to Hoenggye, a remote town located in the mountains, where his office is little more than a dinky shop that functions as a storage facility housing boxes of his failed project, K'ŏmp'yu-mi II.

Sex and desire are closely entwined with death, and because he has relentlessly pursued sex, death — which was temporarily delayed — awaits for Pan-ch'ok once he is through with pleasure, following the pattern of the New Korean Cinema invoked in this book's introduction. This is actually the only film of Jang Sun-woo where he opted for an ending that dramatically kills the male protagonist for whom a lifetime goal for success is thwarted. No other characters in his films of the 1990s are as ambitious as P'an-ch'ok. In the last scene, he races in snowy weather through the curvy mountain road, only to slip and fall off the road. The last scene of the film cranes out from the scene of the accident where a police car, an ambulance, and a tow truck arrive, only to confirm P'an-ch'ok's death. How are we to consider the death of a man driven to succeed, a worshipper of Hitler's ideology, but nevertheless a protagonist of the film who must also be considered a victim of circumstances? Is the film applauding or mourning his death? What must also be evoked is the location of his death, Kangwon Province, where he was born into a broken family, raised by a single father who was uncaring and always drunk. Earlier in the film, P'an-ch'ok's ill-fated youth is explained in detail in a conversation with Sobi. He confesses, "I waited in hunger for Dad, but he always came home drunk and empty-handed. How disappointed I was. Dad asked me to unwrap his fist, to see if he was hiding a penny or something to eat, I uncurled his fingers one by one only to find out that he had nothing. I cried and cried. I grew up detesting his incompetence, laziness, drinking, and harassments." Like many other protagonists in Korean fiction, the memory of childhood is hardly comforting. The contempt for the father — rather than the sympathy for him — is the very place where P'an-ch'ok's desire to succeed originates. He refuses to reconcile with his father and with his past, for they both make him frail for generating self-pity. At one point in the film, P'an-ch'ok proclaims, "Weakness is a sin — it only generates cheap sympathy." Faced with self-pity and narcissism, P'an-ch'ok — unlike Pyŏng-t'ae in Pae Ch'ang-ho's *Whale Hunting* (1984) — chooses narcissism. Once he adopts a narcissistic attitude, it is only a matter of time until death arrives at his doorstep. P'an-ch'ok's childhood trauma is a lingering legacy — like that of the two working-class characters, Ch'il-su and Man-su, in Park Kwang-su's first feature — where desire evaporates. He returns to the site of his birth only to meet death.

At this point, the use of the death of a protagonist as a final image of the film must be further elaborated since it is a narrative strategy that commonly threads the South Korean films produced at the time. The two early films by Park Kwang-su, *Chilsu and Mansu* and *Black Republic* (*Kŭdŭl do uri ch'ŏrŏm*, 1990), as well as some of the most representative films of the New Korean Cinema that have fared well in the international film festival circuit, *White Badge* (*Hayan chŏnjaeng*, 1992) and *Out to the World* (*Sesang pakkŭro*, 1994), all feature protagonists' deaths that signify despair, loss of innocence, and crisis. In the merger of death and violence, they also seek a possible renewal, a rebirth that can cleanse the soul and body contaminated by war, crimes, and corruption. That the shot of a Catholic chapel and a priest in his formal attire appear in the concluding sequence of *White Badge* where the mentally ill Vietnam vet is shot is not accidental. Once it is clear that P'an-ch'ok's trauma from his youth is interarticulated through the present symptoms of narcissism, greed, contempt, and inhumanity, with no hope of restoring his innocence and a stable family, the film finally settles for his death in the snowy mountains.

To You, from Me

Jang Sun-woo is an exile in his own native land — a country that had difficulty accepting him — but produced many works that collectively embody the New Korean Cinema. To argue that Jang's films constitute a form of exile cinema may be mystifying because, unlike Luis Bunuel, a "paradigmatic case of exile" who has represented "the Spanish cinema" by working outside Spain,[28] Jang has never left Korea for a significant length of time. Unlike other directors of Korean cinema in his age group who spent time abroad studying film (such as Park Kwang-su and Pak Ch'ŏl-su), Jang Sun-woo always remained close to Korea. Yet he has suffered from a "state of unbelonging," in the words of Hamid Naficy, since his films have had problems drawing critical appraisal from the domestic press, and censorship difficulties from the local authorities.[29] Jang Sun-woo had to generate international fanfare or positive reception at international film festivals in order to continue making his films and bolstering his reputation as an art filmmaker. Of course, one of the factors that crucially distinguishes Jang from Bunuel or Oshima is the historical conditions in which he worked. Whereas Bunuel and Oshima worked in environments that were perhaps more conducive to art cinema of the 1960s and 1970s — with Bunuel also beginning his career in the 1930s as a member of the international surrealist art movement and ending it in France as one of the leading filmmakers of the postwar modernist cinema — Jang's emergence was primarily in the 1990s, when experiments in cinema did not transgress much beyond the realm of commercial and postmodern film production praxis. By the 1990s, the popular insurgence for democracy in Korea that ushered in political reform was also mostly dormant. Though impetus for social change produced a series of tidal waves that many cultural activists briefly rode in the 1980s, it produced only a quiet rustle during the ensuing decade, discouraging artists from using it as an occasion for creative inspiration beyond the nostalgic effect.

To You, from Me, the first of two adaptations of Chang Chŏng-il's novels (the other being Lies), is a work that cynically reinterprets the 1980s with a "postmodern" twist.[30] However, the use of the term, "postmodernism" needs further qualification. If "postmodernism" is attached to the sensibilities of the "waning of affect," as defined by Fredric Jameson to describe the contemporary cultural condition, then it must be used with extreme caution when considering this film.[31] There are many postmodern references in the film that—along with The Road to Racetrack and A Petal—perhaps best allegorize the spectacular, yet repressed radical agency that was born in the 1980s, an inerasable decade in Korean history. The solemn statement of the bank clerk that he is writing on "something to simply kill time, that lacks a worldview or an understanding of humanity that is a necessary ingredient in the makeup of a great novel" suggests that a "great divide" has been crossed.[32] But a careful consideration of the film, which explores the question of human desire (in a vein similar to the one Bunuel dramatized decades earlier), denies the account that Jang Sun-woo has become less "affective" than his modernist precedents. In Jang Sun-woo's films, surreal components that surprise viewers with outrageous, absurdist, and dreamy situations—where, for instance, an ostrich and a postman appear in a bedroom without either being clearly distinguished from reality—are not present. The social atmosphere in which Jang was raised was far removed from the vibrant modern environment of Western Europe that had inspired modernist works. But To You, from Me is nevertheless successful in depicting the contradictory conditions of postrevolutionary Korea, where the bourgeois dream of a proletarian worker is promoted as protest art exhibited in a corner of a museum, where porn novels are sold by street vendors under the disguise of revolutionary North Korean titles, and where student activism is symbolized by a character who is arrogant and sadistic. Instead of an isolated hero who overcomes insurmountable odds and remains romantically engaging for the viewers, Jang's films are populated with perverts, addicts, liars, and hoodlums—in other words, characters who are a closer reflection of the real world than those in other films. So real are these characters that we become surprised when the writer at the end of the film accepts his role as a chauffeur though he has a job—more ordinary and believable in the real world than the one succeeding in writing a groundbreaking novel.

These instances of radical break or social schizophrenia, when the visual signifier does not correspond to a meaningful signified, are not naturalized in the film as occasions for celebration. Three major characters suffer from traumatic experiences that have separately impacted them. The writer is an award-winning novelist whose award is rescinded when his novel is publicly denigrated as a copy of a Latin American novel.[33] The accusation he suffers dries up his writing talent, and he will remain a writer of porn novels until he is forced to retire from writing. Paji, his girlfriend, is a factory worker from a rural background, representing a conventional by-product of Korea's rapid industrialization drive, which imported large numbers of farm girls into the city and turned them into assembly-line workers. Despite her limited educational background, she is intelligent, capable of writing articulate essays on the status of the global economy in a post–cold war era. Yet, she has suffered from her own trauma after being constantly humiliated and sexually abused by her former boyfriend, a violent student activist. The abuse eventually leads to depression and anorexia, to a point where she has to be hospitalized. Her refusal of food parallels the sexual failure of a bank clerk, the writer's eccentric friend who, after having suffered from a trauma of his own, is impotent. His flamboyant flair in social situations is contradicted by his monotonous everyday activities at the bank, where he works merely changing money for customers.

The losses symbolized by the writing block, anorexia, and sexual impotence all produce melancholic fetishes that commonly bind their identities. The writer, desperate to compensate for the loss of his talent, is keen on remaining close to Paji, even after he has given up his career. For the writer, Paji is the only thing worth living for. Paji's fear of becoming obscure and isolated drives her once again to fetishize miniskirts in order to gain attention (it's an irony given the fact that her name literally means "pants"). And, eventually she will use her impressive body to become a celebrity in Korea. The bank clerk, who still lives with his mother, fantasizes himself as a character in an American film, *Bonnie and Clyde* (Arthur Penn, dir., 1967), to temporarily forget his misery of having to hopelessly work in a bank and remain sexually impotent. But, while Bonnie and Clyde enjoy their escapades out in the open country, there is not one single place to which the clerk can escape. The rural road in the Korean cultural tradition hardly connotes a Kerouac-ian form of freedom. Only suffering, hardship, and death await in Korean roads, and the Buddhist road film Jang made immediately before *To You, from Me*, *Hwaŏmgyŏng* (1993), certainly underscores this fact.

Jang Sun-woo (right) directs Yŏ Kyun-dong as the bank clerk.
To You, from Me (1994).

It is not coincidental that *Bonnie and Clyde* is chosen as a film text that is self-referentially interweaved in *To You, from Me* since both films' subjectivity pivots upon lack. Here, I use the term "lack" to denote the loss of the phallus as only perceived, rather than being actual. In *Bonnie and Clyde*, the male lead is a figure who not only challenges the Establishment by robbing banks, but also literally cannot perform his masculinity through sex. Clyde's impotence is discussed not only as a topic in one of the dialogues in *To You, from Me*, but it is parodied since it is the bank clerk — not the bank robber — who suffers from sexual dysfunction. In *Bonnie and Clyde*, Clyde's penile malfunction is ironically the symbolic overvaluation of his male narcissism that can only be substituted with a gun, a synecdoche of sexual potency and freedom. For the clerk in *To You, from Me*, however, such freedom cannot easily be pursued since his rebellion could only be staged in the confines of his own bedroom in a house he still shares with his mother and his younger siblings. He is captured in a world of *imago*, fantasizing hallucination, and his delirious inclinations prompt him to smoke dried banana peels believing erroneously that they would make him chemically high. Like a child, he moves around in his room in his boxers and undershirt while holding a fake gun, emulating gunmen in iconic American movies.

The bank clerk's arrested development and captivity in the pre-Symbolic stage is linked to his adolescent trauma. While sharing his innermost secrets with Paji, he reveals to her that he has been impotent since high school, when he was then renting a room from a landlady who was frequently battered by her husband. The clerk tells a story of how he fell in love with a young housewife who was always screaming and moaning in pain. Unable to squelch his lust, he decides to discreetly leave a love note for her. The secret note is however found first by the husband, offering him a reason to again beat her. This violence terrorizes not only the woman but also the clerk, who can only furtively watch this scene of horror from his room as a peeping tom. After the husband leaves her, she — wearing only undergarments — crawls inside his room, asking him to seduce her without saying a word. The clerk makes love for the first time with the very woman he secretly desires, but with her body painfully bruised. Soon after, he will contract venereal disease and lose his virility.

If his impotence reflects the severity of his psychic shock, it must be determined that the phallus is the site of his trauma. What is actually in effect is a disruption of the oedipal triangle — the violent father, the masochistic mother, and the sexually-deprived child — during the moment when he has sexual intercourse with a woman twice his age, a mother-figure who breaks the social taboo by slipping inside the child's "bed." Like the writer who had earlier in the diegesis entered a masochistic relationship with Paji, the figuration of cold and cruel mother — through his story — unlocks the mystique of incest. The clerk however cannot continue to have an affair with the older woman whom he fancies and cannot commandeer a narrative of his own because the presence of her violent husband denies his entry into a social realm, indefinitely mummifying him as a child. Trapped in the pre-Symbolic, only when he is able to articulate his experiences through language and writing at the end of the film will he be able to leave behind the Imaginary — the world composed of images and mirror — and regain his masculinity. When he later meets Paji, who has become an anchorwoman of an entertainment news program, for an interview, the clerk laughingly informs Paji that his penile power has been recuperated. His ability to articulate his trauma through words has cured his sexual dysfunction and caused him to gain a literary reputation that had ironically eluded the writer.

Paji is a character who is unconventional in Korean film history, for she displays her promiscuity and immorality without being punished in the diegesis. When she first enters the film, she is introduced as a woman who can hardly be molded according to the preexisting conventions of Korean cinema, which has throughout its history portrayed women either as prostitutes who own dirtied bodies or as nurturing mothers who are prepared to sacrifice themselves to protect the phallocentric order.[34] In reading the works of Shin Tong-yŏp, one of the most renowned postwar nationalist poets in Korea, Chungmoo Choi argues that in his poems the "prostitutes represent commodified bodies, and the purchase of these women's bodies metaphorizes the neo-colonial accumulation of capital and expansionism that replaces the archaic form of colonial invasion, especially that of Japan."[35] If one of the most prevalent literary discourses available hinged on a negative perception of women where the interests of both capitalism and neocolonialism cohered, at the opposite end of the representational spectrum stands a nurturing and sacrificial motherhood that vies to reconstruct a patrilineal heritage that has been threatened by colonial conquest. Even in *T'oji* (*Land*) by female writer Pak Kyŏng-ni,[36] perhaps one of the most popular novels in Korean literary history that epically spans all of the thirty-five years of Japanese colonialism (1910–45) and revolves around a matriarch, Sŏ-hŭi, the women are not free from their overarching responsibilities as mothers compensating for the loss of husbands. Yi Sang-jin, a Korean feminist critic, states, "the writer depicts the sacrificial affection towards their offspring and their chastity for their husbands of these [female] characters in positive light." In this way, the motherhood in *T'oji* is the first to maintain the familial relations, possibly as an "intimate mediator of patriarchy."[37]

Paji deviates from these two polar images of womanhood, which are either being complicit with the colonial machinery by "sleeping with the enemy" or being resistant against it by protecting her chastity. She proposes a radical break with the stereotypical conventions of ideal woman in Korea *not* by completely severing from these oppressive female figurations, but by conflating the two categories. She is a figure that condenses many typical characteristics, simultaneously a woman with questionable sexual morality as well as a nurturer who coaches the writer's resurgence through the literary ranks. She is sexy and savvy, but she is also a devoted person who initially wishes to devote herself to supporting the writer. Only when it is clear that he is going to give up writing and be satisfied running a love motel in the countryside does she leave him to cultivate her own career in modeling. What is missing of course is a desire to bear a male child and continue a familial lineage, which is replaced with her own self-determined ambition to succeed. Nevertheless, it is her "voluptuous ass" rather than her brain that gives her a break. The film eloquently replays the paradox of late capitalism where media, sex, and gender are entangled. Times have changed and the women's success no longer hinges on the protraction of a patrilineal line through the bearing of a son. But as it was during the colonial period, the prostitution of the woman's body remains a signifier that furthers the interest of capitalism and its profit. Does Paji need to apologize, if it is the masculine rules and logic of capitalism that urge her to create a career through the entrepreneurial use of her body? Isn't prostitution or commodification of the female body the very engine that bears the fruit of capitalism and media? This is the question that becomes an almost irresolvable riddle in the majority of Jang's films.

One of the first efforts from a Korean feminist perspective to seriously theorize female bodies as literary sites, Kim Mi-hyŏn's *Hanguk yŏsŏng sosŏl kwa p'eminijŭm* (*Korean Women Writers and Feminism*) draws on the works of Luce Irigaray, Hélène Cixous, and other Western feminists to rethink the function of the uterus. Citing the work of a female Korean novelist during the Japanese colonial period, Kim writes that the "uterus" is both an "unwanted pouch" and an essential part of the body where "motherhood" can render a meaning.[38] It is, in other words, a site of both horror and joy, two experiential extremities that correspond to both conventions of womanhood: the whore and the mother. The uterus is a "horrible" place where violent sex is performed, but it is also where a child is reproduced. What feminist sociologist Nancy J. Chodorow argues is that coitus, pregnancy, and parturition are inseparable for woman, unlike man who refuses to believe that his sex partner can be his mother because of his oedipal anxiety. On the contrary, women's participation is "dual" in heterosexual sex. "First," Chodorow writes, "a woman identifies with the man penetrating her and thus experiences through identification refusion with a woman (mother). Second, she becomes the mother (phylogenetically the all-embracing sea, ontogenetically the womb)."[39] Despite Chodorow's insistence on assessing the gender through a conventional Freudian framework, such crisis or rupture between men's resistance of motherhood and motherhood itself prompts a worthwhile consideration of the women's perspective on sex and reproduction that are often assumed to be intimately associated.

It is here where a discussion on *To You, from Me*'s representation of Paji's body must begin. As noted from her name, she wears revealing clothes that emphasize her buttocks. Her slim body makes it even more conspicuous so that even from her prepubescent days, she recalls, it was an object of both sexual desire and peer taunting. She asks, "How would you feel if the boys' room was filled with graffiti that made fun of your thirteen-year-old body?" A previously sanctified place because of either oversexualization, which implies a "whore" that so closely identifies with foreign colonial occupation, or undersexualization, as a mother's womb, women's buttocks anatomically holding anus, vagina, and uterus are represented as a site of social ridicule. The crisis that began with her extraordinary bodily proportions will soon lead her to a world of bizarre sexual encounters. Narratively framed by a game of truth and dare between her and the bank clerk, the film recounts Paji's past. A poem that young Paji wrote when she was a worker was selected by a literary group that promoted *nodong munhak* (proletarian literature), and it was exhibited along with minjung art in a gallery space. There, she meets an underground activist intellectual with a pseudonym, *Oman kwa chabi* (Arrogance and Compassion), who wished to represent her. She remembers Oman telling her, "Good poems honestly reflect the poet's experience in real life. We call them realism." Young Paji immediately questions him, "But how could my poems be realism when poetry is something I never tried to write?" Her question triggers a rhetorical response from *Oman* who speaks very fast, so rapidly that it is only decipherable through English subtitles. When he reaches a conclusion that her poetry discloses the contradictions of labor and social inequity through the expressions, "lamenting 'my poor legs!' while hiding in the bathroom," "eating black rice and soup," and "she weaved beautiful poetry in her blue uniform," Paji responds very quickly that she—through her poetry—was simply trying to communicate her desire to wear miniskirts.

Her fetishization with miniskirts is visualized in the film by their omnipresence and her impulse to go out to shop for them at a moment of domestic crisis. When the writer becomes emotionally unstable because of his prolonged writing block, she slips out of the house and gets a miniskirt in exchange for a sexual favor with a storeowner at a shopping district. What is the reason behind her obsession with miniskirts? Although Paji had worked in a bicycle factory and was forced to wear dull working clothes, the desire to wear a miniskirt should not just be interpreted in Marxist terms as a fetish that can displace her identity as a worker. The rejection of her desexualized, plain blue overalls must precede the expression of her sexuality as a woman with a voluptuous body. Just as the fetish, according to Freud, is "a substitute for the woman's (mother's) phallus which the little boy once believed in and does not wish to forego,"[40] the miniskirt substitutes for the invisible phallus that Paji has imagined to have existed. Her affair with *Oman* when she turned nineteen is disastrous and exacerbates her fetish. After their meeting at the gallery, she lives with *Oman*, but she soon becomes miserable when she is mistreated as a woman with an inferiority complex. Upon returning from a demonstration rally where they nearly suffocate from teargas, *Oman* rapes her when he becomes temporarily insane. As he penetrates her anus, provoking her painful screams, he yells the anti-imperialist slogans popular during the minjung movement, "down with fascists" and "down with the Yankees." Although *Oman* is not a developed character in the film, this scene suggests that his political hatred against fascism is not genuine, but instead is a fetishistic impulse against his own wealthy background with a penchant for sadism that represses his familial crisis. *Oman's* "antifascist" violence, which explodes as a form of misogynistic rape, indelibly inscribes the paradox of the 1980s that could not easily mobilize a salient subjectivity, despite a clear void for one after long-time dictator Park Chung Hee was shot in 1979.

The exhibition of the intellectual as either a sadistic beast (*Oman*) or an unproductive masochist (the writer) defies the tradition of Korean literary culture that had sanctified the student or the intellectual throughout the twentieth century. As the center of social movement for national independence during the Japanese colonial period and for democratization during the period of postwar military dictatorship, they were frequently depicted as ideal protagonists. The psychic agony of a powerless half-nation often became emblazoned in the figure of young students or intellectuals who continually displayed a flair for active social engagement, a pursuit that was frustrated in the end. Despite such disappointing results rendered in the novels by Yi Kwang-su, a national intellectual icon during the early 1900s, and Kim Sŭng-ok who wrote his cynical stories mostly in the 1960s, the pursuit of salient subjectivity ceaselessly continued through the young educated characters. What is so extraordinary about Jang Sun-woo's male characters (as brethren of writer Chang Chŏng-il's characters) is the director's willingness to break the powerful masculine mystique of the intellectuals in Korea by acknowledging the splintering of subjectivity through historical trauma. To reconcile with trauma is to revisit the sight of acute pain through the means of language. In Kaja Silverman's reading of Althusser's theory, she proposes that there are two laws that structure the Symbolic order: "the law of language," and "the law of kinship structure."[41] As argued in the Introduction, the successful writing of either history or a novel constitutes and defines the subject, who has overcome and/or reconciled the male lack, as a coherent identity and as a gendered family member. This is not something that is categorically denied by Jang Sun-woo as he characterizes men—intellectuals included—in impaired, unstable states that must oscillate between pre-Symbolic and Symbolic, between a member of a family and an isolated individual, and between a masochist and a sadist.

Only by marketing her sexuality can Paji retain her autonomy and subjectivity, which is defined in relation to the male gaze and social value contingent to and confined to the value of the marketplace. Can the woman be the author of her own image? This is not a simple matter especially when considering the characterization of a woman who models for a living. But the self-imposed reification of the image that uses the regime of the gaze in a performative mode enacts a profound ambiguity and rupture that cannot remain completely obedient to the masculine prerogatives.[42] That women are subjective, emotional, and hysterical is left in abeyance not by resisting such conventions, but by debunking the mystique of men's genuineness and their capability to control their surroundings. Men are instead vulnerable, irrational, and violent, capable of destroying the women. After Paji is raped by *Oman*, she remains traumatized, refusing to eat and spending her day only reading books. Anorexia is a defense mechanism that ruptures the modern masculine discourse that fetishizes the slender body of women.[43] Her refusal to eat institutionalizes her, ironically freeing her from the tyranny of *Oman* who cannot possibly understand the reasons behind her anorexia. When she reads the controversial novel of the writer whose literary award was rescinded because of accusations of plagiarism, she realizes that she had once a dream just like his. She leaves the hospital care, and visits him — suddenly we are looped back to the opening scene of the film. Herein lies the motor of the film's narrative theme that is thrust forward only when Paji recovers from her trauma and refuses to remain a victim of masculine violence. It is Paji who drives the story forward, and remains at its center from here onward, placing the crisis at its past and allowing the writer to assume his natural condition as a masochist subservient to her. *To You, from Me* — as the title would suggest when a shift of "I" occurs through the transference that is passed on from "me" to "you" — acknowledges the modern dilemma of the difficulty in stabilizing the self. What is clear at the film's end is the reclamation of the subjectivity in the voice of the female that urges the male protagonist to resume writing. When the writer refuses it, the self, as discussed earlier, remains diffused and de-centered.

Although unexposed in the diegesis, the dream is central to the film's narrative since it is the crucial element that knots the writer to Paji. There is a dream — invisible yet significant to the story — that has inspired the writer's novel, has the award revoked because the novel is accused of being a simulation of a foreign novel, and has reawakened Paji from the severe case of trauma and anorexia. The "dream," which is central in the lives of the two protagonists, remains illusive to the viewers, crossing the boundary of the real (so much that it was given the prestigious literary award) and beyond the simulacrum (for being only a copy of a foreign novel), perfectly striking the "postmodern affect" that makes an impact across linear time and space and transgresses the boundary of the real and the fictive. Here, the dream — unsubstantial yet powerful — is a symptom that is permeated with a Lacanian *jouissance* that functions as a sublime object, which in the words of Žižek is "a positive, material object elevated to the status of the impossible Thing."[44] The Thing is the Lacanian Real, which is so deceptive and elusive that any effort to map its coordinates ends inevitably in frustration. The dream will only remain a "thing," like the political period of the Eighties that was both fascinating and slippery, and permanently forge the relationship between Paji and the writer; it will traumatize the writer with the accusation of plagiarism and also free Paji from her trauma, eventually leading her to media stardom, with the writer happily by her side as her assistant.

Bad Movie

Though the uses of extratextual, noncinematic elements proliferate through-out Jang's oeuvre,[45] *Bad Movie* is perhaps the first film where he explicitly challenged the fundamental limitations of narrative cinema as an apparatus of the pleasurable, voyeuristic gaze. He does this not by eliminating sex from his films, but by showing raw, crude images of sex and violence. Unlike the graphic portrayals of sex in his earlier films that sometimes tilted toward gratuitous titillations, the sex scenes in *Bad Movie* seriously engage the question of sexual representations. *Bad Movie*, to use the words of Bill Nichols when discussing reality TV programs, is "rebuke, not companion, to the simulacrum"[46] because it makes us shudder with horror as we experience over and over the brutal and pornographic footage shot in documentary style. It is important that many scenes in the film are structured like a documentary — grainy, unrehearsed, unstaged, and unscripted — because we generally assume that all documentaries are real. Usually jettisoned in the praxis of watching a documentary is the notion that "every documentary representation depends upon its own detour from the real," and the truth of documentary is "qualitatively akin to that of fiction."[47] The subversive use of the documentary element, the explicit, pornographic portrayal of sex, which André Bazin once termed as "perversion of cinema," and the taboo subject of runaway youth from the ages of fifteen to eighteen, all coalesce in the making of *Bad Movie*. The film is quite possibly the most controversial and ruptured film text in the history of Korea.

Bad Movie is loosely structured around segments of stories narrated by a group of actual "problem youth" who also star as themselves. To heighten the "reality" of these stories, Jang veered from the conventions of fiction film-making. Employing video and 16mm cameras as well as the standard 35mm panavision camera and using minimal artificial lighting, the film often slips out of its fictional realm by self-reflexively acknowledging its own ontology as a film. This self-referentiality breaks the gap between reality and appearance, between performer and filmmaker. Although it embodies many of the features of postmodern aesthetics by playfully listing less-than-affective questionnaire games through multiple-choice questions and intertitles, to suggest that the film remains indifferent to the social problems would be misleading. By carefully engineering an ethical theme that examines crime and repentance beneath the surface of an immoral and cruel world where many of these kids and homeless live, the film exposes the ambiguous boundaries between pleasure and despair, between good and evil. There is an inherent resistance against barbarism that lurks around the violent impulses of the youth despite the fact that they target all institutions of authoritarianism. Throughout the film, Jang assumes an iconoclastic position, and tries to dismantle one of the cross-cultural social taboos that prohibit critical interpretation of the young.

That many of the representative films that anchored new film movements depict corrupted youth is hardly surprising. Through their cruelty, deception, and violence the loss of innocence is reaffirmed, just as is the need to renew a hope for humanity. Yet, as films like Luis Bunuel's *Los Olvidados* (1950), Francois Truffaut's *400 Blows* (1959), and Oshima Nagisa's *Burial of the Sun* (1960) also attest, while seemingly understanding the tension between desire and repression, there is a sense of strict moral behavior that distinguishes criminals from the innocent.[48] Because *Bad Movie* was largely motivated by actual stories told by the teenagers themselves, it refrains from the moralistic framing of villains or crimes, neither exonerating nor condemning them. What is even more surprising in Jang's film is that when the kids commit a rape, Jang refuses to tell us why and, upsetting the moral conventions of feature films, offers no punishment for them. Like Oshima who "looked to the opposite of the educated radical to display . . . his critique of society,"[49] Jang, a graduate of the most elite university in Korea (Seoul National University) and a former student activist, explores the inhumanity of today's society by closely documenting homeless hoodlums, youth gangs, and bar entertainers. Although the characters are intimately depicted, it is extremely difficult to individualize each of the characters since they are assigned roles without a conventional lead. The shaky camera movement, the surprising insertion of violence, and the careful orchestration of a visual mise-en-scène that undermines conventional narrative logic make for one of the most daring and experimental feature films produced in Korea, despite the fact that many of the scenes are staged and reproduced with a large budget.

Like *A Petal*, where three separate narrative strands were interwoven, *Bad Movie* is largely organized around two separate narrative strips: the teenagers' stories are mostly reconstructed from their real-life stories, while the stories and everyday activities of middle-age vagabonds are mostly featured through documentary footage. Looping the two together are several scripted scenes written by Jang and his screenwriters that shape the narrative structure of the film.[50] The prologue begins with the assistant director, and the director himself narrating their reasons for making the film. The credit titles roll and insist that the film was

Street racing. *Timeless, Bottomless Bad Movie* (1997).

made without set direction, script, or production plans. Meanwhile, a group of young runaway teenagers are pictured in the background hallucinating from chemical fumes wafting from industrial-strength glue, a common way to get high in Korea. An impromptu motorcycle race on the street comes immediately after this prologue. The emotive *cinema verité* quickly impacts the viewers as the camera weaves through the crowd in the street. In the crowd, young female bystanders wearing stylish baggy pants, bright t-shirts, and thrift-store jackets enthusiastically yell "How bout a ride?" or "Pick me up, bastards!" The police helplessly and impatiently observe the unruly punks racing on motorcycles until the bikers accidentally fall. They then lurch toward them, beating them with their clubs before arresting them. With the audio cranking up the sound of the approximately twenty motorcycles running at full speed, the mood of the scene is high. The camera follows an interviewer who randomly asks the bystanders their response to such a dangerous hobby and the police brutality. The sequence introduces one recurrent character, Ttongjaru (Shortie), who will appear several times in the film; but since the film indiscriminatingly features about fifteen characters, it is difficult to separate her from the rest of the crowd. Shot at night, the motion of the camera that follows the crowd is rough and jerky. It jostles around the protesters and captures both the interviewees and the young female interviewer, who holds a large boom microphone in front of her subjects, rendering images that all but eliminate the artificiality of an industry film. That this is actually the most expensive sequence in the entire film, involving hundreds of extras, the rental of high-speed motorcycles, and even stunt action, remains ironically unrecognized even to the trained eye.[51]

This opening scene acknowledges that there is not a coherent center from which the "film within a film" emanates, confusing the spectators who assume that there is a "truth" implied in this "documentary" footage. Not only is this scene "fictionally" rendered, but the female interviewer with a microphone also does not appear again in the film, diffusing the film's authority even more. It is not surprising that *Bad Movie* was initially banned by the domestic censor, had premiere screenings that generated jeers and rage from its viewers, and was allowed theatrical release only after twenty-four minutes were excised from the original director's cut. From the moment the film was tested before an audience largely composed of the press and industrial personnel in July 1997, it was met with public outrage. Many of the dismayed viewers left the screening rooms in disgust and questioned Jang's intention behind making an "indecipherable" and "offensive" work.[52] The film leaves the audiences confounded and shocked not only because it refuses to resort to coherent narrative strategies and deters an interpretation of the youth that rests on innocence and naivety, but also because it openly suggests that the youth are capable of committing adult crimes—rapes, thefts, and murders—that are unacceptable even for someone with liberal-progressive politics. The film was caught in a public controversy throughout the summer of 1997 over its right to be screened for the paying public. It was only released in late August after many of the sexual and violent scenes were excised "voluntarily" by the production company. Included in this butchery was the crucial conclusion without the director's approval. What fueled the public outcry against *Bad Movie* even more was the intolerant social climate of the day against the sexual depiction of underage teenagers.[53]

It is not coincidental that Jang Sun-woo's film on teenage rebellion was completed during the month when the state was most intolerant toward the sexual portrayal of youth, since Jang's work always had brushed up against the social mores and the state's forbearance. The film's polyvalence and discursivity that defy ethics and logic, as in *A Petal*, on a politically sensitive subject matter irked not only the state but also the progressive intellectuals who sought to place the rebellious youth in their immunized *haebanggu* ("liberated zone") to hail them as the essentially anti-authoritarian subject. Formulating a discourse on a particular social cluster and representing it requires an ideology, which according to Louis Althusser, is "not the system of the real relations which govern the existence of individuals, but the imaginary relations of those individuals to the real relations."[54] Yet there was an intellectual fervor in Korea during the 1990s bent on labeling particular social groups as if they can champion social change. After the fever for Korea's democratization subsided in the early 1990s, when Kim Young-sam became the first civilian president since the early 1960s, the word *sinsedae* (new generation) appeared in the public arena with frequency and regularity.[55] The word was projected in the popular media, everyday conversations, and intellectual forums that grew wary of the depoliticized, consumerist, and individual-oriented youth that were completely different from the politically inclined youth of the 1980s. But many young intellectuals who participated in the 1980s leftist movement and were despaired by the sterile and self-righteous tendencies of the leftist camp also embraced this new form of agency that was far less regimented than the images of their own past. The emergence of sinsedae was politically manifested by a number of journals of social commentary and articles in popular media, including a book written by a group of young intellectuals, titled *Sinsedae, ne mŏt taero haera* (*Sinsedae, Do Whatever Pleases You*).[56] The emphasis on freedom invoked in this propagandistic title already presumed that the acquisition of individual freedom is the crucial identity that can mobilize changes in a society that has for far too long emphasized only collective mentality and discourse. The search for the self was now only possible through an understanding and an expression of private desires, a pursuit best engaged by the so-called sinsedae. However, not often pointed out was the foundational condition of a slippery agency that will always resist any form of representation and social underpinnings.

What is so beguiling about *Bad Movie* is its provocation of the slippage between sinsedae as ideological formation by intellectuals and the youth as they choose to represent themselves. The freedom imagined by the intellectuals to be embodied in the subject of sinsedae is severely contradicted when they are presented in the film. The youth are just as weak, violent, and complicit as the adults; they are capable of stealing, killing, lying, and raping others. Jang intends an unflinching and nonjudgmental portrayal of amoral youth, not by "frankly" depicting them, but by self-reflexively displaying the impossibility of representing his subjects without manipulation and biases. He creates a world where scams and extortions prevail, stripping away any form of romanticism with the youth as the last bastion of pure anti-authoritarian struggle. They not only use violence and lies to extort money and goods from random pedestrians, but they also cheat and betray one another. As the film progresses, their penchant for scamming and physically injuring each other becomes more and more uncontrollable. Surely their baggy clothes, grimy parkas and ripped jeans, gaudy jewelry, and bleached hair all turn, to use Dick Hebdige's phrase, "narcissism into an offensive weapon," where the values of capitalism, efficiency, conformity, and respect for order can hardly be emblazoned even though the brand names of their outfits are objects that can ironically induce capitalistic desire.[57] There is hardly loyalty or bondage between them, separating their world from the one of gangsters, where intrafamilial betrayals are represented in movies as the biggest sin of all. Perhaps the most anarchic group of youth so far pictured in Korean cinema, they continuously undermine every discourse that attempts to snare and classify them. But their obsession of the self and their penchant for narcissism also allowed the cameras, lights, and the crews to follow them in their stories and everyday lives, combining to produce a radically ruptured piece that is halfway between narrative and documentary, a film that floats somewhere between truth and fiction.

Brutality and violence maintain its repetitive crescendo until finally the film ends with a prayer for salvation and forgiveness. What first starts as harmless horseplay and practical jokes played on one another gradually produce much more serious injuries as the narrative progresses. The youth have courage and do not fear authoritarian figures such as the police who forcibly demand compliance. But what dismantles them is not an external force, for no authorial power can genuinely delimit their transgressions. It is their own unruliness, mutual abuse, and intolerance that pose the biggest threats to their survival. The real-life romance, the subsequent breakup, and jealousies also play crucial parts in creating tension-filled moments in the film. At one point, a group of girls break into a trendy bar after its business hours and start partying. It is here where the two female characters, Yippŭnyi (Beauty) and Alppon (Druggie) engage in a fight over a boy, Redŭ Pyŏn (Red Shit). The physical altercation between the two girls is not trivial, as their pride—something they cannot negotiate—is on the line. The shattering of bottles and glasses, the desperately extended skinny arms of the young girls aiming to injure each other, and the shrill sounds bellowed by the two in the empty and otherwise-silent bar remove any trace of idealism potentially sought in the sinsaedae. For them, the fight over a boy is a matter of life and death where everything—including the music—has to stop. Violence is hardly as romantic and lush as in another film on teenage violence that was released around the same time, Beat (Kim Sŏng-su, dir., 1997). It is as close to the real as it can get, disorienting and discomforting even the contemporary art-film viewers who are familiar with violence aestheticized in cinemas of Wong Kar-wai, Quentin Tarantino, and Kitano Takeshi.

Mostly high-school dropouts between the ages of fifteen and eighteen, these boys and girls are caught between adolescence and adulthood. Lacking motivation to study and work, they have prematurely declared their independence

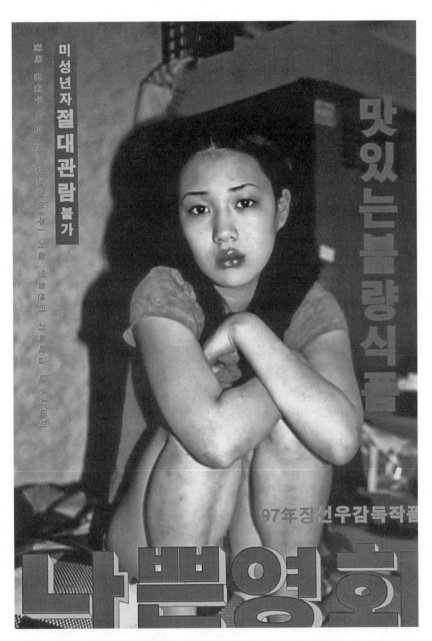

A poster for *Timeless, Bottomless Bad Movie* (1997).

(or have been forced out into the street) from their parents and are in desperate need of cash. They mostly work in hostess or host bars, but since their work is unsteady and humiliating, money always falls short. Because they do not possess any skills, their cons only work when directed at themselves, and only primitive violence will be effective in prying money out of others. The use of violence to steal money provides a significant break from conventional ethics since they are then framed immorally, but Jang manages to steer the audience from either rooting for the crimes to happen or hating the teenagers for what they have done because the violence depicted in the film has gone beyond the "natural" — an action of sequential movement that is familiar to moviegoers — and falls into the serene milieu for actually being too real. The film features two scenes of thefts. In the first sequence, titled *Arirang P'ŏk*, Kamja (Potato), Redŭ Pyŏn (Red Shit), and P'ŭrinsŭ (Prince) follow a drunken middle-age man to a dark alley. Shot from an aerial angle, the gang violence committed against a man who can hardly retaliate the countless punches and kicks is definitely more affective than the stylized violence of, for instance, Wong Kar-wai films, which tend to break down the action into smeared fragments using a slow-motion technique known as the step-printing process (where movements and action bleed and drag saturated colors). Instead of slowing the action down and intimately hugging the subjects of violence through extreme close-ups where even drops of blood are magnified and stylized, Jang uses a long aerial shot in a long take, and even drops frames of the film stock to create a fast-motion image throughout the entire scene. What he creates is a deliberate move to counter the contemporary tendency in both Korean and Hong Kong cinema to aestheticize violence.[58]

Perhaps the most prominent trope that conditions the teenagers' identity is sex. Constantly mobile and potentially explosive, violence and sex are the only outlets through which their energy can be released. What is also clearly manifested in the film is that the sex is not deployed as either escape fantasy or fulfillment of romantic desires. Its only association is with money, the "thing" congealed and condensed through sex. Sex is instantaneous and mannered, as it is bartered in clear calculable sums of money that functions beyond the romantic union. In the film, there are three places where sex is articulated as work that generates "dollar signs." First, one of the girls, Sae (this nickname is abbreviated from *Sae taegari*, which literally means "bird-brain") finds work in a hostess club to escort men who drink in private rooms. Given a little advice from her female seniors, she is conveyed into a room where she joins several men drinking. Her short blonde hair and flamboyant boyish looks have already undergone a complete makeover as she is now seen in a black wig and a revealing black dress. Once Sae's style assumes a 180-degree turnaround, her portrayal emits an undeniably solemn mood. Her dyed hair, cut-up jeans, and colorful t-shirts are more than simple fashion statements; they are her symbols, means of communication, and identity makeup intent on defying and offending conformity. More than upsetting the wardrobe, Dick Hebdige claims that the punks "undermined every relevant discourse" through their style.[59] Although Sae now has a look that accommodates, she is neither witty nor charming, displaying none of the sexual innuendos or flirtations normally seen in these private rooms where sexual fondling of the women is common. In the next shot, framed from a camera placed under the table, a grainy shot captures her in a room alone with a middle-age man who reaches for her genital area, fondles it, and licks his fingers. Sae uncomfortably keeps inching backward, but there is simply no place to hide from her client. While she is being chased by the man, her narration reveals that she had to quit because she could not put up with strange men touching her. Because it is not the man's body but Sae's that is being touched, the woman's sexual pleasure seems to be at stake in this scene. But Sae's pleasure is absent from the sexual exchange, destabilizing the conventional viewing position that is aligned with the peeping pleasures of the voyeuristic camera. Sae, in an indifferent and unemotional tone, concludes her story by telling us that she now wants her job back because she is again in desperate need of money.

Sexual pleasures are solidly tied to a system of exploitative and perverse capitalistic exchanges that make the youth — in need of money — vulnerable. Elsewhere in the film, Aimttŏk (Rice-cake) rushes into his workplace, a private room in a host bar where two middle-age women wait for him. His job, like Sae's, is to entertain them. Performing a few stage tricks, singing songs, and dancing, he — with the aid of a few of his colleagues — is in charge of making the party fun. A woman in a fur coat yells, "Play, play, that way you will see mo' money!" Soon the song-and-dance festivities switch gears into an orgiastic party where the half-naked body of Aimttŏk is sandwiched between two women in a sexual embrace. Despite the jubilance the sequence generates, like the shrill, mechanic sound of the cheap karaoke microphone through which their voice travels in the disco-light lit room, the enactment of pleasure is artificial and coy.

In the film's third sex scene, Sae walks into a small electronic store and asks for the price of a new Walkman. She is however immediately identified by the storeowner as the thief who had just last week stolen the exact same Walkman she has described. Sae tries to run away from him, but gets caught after taking a few steps from the vendor. In the next scene, she is in a kneeled position in a public bathroom, fellating the storeowner. Needless to say, they have come to a repayment agreement. When he ejaculates, Sae gets up and asks him whether she can have "(another) Walkman." He responds to this question by slapping her cheek hard and then tells her, "If you come and blow me off again next week, who knows?"

Significant in all of the three sequences above, sex enacts unequal power relations where it has become an integral component of hegemonic social order. Sex is quantifiable in these scenes, measured in specific financial terms such as a "Walkman," where the material desire of youth and the sexual pleasure of an adult can explicitly be bartered. Referencing Luce Irigaray's essay entitled "Women on the Market," Linda Williams states how "desire, in the context of exchange, 'perverts' need, 'but that perversion will be attributed to commodities (merchandises) and to their alleged relations.'"[60] What Williams attempts to define in this passage is how difficult it is for the Western hard-core pornographic films to represent what women's pleasure exactly is despite the fact that many hard-core films are obsessed with it — as the case is with *Deep Throat*. Each of the scenes from *Bad Movie* described above displays various tropes of sexual perversions, but they proliferate only because "the implantation of multiple perversions," as Foucault says, is an "instrument-effect" that isolates, intensifies and consolidates "peripheral sexualities." The term "peripheral sexualities," for Foucault, signifies multiple modes of conduct where sexualities are branched out beyond power, but something that is not exactly "taking revenge" against a power that has sought to naturalize it through "repressive law." *Bad Movie* — though sex is fetishized and negotiated where it only affirms the double agencies of power that can repress sex but also seek pleasures from it — is aware that no effective resistance can be mobilized against the power that commodifies sex. When a smile appears on Sae's face as she gets up from her kneeling position in the bathroom and hears that she might get her Walkman if she returns to fellate the storeowner again, it is difficult to determine the position of agency in the relation between the two. Is she satisfied because the price of a Walkman can be negotiated with her sexual labor, something unlike money that she can control? Is she now in some mediation of her agency despite the wretched, humiliating condition she was just placed in?

Not only satisfied in featuring youth, the film, through the stories of the middle-age homeless, creates a socio-temporal rhythm that oscillates between stasis and dynamism. Both subjects, the youth and the vagabonds, are radically different in terms of their style and manners, but they share common grounds since they both have no place to go. Unlike the youth who are restless and always on the move, the homeless men who congregate around the Seoul

Sae (kneeling) exchanges a "favor" for a Walkman.
Timeless, Bottomless Bad Movie (1997).

Railway Station are usually immobile. Played by real homeless people, they are usually motionless; their movement is restricted and time seems to stop when they are framed on screen.[61] In other words, their time and space differ radically from those of the youth, despite the fact that the social perceptions both groups generate from the public are similar. (They are both shunned by society and constantly hassled by the authorities.) The kids are never motionless, as they seek pleasure in motorcycle races, dance beats, and sex—all of which must accompany immaculate control of movement and speed. Even when they are simply walking down the road, they are constantly in motion: shaking their bodies, relentlessly fidgeting, hopping on the rails, and singing songs. Randomly inserted throughout the film, a simple pass across the subway station gate becomes for them a challenging game since they—without a ticket—need to zip through the checkpoint without getting caught. Every space they occupy, including their abode, is a place of transience that can hardly contain them. The homeless are also fated to be constantly traveling since they are without homes. But, their engagement with, for instance, the subway station where they sleep differs radically from the one of the youth. They are constantly seen from the squatting position, made even more immobile by the placement of the camera that frequently captures the subject from ground level. For those who have no other place to go, the subway stations are hardly areas to rush through. Halfway into the film, in a crucial scene where the homeless and the youth cross paths, they display affinities yet repulsions. Sae jumps out of a sixth-floor window into a sidewalk dumpster to avoid paying for the bowling fees. Apparently not seriously injured from the fall other than a few cuts and bruises, she walks into a convenience store and is caught shoplifting by the storeowner. She is publicly humiliated by the owner and is forced to stay kneeling in front of the cash register. A homeless man, who is also in the store picking up liquor bottles, places his money in front of her. Wearing tattered clothes and sporting uncombed hair and a grubby face, the homeless man has taken pity on her and gives up his bottles to pay for the bags of snacks Sae had intended to shoplift. In the only instance where the two—the homeless and the youth—actually intersect, the film demonstrates that it is the homeless who are more humane and even freer than the youth. While he possesses nothing other than a few coins, he unhesitatingly gives them up so that she can be freed. He has willingly exchanged his booze, the only material good he desires, for her freedom.

The insertions of footage shot through alternative mediums in a feature film production allow the cast to be performative: motions and behaviors leading to spiritual salvation. The use of multiple formats that range from digital video to 35mm film, the casting of real homeless and runaway youth with no prior acting experience, and the insertion of documentary images though many of the actual stories are reenacted for the film make *Bad Movie* scrupulous with regard to its own limitations. After the *cinema verité* style initially used in the motorcycle race scene, it is elsewhere abandoned, but the medium of video is spontaneous, sometimes positioned as the primary camera in the scenes that figure the homeless. Since much of the film retells the actual experiences of the characters who make confessions of their most intimate and humiliating moments in their lives, the use of the video is hardly surprising. After all, video has been widely used for documenting autobiography in the era of electronic media and personal camcorders. As Michael Renov argues, since the development of the Sony Portapak in the mid-1960s, many independent artists and home consumers have chosen video as their medium to record their diaries because the "systematic solipsism and 'immediacy' of video . . . suit it so well to the confessional impulse."[62] Ubiquitous in *Bad Movie* are the "confessional impulses" many of these characters bring to the film. They constantly talk about themselves and their experiences. One of the homeless explains to the camera how his impotence and alcohol addiction led to the failure of his marriage. Yip-pŭnyi also confesses to a panel of filmmakers, including Jang, how in front of a video camera she was kicked out of her own home without a single piece of clothing other than her underwear. These and other stories about suicide and hallucinations are confessional first-person accounts that solicit intimacy with the viewers. Because video confessions are primarily composed of narcissistic drives as well as spiritual impulses to reconcile with one's self, they become performances and narratives to engage personal traumas.

The performative elements end up usurping the power relationship between the subject and the camera, which assumes an authorial position during a confession. The confessing subject creates havoc. Man-su, one of the central homeless characters, in a highly public area in broad daylight looks directly into the video camera held by a camerawoman and tells her how his "thing does wonders." Man-su remains indifferent to the camerawoman's response that she is already married, and tries to expose his penis to her. At this instance, the film cuts away rapidly from the video to a film camera that from a distance is framing the surprised camerawoman moving backward. When the camerawoman momentarily becomes nervous and feels threatened by Man-su's obscene action, the usual authorial position of the video camera breaks down, and it accepts — instead of the framed subject — a submissive role reassigned by the homeless man's improvisations. What is intriguing is that this scene affirms the film's insistence on shuffling different mediums of fiction, *cinema verité*, and video confessions. By so doing, the power dynamics between the representational subject on screen and the authorial subject behind the camera continually reshift so that the articulation of Truth becomes indecipherable, and with it the location of subjectivity muddled.

One of the elements that separates Jang's work from those of Bunuel, Oshima, and Truffaut that similarly frame societal failures through a corrupted youth is his refusal to end the film with the death of one of his malicious characters (symbolic or real) through which renewal or rebirth is suggested. The final twenty minutes of the film provide an ending that is unique in narrative film history. From a rape sequence that takes place toward the end of the film to the death of one of the anonymous homeless that officially concludes the film, *Bad Movie* explores the boundaries between moral and immoral, life and death via a stylistic mode that rejects the structural bifurcation between real and fiction, and between diegesis and extradiegesis. Death does occur in *Bad Movie*, but it is actually one of the harmless homeless who suffers death, not one of the aggressive boys who commits crimes of rape and assault. In one of the concluding scenes, Ppaen, Red Pyŏn, and Aim Ddŏk get together in an arcade hall and casually plan on gang-raping Kongju (Princess), a fifteen-year old girl, who is still a virgin. After getting her drunk, the three boys take turns raping the girl who is half-conscious. The festive mood rendered by the boys during the rape, the disco music soundtrack, and their guilt-free faces shock the viewer because of the casual and indifferent manner of their crime. The unspeakable shock produced in this film reaches far beyond the one generated in the classic sequence of *A Clockwork Orange* (Stanley Kubrick, dir., 1973) where Alex rapes a suburban woman while joyfully singing "Singing in the Rain" and forces her husband to watch his heinous crime. While this scene from *A Clockwork Orange* replaces realistic elements with a modernist filmmaking style and props, Jang's rape sequence is shot with a handheld video camera, generating a jittery and gritty look that enhances its quasi-documentary quality.

So shocking is this scene of rape that it is difficult to immediately vilify the boys and pity the girl. Emotions are rendered numb and unaffective. The flamboyance exuded by both the boys and the girls even when they are stealing and prostituting for money is forgotten when this act of gang rape takes place. Perhaps even more surprising is what Jang does *after* the rape scene. After showing simulated sex and naked bodies, the film ventures outside the diegesis to portray a couple of reactions after the take of the same sex scene. Kongju, now fully clothed and seated on the bed, sips on her water and begins to cry, unable to control her emotions. In this scene, we see her in full close-up for the first time, which informs us of the emotive and stressful conditions in which the film was shot. The film then cuts to one of the still photographers hired to take promotional photos of *Bad Movie*. The real exchange between the director and Hajin, the still photographer, unfolds as such:

Jang: Hajin, why did you not take any photos?
Hajin: Because it was bad.
Jang: You mean that it was bad to shoot?
Hajin: Yes, it's bad.
Jang: Shooting this film or taking still photos?
Hajin: I don't care about the movie. I have nothing to do with it. But taking photos is bad. (The video camera that had closely framed her face at this point, tilts down to show her still camera.) It's a "bad movie" anyway.
Voice of another male crew away from the camera: It doesn't matter if the pictures were not. It's funny how everyone has a different interpretation of the word "bad."
Jang: From here onward, there are many more scenes like this. Would you continue not to shoot them?

Leaving Hajin awkwardly laughing, the film cuts to Ppaen who, in the midst of taking off his clothes, also protests to the director who wants another take of the scene, "Why must we go through this again? Is it necessary to get completely naked?" He also adds, "Do you think we would actually do this sort of thing?" His reminder that this is a scene that they had not scripted but was inserted only because the director himself wanted it is a mystifying break for the viewers who so far had believed that the youth had scripted much of the film. The astonishing race toward the end continues once the film returns us back to the diegesis where Redŭ Pyŏn is confronted by Yippŭnyi, his girlfriend, who meets him out in a dark alley. She fiercely protests, "How could you call yourself a human being after raping a young girl? How could you possibly gang rape her?" Her rage, delivered in a shrill voice, is met with another round of violence unleashed by Redŭ Pyŏn. Redŭ Pyŏn cannot possibly come to terms with the fact that he has committed an atrocious crime, and because he is not ready to repent (or Jang doesn't want the scene to be cathartic), he again resorts to violence, beating his girlfriend to the ground and kicking her hard even when it is clear that she is incapable of retaliating. Just like Kongju, she remains helpless and just accepts his cruel violence, blow after blow. While the stable camera remains distant, this graphic and misogynistic violence will be the final image of the youth we see in the film.

Why were these "bad" scenes filmed in the first place? How did they survive the editing room? Why were they presented to us as only the self-referential exposure of the director who insists on misrepresenting the truth and the youth as rapists? Both scenes of rape are hardly gratuitous. Shot mostly from a long position, the scenes do not reveal visceral excitement, but leave — even for a crew member who was present during the film's production — only anger, frustration, and confusion. Yet the film brims with ambiguity, and these intense reactions all intermingle because the film has self-reflexively displayed for us that the young boys who have been involved in the sex scene have only been reluctantly acting it out, following the direction of Jang who personally wanted the scene. By offering amnesty to the runaway youth and preventing them from being depicted as sexually driven characters, the film leads us to believe that it is the director Jang himself whose moral intentions must be questioned. The film's Brechtian "distantiation," which intends to break the audience's emotional identification with the fictional characters, does not diffuse the highly charged emotions but redirects them against the director himself who has intentionally made the teenaged actors participate — albeit fictionally — in this atrocious and inexcusable crime against women and humanity. The film's placement of the themes in the playful postmodern context dumbfounds and discomforts the viewers even more. By exposing his authority and control over the means of the production and the content of the film, Jang, the director whose ultimate aim is to remain true to the spirit of iconoclasm, dismantles and disclaims his own authority to salvage the youth. The icon he set out to destroy is revealed to be him; the cynicism echoed in the self-reflexive mechanisms and playful styles is aimed at none other than Jang. The film ends with Man-su praying before the camera, "Lord, bless the health of my brothers and sisters. Dear my Father, Lord. Forgive my sins. Hallelujah. Father! Lord!" Christian hymns are sung in the background. The concluding intertitle mentions that Man-su, a real vagabond, was arrested during the film production for reasons that could not be identified: an apt ending for Jang Sun-woo who was publicly condemned by the state and critics after the film was complete.

7

Too Early/Too Late: Temporality and Repetition
in Hong Sang-su's Films

In all four films directed by Hong Sang-su, scenes of waiting are repetitively structured as sublime moments that define both the characters and the central thematic motif. In Hong's first feature, *The Day a Pig Fell into the Well* (*Tweji ga umul e ppajin nal*, 1996),[1] Tong-u, a plain married man in his thirties, visits Chŏnju (a four-hour bus ride from Seoul) on a business trip. From the moment he hops on the bus, he is forced to spend the entire day waiting. The actual business meeting never takes place in the film's diegesis; instead, the narrative spends much more time recounting the man's journey. When the passenger seated next to him vomits, Tong-u is forced to spend extra time in the bathroom at a stopover to clean himself. The bus leaves without him on board, requiring him to wait for the next bus. He finally arrives at a department store in Chŏnju where the office of his business partner is located, but the partner is away for a meeting and will be back only after lunch. Reluctantly, Tong-u, a salesman for a mineral water company, has lunch by himself, only to find himself out-of-luck again. After lunch, he narrowly misses the man he needs to see for he has stepped out momentarily to take care of an "errand." Unwilling to wait at the office, Tong-u calls a friend who lives in the city's suburbs; he then spends more time waiting for him. When he returns to the office for the third time, the receptionist relays a message to him that the partner won't return to the office. The meeting will have to be postponed until the next morning. What has previously been referred to as an "errand" is now an "important affair" that keeps the man away from his desk. Tong-u's patient waiting has been for naught. He will have to spend the night at a motel in a strange city, and the unfamiliar setting exacerbates his anxiety. Tong-u solicits the service of a call girl to his motel room. The call girl is suspicious of the motives of Tong-u who initially only wants to talk. After an awkward moment of hesitation, they have sex.

Particularly interesting is the conversation that takes place between Tong-u and the prostitute before intercourse. One of the reasons Tong-u ends up having sex with the call girl is because they were not able to find a topic to discuss. In other words, their inability to verbally communicate to each other is one of the preconditions for physical consummation. When the woman enters the room, she is surprised to hear Tong-u's suggestion, "Could we just talk?" Though they agree to initially "just talk," they drift through uncomfortable pauses, callous answers to pointless questions, and contradictions to presumptions. (Tong-u replies "no" to the woman who asks, "Do you like to be in the dark?" The woman also tells Tong-u that she doesn't come from the café across the street as he had thought.) The continuity of their dialogue is ruptured because it is a "talk" that is closer to a double monologue. Tong-u's request, "You talk about whatever you want and I'll do the same," diminishes or eliminates the role of the receiver in a verbal communication. The de-centering of the other (the receiver) complicates the location of the self's subjectivity. Without the person listening, the speaker only remains an infelicitous enunciator without a point of reception. The "talk" initially insisted upon by Tong-u lays the contradictory foundation of the relationship between the two also because he has hailed her as a prostitute and is now hesitant to become her client. The self/other role between sender and recipient is then framed by awkwardness, suspicion, and threats of leaving, as well as the impossibility of conjecturing a rational structure of communication in the barren, filthy motel room. Tong-u's subjectivity is split between the desire for real companionship and the impossibility of creating one outside the circuit of money (which is chained to the act of sex).

Sex is both the explicit and implicit purpose of the woman's visit. She is a prostitute, but she is "officially" there to deliver him coffee since prostitution is illegal in Korea. Therefore, if sex is deduced from their relationship, the woman's role is ironically forced to return to her masquerade, a waitress who is simply there for room service. The cutaway shot to the sperm-stained blanket on the television set suggests a temporal leap, but one that has produced no real progress in their relationship. Instead of continuously floating in the circuit of meaninglessness, the anonymous call girl gives Tong-u an ultimatum: he is to make up his mind whether to have sex or not while she leaves for the bathroom. She is tired of waiting since only sex — and not talk — can be quantified into labor and an exchange value that entails her wage. No longer able to continue to mull things over in passivity, Tong-u picks from his wallet a small photograph of his wife and kid. Tong-u's desire stems from an absence that has long traumatized him. Tears flow from his eyes after he shakes his knees in a state of violent anxiety. The origin of his sadness is later revealed as the death of the child, which has led Po-kyŏng, his wife, to an adulterous affair and to an eventual suicide.

During intercourse, Tong-u yells, "I would like to love you," a phrase that is repeated by the call girl who says, "Me too. I would like to love you."[2] The exchange of "I love you" — with the use of a conditional clause — constitutes a sign that is one-half signified in the state of longing; the other half is trapped in reality that is self-conscious that it will "never happen." J. Hillis Miller in *Speech Acts in Literature*, discusses Derrida's exposition of the phrase, "Je t'aime" as an exemplary of the speech-act theory that is an "explicit performative,"[3] a special kind of testimony that needs the bearing of a witness. What I find interesting about the citation of "Je t'aime" or "I love you" is that it is punctuated not only through the gestures of seduction, affection, and act of faith, but also through its threats and dangers. In Hong Sang-su's films, the utterance or the nonutterance of "I love you" also bears importance as a play not of romance but of power. The underscoring of the signifier as a performative far overrides its signified or the meaning of "I love you," for when and how this is stated is far more important than its actual meaning. The utterance is dependent not only on the possibility of this phenomenon but also on the impossibility of the recipient's knowing the credibility of this proposed testimony. Complicating this situation even more is that this verbal utterance constitutes an indeterminate temporal condition that neither thrusts a movement forward nor remains fixed in a present stasis. Tong-u — by verbally stating these words — is not released from his state marred by crisis and anxiety but is further bound by it. The desperate expression of the need for love to a prostitute whom he has just met underscores Tong-u's current affair: the vanishing of affection and the repression of sex with his own wife, which will be revealed in the story of his wife separately told later in the film.

During the postcoital aftermath, Tong-u discovers that he had been using a defective condom. In the very next scene, he is back in Seoul, receiving a needle injection at a health clinic as a precautionary measure to prevent the contraction of disease. (It is unclear however whether an injection after the fact can actually help prevent contraction of the disease. Isn't it too late if one receives the treatment after sex?) The subject remains restrained in this cyclical path that strays near pleasure and death, but he never quite arrives at its fatal destination. The death will be delivered only at the very end of the film.

The strength of this scene lies not on the sex act but on the structure of alterity or the *différance* that is sharpened by both the impossibility of the two to verbally communicate to each other and the postponement of sex. Both the multiple layers of difference (precipitated by the verbal miscommunication, identities, and the meaning of love) and the temporal delays (of the business meeting and sex) constitute the dual signified that already preconditions différance, the term which is central to Jacques Derrida's theory. The notions of self-differentiation and postponement, taking his cue from Husserl, allow Derrida to cross out the determination of absolute subjectivity to a point where the very concept of subjectivity and its constitution must be deconstructed.[4] Both "difference" and "deferment," the two terms that structure Derrida's concept of différance, underscore also the crisis of meaning and subjectivity that shapes Hong Sang-su's work.

The différance of temporality is signified in Hong Sang-su's films as waiting (deferment of the event) and the repetition (which becomes the mode of alterity that is so central in différance) that is precisely made possible by this temporal delay. The exact reasons why his characters wait are of little consequence. The affair that has initially prompted Tong-u to travel far, for instance, remains unclear in the film, and its significance is superceded by that of the suspense created by the vacuum—both temporal and ontological. The meeting between Tong-u and the store manager never takes place, affirming that it is significant only in its absence. The wait has forced Tong-u to loiter in a strange city, far from his family and his familiar environment. Hong Sang-su exploits this vacuous intermittence—the temporal gap when people are forced to tediously sit—to create his drama. Even when people are "working," Hong's characters constantly procrastinate, hindering productivity and instead daydreaming of escaping the monotonous everyday. Whether early or late, his characters are never on time, and it is precisely during this idle moment when providential encounters, egregious jokes, and tempting situations that are so central in his films take place. There are many reasons why people wait; mismanagement of time, indecision, bureaucratic holdup, traffic congestion, unexpected phone calls and meetings, plain irresponsibility, and forgetfulness all potentially fill the list of reasons why people are forced to constantly wait in Hong's films. All of them constitute symptoms of a modern society, which makes the order of things necessary but impossible. Hong, by creating the suspension of temporal delay, compels the viewer to ask, "What is going to happen after the wait?" Of course, more often than not nothing happens, or, even when something does happen in the end, a neat, tidy closure is resisted. Hong insists that there is something always interesting to say even during an interval where people are forced to wait and "nothing happens."

Time is of essence in the modern era, especially in Korea, which had a late start in the process of industrialization and is eager to catch up with the West. When the clock ticks, everything—including money—has a chance to become obsolescent if it sits idly even for a moment. Hong depicts ordinary characters who are anxious that idleness might be converted into loss of productivity or value. So, instead, they impatiently try to squeeze in errands, activities, and other meetings while they wait. Often these efforts to engage in multitasks— moments that "free" them from waiting—backfire as they have to then be "re-queued." For example, in Hong's second feature, *The Power of Kangwon Province* (*Kangwon do ŭi him*, 1998), the film's protagonist Sang-gwŏn and his friend are placed on stand-by when they try to fly home from their vacation in Kangwon Province. Because they are impatient during their wait at the airport, they are unable to resist the temptation to see more of the site. They hop in a taxicab for a quick tour of a Buddhist temple, only fifteen-minutes away from the airport, and thus jeopardize their spots on the stand-by list. When they return, only one of them can go onboard, and thus Sang-gwŏn—like Tong-u—is forced to stay another night in a strange city alone.

Hong Sang-su's unorthodox approach to time motivates a departure from the conventional narrative form. He tends to muddle the structure of his films, resisting the order of a beginning, a middle, and an end. His leaping over the boundary of linear time also affects the recovery of the truth, one that is closely related to the question of historiography, something that is significant in his films, though they are not accounts of public history. *The Power of Kangwon Province* and *Virgin Stripped Bare by Her Bachelors* (*O Sujŏng*, 2000) adopt a "forking-path" narrative form where two separate narratives split from the same original point.[5] Normally in these narratives, the alternative story produces an ending that is different from the initial plot. Frank Capra's *It's a Wonderful Life* (1946), Krystof Kieslowski's *Blind Chance* (1981), and the *Back to the Future* series (Robert Zemeckis, dir., 1985, 1989, 1991) all testify that the endings would be different if the trajectories of these stories were altered. What is radical about Hong's films is not the use of a forking pattern, but that the varying plotlines do not have any impact on changing the ending (nor do they threaten to change the history of the world). The subversive power of Hong's films relies on its insistence that nothing will change the present, even when the past is varied. Hence, Hong often repeats the same story from multiple perspectives in order to acknowledge that even when there are differences from one memory to another, the end result will still be the same. This narrative strategy not only terminates the possibility of hope and optimism, but also proposes the impossibility of despair since life, he insists, still has to be lived.

Derrida's concept of "trace"—the "mark of the absence of a presence, an always already absent present"—necessarily marks the presence of a subject, a Being, but one that lacks his or her origin. The inability to find the origin or the impossibility of a Being to recuperate his or her Whole equates with neither death nor nihilism. Hong's castrated characters are similarly placed in a ceaseless shuffle between Eros and death, but they almost always do not arrive at their destination. Hong's films shatter what Gayatri Spivak in her introduction to *Of Grammatology* states is "humankind's common desire . . . for a stable center, and for an assurance of mastery" and a narrative's structure of beginning, middle, and end that satisfy that desire.[6] By daring to repeat a banal story of anxiety, hardship, and contempt in each of his films, he denies the pleasure of a closure and instead splits it, interrupting the narrative progression and constructing a subject who is often an amnesiac and a mimic (Hong's characters often suffer from chronic forgetfulness and mimetic impulses) who is caught somewhere between Being and nothingness. The stories of people who desperately try to release themselves from their traumas never quite reach their sense of fulfillment precisely because he or she can never fully undo in the present what has been done in the past.

"After Politics, What Next?"

Through his four films, *The Day a Pig Fell into the Well*, *The Power of Kangwon Province*, *Virgin Stripped Bare by Her Bachelors*, and *Turning Gate* (*Saenghwal ŭi palgyŏn*, 2002), Hong Sang-su became a local film critic's favorite at a time when Korea had passed through its most intense political period of the late 1980s and the early 1990s. No longer were masses of protesters commiting self-immolation, dissenters being tortured and killed, and sightings of an army in riot gear everyday instances in Seoul. The revolutionary fervor that swept the nation had faded into a melancholic memory. The year of Hong's directorial debut, 1996, is around the period when the questions like "After politics, what next?" became fashionable.[7] The year marked three years beyond the inauguration of the first civilian president in Korea since 1960. Yet, the certainties to which earlier eras were accustomed through remarkable double-digit annual economic growth and a stable political system under military dictatorship (after all, if not stability, what else does a dictatorship guarantee?) had well come to an end. The question, "After politics, what next?" and the identification of Hong's films as an exemplary of a convention or a model that uses a prefix of "postpolitical" presumes a number of things. First, the naming of a film to be either nonpolitical or postpolitical assumes that there exists a cinema that is capable of being political. Second, it also presumes that the de-centering of a subjectivity or the withering of the *telos* as a marker of history that is easily identifiable in Hong's films necessarily entails a process of depoliticization. But isn't Hong's attempt to make a deconstructionist film in the historical context of a Korea that is located outside the West sufficiently political? Another question that also complicates these presumptions is: If Hong Sang-su's films and their popularity in South Korea testify that Korean cinema is now producing films that are closer to the postwar European art-house cinemas, then could his films be considered as a cultural coda that aesthetically corresponds to Korea's late stage of modernization and industrialization?

These questions are perhaps impossible to answer because the dynamics of history always resist a clear marking that divides modern from postmodern or the East from the West. But what also holds undeniably true is that the withering of subjectivity is intricately tied to the crisis of meaning in language that is underscored as the central motif in all of Hong Sang-su's films. Verbal miscues, infelicities, and awkwardness compound the complexities and contradictions of dialogue where the interlocutor or the receiver is often bid farewell. Hong Sang-su and Derrida both share the concern that this linguistic crisis is punctuated by the absence of multiple positions, the receiver, the context of production, the signified, etc. Derrida writes, "If while looking out the window, I say: 'The sky is blue,' this utterance will be intelligible. . . . even if the interlocutor does not see the sky; even if I do not see it myself, if I see it badly, if I am mistaken or if I wish to lead my interlocutor. Not that this is always the case; but the structure of possibility of this utterance includes the capability to be formed and to function as a reference that is empty or cut off from its referent."[8] The *différance* between intention and meaning, between the sign and the reference, and between Being and non-Being structures the primary tensions in Hong Sang-su's films that end up splitting the questions of ontology as well as temporality. The protagonists in them desire love and they wait for it to be uttered; but when "love" is uttered, it is "empty or cut off from its referent."

There is an intricate connection between Hong's meticulous depiction of everyday life and his characters who are incapable of recuperating their subjectivity. In other words, Hong Sang-su's films underscore the importance of style (by minimizing the use of insert shots, dramatic music, and exaggerated dialogue) that must slip out of its conventional form in order to complement a mechanism of nonmelodramatic pathos and theme. Hong's characters never seem unnatural though they constantly fail to live up to the audience's expec-

Chi-suk buys a newspaper. *The Power of Kangwon Province* (1998).

tations of unity and harmony during the closure. By repeating the everyday occurrences as his primary drama, Hong's narrative trajectory often loses its momentum forward and reiterates the circular motion in the spirit of realism, constituting what Brian Henderson called the "iteratives."[9] The use of iteratives frees Hong from the limitation imposed by the temporality of plot. The scenes of Min-jae, the ticket-seller in *The Day a Pig Fell into the Well*, waking up in the morning; of Sang-gwŏn, the university lecturer in *The Power of Kangwon Province*, looking for his pager at his apartment; and of Su-jŏng, the assistant to the director in *Virgin Stripped Bare by Her Bachelors*, playing electronic keyboards in her office are special only because they are typical everyday instances.

The portrayal of everyday banality deflates the masculine ego and subjectivity without the possibility of its recuperation. The impossibility of resolving the psychic lack (which leads the characters to desire), the continual insistence of a subject to slip outside the temporal linearity or linguistic meaning, and the tendency of the characters to constantly forget and mimic each other all punctuate a male crisis.[10] Rather than privileging the trajectory of a man fully recovering from his trauma, the nomadic characters (like Kyŏng-su in *Turning Gate*) become further entrapped by their retroactive circuit. Lured by their *objet petit a*, their movements fail to thrust forward and return only to the point of origin even after their desires have been physically fulfilled through sex.

Virgin Stripped Bare by Her Bachelors

> ". . . the trace is *nothing*, it is not an entity, it exceeds the question *What is?* and contingently makes it possible." — Jacques Derrida[11]

Two people meet and fall in love. Where and how this first began is a question Hong Sang-su focuses on in *Virgin Stripped Bare by Her Bachelors*, his third film. In tracing the origin of this phenomenon, he tries to explain that there is no essence through the two scenarios that are separately plausible but mutually conflicting. The two different stories — split on the basis of intention and of coincidence — force the characters to slip outside the question of "what is" that has always functioned in linear structure and ontological form; what is instead asked at the end is "Does it matter?" In a divided nation with a history of hot and cold wars, where the two sides presently still seek to authorize their legitimacy by disclaiming each others' past origins and ideological essences, this deconstructive question cannot be constituted away from its political implications. Neither nihilistic nor optimistic, this narrative structure "vulgarizes" a sensible, intelligible perception of truth, disavowing the possibility of a subject and thus the reproducibility of its power.

Many scenes in *Virgin Stripped Bare by Her Bachelors* (hereafter *Virgin Stripped Bare*) are repeated, without clearly indicating whether they are flashbacks of the past or contested memories between different characters. As in his other films, *Virgin Stripped Bare* features neither a voice-over narration nor an authoritative figure whose point of view remains central, omnipotent, and reliant. The love story between a rich, eligible bachelor (Chae-hun) and a young female office clerk from a poor background (Su-jŏng) is divided into two parts, "Perhaps Coincidence" and "Perhaps Intention." These two parts are framed by two scenes: the prelude and the climax of the film, which are the only scenes that take place in the "present tense." These scenes will anchor the two splitting plots, where the same story will be told twice and create mismatches. The repetition of the same story functions to iterate the veracity of the event twice for the purpose of muddling it.

The mismatch created to account for the two different versions of the same event is fundamentally different from the multiple perspectives of the truth offered in a film like Akira Kurosawa's *Rashomon* (1950). In *Rashomon*, the truth is varied, yet each and every story remains irreducibly absolute through its differences. The gap between the memories of each character, the bandit, the Samurai, the Samurai's wife, and the woodcutter, remains permanent and irreconcilable because they each manifest self-conscious ego and its individual interest. Kurosawa laments the selfish nature of humans, which comes across

"How 'bout if I become your girlfriend only when we drink?"
Virgin Stripped Bare by Her Bachelors (2000).

through the priest in *Rashomon*, who states, "Because men are so weak, that's why they lie. That's why they must deceive themselves." Hong Sang-su's film departs from this rigid division between fact and misrepresentation, and declares that the integrity of individual ego may not be relevant in clarifying the difference between the truth and the lie. And instead he playfully coordinates the two different perspectives so that their conflicts can be seen as either chance or intention. The two stories, "Perhaps Coincidence" and "Perhaps Intention," become characterized by their interchangeability and playfulness. This flexibility is possible because the film understands the two concepts, "coincidence" and "intention," as not absolute terms, but coterminous categories. In every intention, a trace of chance can be found.

The interchangeability or the play between coincidence and chance in the film becomes further materialized by common human traits like forgetfulness. One cannot always mean what he or she intends or says, because he or she forgets. "Iterability," Derrida defines, "alters, contaminating parasitically what it identifies and enables to repeat 'itself'; it leaves us no choice but to mean (to say) something that is (already, always, also) other than what we mean (to say), to say something other than what we say and would have wanted to say, to understand something other than . . . etc."[12] The impossibility of identifying the origin of the desire that is embedded in the story where Chae-hun tries to consummate sex to no avail and the difficulty of distinguishing the romance between the two as intentional or chance constitute the différance (in the form of both repetition and waiting) that is governed by the ego unsure of its intentions. The impulses of desire and the forgetful mind that are so ubiquitous in Hong's films make the modern subject's accountability for his words something of an impossibility.

Virgin Stripped Bare begins when Chae-hun alone enters a love motel located in the outskirts of Seoul. In the corridor, he spends some time waiting for the housekeeper to finish cleaning his room. Chae-hun receives a phone call from Su-jŏng, who tells him that she is not feeling well and would like to postpone their rendezvous until a later date, a proposal Chae-hun immediately refuses. Su-jŏng reluctantly comes out of her house but delays her date with Chae-hun by getting on a cable car at Namsan, a mountain located in the heart of Seoul. The cable car — as if to emphasize her hesitation and indecision — suffers a mechanical failure. It leaves Su-jŏng dangling in mid-air and high above the ground. This is the moment where the film "rewinds" back to the first meeting between the two principal characters, beginning the first part: "Perhaps Coincidence."

When the same events — not the iteratives of ordinary events that habitually take place everyday but "singulatives" that supposedly only happened once—repeat themselves with slight change, we, the spectators, are forced to ask whether the contradicting stories are matters of significance or triviality. Early in the "Coincidence" episode, Chae-hun accidentally runs into Su-jŏng at Kyŏngbok Palace, located only a short walking distance from his gallery. This is a random meeting that unites them after their first meeting where they were introduced by their mutual friend, Yŏng-su. Yŏng-su is a director-producer of corporate videos and Su-jŏng is his assistant. Chae-hun remembers her name, and proudly boasts that his memory is reliable. (This will prove to be false, as he constantly forgets and even confuses Su-jŏng with another woman's name at a crucial scene later on.) As chance has it, she is holding Chae-hun's gloves, which he had left behind at a bench on the palace grounds. To Su-jŏng, who remains indifferent and almost disinterested, Chae-hun excitedly exclaims how wild and unexpected this meeting has been. When the same fortuitous encounter is restaged in the second part of the film, "Perhaps Intention," a couple of changes are made.

The "Intention" section restages the same scene depicted in "Coincidence," not only to abolish the temporal shifts that occur between the present and the past, but to affirm that the seamless relationship between the past and the present that most narrative films aim for is impossible. The alternative sequence of the random meeting begins in a company van where Su-jŏng, who has earlier heard from Chae-hun that he eats lunch at Kyŏngbok Palace almost every day, insists that they shoot the additional video footage they need at the palace. The meeting is "intentionally" arranged by Su-jŏng since she was adamant about going to the spot where Chae-hun eats lunch. But had it not been for the gloves that Chae-hun randomly left behind at the site, they would not have met.

Every intention is accompanied by chance, and every repetition underscores alteration. Framed from a slightly different angle while retaining the two-shot paradigm at the same exact location, they restage the same scene involving the "fortuitous" meeting between the two. While the dialogue centers on the same subject of Chae-hun's lost glove and the randomness of their encounter, Su-jŏng is no longer frigid as she had been in the first staging of the same encounter. She is more animated and jovial, and excited about their meeting. The reversal of the dynamics between the two obfuscates the truth of what really happened during their first meeting. Was it chance or was it coincidence that they had met? Neither Su-jŏng nor Chae-hun can perceptibly distinguish the difference between the two. This difference fragments the social totality that is facilely constructed in the modern world as the absolute.

This encounter between Su-jŏng and Chae-hun will blossom into a romantic

Su-jŏng returns Chae-hun's gloves.
Virgin Stripped Bare by Her Bachelors (2000).

relationship, but it will be affected by several factors. The first hurdle between the two that needs clearing is their class difference. Chae-hun, an art gallery owner, comes from a rich family and does not need to work for money, while Su-jŏng is only a clerk/assistant who really has no hope of moving up. Like Conchita in Luis Bunuel's classic, *That Obscure Object Called Desire* (1977), Su-jŏng frustrates her pursuer by constantly delaying her commitment to sleep with him if and when she is ready. She tells him that she is a virgin and simply needs time to make up her mind. But Hong Sang-su makes it clear that the film is not symbolic about the gap in economic class. Chae-hun's sexual frustration, unlike that of Matteo in *That Obscure Object Called Desire*, is discursively figured and cannot easily be read as an allegory of class. Chae-hun, despite his courteous and gentle mannerisms and ownership of a BMW sports sedan, does not consider Su-jŏng just his plaything. And Su-jŏng also does not have the qualities of a charming but sly fortune hunter who typically figures as a protagonist in, for example, Henry James's novels. The inability of the two to sexually consummate their relationship goes well beyond the matters of class symbolism. Su-jŏng's refusal to have sex with Chae-hun is a ploy that makes the entire film a narrative of waiting in which the theme of repetition congeals. Only when Su-jŏng denies Chae-hun's tenacious demand of her body can they return the next day to struggle with the same issue again.

Su-jŏng kisses Yŏng-su in an office.
Virgin Stripped Bare by Her Bachelors (2000).

Second, complicating the relationship between Su-jŏng and Chae-hun is the presence of Yŏng-su, Su-jŏng's boss, who had initially introduced her to Chae-hun. Although most of the film centers on Chae-hun's pursuit of Su-jŏng, Yŏng-su, despite the fact that he is married, plays an integral role by also chasing her. Slightly older than Chae-hun, Yŏng-su is a director working for a small video production company, who has a lofty dream of making his own feature film one day. In the middle of the film, he discusses the possibility of procuring financial sponsorship from Chae-hun for his film project. Chae-hun initially tells him that he would gladly finance it. Yet, Yŏng-su lacks the determination and dedication to make his dream come true. He is imprudent yet timid, and intemperate yet passionless. (At one point in the film, he withdraws from a ping-pong match against Chae-hun after falling behind late in the game; he would give up rather than suffer a humiliating loss.) He desires his assistant Su-jŏng, but his unwillingness to give up his marriage commitments prevents him from cultivating the relationship between the two beyond a flirtatious fling. He is reluctant to risk his stable and complacent life as a husband to a woman from a wealthy family (which owns the company he works for) by having an extra-marital affair with his assistant. The reason that hinders his pursuit of Su-jŏng also similarly prevents him from dedicating himself to his film project, which will always remain a futile dream.[13]

Freedom from the cycle of desire and futility hardly awaits them even when Su-jŏng finally heeds Chae-hun's demand and allows him to have sex with her. After twice deferring the immanent, the sexual union between the two does finally take place. The concluding sequence where sex occurs is satirically called, "Naught Shall Go Ill When You Find Your Mare," constituting an ending for both "Perhaps Coincidence" and "Perhaps Intention." The cable car carrying Su-jŏng that had been malfunctioning begins to move again after the film has twice recaptured what has happened between her and Chae-hun. Shot in a single long take from a long shot, their first sexual intercourse is hardly pleasurable for either Su-jŏng or the viewers. Su-jŏng screams in pain, "It hurts!" as Chae-hun—after several tries—awkwardly inserts his penis into her body. He keeps telling her that he will be gentle, but her sharp screams that continue throughout the scene contradict his word. After a consummation that waylays any romantic feeling, they find the bed sheet stained with blood, a sign that confirms her virginity. This prompts Chae-hun to cruelly joke about taking the sheet stained with her blood home as a memorabilia while washing it in the bathroom tub. The film concludes with the two of them engaged in small talk about what to eat for dinner and who would be responsible for cooking duties once they get married. The foreboding of marriage is not a celebratory instance; on the contrary, it is a grim prospect of facing another obsessive cycle of the game to which they are now eternally bound. The film's ending leaves a bitter taste by provoking the question, "What else do you expect in a world where the meaning of romance has lost its intrinsic value?" The utterance of "I love you" remains dangling in air somewhere between performance and sincerity, and also between necessity and impossibility.

The Power of Kangwon Province

The futility of dreams leads Su-jŏng and Chae-hun to drink excessively, and becoming obstreperous drunks frequently at dinner parties impairs the credibility of the stories told by them. "How 'bout if I be your girlfriend only when we drink?" asks Sujŏng to Chae-hun in the early stage of their relationship after having coldly rejected him a sequence earlier. Her question posed in a taxicab after another night of drinking is soon followed by an intimate scene at an empty park where the two embrace in a long kiss. Her proposal to become intimate only when they are drunk is fitting since they keep their relationship secret from the public, especially from Yŏng-su. Furthermore, their clandestine affair, which is only validated after intoxication, thematically affirms an air of what I call the "insobriety" of Hong's films.[14] Hong's characters are always

Chi-suk (right) and her friends sing "My Darling Clementine" on the beach.
The Power of Kangwon Province (1998).

conniving, never "direct, immediate, [and] transparent" in their relationship to the real, and can only reveal their true feelings after a few drinks.[15] The desire and the will that have been restrained and ordained by bureaucratic order, social decorum, and formal etiquettes seep out of their repressive containments when their words become slurred and their body movements staggered.

A trait that crucially impinges the discourse of insobriety is forgetfulness.[16] As much as waiting motivates a narrative of repetition, so too does forgetting usher in an iterative cycle. In the beginning of *The Power of Kangwon Province*, Chi-suk and her two friends sing the Korean-versed "My Darling Clementine" together while sitting on a beach. A small quarrel breaks out between the two friends over the words of the song. The correct words are "*yŏngyŏng* ŏdil katnŭnya" (forever gone), but one of them insists that "*nŏ nŭn* ŏdil katnŭnya" (where have you gone) is a more appropriate phrasing for the song. The debate over the words of the song underscores the theme of *The Power of Kangwon Province*, which tells a story about the inability of leaving behind love that is out of reach. It appears at the end of the film that love can "smell foul" when one does not accept the fact that love too has an expiration date.

Chi-suk, a twenty-two-year-old woman and a recent college graduate, visits Kangwon Province, a region known for the serene beauty of its mountains, mineral water spas, temples, and shoreline. She is on her summer vacation trip with her two friends. A couple of months have passed since the termination of a relationship with her former teacher, a married man, and she wants to heal her wounded heart. She is stubborn and proud, yet vulnerable and emotional. In a conversation with one of her friends, Chi-suk, while drunk, asks, "Don't you see that in life there are things you can have and things you can't? I see them all the time. I reach out for the things I can get and give up on the rest. That's why I get hurt so much." But instead of scrupulously following her principle of giving up "what she can't have," she becomes intimate with another married man whom she has just met after drinking all night. The one-night affair propels Chi-suk to return to Kangwon Province in a matter of days. (As a result of the affair, she becomes pregnant, and will later be forced to abort the child.) After her trip, she cries on the bus that takes her back to Seoul because she — contrary to the position she has so confidently stated earlier — cannot easily leave behind what she cannot have, something that will become apparent at the end of the film.

Waiting and indecision are two major themes through which the film maneuvers its romantic affair between Chi-suk and Sang-gwŏn, a university lecturer who is married with a child. Also taking a trip to Kangwon Province, Sang-gwŏn and his friend are on the same train that Chi-suk is on. Though they do not meet until the end of the film, when they are both back in Seoul, they are seen several times visiting the same sites in Kangwon Province. *The Power of Kangwon Province* introduces another spliced plot, two stories that separately feature Chi-suk and Sang-gwŏn within the same temporal span. No omniscient narrator simulates the story from a privileged position in the text, nor does the film offer viewers the pleasure of knowledge that is otherwise inaccessible to the characters not in the scene. The spectators are not sure whether Chi-suk and Sang-gwŏn are each other's absent objects of desire — unless they had been paying attention to small clues — until the concluding sequence. At a first glance, the simultaneous temporality repeated in the film disorients the viewers who are asked to knot the two narratives of Chi-suk and Sang-gwŏn that are told separately. But the structure of interweaving several narrative strands into one, which Fredric Jameson has termed "the narrative of synchronous monadic simultaneity" in his analysis of *The Terrorizer* (*Kongfu fenzi*, Edward Yang, dir., 1986),[17] allows the film to tweak an otherwise melodramatic plot involving an extramarital affair, separation, and pain into a sophisticated, peculiar narrative that resists sentimentality. Unlike *Virgin Stripped Bare* where the truth between two competing stories remains obfuscated, a sense of unity is achieved in *The Power of Kangwon Province* by disclosing at the end the missing knot between the two ex-lovers.

Hong uses mise-en-scène and film language that complement his unorthodox narrative structure. Even the most dramatic "singulative" event is framed as if it is an iterative, banal everyday instance in *The Power of Kangwon Province*, neutralizing the impact of sentimental and spectacular impulses. One of the most romantic forms of communication often exploited in cinema is the leaving and writing of memos between two lovers. Hong creates such exchange, but even this sight of intimacy strips away its romantic elements. Chi-suk, on her way back home from a public sauna after returning to Seoul, finds writing on the wall next to her apartment entrance. Without expression, she erases the graffiti that states, "Breathe deeply, let us wait just a little bit longer." The film does not provide music or any form of artificial lighting to heighten this moment of drama. At this point, the author of the writing on the wall remains veiled since he has yet to appear in the film. Only toward the end of the film will the audience see Sang-gwŏn, her former lover, leaving the very memo seen earlier in the film. The film asks the viewer to remember Chi-suk's pain while trying to erase the sign, a memory that is already irrecoverable, at the moment of its inscription by Sang-gwŏn. In putting the two events—the inscription of the sign and its erasure—backward, the film ruptures temporal linearity and disorients the viewers' romantic engagement with the text.

What is intriguing about the film is that much of it takes place in Kangwon Province. But there is hardly anything bucolic about a few young urbanites spending their vacations in the countryside. The intensification of the urban—the paradigm of the immoral and the overpopulated—impacts the previously pristine, pastoral region of Kangwon Province. The film nullifies the traditional dichotomy between the countryside and the city. The random meetings, the solicitations to hostess bars, and the luring circumstances are as equally possible in Kangwon Province as they are in Seoul. What was known intractably as a rural experience is no longer possible, as the urban has overwhelmed the countryside to a point where it is erased. Looking out to a vast, misty mountain covered with fully bloomed trees, Sang-gwŏn asks, "How many people do you think that one mountain can hold?" He answers his own question by saying, "How 'bout a million? If you have them serried, it's possible. . . . Then just fifty of those would then be enough to hold our entire population." The vision of a majestic mountain is instantaneously reimagined as boxed dwelling spaces.[18] No longer does the beauty of the mountain—its color, fragrance, and texture—impress Sang-gwŏn. To him, the sheer size of unpolluted space offers only the possibility of intense habitation and a crude solution to overcrowding. Equally persistent is the vanity and vice that have followed Sang-gwŏn to the confines of Kangwon Province, which has been stripped down to a vacation spot for urban dwellers. Prostitution, anxious discussions about Sang-gwŏn's job prospect, and obstreperous behavior after getting drunk are just as ubiquitous and familiar in the region of clean air and magnificent nature. The power of Kangwon Province's natural environment becomes ironically conspicuous only through its negation.

Sang-gwŏn's narrative is as equally pessimistic as Chi-suk's and the space they simultaneously engender. He is fast approaching forty but still has not found a permanent teaching position. Time is no longer on his side as even his junior colleagues have found tenured employment in academia. The new position that has been advertised at a university in Ch'un-ch'ŏn (also located at Kangwon Province), as his friend tells him, is the "last opportunity [he] will ever have." But he must wait, as all of Hong's other characters are required to do, until the university makes a decision. Before departing to Kangwon Province, Sang-gwŏn follows the advice of his friend and visits the home of his former professor who is capable of influencing the decision. After a bit of dialogue that reveals nothing about the actual matter for which he is visiting, Sang-gwŏn gives him a gift: an expensive bottle of whiskey (Johnny Walker Blue Label). But, even after the offering, he cannot broach the actual subject of the new faculty hire. It is this wait during which he receives an invitation from his friend to join him in a short trip to the Kangwon Province. Leaving his wife and his young child behind, he hops on a train departing Seoul, temporally repeating the opening sequence of the film from a different perspective of Sang-gwŏn—Chi-suk riding in the next compartment. Nothing really happens on the trip as far as the two major tensions in the film are concerned. The reunion of Sang-gwŏn and Chi-suk fails to materialize, and there is no further development of Sang-gwŏn's employment situation. During the trip, Sang-gwŏn and his friend instead visit the popular tour sites, party at an expensive hostess bar from which escorts are taken to their hotel for meaningless sex, and are forced, once again, to idly wait. (They wait for a woman whom they planned on meeting and for the seats in the plane on their way home.)

Sang-gwŏn walks around the same venues to which Chi-suk had traveled in the first part of the film, but he never encounters her. *The Power of Kangwon Province*, instead, slips out of its main plot that involves wasted love between the two and adds a mystery subplot that involves death (possibly a murder), a witness report, and an arrest (possibly the solving of a crime). Although underdeveloped, this is one of the crucial linchpins that tie the two separate narratives of the former lovers. In Chi-suk's story, we first hear of an accident involving a woman who fell from a cliff in Kangwon Province. The policeman, whom Chi-suk ends up dating, cannot join the rescue team because he had been drinking with Chi-suk and her friends. When Chi-suk next visits Kangwon Province, she is casually told by the policeman that the primary suspect responsible for the woman's death has been arrested, courtesy of an anonymous witness report. In Sang-gwŏn's story, we meet all three people (the accused, the dead, and the witness) involved in the mystery of Kangwon Province. Touring the same sites with Sang-gwŏn is an unknown female traveler, an enigmatic character, who is first alone, then seen later with another man. Sang-gwŏn and his friend propose a meeting with her, but it doesn't materialize. Upon his return to Seoul, he reads a newspaper article about the death of the same woman, who had fallen off a cliff on the day they had met. Without using dramatic effects or an exaggerated music score, the camera in a long shot frames Sang-gwŏn entering a phone booth and making an anonymous call to the police. He has not witnessed the scene of the crime but remembers the name of the man with whom she was last seen. The crime is solved, but there is no cathartic release even though the mystery of a crime has been cracked because of Sang-gwŏn's good memory. The matters of murder, arrest, and the possible trial that form the backbone of a mystery film are visually erased here. Only a witness report is represented as if it is an iteration of an everyday instance, subverting the conventional narrative film's frivolous tendency to overdramatize the crime or court trials as spectacular instances.

"The doctor has advised me not to have sex," desperately pleads Chi-suk to Sang-gwŏn during the film's climax. The film finally brings together the two ill-fated lovers, but warns us of the consequences when the lovers fail to recognize that their love has gone past the expiration date. In the final sequence of *The Power of Kangwon Province*, Chi-suk and Sang-gwŏn meet for the first time; yet no flurry of emotions underscore this rendezvous. On the day Sang-gwŏn celebrates the announcement that he is the new professor, they meet. After bidding farewell to a group of his colleagues who had gathered to congratulate him, Sang-gwŏn calls Chi-suk and they proceed to a motel. Sang-gwŏn's urge for intercourse is compromised when Chi-suk reluctantly fellates him. She explains to him that she had an abortion surgery earlier that day—to erase the "fetus" borne of her affair at Kangwon Province—and cannot have sex for several days. Chi-suk knows that she is making a mistake by sexually entertaining him, but she cannot say "no" to the man whom she once loved. The camera frames from behind Chi-suk slowly bobbing her head up and down around Sang-gwŏn's crotch area, and it ironically becomes the image that stamps the pact of love between the two—something that has long been gone, and is extended only by its anticlimatic sexual gestures. The long wait they have endured has failed to produce anything solid, only passionless sex in a state of inebriation inside a cheap motel room.

Unlike Jang Sun-woo who has dramatized scenes of forced sex to flirt with the masculine principles of the Korean society,[19] Hong Sang-su does not create sex scenes as instances of rape, nor does he eroticize women's body parts (unlike the rounded breasts or curvy waistlines of women in tight skirts that are so embellished in Jang's films). But the sex scenes are nevertheless explicit, remitting complicated signals that are separately justifiable, but mutually conflicting. Sex is never an impassioned affair between two lovers, but a site where power is constantly negotiated. Women constantly desire in Hong Sang-su's films, but once they are in bed, they are either reluctant to have sex or, if they are having sex, do it only for money and other personal gain. In other words, they are either virgins or whores, a reaffirmation of the stereotypical representations of women that so patented Korean cinema. In so limiting the paradigm through which his female characters manifest their dreams, Hong's cinema may be irreconcilable with feminism. But what must not be negated is his films' critical intervention with the very repressed condition of Korea, a society that demands no ambiguity between the two conventions of women. The female characters who defy the social mores and desire to freely express their sexuality eventually end up being a victim of circumstances (Chi-suk) or a victim of death (Po-kyŏng in *The Day a Pig Fell into the Well*)

The Day a Pig Fell into the Well

In the postindustrial and ultraurban spaces Hong depicts, no one is immune from the symptoms of varying diseases that permeate the zoological Seoul. As in his other films, Hong finds personal dramas within the confines of the impersonal spaces of "love motels,"[20] taxicabs, and even elevators (in an elevator Tong-u earlier runs into the man who is having an affair with his wife without both of them knowing each other) in *The Day a Pig Fell into the Well*. The juxtaposition of pure human emotions of rage, joy, and sadness against the backdrops of desolate and depersonalized landscapes creates an irony that is now all too familiar in Hong Sang-su's films. *The Day a Pig Fell* also projects Seoul as a space where men and women work predominantly in the service sector. Hong has affinities to the people who hold menial jobs in the service industry. (Minor roles such as the company driver in *Virgin Stripped Bare* or the airline receptionist in *The Power of Kangwon Province* are given exposure more critical to the plot than is necessary.) Rather than juxtaposing the primary tension between the all-too-common conflicts between the country and the city, labor and capital, and tradition and modernity, the postrevolutionary society is depicted as an arena where fervor and passion are replaced with ennui and boredom. *The Day a Pig Fell* is perhaps the most serious film Hong Sang-su has made because passion and rage animate characters who are struggling to deny their sense of alienation in the heartless city. The film visualizes an urban space where the radical political impetus has lost its historical momentum and reappears in the form of intellectual vignette. A publisher, for instance, randomly begins to discuss an absurd idea for a novel by fictionalizing Chuang-tze and Marx as cartoonlike characters. Loss of innocence and hope are signified by the mystifying disappearance of a baby and the contradictions of young Min-jae, who is barely in her twenties. The logic of late capitalism has produced desires, emotive and innate, that can seal and dig a person's fate and grave. The lies, jealousies, temptations, obsessions, betrayals, and abuses, however big or small, all pile up before the horror; and the monstrosity of them collectively assembled translates into a destructible force, surprising us with the violent ending where every major character, with the exception of Tong-u, is killed.

Because of its discursive web of people populating the modern city, *The Day a Pig Fell* suggests that it is common to find two people who do not recognize one another, yet whose lives are profoundly affected by each other's existence. Struggling against isolation and indifference, the characters in the film desperately cling to the hope of intimacy. Intimacy is almost an obsession, an elusive *objet petit a*, which exposes people's vulnerability precisely because the desirable object is most often unattainable even when it is staked at the risk of death. The motif of death — both as a fantasy and as a real matter — crucially underpins the theme of intimacy the film explores. *The Day a Pig Fell* figures a coincidental interweaving of multiple, contingent plots of four main characters: Hyo-sŏp, Tong-u, Min-jae, and Po-kyŏng. These four characters are bound by romantic affairs that lead to betrayals of one another in a long reactive and discursive chain. The salesman Tong-u (a character discussed at the beginning of this chapter) has a wife, Po-kyŏng, who is having an extramarital affair with a writer, Hyo-sŏp. Hyo-sŏp, because his relationship with Po-kyŏng remains without a firm commitment, also keeps a young girlfriend, Min-jae, who is awe-struck by his work. (At the film's beginning, in a self-reflexive manner Min-jae, reads the novel Hyo-sŏp has just written and tells him that the characters ought not to die in the end.) The four sections separately narrate a day and a night in the lives of these four characters. But since they are intimately tied to each other's lives, they appear in each story as either supporting or minor characters. As in his other films, Hong offers no explicit linguistic cues, such as dialogue hooks and intertitles, for smooth transitions between the four sections.

In the film's opening, Hyo-sŏp, the writer, enters the frame by coming out of his apartment located on a building rooftop. In this scene, as he would everyday, Hyo-sŏp reaches out for the small fruit tree located in the adjacent building. Checking to see that no one's around, he quickly consumes a fruit or two. Both of his traits, insecurity and deception, are exposed in this scene, which is otherwise typical and habitual. Hyo-sŏp, like other characters in the film, is torn between hunger and pride. The camera follows him for roughly twenty-four hours, capturing him going through his daily routines that include dates with his girlfriends (first with Min-jae, a young ticket-seller, then with Po-kyŏng, a woman closer to his own age), meetings with his editors, where he is denied his request for an advance against royalties, a fortuitous encounter with a friend, a dinner party with his former classmates, a fight with restaurant workers, and a humiliating court verdict that finds him guilty of assault the next morning. Hyo-sŏp tells little lies, displays his short-fused temperament, and is finally punished by a sentence of five days in detention when a little incident of a waitress spilling kimchi on him escalates into a fight with the restaurant workers. By ending his day in the courtroom, where for the first time a moral judgment is decisively handed out, the film places its viewers in a dilemma. The verdict may be an excessive punishment for his incontinence. After spending a day with him, it is difficult to morally denounce Hyo-sŏp, who is clearly neglected and disrespected by his peers. But he is also hardly likeable, since he is cheating on two women — abusing a young girl materially and emotionally while pursuing a woman out of his class. His short-temper and conceit also make the irritation of his peers not entirely unjustifiable. But when the judge's sentence is read, the film centers him in the vast and nebulous moral spectrum that lies somewhere between pity and condemnation. Hyo-sŏp, after the verdict, reveals for the first time a humane side. He gives 20,000 won (approximately U.S.$20) to a less fortunate man in the courthouse who is in need of quick cash to pay off his fines. Although his basic nature may be kind, it has been masked behind his pride and everyday frustration. Mounting quotidian pressures force him to pick quarrels, to make threats on others, and to wreak havoc. Although violence and abuse, especially committed later against the person dearest to him (Min-jae), cannot be condoned; whether to condemn him is another question since the film has carefully shown that humanity lies on the opposite side of pride, prejudice, and contempt.

The film strikes a pose between disapproval and condemnation, between pathos and farce, and its moral complexity exceeds the sum of its individual characters. Hong imbues his characters with affective yet condescending attitudes, and the subtleties in everyday arguments, lies, and excuses delineate the suffocating urban environment where nothing seems to happen even when things do happen. Alluded to by her reference to her mother who still lives in the countryside, Min-jae is the only character among the four principal characters who is a migrant dweller in Seoul. She holds three jobs: in the morning, she is a live wake-up caller, making morning telephone calls to people she doesn't really know; in the afternoon, she works inside the ticket booth of a second-run theater, selling movie tickets again to people she can hardly see; and at night, she dubs Korean in Japanese game software programs and porn films for an underground company, communicating with consumers she will never meet. Min-jae is featured after the story of Tong-u's visit to Chŏn-ju. She is charming and sensitive, yet common and poor. She works hard but nonetheless has to camouflage her own fear of being ridiculed because of her wretched social identity. Though they both share the same rural background of struggling in the city, Min-jae, unlike the maid in the *Umberto D*, is not particularly likeable. She suffers from the insecurities of living alone in a maddening city, and her moral fiber has been zapped. She never tells the truth to anyone. She lies to her boss, her coworker, and even a random shopkeeper, to whom lying is completely unnecessary.[21] The only person she cares for is Hyo-sŏp, who unfortunately does not reciprocate her love. To win respect and love from Hyo-sŏp—who is equally poor but nonetheless enjoys cultural capital and an educational background far superior to her own—she voluntarily offers her labor to him. The lack of proper education does not stop her from copyediting Hyo-sŏp's novel, meticulously polishing it and soliciting assistance on grammar from a friend over the phone. Working mostly behind the counter of a ticket booth at a second-run theater, Min-jae's face glows under yellow rays refracted by the tinted counter window behind which she works. Yellow symbolizes her dream and jubilance, but also accentuates her imprudence and indiscretion; it suits Min-jae who follows a dream and is willing to pay any price to attain her love that remains for now unrequited. Further complicating the relationships between the four principal characters, Min-jae is pursued by her theater manager, Min-su, who comes from a background similar to hers and is therefore not within her remote frame of romantic interest.[22]

Min-su is radically different from every major character created by Hong in all of his four films, for Min-su retains a sense of justice and a will to execute it. Even though a felon and a would-be criminal, Min-su is the only character in the film who is driven by moralistic responsibilities. After a draining day at work, Min-jae makes an unannounced visit to Hyo-sŏp's apartment to surprise him on his birthday. Holding the box of shoes she has carefully chosen for Hyo-sŏp, she realizes that he is already with his other lover, Po-kyŏng. Po-kyŏng recognizes that she is in an awkward position and quickly departs. After chasing her unsuccessfully, Hyo-sŏp becomes infuriated that Min-jae interrupted his moment of intimacy with Po-kyŏng and makes it clear to her that he prefers Po-kyŏng. Hyo-sŏp displaces his frustration onto Min-jae by violently throwing her — and her pride — into the street. The camera pans to a dark street corner where Min-su intently observes this scene of violence. He had been silently stalking Min-jae. He knows that intervening at this very moment could further jeopardize any chance he may have with Min-jae, for she will surely reject his pity. But his raging anger against both (Hyo-sŏp for abusing Min-jae, and Min-jae for rejecting his love and instead allowing herself to be abused by Hyo-sŏp), will linger and resurface uncontrollably later on.[23] The rage exhibited by Min-su is not different from the one shown in Robert Bresson's *L'Argent* (1983) by the main character Lucien, who has a reason to inexplicably kill an entire family before turning himself in.

Po-kyŏng — Hyo-sŏp's lover and Tong-u's wife — returns in the film's final segment as a listless drifter who is lost in an urban space with which she is familiar. She holds a suitcase and waits at a bus station for Hyo-sŏp's arrival. When he fails to show up, Po-kyŏng, like her husband who earlier had to constantly wait for his business associate to arrive, spends the entire day waiting. To make matters worse, Po-kyŏng's purse is pick-pocketed and she is forced to ride buses around Seoul. Without money, the habitual and intimate sites immediately become places of unfamiliarity and hesitation for Po-kyŏng. She is lost in a state of unpredictable transition. When the door of the bus she has been waiting for flings open before her, she is unsure whether to get on it. Loitering around Seoul, her time is not one that thrusts forward, but one that lingers, suspended by the sudden disappearance of her boyfriend, with whom she planned an escape. She sits on the bus, without a destination. Her bus moves, but her mobility remains restrained. Po-kyŏng has become a "nomad" in a "striated," urban space, to follow a Deleuzian term, for she has a home, but one that is uninhabitable.[24] She visits her husband's business district in the hope of borrowing money from him, without telling him what has happened. But Tong-u informs her over the telephone that he has an important meeting and won't be available to have lunch with her. On her way out, she coincidentally finds him on the street and follows him to the urology department of a hospital. She there learns that he has been receiving treatment to cure his venereal disease, something he had contracted in Chŏnju.

The discourse of insobriety that accounts for counter-memory, repetition, and forgetfulness also tends to obfuscate the truth by introducing a fantasy sequence in *The Day a Pig Fell* where reality further wanes from its remorseful frame. At her friend's apartment where Po-kyŏng finally gets some money, she takes a short nap. The film for the first time slips out of its narrative capsule and transports the viewers elliptically to an unconscious realm where the four principal characters all meet. They rendezvous in a wake ceremony where Tong-u and his several friends are mourning the death of Po-kyŏng. Hyo-sŏp and Min-jae, each dressed in black attire, enter the apartment to express their condolences to the widower. At this point, Po-kyŏng, who had been sleeping in the next room, wakes up, and goes to the living room to calmly greet them. Breaking out of the fantasy, the film then returns to the main narrative where Po-kyŏng wakes up from her dream. This scene, both cerebral and surreal, shocks the viewers who have not yet been offered a clue as to what this sight of death signifies.

Hong Sang-su's films feature too many elements of postmodernism to be classified as existentialist; too much rage and sincerity for postmodernist; too much cynicism for romanticist; and, perhaps most importantly, too much passion for nihilist. In this discursive constellation where subjectivities, lives, and hopes remain uncertain lies the very fantasy that guides us past the unmappable, and impalpable realities. Like Žižek's notion of fantasy that rests closer to everyday reality than it seems,[25] Hong's world is one where reality and fantasy are indistinguishable from each other. The moment Po-kyŏng awakens, she returns to "reality," but the "real" time and space reminds her of only illusions of marriage, faith, and life that she understands she is falsifying. Only inside her dream is the Real of her desire articulated where death, life, marriage, and love erase their bifurcating other-ness. Truth is bound to this wakening reality, which ironically realizes itself in the dream.

The iterative power of banality builds to a crescendo until a cataclysmic event finally erupts, a scene of unruly violence that had been lurking beneath the serene, habitual surfaces all along. In the scene where Po-kyŏng returns to Hyo-sŏp's apartment for the last time in an attempt to resolve the mystifying question of why he has failed to keep their promise to elope, the deferred significance of the preceding dream sequence becomes all too clear. When Po-kyŏng reaches the apartment, the film slips out of the first-person perspective, allowing the camera to move inside the room while its interior remains veiled to her. The viewers are surprisingly exposed to a murder scene where both Hyo-sŏp and Min-jae lay dead, slashed by Min-su. He is still in the room, with a bloodied face and a blood-dripping knife in his hand. The lights of the neon signs seep into the unlit room selectively. In a shot that frames the dead bodies of Min-jae and Hyo-sŏp, the color blue dresses the naked Min-jae while her similarly fated lover lies dead on the yellow floor. Never has the cheap yellow, laminated paper flooring that appears in so many rooms of a typical Korean home radiated so much primal rage. The cruel twist of plot has now finally unleashed its terror through an unmercifully bizarre nightmare. Love has lost its innocence and sanity, and has instead ruthlessly unpacked jealousy and madness that have produced a double murder, a justice personally delivered by Min-su, but surely deemed senseless by the authorities.

The most dramatic element of the plot that had been latent or suspended will become particularly salient at the end of *The Day a Pig Fell*. The fleeting premonition of Po-kyŏng's death in the fantasy sequence is crystallized. With her lover now lost and her feelings for her husband also long dissipated, Po-kyŏng, despite having a husband, really has no one else to turn to. Among the principal characters, she had been the only one who remained mostly unaffected by the euphoric condition. It is only a matter of time before she finds out that her time has run out like the rest of them. Before visiting Hyo-sŏp's apartment, Po-kyŏng was at a loss for words after seeing a photograph of her in the display window of a photo studio in her neighborhood. The colossal-size family photograph showed Po-kyŏng, her husband, and their baby, all of their faces almost surreally and unimaginably content. The absent, fictive family visualized in the picture reminds her of an unbearable past that must be violently destroyed. Po-kyŏng later visits the studio and recovers the photograph with the money she received from her friend. She destroys the picture frame and tears it apart in the store, making a statement that her marriage, once a dream, will remain in its shattered form. Because the film elsewhere supplies no mention of the child, we can only presume that their child has died. Upon returning home, she finds out that her decision to end her marriage with Tong-u has to be postponed at least on a sexual term. Her husband rapes her, insisting that he now trusts her to be a "clean woman." She is unable to either confront his secret (his trips to the clinic) or confess hers (her plot to run away with her lover).

Using a moment alone while the husband goes out to fetch cigarettes, Po-kyŏng—still unaware that Hyo-sŏp is dead—places a call to him, but he of course cannot be reached. She takes a shower while the newspaper is delivered. Sitting in the barren living room, she reads the morning newspaper, which presumably contains the report of their deaths. She silently lays the newspaper out, page by page, across the living room floor, moving toward the apartment balcony as if she is doing a habitual morning chore. It is a sensually affective mo(u)rning scene. The stationary camera then captures Po-kyŏng in a long shot. She moves indifferently toward the balcony and opens the window. Like other elliptical sequences where the final climactic action remains unframed, the film ends here with a violin and a cello supplying the high-pitched minimalist music score; it denies us the visual pleasure or pity of watching her throw her body out of the high-rise apartment. Hong's elliptical editing style opts to skip over the spectacular sight of death and leaves us with a banal image of Po-kyŏng—with her hair still wet—greeting the morning sunrise. The repetition of the mundane, oppressive everyday life of the four characters reaches its completion when Po-kyŏng chooses to follow the fates of the others by voluntarily lifting up the repression of death.

A Mockery of Small People

Slavoj Žižek once noted that the Czech films Milos Forman made during the early part of his career were subversive because they mocked "small, ordinary people: in showing their undignified ways, the futility of their dreams . . . and this gesture was far more dangerous than making fun of the ruling bureaucracy."[26] The mockery of the small, common people accompanies the chance of them being subject to condescension. But Hong's characters are always excessively real, for they are self-conscious dispositions and displacements of the author/director himself or the things he has experienced. Does the self-referential representational mode make possible a construction of agency that resists power and its reproducibility without dramatizing the humanity of common people? Hong depicts common people's frailty, indecision, and deception, rather than their triumph and humanism. Also they unconsciously refuse to make their lives meaningful by choosing to fall into empty, erotic liaisons. Could this be made an occasion of resistance against modernity and its terror? Even when a heterosexual reunion between two lovers takes place (*Virgin Stripped Bare* and *The Power of Kangwon Province*), when the mysterious crime is resolved (*The Power of Kangwon Province*), and when justice is executed (*The Day a Pig Fell into the Well*) at the end of the film, the results veer away from redemptive catharsis. His films display a power of cynical repetition, one—like Samuel Beckett's *Waiting for Godot*—that settles for the faded hope of salvation and renders a new meaning to the phrase, "nothing happens." But this "nothing," this futility, reminds us *once again* that it is impossible to draft a subject—imaginarily Whole, that is capable of offering a false sense of optimism in the era of condensed modernization and intense competition.

III

FIN-DE-SIÈCLE ANXIETIES

The last two chapters consider the latest trend of the Korean film industry, which has seemingly rebounded from the humiliating slide and turmoil suffered during the 1970s and the 1980s. Even American critics have taken notice of the rising box-office revenues and the quality of films, as evinced by the *Hollywood Reporter*'s front-page declaration in 2000 that "Korea, [once a cinematic backwater], drives World Cinema."[1] The rapid rise of export figures, the increase of domestic film audiences, the clear visibility of Korean cinema in art-house festivals across the globe, and the emergence of Korean film stars as matinee idols in show business across Asia have all contributed in reviving the Korean film industry that many local critics had proclaimed dead as late as the mid-1990s. This section seeks to understand the problematics of gender as it is particularly inscribed within the commercial success of Korean films.

If the 1980s was a period of male masochism for Korean cinema, by the end of the 1990s men freed from anxiety, fear, and trauma dominated the cinema. What had been only fantasized in the previous decade as a dream of Pyŏng-t'ae (the male protagonist in *Whale Hunting*) — the confident, chic, romantic man capable of receiving undivided attention from women — has become a reality at least on-screen as Korean cinema became one of the most popular forms of entertainment at the end of the century across Asia. Recalling the glamorous actors of the Golden Age, the young male actors of Korean cinema, Chang Tong-gŏn, Song Kang-ho, and Yu Chi-t'ae, have emerged as now legitimate pan-Asian stars who have superceded Chow Yun-fat and Jet Li, the marquee names in movie business in metropolitan areas of Asia. The impulses — which previously mobilized the recuperation of masculinity through the innumerable depictions of men who appeal for self-pity and attention—have been oppositely refigured as they are now splendid, aggressive, and confidently violent in blockbuster films. All along lurking beneath passivity, as if the flip side of the same coin, was the fascination for aggression: the ideal trait of masculinity that cinema of the 1980s desired. Both self-hate and self-love were bound by an obsessive drive—one that is equally dangerous and pitiable.

Two tropes that have ushered in the Korean cinema's renaissance are given attention in this last section of the book: the domestic space and the national division. Although they seem worlds apart from each other, the domesticity and the partition of the nation commonly bound by the conventions of melodrama are dispensed to strengthen both box-office formulas and stable gender anxieties. The killings of women are figured crucially in both blockbuster hits featured in the last section: for instance, *Happy End* (1999), a film about the murder of an adulterous woman, and *Shiri* (1999), which brings to fore the tragedy of the divided nation through the revelation of the female lover as a North Korean agent who threatens the security of the nation. It is not coincidental that both female protagonists—attractive, highly professional, and even more confident than men—are identified as *femme fatales*, or as sirens (in Homer's *Odyssey*) who threaten to dismantle the foundation of home and must be destroyed at the very end of the respective narratives in order to restore the peace at home and for the nation. Taken separately, the domestic melodramas about adulterous women and the spy thrillers about betraying women depict the anxieties typically cast at the end of the century. The depictions of these "dangerous women" nervously frame—perhaps more acutely than for any other regions in the world—the gender imbalance and troubles in a rapidly industrializing and simultaneously deindustrializing nation that struggles still as the last front of the cold war.

8

Lethal Work: Domestic Space and Gender Troubles
in *Happy End* and *The Housemaid*

Toward the end of *Happy End* (*Haep'i endŭ*, Chŏng Chi-u, dir., 1999), Min-gi, the male protagonist, is seen riding on a train. Wearing a black suit and a tie, he is traveling to Taegu, a city about 150 miles away from Seoul, for the funeral of his old school teacher. He anxiously smokes in the moving train. It is not the death of his teacher that is making him shake, but the death of Bora (Po-ra), his wife, whom he has just killed. Before departing Seoul, he executed a meticulously planned murder of his wife, a bloody affair in which he stabbed her repeatedly with a long jagged knife. He has an alibi though: he was taken to the train station by his friend and was furthermore seen on a train that departed earlier in the day before he got off. He has also been careful to leave no evidence. He has painstakingly removed his fingerprints, his murder instrument, and his blood-stained clothes. By leaving Bora's blood marks in another apartment, he has instead framed Ilbŏm, Bora's secret lover. Min-gi, after having a cigarette, takes his seat, and begins to toy with an elastic band. Across from him sits a young boy who curiously watches Min-gi's game where he constantly twists the band into different shapes. The boy's puzzled and naïve expression offers Min-gi a moment of relief, and he smiles for the first time in the sequence. It is here that any spectator who is knowledgeable of Korean film history feels an eerie sense of familiarity and intimacy. The train, the funeral, the guilty man, the adulterous affair, the violent murder, and, topping it all, the twisting and twirling elastic band evoke the memory of a legendary Korean film, *The House-maid* (*Hanyŏ*, Kim Ki-yŏng, dir., 1960), that features a man, Tong-sik, whose affair with his maid ends up killing them both. Moreover, train imageries—a pumping engine and blowing whistle—are vivid sights and sounds in *The Housemaid* when Tong-sik, the guilt-stricken protagonist, travels to attend a funeral to mourn the death of a woman whose suicide he had indirectly caused.[1] As for the elastic band, it recalls *The Housemaid*'s opening scheme, in which Tong-sik's two children play "cat's cradle" with a ball of yarn before the film turns to a textile factory where the real narrative unfolds.

Happy End's prominent cinematic references to *The Housemaid* are significant on three grounds. First, they signal the arrival of a new generation of Korean filmmakers who are profoundly influenced by their own national cinema and link the Golden Age of Korean cinema of the 1960s to the present-day renaissance of Korean cinema.[2] Korean cinema has only recently come out of its slump, after enduring a long stretch in the 1970s and the 1980s dominated by government propagandas, B-grade quota quickies, and quasi-porn flicks. Over these decades the public seemed to have forgotten the glorious and glamorous heyday of cinema in the 1960s when even the most trivial activities of movie stars were closely monitored, national pathos was popularly expressed, and the cinema earned the respect of artists working in other mediums. *Happy End* demonstrates that the return of cinema once again as a popular and artistic medium is inspired both by national film history and by global developments that have forced Korean cinema to compete with Hollywood and Western art-house films as import quota restrictions diminished during the 1980s.[3]

Second, the themes that thread through the two films allow us to reflect upon transformative figurations of gender and family over this historical period. In both films, the tropes of domesticity, masculinity, and motherhood are intriguingly juxtaposed against the severe financial and social crises comprising the historical moment of each film. *The Housemaid* was made in 1960, a chaotic year that brought down the corrupt Syngman Rhee regime only to have a fledgling democratic government overthrown by Park Chung Hee's coup d'etat a year later; *Happy End* was made in the midst of the national bankruptcy of the late 1990s that led to the International Monetary Fund (IMF) bailout of Korea. In this chapter, I pay close attention to the domestic spaces of the two films in order to closely monitor the representations of gender in them. I propose that both films intently engage the question of gender, unconsciously or consciously, through filmic tensions that tactically reassign the sociosexual division of domestic space. The social uncertainties in the public realm are mirrored in the restructuring of gender, which foremost creates anxiety around the bourgeois family, highlighting its fragility. Intriguing is that both films depict masculinity as a vulnerable and repressed gendered agency, falsely invoking the need to awaken its violent nature. Intensely evoked in both films is the man's inability to adjust to the rapidly changing social and gender organization, including re-arrangements at work and at home with the births of children. This is an environment that permanently captures him in a state of shock. In each case, the man sets out to destroy the woman—misidentified as the root of his problem.

How the terms of gender (the constitution of "masculine" and "feminine" qualities) became a critical index during the mesmerizing social change over the span of four decades is a concern in this chapter, as it has been throughout the book. There is no question that South Korea has economically caught up with even the First World, but whether such frenzied drive has profoundly changed the conventional relations of gender is an issue that cannot be answered easily. When comparing a film released in 1960 with one released exactly thirty-nine years later, most remarkable is *not* the changes that take place in terms of gender representation, but rather the fixity. Much has changed in the last forty years as the society moved from a poverty-stricken postwar economy to a postmodern center of hi-tech industry where one-third of the population have internet connection at home, but the traits of gender as well as its relations remain remarkably unaffected.[4] In a society where the economic structure rests on sexist principles, leading to statistics that consistently reveal that the percentage of women in the upper echelon of public and corporate sectors is among the lowest in any industrialized or industrializing nations, only men can be agents of change, even though men, ironically, are often not very adaptable in an ever-changing work environment. The constant shifts in ideology, ethics, and lifestyles cast these sluggish men as pitiable and lifeless beings, continually alienated and besieged from the public. This leads men to demand more attention at home and more domesticity from the women. This pattern reveals the profound difficulties in gender relations, in societies that underwent intense modernization throughout the twentieth century.

Lynn Spigel writes of the role of television in shifting domestic gender relations in the United States during the 1950s: "Faced with their *shrinking authority* in the new corporate world of white-collar jobs, the middle-class men of the early 1900s turned inward to the home where their increased participation in and control over the family served to compensate for feelings of powerlessness in the public sphere"[5] (my emphasis). The "shrinking authority" of also Korean men in the modern society ushers them to reassert their power in the domestic space. This pattern also demands that women idealize the notion of "feminine passivity" even in the "modern" domestic space. The inclination by men to spend more time with domestic affairs in the twentieth century did not necessarily achieve gender equality in domestic labor or encourage women's further participation in the public sphere, but it simply replaced the masculinity inside the home since its power was ceded beyond the domestic.

A third feature shared between the two films discussed in this chapter is their assembly of desire, illicit love, and murder. Interestingly, extramarital affairs have been popular topics not only recently, but also during the Golden Age of Korean Cinema. Some of the most controversial films in the history of Korean cinema—including Kim Ki-yŏng's *The Housemaid*—have challenged the ethical conventions of their era by focusing on the tension between faithfulness and desire, and between conformity and passion. In the often-discussed film *Madame Freedom* (*Chayu puin*, Han Hyŏng-mo, dir., 1956), the transformation of a professor's wife from a modest mother to a promiscuous businesswoman is depicted, making a scandalous woman of an otherwise ordinary middle-class housewife.[6] As a Korean feminist film critic, Soyoung Kim (Kim So-yŏng), has argued, the sexual identity of the female lead in *Madame Freedom* is inseparable from the increasingly consumerist culture: it is precisely the availability of her new income—disposable to spend and independent from her husband—as a sales manager in a department store that gives her access to freedom and fosters her desire, which is pursued outside the domain of her home.[7] Though their productions were forty years apart, in both films the women's pursuit of work outside home is portrayed as a threat, and furthermore deemed as a sufficient cause to eventually punish the women. The representations of working women are surely inauspicious; not only do they leave their domestic duties unattended, but they also eventually end up having extramarital affairs.

Modern society's need for women to be active both in the work force and in the home created tensions: social prejudice often denied women's active agency in the public sphere during the early stage of industrialization. Although women's desires that result in promiscuity are pathologized in both film eras, there are important differences; the more recent portrayals of extramarital affairs capture Korea's anxiety in another economic period: the deindustrializing phase.[8] What distinguishes the recent films such as *The Day a Pig Fell into the Well* (*Tweji ga umul e ppajin nal*, Hong Sang-su, dir., 1996), *No. 3* (*Nŏmbŏ 3*, Song Nŭng-han, dir., 1997), and *An Affair* (*Chŏngsa*, Yi Chae-yong, dir., 1998) from those of the 1950s and the 1960s that dealt with extramarital affairs is the affirmation of anomie or boredom as the woman's dominant reasons for adultery. No longer is illicit sex referenced solely in terms of the society's unwillingness to accept women as public workers. If it was the frenzied drive to move up the social ladder that invited the seductive maid into the house in *The Housemaid*, and the desire to experience new Western consumerist culture that captured the curiosity of the professor's wife in *Madame Freedom*, now the middle-class conformity and anomie rush characters like Po-kyŏng in *The Day a Pig Fell into the Well*, So-hyŏn in *An Affair*, and Bora in *Happy End* onto the path of adultery. (Bora, unlike the other two, is not a housewife, but, as an owner of a successful business, she does not have a need for an affair with a man who would help her raise her public stature. She is sleeping with her employee.) These female characters no longer need to reestablish their respectability and social refinement in the public arena through their ability to date young men; instead, they are simply bored.

The recent proliferation of extramarital affairs on screen prompts a very simple question that begets a not-so-simple response: Why aren't these women asking for divorces? Wouldn't Po-kyŏng in *The Day a Pig Fell into the Well*, a housewife who falls in love with a writer, or Bora in *Happy End* be better off with their lovers than their dreary husbands? Both characters are not severely bound by motherhood obligations or other familial restraints. Po-kyŏng's only child is presumably dead, and Ilbŏm is willing to adopt Bora's child. Also absent in both films is the pressure from the elders to sustain their marriages. Yet, they are unable to leave their husbands, which leaves them susceptible to the deaths that befall them. The difficulty for them in leaving their husbands, even though their marriages are clearly failures, suggests that families today are contentious institutions bound by repressive rules even as the divorce rate rises every year. Many of the recent film images of middle-class women having affairs portray women's desires to escape from family obligations, maternity, and housekeeping. The social reluctance to break completely from orthodox perspectives on marriage leaves many of these characters dangling still between older and changing mores even though the public perception is that Korea has entered a condition of postmodernity where such tensions putatively ceased many decades earlier. The institution of the marriage testifies that it is one of the most regressive social apparatuses that binds Korea's movement forward and creates anxieties where women attempt extramarital affairs at the risk of death.

Could This Be a Happy End?

Made during the height of the 1998–99 financial crisis that burst Korea's so-called postwar economic miracle, *Happy End* features a married couple in their thirties, Min-gi and Bora, whose lives are impacted by the economic troubles. The massive layoffs that skyrocketed the unemployment rate from 2.3 to 8.2 percent in a period of less than a year (1997–98) have disfigured the family of Min-gi, Bora, and their baby daughter, Sŏyŏn, who was most likely born around the time when Korea signed the humiliating IMF loan treaty on Decem-

Bora, Min-gi, and their baby. *Happy End* (1999).

ber 3, 1997.[9] Min-gi, a former bank employee, is jobless,[10] and he spends his day reading in bookstores and parks. He is also responsible for childcare, on top of being the principal domestic worker in the house. He picks up Sŏyŏn from the daycare center, feeds her, cooks, vacuums the house, does laundry, and cleans the car. Although he is out of a job and his employment prospects are dim in an economy that is downsizing, the family's middle-class life is sustained because Bora is a successful businesswoman. She runs a popular modern after-school English institution for little children. Korea's struggle against the global tide of recession has not diminished its interest in the West; on the contrary, the desire to learn from the West is even more clearly manifested by the crowded classroom at Bora's institution that employs American teachers. Bora and Min-gi are able to keep their spacious apartment, drive their sedan, and occasionally dine out because Bora will continue to provide opportunities for economically privileged children to "learn to speak English as well as if it was their first language."

Bora's success reverses the conventional gender roles, where she—the breadwinner—now does not feel guilty for demanding that Min-gi become more active in childcare and housework. Moreover, while Min-gi retreats to his sofa at night to watch television soaps and to the park bench during the day to read pulp fiction, Bora is publicly visible, referred to as the "President" by her staff and her clients. These "troubled" gender roles endanger their marriage and are compounded by Bora's extramarital affair with her former college classmate,

Ilbŏm, which thickens the plot. The obsessive and mad nature of this lustful relationship cannot be contained in Ilbŏm's small apartment. Ilbŏm visits Bora in the office, takes her out to the beach, and even loiters around Bora and Min-gi's apartment, pressuring her to move in with him. Bora enjoys the pleasures and thrills offered by illicit sex, but she is unwilling to leave the security provided by her marriage and the family. Also, in a culture where stigma is permanently attached to a divorced woman, divorce is not an easy decision even for an ambitious and financially independent woman like Bora.

Min-gi grows suspicious of Bora's late returns from work, the excessive mileage on the car, and an unidentified key he finds underneath the car carpet. Using the key, he enters Ilbŏm's apartment after waiting for him to leave his home. In his studio apartment, Min-gi finds half-naked pictures of his wife. Initially shaken, he is unable to even bring up the matter with his wife. But Min-gi eventually decides to kill Bora after discovering that she had placed their daughter's life at risk by giving her a sleeping pill and leaving her unattended to meet Ilbŏm. Bora has failed to be not only a "good housewife," but more importantly the "good mother" that Min-gi had expected of her.[11] When Bora drugs her child and then risks her health, she has completely abrogated the expectations of motherhood, committing sins that are unredeemable and unforgivable. Portraying a woman who chooses her own sexual desires over her maternal duties, the film condemns Bora based on its conviction that "women's mothering . . . [is] a natural fact."[12]

After saving his baby's life and accidentally witnessing Bora in a heated moment with her lover (without them even recognizing him), Min-gi plots to kill Bora. Having first arranged an alibi (his apparent departure for the funeral in Taegu), he remains in Seoul and breaks into his own apartment. He holds Bora's body down on the same bed where they sleep together every night. Drops of red blood make a stain, and before long Bora's white shirt is drenched in blood. As Min-gi repeatedly stabs Bora, who is gagged, her shudders cease and her muted cries for help fade. The only person in the house who is normally in a position to help her is unfortunately the very person delivering the fatal blows. If Min-gi had failed to sexually impress Bora, as instanced by an earlier sex scene between them where she blankly stared at the ceiling, he has certainly secured her attention in this encounter, entering their bedroom as a criminal, and striking her until she is dead. Without saying a word, Min-gi dials Ilbŏm's cell phone so that he can hear Bora's dying moans. Recognizing the dire situation Bora is in, Ilbŏm will soon rush to the apartment where he will find her dead, and so he will fall into Min-gi's trap, leaving his fingerprints all over the site of the crime. As the bedroom is rendered the site of a horrifying murder, we are not sure how to respond to the pool of blood, with relief or grief. Bora's extramarital affair, the cause of the familial demise, is now over, but it required her death to conclude in a "happy end." Unlike *The Eel* (*Unagi*, Shohei Imamura, dir., 1998) where the murder of the adulterous wife takes place compulsively in the middle of the act of intercourse between her and her lover, Min-gi's murder is premeditated and meticulously planned such that Ilbŏm will be arrested and tried in his place. The unfaithful wife and the jealous lover will both die, leaving only the murderous husband alive. In the last shot of the film, however, Min-gi wakes up from a nap in his living room, leaving us to wonder about the veracity of the murder.

Thou Shalt Not Cheat on The Housemaid

Kim Ki-yŏng's *The Housemaid*, as is well known, also frames an extramarital affair and a consequent murder in the fantastic structure of a dream. *The Housemaid* catapulted Kim into global art-house stardom when it was rediscovered in the late 1990s, thus generating international fanfare almost forty years after its original release.[13] After the film was showcased in a retrospective at the 1997 Pusan International Film Festival, it—along with several other Kim Ki-yŏng films—was immediately screened in film festivals in Berlin, London, Belgrade, San Francisco, and Hong Kong, among others. A website pays tribute to him, "The House of Kim Ki-young,"[14] and since his sudden death in 1998 he has been posthumously honored through retrospectives of his work. Kim was an exceptional filmmaker, making hybrid genre films well before they became fashionable not only in Korea but also in the global cinema. If the national cinema aesthetics of Korea are characterized by the thematic motifs of han (pent-up grief), mise-en-scènes of rural mountainous landscapes, and understated emotions that are frequently projected in the works of Shin Sang-ok and Im Kwon-Taek, Kim Ki-yŏng is a filmmaker who falls completely outside this framework.[15] Instead of sublimating han, his characters plot revenge; instead of featuring mountainous rural landscape and thatched roofs, his films display overpopulated asphalt boardwalks, neon lights, and Western mansions with cubist paintings; and instead of understated emotions, he prefers stylistic excesses.[16] Freely mixing absurd fantasy with bizarre plots and exaggerated sexuality and violence, his films—including *Insect Woman* (*Ch'ungnyŏ*, 1972) and *Killer Butterfly* (*Sarin nabirŭl tchotnŭn yŏja*, 1978)—display the psychological angst and anxiety behind the nation's rapid pace of industrialization. Central to this paranoid pathos and grotesque visual style are unconventional and absurdist props such as dead rats and an out-of-control Korean ricecake popper that in several of his films whet the sexual appetite of his characters even more.

Compared to the films from the 1970s where Kim Ki-yŏng took cinematic "excesses" to a greater height, *The Housemaid*, his early film, shows both stylistic and narrative restraint. Yet, Kim's stylistic conventions and plot progression that belie expectations and conventions are already very well at work in this film. The film displays a crisis—a staple in family melodrama—provoked when a housemaid is employed in a middle-class home. The maid is first hired to help manage domestic affairs in a home where the mother falls ill after overwork from her in-house job as a seamstress. The recently acquired two-story Western-style house is simply too big for the ailing *patrona* to maintain. But the maid (never named), soon turns out to be a wicked nightmare for the family. Kim Ki-yŏng's maid hardly has any of the qualities of Douglas Sirk's Annie Johnson in *Imitation of Life* (1959), whose immaculate and sacrificial execution of domestic duties allows her employer Lora to concentrate on her public role and become a star. On the contrary, the maid's nagging sexual seduction of the father, Tong-sik, distracts him from his work—teaching music to young female factory workers. The maid threatens Tong-sik that she will expose their adultery, so that he will lose his job, and never see the light of the day as a star musician. Her long hair, slim face, light sensuous lips, dark eye-shadow, and tight revealing dress place the maid closer to Annie Johnson's tragic mulatto daughter, Sarah Jane, than to Annie.

Despite the casting of the maid as the central character whose psychological complications add depth to the story, *The Housemaid* is undoubtedly a masculine drama in which the film's crisis revolves around Tong-sik's fall as a teacher in the public sphere and as a husband in the private one. In the film's beginning, Tong-sik suffers from a guilt complex after one of the students in his choral class commits suicide. Her suicide was precipitated by her being suspended from school after Tong-sik exposed her naïve love letter for him to the company executive. After attending the student's funeral, Tong-sik feels guilty. Playing on this vulnerability, the maid tries to sexually seduce him on the stormy night of his return from the funeral. Already feeling responsible for the death of one woman who tried to seduce him, Tong-sik cannot possibly refuse another woman's advance.

After their bizarre sex—immaculately photographed—materializes,[17] the maid now transforms from a helping hand to a dangerous threat, who must be eliminated in order for the familial stability to be restored. Yet, matters cannot easily be resolved as the maid reveals to Tong-sik that she is pregnant with his child. Tong-sik is psychologically torn, and we glimpse this dilemma in a taxicab ride. The taxicab scene recalls Ch'ŏl-ho in *The Stray Bullet* (*Obalt'an*, Yu Hyŏn-mok, dir., 1960), the film voted by the critics as the best Korean film of the last century, who at the film's end half-consciously wanders the streets of Seoul also in a taxicab.[18] Tong-sik tells the cabdriver to go "anywhere very fast. Let's run away from the earth or crash into something." While Ch'ŏl-ho in Yu Hyŏn-mok's film was sedated by the anesthetics given to him by the dentist preceding the ride, here Tong-sik is drunk from the bottle of gin he has just consumed in order to forget his troubles. The display of recklessness and fearlessness in this scene suggests the potential for masculine rejuvenation, but it also points to masculinity as a "self-deluded state." Heavy drinking, argues Yuejin Wang in his discussion of *Red Sorghum* (Zhang Yi-mou, dir., 1987), "can be a transgression of decorum, an act of defying convention, a route to visionary intensity for transcendental possibilities and poetic ecstasy, or a way of achieving autonomy," but it is also an embodiment of "spiritual degradation, over-indulgence, moral corruption and social irresponsibility."[19] The drunk Tong-sik aimlessly swaggering in a taxicab that lumbers through the neon lights of Seoul symptomizes the very contradiction echoed in the perception of masculinity that can only be attained in such a delusional state.

Unfortunately, Tong-sik cannot hide from his domestic trouble much longer as he will soon wake from his stupor. He ignores the advice offered to him by a friend, and ends up telling his pregnant wife that he has committed adultery with the maid. Surprising her even more, Tong-sik tells her that the maid too is pregnant with his child. The family was once happy when exotic meals for the whole family were prepared by the father and the delivery of the television set had prompted the small son, Ch'ang-sun, to declare that they are the richest family in the neighborhood. It now awaits its total collapse. The mother will not tolerate the scandalous birth of two children fathered by the same man, and persuades the maid to abort her child. Opting for the most primitive and violent method of abortion, the maid reluctantly throws her body down the staircase and, in so doing, aborts her fetus that was destined to be a bastard born out of wedlock. Following the doctor's declaration of the maid's abortion and soon afterward the mother's safe parturition of the baby, what began as a melodrama quickly deforms into a horror film in which the maid plots a blood-curdling revenge against the family. She literally invades the married couple's bedroom, and demands the father to sleep with her in order to amend the grief she has suffered. She protests, "Why did you kill only my child? Where is justice when one woman is allowed to keep a child while the other woman cannot? How can you treat my body like a toy? The two babies are fathered by the same man—they should live or die together." She picks up the baby who has just been born and motions as if to throw it to the ground as Tong-sik and his wife watch in horror. Despite the fact that the maid's rage is not incomprehensible, the film seems to take a phallocentric perspective, one that denies the maid a role other than that of the vamp who seeks blood to avenge the loss of her child.

Soyoung Kim reports that when the film was first released in 1960 the audience—especially the female audience—was openly hostile to the maid character. During the scene where the maid lures the father, the audience reportedly responded by screaming, "Kill the bitch!"[20] This identification of the then female spectators who sympathized with the father rather than with the maid seemingly testifies to the difficulty of rupturing a masculine orientation even in a women's genre like melodrama. But this audience reaction is hardly abnormal when considering the U.S. audience reaction to American melodrama. Linda Williams attempted to explain why the "device of devaluing and debasing the actual figure of the mother while sanctifying the institution of motherhood is typical of 'the woman's film' in general and the subgenre of the maternal melodrama in particular."[21] Using the psychic term, "fetishistic disavowal," she argued that the viewing position is never simply unilateral even when the audience at large debases and condemns the woman who revolts and instead opts to sympathize with the victimized woman. Williams disagreed with E. Ann Kaplan's reading of *Stella Dallas* in which female viewers, like Stella who at the end of the film remains outside the window at her own daughter's wedding, were argued as powerless agents; and she suggested that the "female spectator does not necessarily acquiesce in the necessity of this sacrifice, nor does she identify solely with the effaced Stella at this final moment."[22] The debate encircling this American melodrama classic would have to be refigured in the case at hand here—that of a "vamp" maid, a femme fetale, who refuses to remain a victim of circumstances.[23] What remains is the fact that the then Korean female audience, who were presumably more socially aligned with the maid than the bourgeois housewife living in a Western-style mansion, did not cheer for the maid who had ample reason to be angry at Tong-sik. But the display of anger, like the feeling of pathos invoked by the American spectators watching *Stella Dallas*, can be used as a point of reference to locate the potential for rupture that transgresses the boundaries of normalized identification with the abjected subject on screen. The female audiences would have had to "overidentify" with the female antagonist who embodies and realizes their own transgressive desires and fantasies (sleeping with a handsome master and then killing him for violating their bodies) for their feelings to have violently resurfaced. In other words, the "bitch" that they were so enraged at points to nothing other than their own narcissistic ego that desires to break free and freely rummage through the repressive social structure.

As the plot turns, the piano that had previously produced harmonic choral music begins to produce dissonant sound at night. The maid's untutored fingers randomly strike piano keys, awakening the soundly sleeping family with an unbearably disruptive sound, yet one eerily memorable to the contemporary audiences who are familiar with the cacophonous modernist soundtracks of horror films from the seventies. The adorable son, Ch'ang-sun, soon pays the price of his father's transgressions when he is killed by the maid. Like the maid's fetus that suffered its death by crashing down the staircase, he too dies from falling off the top of the staircase. Despite witnessing the murder of their child, Tong-sik and his wife cannot turn her over to the police because the affair between Tong-sik and the maid will be scandalous once the public finds out and will jeopardize Tong-sik's reputation and his job. The maid, who never had much authority in the house, emerges suddenly as its master and starts to give orders to her employers, instilling fear in them. The power dynamics between the mother and the maid tilt heavily in the maid's favor when she openly sleeps with Tong-sik and her meal is served by the wife.

This subverted familial structure cannot last forever. On a fatal night, Miss Cho, one of Tong-sik's students, visits his home for her piano lessons. Cho, the person who had initially introduced the maid to the family, had long been trying to seduce Tong-sik without success. When she visits, the maid cannot conceal her jealousy, and takes a knife out of the kitchen. The maid climbs up the staircase—filmed as a space that elicits psychic anxiety—and, in a fit of uncontrollable rage, strikes Cho in the piano room.[24] After Cho is driven away from the house in pain, blood dripping from her shoulder, the maid proposes a double suicide with Tong-sik. He accepts her proposal in the same piano room where they first seduced each other. Drinking rat poison together, they die. Rejecting the maid even at the moment of death, Tong-sik crawls down the staircase to share his last breath with his wife.

The film is extraordinary in many regards; the constant movement of the camera, exquisitely composed close-ups that evoke expressionist styles of Weimar German cinema, a vigorous orchestra soundtrack, and the use of shadows and special lighting effects all demonstrate the cinematic talent of Kim Ki-yŏng who had independently produced the film while serving as the film's screenwriter, music supervisor, and editor. So extraordinary in its affirmation of Kim Ki-yŏng's filmmaking imagination and talent, *The Housemaid* also testifies to the overarching extent of the suppressive military governments that

The housemaid peeps at her master seducing Miss Cho.
The Housemaid (1960).

have since 1960 delimited Kim's creative freedom, disallowing Kim to make films of equally high standard consistently throughout his career. What is even more astonishing is the very ending of the film that returns to the opening scene where the family—Tong-sik, his wife, and the two children cast by the same actors—is enjoying a conversation about a newspaper article on a man who committed suicide with his maid, a woman with whom he was having an affair. Tong-sik defends the man in the newspaper story against his wife who is complaining that all men are no different from "beasts." Just when the debate between the two is heating up, the sliding door opens, and in enters the character who has terrorized the family. She, not unlike Dr. Caligari in the final scene of *The Cabinet of Dr. Caligari*, is now a changed character.[25] We can no longer find any glimpse of the killer as her hair is neatly pulled back and her manners are obedient when serving her master tea. Yet, having a young woman in the house, according to the mother, is like "offering raw meat to a beast." After the maid is driven away from the room, Tong-sik looks directly into the camera and addresses the audience, saying "Dear sirs and madams, when men age, they spend more time thinking about younger women. This is why we men become easy prey to women and end up embarrassing the whole family." Humorously pointing his finger at the camera, Tong-sik continues, "That's right, *you* are no different . . . and *you* there, shaking your head, sir, this concerns *you* too."

Jinsoo An (An Chin-su) writes that "[Tong-sik]'s death signifies the symbolic reunion with the mother/wife and a regression to an infantile stage. The distant and brief sound of a baby's cry after his death affirms this point."[26] This allusion to the infantile stage and the desire to return to the mother's womb were also registered in *Happy End*, which features a fantasy sequence involving Bora and a balloon that was inserted just before the last scene in which Min-gi wakes up in the living room with his baby by his side. The strong death motif—present in both films—points to the anxieties of the self and to the frustrated efforts of men to claim an autonomous domain. This assertion of masculinity is a pursuit that was already doomed to fail since Tong-sik was forced to play too many roles: an object of desire to his female student, a perfect husband to his wife, a nurturing father to his handicapped daughter, and a sex machine to the promiscuous maid. What forges the *stable* and ideal manhood out of Tong-sik is the relative *instability* of the women spurred by the psychological hysteria and physical dysfunction that are pinned by the film as feminine conditions. The wife is a distressed, overworked woman who must rest in bed, the female students are restless workers in an urban factory who have their ties severed from their rural homes, the daughter is a physically handicapped girl who is invalid from the waist down, and, of course, the sexually-deprived maid is threatening to kill all of them if he stays away too long. Positioned to remedy all of these ailing "feminine symptoms" of paranoia and hysteria with references to the dilapidated economy and the demoralized war-stricken nation, Tong-sik is doomed to fail in each case, as a teacher, a husband, a father, and a lover.

The use of narrative frames by both films serves both to assure viewers that the stories of adultery and sex are only fictions, and to forewarn them that the governing realities of a bourgeois family are very unstable. Tong-sik's last statement, in which he looks into the camera and addresses the *male* viewers, is important because it implies that every man—including those in the audience who are inclined to exempt themselves—is susceptible to lust and desire. This crisis, impinged beneath the humorous scene, is still threatening as it can cause the failure of patriarchy and lead inevitably to death. Here, sex and death become intricately connected as an irrepressible force, eventually thwarting and contradicting the male subject's aspiration to disavow the crisis, to cure the "feminine" ailments, and to reestablish familial sufficiency and authority.

Staircases and Elevators

The Housemaid and *Happy End* are both visually suffocating because the domestic confinement of the male protagonists is so meticulously depicted and spatialized. It is inside their homes where the male agency is threatened, and this clarifies and spatializes the mechanisms of the psychological besiegement. From the staircase and the piano in *The Housemaid* to the special attention paid to everyday machines such as the elevator and the television in *Happy End*, I argue that modern appliances, instruments, and utilities reinscribe gendered power dynamics. Throughout the remainder of this chapeter, I will discuss the domestic space and those of household appliances that most centrally refigure family relations, as they are very sites in and through which the gender norms are both threatened and recovered. For instance, the spatialization of kitchen, from a space segregated from the rest of the communal living space in *The Housemaid* to the "open plan" space featured in the modern apartment of *Happy End*, I argue, renders visible evidences to the shifting patterns of domesticity and the crisis of gender and familial relations. Perhaps this comes as no surprise since kitchens, televisions, and pianos are already heavily prefigured in terms of gender. They emerge in these films even more as active agents of change, often disrupting and threatening the preexisting order of things. The simple placement of men inside the kitchen or in front of televisions or pianos symbolizes deepening gender crisis.

The staircase in *The Housemaid* is where the desire for class mobility is both imagined and thwarted—becoming finally the setting for despair and death. The first time we are introduced to the Western-style house, the family has yet to move in. The house is still under construction, with plywood, ladders, and construction materials scattered all over the house, mirroring the war-stricken Korea of the day. The first space the camera captures is the staircase where Ch'ang-sun, the younger child, taunts his handicapped sister on crutches and dares her to walk up the stairs to take away a bag of cookies from him. She slowly hurdles up the stairs, step by step, with great struggle, before collapsing halfway. The audience is forced to wonder at this very point: With the daughter handicapped by polio and her mobility severely restricted, why would any family move into a two-story house with a long staircase? And, what is the significance of this particular scene where the young disabled child desperately climbs up the stairs to get a bag of cookies from her brother, while her father observes silently in the dark?

The daughter's restricted body movements, the sweat dripping from her face, and the bag of cookies waving in front of her as a fetishistic reward for her desperate labor crystallize both the ambition and inhumanity such a simple housing structure can thematize. The father's statement, whispered to Miss Cho who is sympathetic to the child, "Let her go up by herself. Exercise is good for her leg muscles," further confirms the cruelty and pain that one must face in any desire for physical rehabilitation or national redevelopment. Such an introduction of the staircase in the film dramatically deploys its central themes: the fetishistic desire for an unattainable object, struggle to succumb against odds, and the cruelty and humiliation one must face before, during, and after the climb. In other words, the handicapped girl climbing up the stairs elicits sympathy from others, but it is not an easy choice whether to cruelly leave her on her own or to help her at the risk of humiliating her. The complexities of human emotions in a competitive modern environment — with its prejudices against the less unfortunate, those born with either a physical or a material handicap — are thus conjured up in the film. And all hopes of moving up — either the staircase or the social hierarchy — will require discipline, sacrifice, and even the risk of death.

In *Happy End*, the story is situated in a modern high-rise apartment where no sweat needs to be toiled in climbing up flights of stairs. Min-gi and Bora's apartment compound is just as familiar and common as any of the newly built residential high-rises that were passionlessly built in the last thirty years of the never-ending mass urbanization. Crammed parking lots, tiny mandatory playgrounds, and narrow driveways all mirror the suffocating pace of Korea's industrialization. The metallic elevators are just as heartless as the staircase in *The Housemaid*. Yet, because elevators, unlike staircases inside the house for the family use only, are integral devises of communal space, many people randomly enter and exit. They become a primary venue where meetings — both cheerful and dangerous — can be occasioned. The up-and-down function of the elevator invokes the utility of the staircase that signified both the hope and the failure of class mobility in *The Housemaid*, but its compressed and automated condition removes the struggle involved during the industrialization process. Better suited as a machinery that symbolizes the postmodern condition of Korea, the elevator dramatizes the society's unpredictability as it moves randomly up and down and radically shifts from an open public facility that gives people access to their destinations to its suddenly closed, crammed confinement. The opening and closing of an elevator are dramatic and instantaneous, and strangers often have to share standing-room only space. In Seoul, one of the most densely populated cities in the world, elevators are a ubiquitous, crucial part of everyday movement at home, at work, and at leisure.

In the elevator featured in *Happy End*, we realize that time and space are structured in a gendered mode. This particular elevator serves a residential route. Yet, even in this residential apartment elevator, work is performed. In the beginning of the film, Min-gi picks up his child from the day-care center and enters his apartment elevator. He is carrying the baby, his bag, and the baby bag, and thus the simple press of the elevator button is difficult. Then a thirty-something woman runs into the elevator also with countless shopping bags in her hands. Here, between a man — albeit in business attire — holding a baby and a woman carrying loads of grocery bags, a social and gender alliance is forged in the elevator. Their sex may be different, but their domestic labor commonly binds them and links them through its conventional "femininity." As if to affirm such an alliance, they recognize each other as friends from college. The woman, Mi-yŏng, will soon become Min-gi's buddy, much as if they were same-sex friends. They will soon shop together, help each other with childcare, and gossip on the telephone about television soap programs. The meeting between Mi-yŏng and Min-gi in the elevator is not coincidental as their everyday rhythm follows gendered time. It is near sunset, but for the two of them, their workday is far from being over since they have only a couple of hours before their spouses, with public work, will return home expecting dinner.

Also remarkable in *Happy End*, like *The Housemaid*, is that the waning of male authority is visually captured through the use of the surrounding space of the apartment as an anxious site. Provident meetings in the elevator are not only pleasant, but also dangerous, as the film later demonstrates. In the scene where Min-gi finds out that Bora risked the life of their child to rendezvous with Ilbŏm, Min-gi returns haggardly from the hospital emergency room where the baby was treated. Clutching the baby in his arms, Min-gi enters the same elevator that he rides every day. It is well past the busy hours of the day and no one else is in sight. The camera follows Min-gi from the parking lot into the elevator, and finally into the apartment corridor. It is here in the corridor where Min-gi witnesses Bora — who had rejected her role as a "mother" — embracing Ilbŏm. Had Min-gi arrived a few minutes earlier or a few minutes later, they would have met inside the elevator. Min-gi already knows that they are seeing each other, but to ask him to be a "peeping tom" of their escapade is yet another humiliating blow to his self-esteem. The lovebirds are both drunk and hardly discreet. The depiction of Bora as an intemperate drunk in this scene further affirms the gender reversal depicted by the film. Lost, Min-gi takes a few steps back to the elevator, and hides in the adjacent staircase to it until he hears Ilbŏm's footsteps move toward him. When Ilbŏm finally staggers inside the elevator, Min-gi comes out of his hiding place and checks to confirm the elevator's descent before "safely" returning to his own home. It is difficult for the audience not to sympathize with Min-gi at this point. Holding a baby in his arm, he has lost not only his wife and the mother of his child, but also clear access to his home: the corridor and the elevator. The moment he decides that he can return home only after confirming Ilbŏm's departure, his claim as the "man" of his house is denied.

In *The Housemaid*, the staircase is the space where the struggles for power were visualized. The maid continues to struggle to vie for her authority using the staircase. It is the very site where murders are performed and lives are claimed: a place where the maid throws her body to abort her child, where Tong-sik's son is pushed and found dead, and where before dying Tong-sik desperately crawls to see his wife who is in the ground-level bedroom. In *Happy End*, Min-gi lurches himself across the corridor and reaches for the metal door of his apartment. With the baby in his arm, even the simple task of twisting open a lock is cumbersome. The camera remains static, and does not reveal to us what exactly he sees the moment he opens the door. But, from Min-gi's reaction, we know that his wife is having sex with Ilbŏm. (What Min-gi didn't know is that Ilbŏm had rushed up the stairs on the other side of the building after stopping the elevator, which had descended only one floor.) Their intercourse is so passionate that even the presence of Min-gi goes unnoticed. Min-gi's demise is complete when he doesn't—and can't—even intervene. The primal scene between Bora and Ilbŏm pushes Min-gi and the sick child out into the dark, damp concrete fire escape.

Rats in the Kitchen

Perhaps the pervasive anxiety that stretches throughout the entire lengths of the two films, *Happy End* and *The Housemaid*, is most effectively articulated in the space of the kitchen. In *American Domesticity*, Kathleen McHugh argues that staple narratives of American melodrama, including *Imitation of Life*, *Stella Dallas*, and *Mildred Pierce*, "engage modern cultural beliefs concerning gender and labor by bringing women and their love into explicit relation with what are characterized as public and masculine concerns: work, money, ambition, and success."[27] This effort to associate women's success with what is typically a masculine agenda has led to the absence or invisibility of domestic labor in many Hollywood melodramas in the last century. But, as McHugh later acknowledges, kitchens, housework, and domestic femininity are sufficiently and creatively represented in other forms of cultural discourse in the West: feminist art and films that range from Yoko Ono's conceptual art to Chantal Akerman's experimental films. Korea has never been host to a vibrant avant-garde culture where such imaginative variants of domesticity were attempted, but *The Housemaid* and *Happy End*, both commercial feature films, intriguingly make a case for a vivid representation of domestic labor. In the two Korean films, the kitchens receive critical attention as a space where domesticity is not only performed, but also where the social tensions, upward class mobility, and middle-class conformity are perhaps most effectively expressed. Both Korean films startle the viewers by placing men inside a kitchen, a spatial arrangement that is extremely rare elsewhere in Korean cinema. The sharp differentiation between public and private spheres becomes less distinct as work is performed by both the man and the woman in the films (Tong-sik teaches piano and the mother sews at home, supplementing their income in *The Housemaid*); and the fathers engage in domestic labor (Bora brings home work from her office while Min-gi takes care of the housework in *Happy End*). Perhaps it is this rarity that makes the family relations in the two films both exceptional and dangerous.

The function of "work" and the spatialization of the kitchen where this work is performed are clearly important to the themes of the two Korean films. The kitchen in the 1960 film, *The Housemaid*, is a clean Western-style one installed with a bright electric lamp, wooden cupboards, a sink with two faucets, and a gas stove, all extreme rarities in South Korea at the time.[28] The mother tries to organize the kitchen after moving into the new house; she opens up the cupboards and stacks things in them. These are the happy days for her: the sound of the beginner's piano indicates that her husband is teaching a student upstairs (generating income), and there are also the sounds of children playing (signifying successful childrearing). The fruits of her hard labor as a seamstress and a mother in the last ten years have finally paid off. At this moment of happiness, all of a sudden, a rat appears in front of her. Letting out a sharp scream, she falls, forcing everyone in the house to gather around her. The rat is soon gone, but the shock lingers on, as she cannot easily recover from her fall. In order to prevent rats from encroaching upon the house, the family sets traps: food garnished with rat poison. The poison purchased to get rid of the rats ironically will end up killing the people themselves.

The appearance of the rat first destroys the mother's happiness, then the kitchen's cleanliness, and eventually the family's lives. Because this is a film by Kim Ki-yŏng, an avid reader of Freud, it is not coincidental that the rat appears as a visual symbol of familial anxiety. Freud observed in his famous "Rat Man" case, that the symbols of both money (material) and syphilis (sexual) converged in rats, disgusting animals that carry many infectious diseases.[29] Both material and sexual anxieties play a big part in instilling the fear of Tong-sik and his family, who purchased a new piano in monthly payments and hired a sexually promiscuous maid. Despite the family's effort to exterminate the rats, they would not easily be removed from the kitchen. When the new maid first visits the house, she walks into the kitchen alone, a space segregated from the rest of the house. The maid surveys the room, sampling food and opening the cupboards, familiarizing herself with the only facility that she will now rule. The rat again appears in the cupboard. Unlike the mother who had screamed and fainted at the sight of the rat, the maid curiously picks it up by its tail, and sticks out her tongue at it, and sets it down on the floor as if it's her pet. However, as soon as she finds a small wooden bat used for cooking, she strikes the rat with it. When the family, surprised by the sound of the bat, congregates in the kitchen again, she proudly holds out the dead rat in front of the astonished crowd. Differences in class, region (rural versus urban) and delicacy are clearly established in the maid and the wife's different reactions to the rat. Further, the maid is able to catch and overcome the rat, creating an even bigger illness for the wife. She soon becomes more dangerous and threatening to the family than even the animal, her rabid sexuality seemingly invited into the home by the family's aspirations to social mobility.

Tong-sik, in an indifferent voice, tells her that rats should be trapped with rat poison and gives her the bottle that will later seal both of their fates. Both the intimacy and the cruelty she displayed in her relationship with a rat presage the complicated nature of passion and jealousy that she will soon exhibit in her relationship with Tong-sik. Her action declares that she is in full command of the kitchen, a critical space that contains and serves both food and poison, not unlike Korea's industrialization that will soon bring prosperity, but also simultaneously produce environmental pollution and contamination, economic dependence to the West, and class contradiction.

Just as important as the staircase where power is constantly contested, the kitchen, a part of the house where only women would have previously performed denigrating work, is refigured as an important and powerful space. The hiring of the maid not only allows the mother to recover and concentrate on her work with the sewing machine, but also releases the father from the kitchen. The father had been cooking for the family just prior to the maid's arrival. Wearing a checkered shirt with the sleeves rolled up and an apron around his waist in a Western-style kitchen, Tong-sik is a "modern man" who is capable of providing for the family both outside and inside his home. The availability of stove, cabinets, china, and Western recipes (e.g., for curry rice that had become a convenient Western-style dish) has transformed at least a segment of domesticity into another social function. And thus it is fitting that the man should now be inextricably tied to the kitchen. Is it a matter of trivial coincidence or imperative significance that the mother collapses the first time she enters the new kitchen, requiring the father to substitute for the woman before he finds a housemaid? This is a kitchen that has many modern appliances and utilities, things out of sync with the mother who is dressed in traditional Korean clothing. The mother's collapse signals her total unfamiliarity with the offerings of a modern kitchen meant to promise convenience and comfort.

If there is one space in the house, wherein a family with two young children live, that cannot be left alone, it is the kitchen, and the need prompts the father to cook and temporarily resume housework. Even though he is a "better cook than mom," the alignment of domesticity and masculinity in the social context of 1960s Korea simply seems out of place, if not threatening to the prevailing gender division of labor. This illustrates the confusion of the period when Korea is straddling war-stricken poverty and the nascent stage of Western-style industrialization, tradition, and modernity. Thus a crevice is left open through which destructive elements will seep inside, destroying a family that gets caught in the liminal space between tradition and modernity, male and female.

The one other domestic space that is as highlighted as the kitchen in *The Housemaid* is the piano room, which also functions as a family room. There is perhaps no material object more highly prized than the piano since it is positioned as an object of fetishistic desire that not only generates income for the family but also sorrow. Although Korea is today one of the world's leading manufacturers and exporters of pianos, and although pianos are staple items of many middle-class homes,[30] they were not easily accessible to the public in 1960. Tong-sik's occupation as a music teacher, with complete command of this elegant instrument, cannot be separated from the fact that he is an object of romantic gaze by all of the women around him. Precisely because Tong-sik is an ideal male figure, his masculinity becomes fraught with anxiety when he tries to please all of his female admirers. To be in control of such a graceful Western machine requires sensitivity, confidence, and cultural sophistication that none of the women working in the factory yet possesses. The moment Tong-sik walks into a baroque-style room where music is taught to female factory workers, he is a center of starry-eyed and envious attention. He has the expertise and talent that women desire and acquire if they are to convey material comfort and graceful cultural taste that stretch further beyond music. The image of ideal femininity projected through the famous Dutch or French paintings during the nineteenth century that explicitly identify the keyboard instrument as a site of seduction appealed to many young Korean women then.[31] As if to aid them in translating their dreams into reality, Tong-sik makes an announcement in his class, expressing his intent to recruit piano students.

Nonetheless, Tong-sik's offer to help the young women achieve their dream of learning the piano also helps him to attain his own material dream. He states,

"I purchased a piano in installments, and would like to get some return on my investment," acknowledging that the piano is not only a dream machine, but also an expensive material investment that usurps other dreams. From then onward, the piano—like many other props in the film—serves a dual function. It is an object of desire, generating fetishistic impulses by virtue that it is rare and delicate. But, because it is so costly, it also generates the film's tragic plot. After the maid becomes hysterical and stabs Miss Cho who has come for a piano lesson, Tong-sik regrets having purchased the piano, and blames it as the root cause of all the family misfortune. The act of learning the piano is narratively integrated in the film that packages a dream of upward mobility, like the way learning English in *Happy End* also symbolizes a similar façade of upward movement in social stature.[32] In *The Housemaid*, Tong-sik prevents his maid from even casually touching the piano. When the maid curiously strikes a few keys, he warns her, "Whatever you do, never touch the piano." Even after they make love, the rules that ban the maid from the piano still apply, as if to gesture that the heartless machine is more sacred than the human body. This however will not stop the fearless housemaid. Her untutored hands will soon strike the piano keys with rigor, producing horrendous night sounds that will wake everyone in the house. Just as the staircase stands as a metonymy for the family's economic ascendance and demise, the piano, the fetishized symbol of Western bourgeoisie and the primary source of income for the family, will turn out to be Tong-sik's "enemy."

Happy End's Open-Space Plan

The modern spatial plan has reconfigured residential apartments, refiguring the previously partitioned spaces, the kitchen, living room, dining room, and hallways, into one open area. Compared to the confined and crammed public urban space seen elsewhere in *Happy End*, as instanced by the elevator, the bookstore, or even Bora's office, the apartment appears spacious. Min-gi is associated with domesticity not only through various housekeeping chores, but also through his inextricable ties to the television. Leslie Regan Shade writes that the television set is an "electronic hearth that replaced the fireplace and the piano as the center of family attention."[33] Television may have replaced *The Housemaid*'s piano at the center stage of domestic space, but the family is no longer there to give much attention to it. Only Min-gi is seated in front of television. When he first enters his apartment, after meeting his old friend from college in the elevator, he cannot easily take his eyes off the television, even though the baby profusely cries, demanding to be fed. His focus shifts between

Ch'oe Min-sik, an actor who usually plays a tough guy,
shows his "feminine" side. *Happy End* (1999).

the soccer game on the television located in the living room, the baby lying on
the sofa, and the powdered milk he's preparing in the kitchen. While Min-gi is
getting food ready for the baby, he realizes that there are small black worms in
the formula, making its consumption impossible. The black worms—like the
rats in *The Housemaid*—will continue to infest the house, especially the kitchen
cabinet, symptomatically rendering once again the anxiety encircling sexual
promiscuity and familial financial crisis.

Min-gi's relationships with the kitchen and television are both conventional
and extraordinary: conventional because domesticity has had a special relation
with the kitchen and with television during the modern era, but also extraordinary given that he is a masculine man who hardly has "feminine" qualities. The
actor cast as Min-gi, Ch'oe Min-sik, is a well-known "tough guy" persona in
Korean cinema, making the character's association with stereotypical images of
femininity even more difficult.[34] *Happy End*'s cessation of the intimacy between
femininity and domesticity radically departs from the contemporary Hollywood films such as *Tootsie* (Sydney Pollack, dir., 1982), *Mr. Mom* (Stan Dragoti,
dir., 1983), or *Mrs. Doubtfire* (Chris Columbus, dir., 1993) that allow men into
the kitchen only by stripping them of their masculinity. In these, for instance,
Dustin Hoffman and Robin Williams had to literally dress up as women in order
to justify their place in the kitchen or their cooking tips. Yet, these transgres-

sions are the very threats, tense and rife with domestic hostility and reversed gender roles, that would eventually destroy the family.

In one particular sequence, Min-gi performs various housework tasks. Sequentially structured, Min-gi prepares a meal, organizes and loads empty cans and milk cartons into recycling boxes, and flips and pegs laundered sheets on the balcony laundry line. This sequence of static shots—without music—that cuts between each housework item is sensual and affective, rendering beauty in simple everyday domestic labor without humorizing or sentimentalizing it, and defying the conventions of gender-bending Hollywood comedies. In the subsequent sequence, Min-gi reclines on the sofa, with a glass of beer in his hand, watching a nighttime soap drama where two famous television actors, Kim Hye-su and Pae Yong-jun, exchange excessively melodramatic dialogues. In tears, Kim Hye-su, the woman, states: "I know it's wrong for me to do what I have been doing. There's not even enough time for me to complain about it. I was a fool." Unable to control her emotions, the actress with heavy makeup breaks into tears, smudging her dark mascara. After having captured the television in full frame, the camera of *Happy End* then cuts 180 degrees to Min-gi who is intently watching the soap. At this very moment, he is temporarily resting after a long day of work. Yet, he is forced to break his concentration from the television program when Bora yells from her room, asking him to lower the volume. At almost the same time, the phone rings and the baby also starts to cry. Not even a moment of peace can be secured for Min-gi when Bora— after her several pleas to turn down the television down go ignored—agitatedly rushes out into the living room. The phone keeps ringing, the baby continues to cry, and the kettle on the stove begins to whistle; these noises intensify the tension between the husband and the wife, whose roles have been reversed.

It is only Bora's work brought home from the office that is valued as "labor," while the domestic labor performed by Min-gi earlier in the day remains invisible to Bora. She only sees that Min-gi is watching television while sipping beer and remains entirely unaware that he too has completed a full day of hard work. In the ensuing family conference, Min-gi sits in the dining chair closest to the kitchen, symbolizing his closer proximity to the kitchen. Bora, seated on the other side, tells him that he must be responsible for all of the housework unless he is serious about looking for a job. She continues to chastise him: "Do you care to know which store has the cheapest juice price or which store has the best bread, or the time the freshly baked bread comes out? Do you care to know? You would rather not care, right? Then, you must start 'work' (*il*) again. Why do you simply sit there, ugly and defeated, like someone who has just lost a war?" Min-gi feels humiliated not only because he is incapable of finding employment, but also because she is denigrating his domestic labor, subordinating it to her own "masculine" work. To Bora, Min-gi's labor in the house does not qualify as il. Her ability to earn money is perceived to be far more sacred and profound than "saving" through "best buy" juice and bread. This is precisely the moment where the terms of domesticity and gender relations shift and become troubled, laying the foundation for the later merciless killing of Bora—a killing that will be emotionally and subconsciously legitimated by viewers, not "because she is a woman," but more importantly because she is "just as bad as any working man." In other words, Bora has to die, for she has all the qualities of a "bad husband" who has an affair with his office staff, ignores the hardship of his wife's domestic labor, and does not believe in the importance of television viewing as a leisure that is crucially integrated within the rubric of domesticity and communal social activity. (As soon as the program is over, Min-gi receives a phone call from Mi-yŏng who asks him what he thought of the soap's new developments.) Of course, had the film insisted on conventional gender relations, such desire for a dramatic and brutal killing would not have been necessitated. In other words, even though it is Bora's masculine insensitivity toward domesticity that allows the film to later prepare us for her brutal death, had she been biologically male—with a penis—Bora's death would not have been warranted. For then, most men would have to die for their insensitivity and for their failure to be good "mothers."

Masculinist/Feminist

The alignment of men in domestic spaces, serious depictions of masculine anxieties, and emphasis on sexuality and desire in *The Housemaid* and *Happy End* all articulate the complexities of gender. Even the punishments of women, the maid in *The Housemaid* and Bora in *Happy End*, can be considered as rupturing instances that may be exempted from the Mulvey-ian critique of the masculine conventions of mainstream cinema. The stylistic excesses in *The Housemaid* cast not only women as monsters but also men as equally hapless and terrible creatures. Also, the attention paid to domesticity and the placement of Min-gi inside a kitchen allow alternative gender readings of these films. Yet, it is precisely Bora's masculine characteristics transgressing the conventional boundaries of gender that necessitate her punishment at the end of *Happy End*. And even though the housemaid is an "active sexual agent," (according to Chris Berry) that disassociates her from the conventional roles of femininity assigned by Korean cinema, as the female spectators then shouted, she is still only a "whore" or a "bitch."[35] This fulfills the mother-whore dyad of patriarchic representation of women, something I raised in the introduction of this book, that Korean cinema has regulated throughout the postwar decades. Further disqualifying these films from the ranks of feminist films is their refusal to question the conventional gender roles; they employ gender differentiation as an integral component of filmic tension that ultimately leads one film's respective narrative movements. In other words, the phallus in these films is *not* used in the Lacanian sense in which its realness is stripped, but is instead where power remains very much condensed.

The threats issued against male potency during both stages of nascent industrialization and deindustrialization have ways of redirecting themselves so that gender relations are, on one hand, destabilized momentarily, but, on the other, restabilized and reorganized through the "normative" function of gender: norms that rely on gender differences and a fixation on "traditional" characteristics. Gender roles have remained remarkably consistent such that the representation of the woman is still caught between the mother and the whore, and the crisis is a male one — in which the man must resort to violence in order to recover himself from trauma. But, this hardly accomplishes anything other than once again affirming gender essences. For instance, even when Min-gi is left in the end alone with his daughter, he can never be a single father who is capable of withdrawing himself from his phallocentric universe despite his dedication to housework and command of domestic space. On a similar note, it is extremely difficult to imagine the mother in *The Housemaid* assuming the paternal role for her children after her husband and the maid kill themselves. Even in these films, where stylistic excesses and refigurations of domestic spaces potentially complicate the conventional notions of gender, gender essentialism cannot and will not easily be dismantled or deconstructed. In the midst of such regressive shoring up of hegemonic relation, any masculinity threatened by social crisis will again be recuperated.

9

"Each Man Kills the Thing He Loves": Transgressive Agents, National Security, and Blockbuster Aesthetics in *Shiri* and *Joint Security Area*

Directors in Iran, Korea, Taiwan and Argentina . . . are also breaking the mold with their stylish and bold movies. More than ever, filmmakers who come from countries suffering through political or economic turmoil are introducing the world to their stories. For instance, Korean director Kang Che-gyu's action thriller "Shiri," about a renegade group of North Korean commandos infiltrating South Korea, was a No. 1 hit not only in Korea but also in Japan and Hong Kong. . . . These directors are not making your typical arthouse fare. Instead they are making entertaining, relevant and energetic films. . . . —Lorenza Muñoz, *Los Angeles Times*

I agree that there have been more things to look at in Korean movies, but I can't shake the feeling that they are imitations of Hollywood. I wonder whether it is significant if the movies Koreans are making are the same as the ones made by Hollywood producers. . . . If there was one thing to be learned from Hong Kong [film industry's demise] it is that movies lacking criticism and creativity will suffer a fate that is no different [from Hong Kong's]. —Tsai Ming-liang, *Cine 21 PIFF Daily*

But it is better to fail in originality, than to succeed in imitation. —Herman Melville

Toward the end of *Shiri*, the film's protagonist, Agent Yu of South Korea, follows his nemesis, Yi Pang-hŭi, a female sniper from North Korea, throughout the streets of Seoul. Yi Pang-hŭi had been responsible for several assassinations of government officials and the theft of a new powerful bomb, and the entire city had been placed on alert. But during a melée between a team of North Korean terrorists and the South Korean agents that took place earlier in the busy business district, she is shot in the arm. For the first time in the film, she is no longer invincible or invisible. When they both approach Yi's point of destination, Agent Yu, who had been furtively trailing her, becomes disori-

North Korean agent Yi Pang-hŭi (alias Yi Myŏng-hyŏn)
in her pet shop. *Shiri* (1999)

ented. He feels dizzy not because he is in a neighborhood that is unfamiliar, but too eerily familiar. This is the district where he shares a small apartment with his girlfriend, Yi Myŏng-hyŏn. Yi Pang-hŭi enters the trendy shop filled with aquariums of tropical fish that Yi Myŏng-hyŏn owns. Once Yi Pang-hŭi takes off her wig, her trench coat, and her artillery inside the apartment annexed to the fish shop, she is revealed as Yu's sweet girlfriend with whom he had planned a wedding next month. During the rampage of terror, Yi Pang-hŭi was the sadistic figure of an omnipresent godhead, with the vision and precise execution of a ruthless warrior. But once Yi Pang-hŭi and Yi Myŏng-hyŏn collapse into one single injured female body, she instantaneously shifts into a masochistic regression. With the sentimental soundtrack sweetening the mood, the "woman beast" who had terrorized the nation is now reduced to a distraught woman torn between two men, Yu and her lover from North Korea, Park.

Yi Pang-hŭi has taken the identity of Yi Myŏng-hyŏn, a woman who in real life has been admitted to a hospital in Cheju Island (off Korea's southern coast) in order to execute her assignment of infiltrating South Korea's intelligence system through Yu. (She had planted small high-tech voice detectors inside pet fishes that Yu had unsuspectingly taken to his office.) The real Yi Myŏng-hyŏn had been segregated from society because of her low immune system (officially called the Innate Immunodeficiency Syndrome) and must avoid direct contact with others. The three female characters (all of them played by the same actress,

Kim Yun-jin)—Yi Pang-hŭi the North Korean Agent, Yi Pang-hŭi/Yi Myŏng-hyŏn the girlfriend, and Yi Myŏng-hyŏn the hospital patient—combine the traits of the violent terrorist, the attractive and entrepreneurial lover, and the useless and irrecoverably sick woman. She is triply constructed within a patriarchal discourse that has set its parameters within the terms of her sexuality and that invokes the "monstrous-feminine," something Barbara Creed has designated in her study of Western horror films. Shifting from asexual Yi Myŏng-hyŏn to sexual Yi Pang-hŭi/Yi Myŏng-hyŏn, and then to overly hysterical Yi Pang-hŭi who would rather destroy herself with booze than confront her reality as a double agent, she is continually forced into a role of a ventriloquist until she is killed. The pitiful sympathy that was once solicited from the audience for Pyŏng-t'ae, the anxious, self-loathing college student in *Whale Hunting* (1984), is redirected to the Hydra-like double agent.[1] Yi Pang-hŭi/Yi Myŏng-hyŏn is distinguished from Pyŏng-t'ae, for she is not only pitied but also desired and loathed. She invites a seductive gaze that fatally turns her seducer into a victim. Through this process, she is left with no other option than self-destruction.

Barbara Creed notes that "when woman is represented as monstrous it is almost always in relation to her mothering and reproductive functions."[2] The two Yi merge into an electrifying yet shocking, violent yet abject, terrific yet horrific monster that transposes the pain of more than fifty uninterrupted cold war years and the equally long military and masculine history of Korea into the pleasurable genre conventions of Hollywood. It symptomizes the fear and anxiety that has built up during the fifty-plus years of cold war. The two lead characters of *Shiri*, Yi and Yu, are draped in the two national flags that equally but separately vie for reunification: Yi follows the order of Park, a commander of a North Korean special force, who desires reunification by plotting another civil war and sabotaging the reconciliatory meeting between the two leaders of North and South; Yu, on the other hand, remains firm in keeping the peace process uninterrupted. It is interesting that Yi Pang-hŭi/Yi Myŏng-hyŏn was carrying a child in her monstrous womb, a fetus that was destined to be a by-product between a North Korean spy and a South Korean agent when she was shot by Yu in the film's climatic scene. Once her life is taken away by Yu and the weight of history crushes any hope for romance, which cannot free itself from rigid ideological stratification, so too erased is her fetus that crucially embodied the reconciliatory spirit between the North and the South.

The agencies of females are adumbrated in the two blockbuster films, *Shiri* and *JSA: Joint Security Area* (*Kongdong kyŏngbi kuyŏk JSA*, 2000) that transform the conventional representation of women—from prostitutes and mothers—to a dangerous *femme fatale*. Transgressive also is the female lead character, Sophie

Agent Yu of South Korea, Yi Myŏng-hyŏn's lover. *Shiri* (1999).

Jean, in *JSA*, who is a biracial woman born between a Korean father who defected to Switzerland as a POW during the Korean War and a Swiss mother. She joins the fictive Neutral Nations Supervisory Commission (NNSC; comprised of Swiss and Swedish delegates) in the politically sensitive area of Panmunjŏm, a symbol of divided Korea in the Joint Security Area. The commission is investigating a shooting rampage that left two North Korean soldiers killed and two South Koreans and a North Korean injured. One million eight hundred thousand troops guard the world's most heavily fortified border. Though Major Sophie Jean is a woman in a heavily militarized space, she is the only person who can potentially transgress the most explosive border in the world to probe the truth behind the shooting incident and diffuse the escalating tension between the two sides. She is a pensive officer with a legal degree, and her racial and ideological background of one-half Korean/one-half Swiss and one-half communist/one-half neutral renders her special access into investigation rooms of both North and South Korean military bases. She also participates in morning jogs with other foreign personnel, wears military uniforms, and spends her leisure time shooting darts to ease her entry into the homo-social space where only men are present. Her objective is to find out the truth, something that remains clustered behind the silence of the two soldiers.

It is revealed at the end that a South Korean sergeant, Yi Su-hyŏk, and a North Korean sergeant, O Kyŏng-p'il, had violated one of the most revered military

Agent Park of North Korea, Yi Pang-hŭi's lover
from the past. *Shiri* (1999).

codes in the two military camps: "thou shall not fraternize with the enemy."[3]
When Su-hyŏk had accidentally stepped on a mine during a South Korean military exercise at the border and was immobilized for hours, Sergeant O had
rescued him by deactivating it. This fortuitous meeting between the two had
forged a friendship to a point where Su-hyŏk and his military companion Nam
Sŏng-sik routinely crossed over the "Bridge of No Return" to fraternize with
Sergeant O and his military subordinate, Chŏng U-jin, while on a night shift
at a military post. The reinstitutionalization of law and order is punctuated by
the entrance of a North Korean officer, Lieutenant Ch'oe, who abruptly breaks
up the party only a few days before Su-hyŏk is scheduled to be honorably discharged from his compulsory military service. Lieutenant Ch'oe, who dutifully
serves the interest of both Koreas' national security, takes out his pistol from
his holster and orders his North Korean subordinates to arrest Su-hyŏk and
Sŏng-sik. A brief attempt to restore peace in the small cottage fails, resulting
in a shootout where Lieutenant Ch'oe, who had rudely interrupted the party,
and U-jin are shot to death. Su-hyŏk — during the mayhem — is also shot in the
leg. Before reinforcements from both sides arrive after hearing the gunshots,
Kyŏng-p'il quickly suggests to Su-hyŏk that he make up a story of a kidnap
and an escape. He also volunteers to be shot in order to persuade his superiors that he had been a victim of a surprise attack by the South Korean soldiers.
In a slow-motion shot, Kyŏng-p'il — with blood dripping from the corner of

The border patrol at Panmunjŏm at the Joint Security Area (DMZ).
Joint Security Area (2000).

his mouth — stands alone in the middle of the shack until Su-hyŏk empties one last bullet in his shoulder. Between the two competing stories of the kidnap (insisted by Su-hyŏk) and the surprise attack (made up by Kyŏng-p'il) lies the truth that is unveiled to Sophie.

The prohibited companionship between the four male soldiers, the breaking of political taboo through games of bodily contact (playing the children's game one-leg wrestling), the exchange of bodily fluid (the spitting game while Su-hyŏk and Sergeant O are on guard at a public area while only a few feet apart), and the use of actual guns and bullets as instruments of pleasure, threat, and eventual killings all post allegories of same-sex eroticism. What is invoked as the ultimate form of tension that had rendered the nocturnal event as an unspeakable, horrific form of encounter between the men is the presence of Lieutenant Ch'oe of North Korea. The Name of the Father he represents anchors the definite linkage between national security and the prohibitive homoerotic codes of *JSA*. He is the symbol of repression that precipitates anxiety. The inconsistencies produced in South Korea between restored civil liberties and the still prevailing national security law (authored by the government to keep communism at bay) render the surplus of meaning in any given text produced at a time of social frenzy (the economic crisis, the first winning of presidential elections by the dissident party in 1997 and the first meeting between the two leaders in 2000). All of these make their impact in the destabilizing of the

Sophie Jean, an agent who transgresses the boundaries of ideology and gender.
Joint Security Area (2000).

dominant conventions of gender. *JSA* successfully utilizes these codes of anxieties—the most feared measures of social prohibition such as the direct contact with North Koreans and same-sex romance—as subversive conventions in a melodramatic narrative.

As much as it is difficult to claim *JSA* as a gay film, it is almost impossible to disclaim the same-sex bonding as the film's primary element that drives the desirable and subversive narrative movement. *JSA* is a "male melodrama" that induces all of the ingredients of pathos, sentimental music score,[4] and emotional experiences of war exercises and camps most Korean men have endured for almost three years of their youth in the military. O Kyŏng-p'il is one of the most highly decorated soldiers in North Korea and even earns the respect of Su-hyŏk, a South Korean. Sergeant O teaches Su-hyŏk that the most important principle in a battle is not how fast one draws his or her firearm, but how graceful one is under pressure. Calm and poised, Sergeant O possesses traits of masculinity that are lacked and desired by Su-hyŏk. Julian Stringer, while examining the function of masculinity in John Woo's Hong Kong films, argues that "male bonding around both passionate violence and passionate suffering can be taken in either of two ways. On the positive side, the loving, anguished, pained look of one impaired male melodramatic action hero at another embodies a same-sex bond of intense feeling to which a heterosexist culture does not normally permit access. On the other hand, such views privilege the male, patriarchal, masculinist, woman-excluding point of view."[5]

If *Shiri* reclaims the masculine power through the destruction and erasure of the North Korean Other that is embodied in the female, *JSA* redeploys and even defuses it by creating a melodramatic longing for the Other.[6] O Kyŏng-p'il is no less detached from "real" than Yi Pang-hŭi as a North Korean character, but his superhuman acts of self-sacrificing heroism and impeccable grace emotionally move the audiences in a direction of desire and fantasy. Though the phallic lack remains overvalued in *JSA*, it induces a masochistic viewing position from the intense feeling of separation between the two men who cannot easily breach the "fifty-year tragic history of agonizing and humiliating division." The very institutions of male bonding and patriarchal power force men constantly to reexamine their closeness and attraction to other men. But by draping themselves in a form of prohibition derived from the name of the nation, which is far more visually prominent, male bonding itself becomes less scandalous. *JSA*'s Sergeant O is equally terrifying and desirable as *Shiri*'s repressed other: the double agent Yi.

Sophie's sexuality is framed outside the realm of desire both within the diegesis and outside of it because she has entered a space that is heavily charac-

Su-hyŏk (left) breaks military taboo by fraternizing with the enemy.
Joint Security Area (2000).

terized by its homo-social activity. Both female leads in the two blockbuster films signify the return of the historically repressed, something the South Koreans want to erase from their collective memory as they celebrate a postwar economic revival and restoration of civil liberties. Through the image of two beautiful women and their corporeality, history becomes embodied; the North Korean terrorist Yi Pang-hŭi is pregnant with the child whose father is the South Korean agent, and Sophie is a daughter of a North Korean socialist intellectual who had defected to Switzerland fifty years earlier. What constitutes the elements of "monstrous-feminine" through the two Yi's in *Shiri* is mostly diminished in *JSA*'s Sophie. Though Sophie possesses a transgressive element, her hybridity is immediately laid bare when she is first introduced in the film, while Yi Myŏng-hyŏn's monstrous real is exposed only through her bodily other (Yi Pang-hŭi).

As David Scott Diffrient remarks, *Shiri's* "callisthenic camera exhibits a resistance to spatial fixity" when it maneuvers through the streets of Seoul.[7] By resisting spatial fixity, *Shiri* produces the trope of invisibility and the phantom-like identity of Yi Pang-hŭi, a double agent who is omnipresent at all of the O.P. (South Korean intelligence system) agents' initiatives yet invisible to them. On the other hand, *JSA*'s spatial identity is defined by the recurrence of the little cottage located on the other side of the "Bridge of No Return" where the nightly rendezvous between Su-hyŏk and Kyŏng-p'il is held. In this clandestine space emptied out and now only stained with blood firmly stands Sophie, who must establish her power not by being invisible, but by pronouncing her presence that is defined by international law, biracial identity, and female body in a masculine uniform. Both female characters (Yi Pang-hŭi and Sophie) are borne of men's fantasy and thus constitute a transgressive double identity, but Sophie resists the characterization of femme fatale, by clearly defining her function that is not delimited by her sexuality, something that becomes inoperative in a homo-social space.

Identifying the historical trauma as woman's monstrosity is one of the most popular remedies prescribed for male hysteria. The masculine constitution of the woman as the other in the form of volatile, impossible, and threatening in the realm of fantasy rescues the male identity that was awry under the constraints and the frenzy of the socio-political condition. Both female leads are pushed beyond the normal state of rational consciousness and into the realm of what Julia Kristeva calls the "abject." What is simplified in *Shiri* as simply the ideologically "monstrously hideous" is actually better mediated in *JSA* where Sophie remains at the calm and rational center of a storm to readjust the masculinity that has gone hysterical. If *Shiri* insists that the masculine rejuvenation requires the woman to be violently extinguished, *JSA* declares the impossibility of the male subject to reacquire its standard of rationalization.

Sophie desires to know what exactly has happened on the night of the murder but Su-hyŏk is not positioned as the object of her desire, contrary to the tendency in most commercial film narratives that desperately seek to romantically knot the two heterosexual leads. Sophie's transgressions not only cross the boundaries of nation, race, and ideology, but also the homo-social community of men. Su-hyŏk tells her the truth about what had really happened on the fatal night. But he fails to recognize one piece of information, which is clarified by Sophie. Contrary to his belief that he had not been directly responsible for any murder, Sophie tells him—based on medical and material evidence—that U-jin, Sergeant O's subordinate who died that night, had been killed by Su-hyŏk, not by Sŏng-sik. After coming out of the dark, Su-hyŏk and Sophie exchange a courteous embrace, but absent is any remnant of sexual longing between the two. Through the negation of the heterosexual desire between the two leads surfaces the quasi-romantic impulses that had underscored the companionship between the North and South Korean soldiers, a game that had been played after defying the threat of death and state prohibition. In the final scene, Su-hyŏk—still wounded from the shot in the leg—is taken away by the South Korean authorities. Before he is escorted into a car, he captures a gun from one of the officers. In a swift move, he kneels, wincing as his injured knee hits the asphalt. Surprised, Sophie runs down the building, but Su-hyŏk has already placed the pistol in his mouth and pulled the trigger. Sophie is terrified and dismayed by the death that has occurred only a few feet away from her. What has motivated Su-hyŏk to commit such an extreme act of violence against himself? Was Sophie's revelation that Su-hyŏk was responsible for the death of Chŏng U-jin, one of his North Korean friends, too traumatic for him to accept? Why is he unable to push himself beyond death even after breaking the spell of silence to Sophie?

"Each man kills the thing he loves," sings Lysiane (Jeanne Moreau) in a song that punctuates the central theme of *Querelle* (1982), Rainer Werner Fassbinder's controversial film made just before his death. The character of O Kyŏng-p'il is compelling to Su-hyŏk and to viewers in South Korea because he represents an image that has long been prohibited: an affable North Korean Communist soldier. He in many ways arouses desire because he has been devalued by the South Korean state as nonexistent beyond the masses of faceless soldiers who mechanically march to the rhythms of military trumpets and pledge their dogmatic loyalty to their totalitarian leader. Yet this is the very place where his aura — unique and fetishistic — can be uncovered, once his veil is lifted and he emerges as a demystified individual. He on one hand is a human, with sentimental emotions (for South Korean pop music) and an appetite for junk food (for cheap chocolate cakes), but on the other holds an exceptional mastery over his corporeality, ideological loyalty, and self-discipline. The combination of these qualities produces a masculinity that is splendid and ideal to those who have grown up in a postmodern environment of South Korea where the penchant for perfect subjectivity is no longer idealized. The "reciprocal acts of violence," which René Girard proposes in his discussion of the Oedipus myth as the condition of "all masculine relationships,"[8] are no exception in *JSA*. Like Agent Yu of *Shiri* who was forced to draw his gun against the "thing he loves," Su-hyŏk consciously pulls the trigger of the pistol pointed at Sergeant O, the North Korean man he admires, in an affective slow-motion sequence that provides the climax of this male melodrama. Because abnegation and abjection are simply categories reserved not only for women but for men as well, the death of Su-hyŏk is awkward in its timing, but appropriate in fulfilling its generic conventions. The murderous apocalyptic finale is the only option left for Su-hyŏk and his comrades, who had participated in the highly charged game that eventually disembodied everyone involved. Denied is the peaceful process toward a salient post-traumatic identity even in the cinematic realm of fantasy. The taming of Suhyŏk's male hysteria by a woman is impossible since the only one who can comfort him is on the other side of the 38th Parallel, with their reunion—like the one between the old man and his family left behind in North Korea in *The Man with Three Coffins* (see chapter 2)—impossible in the near future.

The Emergence of Asia's Hollywood

In the early 2000s, the routine in Korean cinema has been to distribute a film in more than two hundred screens through aggressive marketing campaigns and to maximize the return of opening weekend box-office results.[9] *Shiri*, the most successful commercial film of the 1990s, rewrote Korean film history by selling 2.73 million (5.78 million nationwide) tickets in Seoul alone.[10] *Shiri*'s box-office figure exceeded the annual total ticket sales record of all Korean films in an average year throughout the 1980s and the early 1990s. (In 1989, for instance, seventy-three Korean films released that year sold a total of 2.43 million tickets in Seoul.) The change of distribution patterns made this astounding box-office success possible. *Shiri* opened on twenty-four screens in Seoul alone, eventually maximizing its exhibition outlets to thirty-five screens in Seoul.[11] (By contrast, *Sopyonje*, which held the previous box-office record for a Korean film, was only released on one screen and, even at the height of its commercial sales, was screened on no more than three screens simultaneously in Seoul, a city of over ten million people.) *JSA* and *Friends* (*Chingu*, Kwak Kyŏng-t'aek, dir.), two mega-blockbusters, followed the success of *Shiri* in 2000 and 2001, respectively, each of them breaking *Shiri*'s box-office record with more than 2.7 million tickets sold. These records contributed in strengthening the domestic film industry that was once threatened with extinction. Over 82 million movie tickets were sold in 2001, registering 27.4 percent increase compared to 2000. In 2001, Korean films drew 46 percent of the total audience, a figure larger than that of Hollywood films. (By comparison, in 2000, the Japanese local film market share was 31.8 percent; France, 28.5 percent; Great Britain, 19.6 percent; and Germany, 12.5 percent.) This represented one of the highest shares of domestic movie consumption in the world, and Korea is the only nation during the post-Vietnam history that has regained its domestic audience after losing them to Hollywood products. (Merely less than a decade earlier, only 16 percent of moviegoers watched Korean films. All of the top ten films at the box office in 1993, for instance, were films produced by Hollywood, with the exception of *Sopyonje*.)

The figures are even more impressive when considering that the chaebols (conglomerates) pulled their resources from the Korean film industry after the

IMF pressured the closure and/or merger of many of their inefficient subsidiaries during the national financial crisis in the late 1980s. The so-called "IMF crisis" ironically helped the Korean film industry in its battle to protect the local market. Three factors since the crisis have contributed to the Korean cinema's commercial renaissance. First, because Hollywood films became exponentially more expensive after the local currency instantaneously lost half of its value, the demand for local products rose. Korean film distributors cancelled their agreements to more than one hundred foreign films immediately after the crisis,[12] which allowed Korean films to be more competitive. Second, once the pride of Korea's economic miracle, the chaebols became the target of public rage after it was discovered that they had largely been responsible for the $110 billion private-sector debt. Conglomerates had to restructure, which meant closing many nonprofitable subsidiaries, making their accounting system more transparent, and rendering their management system lean and efficient. SKC, Daewoo, and Samsung officially discontinued their investments in movie entertainment. The withdrawal of chaebol capital allowed the venture capital companies to fill the void in the Korean film industry. The lean structure of venture capital, the Western-style management system, and the short-term oriented goals well suited the ambitions of many producers and directors who sought to follow the Hollywood blockbuster marketing and distribution model. Third, the crisis of national finance revived nationalist sentiment on a popular level and legitimated the arguments for protective measures of domestic products. The filmmakers' campaign to maintain the screen quota of 126 days of Korean film screenings in local theaters each year received widespread support. Despite the constant pressures made by the high-ranking U.S. trade officials to eliminate the quota system and the surge of the domestic market share to more than 40 percent (46 percent in 2001), the screen quota policies remained intact.

Korean cinema vies to fill the vacuum that had been created in the Asian market after the Hong Kong film industry's demise. No longer is Korean cinema characterized by its "hermit" status that previously exhibited mostly cheap exploitation films and government propagandas. The export figures of Korean films that hovered only around U.S.$200,000 annual revenue throughout most of the decades of the 1980s and the 1990s surged in 1998 almost tenfold by recording sales of U.S.$3 million. The annual export figures continually and exponentially increased since then, registering U.S.$15 million in 2002.[13] While much of the Korean films that had interested foreign buyers during the early to mid-1990s were soft-porn products, the most attractive films are materials of much wider appeal. The commercial emergence of Korean cinema in the late

1990s and the early 2000s not coincidentally overlaps the demise of Hong Kong film industry, which lost its status in the Asian market and suffered a massive talent exodus to Hollywood.

The surprising surge of the commercial viability of Korean cinema is attributed to the perseverance of a serious film culture during the last two decades of the twentieth century, the period covered in the book. During the late 1980s and the early 1990s, students were demonstrating in the streets not only for democratic representation through popular vote, but also for free access to media and film beyond the mainstream images. The explosion of visual culture and the popularity of alternative filmmaking and cinephile culture in the urban sectors of Korea had deeply affected the generation of people who were going to college at the time. Most of them were in their thirties in 2000, and they are the newer "386-generation" filmmakers who made their debuts in the 1990s.[14] These filmmakers had not only grown up with Hong Kong and Hollywood action films that dominated the box office in the late 1980s and the early 1990s, but also with art-house films, which were far more accessible and popular than they had ever been. The demand for these films in the early 1990s and the mid-1990s surged to a point where the films of Andrei Tarkovsky, Abbas Kiarostami, and Kristof Kieslowski were released in commercial theaters. The films of Hou Hsiao-hsien, Tarkovsky, and Robert Bresson were also widely circulated in pirate VHS copies, and they ended up deeply affecting the young filmmakers working today.[15] During the mid-1990s, international film festivals, special retrospectives of foreign art filmmakers, and cinephile club screenings also sprouted throughout Korea, regulating screenings of films that by then had become commercially unviable in the West.

The anomaly of Korean cinema during the early 2000s is that its commercial renaissance is threatening to kill any remnant of art-film infrastructure rather than to foster it further. This is ironic since the revival of the popular interest in cinema would not have materialized had it not been for the cinephilia of the past two decades that devoted itself to bringing critical discussions of films in the press, film education, and international film festivals in Pusan, Puch'ŏn, and Chŏnju. The inrush of venture capital that in 2001 made up approximately 30 percent of about U.S.$100 million of annual total investment in local film production has largely been invested in the conventional genre films that curtail cinephile culture.[16]

The demand for the diversification of cinema, which is the central rationale for keeping the quota system alive, has not exactly been effective in keeping film production in Korea diverse. The protest campaign against the U.S. pressure to remove all protective mechanisms in cinema had effectively focused on the argument that cultural products cannot abide by the laws of the market for they will only erase cultural heterogeneity and induce "McDonaldization." The irony of the Korean film industry is that it has localized the conventions and praxis of Hollywood to such a successful degree that it has produced formulaic films that are appealing even to Hollywood.[17] The year 2001, the first profitable year for the Korean film industry in many years, also proved to be an aberrant year. Despite holding firm to the share of the entire market at around 45 percent, most big-budget films in the subsequent year flopped at the box office, driving many investment companies either into bankruptcy or out of the film industry altogether.

A concerned filmmaker like Tsai Ming-liang (whose quote is featured at the beginning of this chapter) or Wim Wenders (who has once stated that "The Americans have colonized our subconscious"[18]) may be able to point that the reason for the decline of American supremacy in Korea is due to the increase of indigenous products that mimic Hollywood. While Korean cinema's commercial viability provided a working environment conducive for the filmmakers who wish to emulate the style of Hollywood, it has stripped the creative liberties of filmmakers who desire to make films that stand outside the convention of Hollywood. Not even the government subsidy that pledged U.S.$200 million for the five-year period (1999–2003) has yet to establish one theater that operates outside the market interest. Already vanished is the diverse movie-going culture that had previously elated foreign critics. Tony Rayns had declared as late as 1998 that Korea was a "cinephile nation," citing a three-screen downtown multiplex that was then showing Jang Sun-woo's *Timeless, Bottomless Bad Movie*, a Hollywood thriller *Anaconda*, and Kiarostami's *Through the Olive Trees* on the same day.[19] In the early 2000s, one is likely to find a multiplex theater to be playing a list of films (many of them occupying more than one screen) that would not be radically different in its character from a typical theater in a U.S. suburban shopping mall. Genre films comprise this list. Even though half of them are films made in Korea, they are mostly conventional works that have domesticated much of the foreign personalities. Outside the film festival circuits and special screening events, distribution outlets for local art films are now more malnourished than ever.[20]

David Bordwell explains that the European art films of the 1960s and the 1970s were able to constitute a distinctive branch of the cinematic institution because of the small nature of the national film industries from which they were derived. He writes, a "small industry is devoted to informing viewers of [art films'] authorial marks. International film festivals, reviews and essays in the press, published scripts, film series, career retrospectives, and film education all introduce viewers to authorial codes."[21] Despite the fact that Korean cinema has enjoyed commercial rejuvenation since 1999, it is only a small market. Its film industry's annual revenue for all of its products is 175.3 billion won (equivalent of U.S.$146 million), which only equals the production cost of *one* big-budget film in Hollywood.[22] Korean films cannot match the commercial successes of Hollywood when there is limited potential for earnings beyond the local revenue. Korean cinema's recent technical fluency in creating the genre of comedies that feature gangsters is not surprising, given the fact that they are the only locally brewed genre proven to succeed in the box office.

Political Construction of Gender in South Korean Blockbusters

It is perhaps not coincidental that two of the most commercially viable film industries of the last twenty years (Hong Kong and South Korea) were built in a region where both hyperbolic activities of market economy and anxieties of political transformation (the 1997 handover of Hong Kong to Communist China and the ushering in of democracy in South Korea throughout the 1990s) conditioned the frenzied state of society and culture. The system of capitalism is intricately tied to the process of shoring up the gender traits to compensate for the phallic lack that is necessitated by social instability. The Korean War and the postwar authoritarianism had unleashed political terror that eventually led to the characterization of trauma through male masochism. But, while the auteur-led cinemas that were showcased abroad in international art-house festivals had cultivated these characters of inefficient male intellectuals, during the 1990s, genre films vied for remasculinization, transposing its own historical pain and gentrifying it into the pleasurable elements of gender relations ready for commercial consumption. The successes of *Shiri* and *JSA* attest that the previously sensitive topics such as the nation's division can now be exploited as a theme that reconciles not the interest of generations of Koreans who were traumatized by the war, but that of the young moviegoers who grew up in a post-authoritarian environment. Rarely would a film today foreground a theme that releases anxiety, fear, and desire within a political discourse without invoking some form of pleasurable entertainment value that dehistoricizes it.

Through the relegation of the political crisis onto the body of a woman, the male subjectivities in a modern environment are born. The disfiguration of the woman covers up their incompetence and instability. The two bullets fired during the climax of the two films, *Shiri* and *JSA*, one aimed at the female other (Yi Pang-hŭi) and the other one at the male self (Su-hyŏk) do not disrupt the masculine order and universe. Instead, they testify and legitimize violence as the normative praxis that disavows the fragile nature of masculine rationality. The narcissistic tendency and the male cupidity transpose the man's lack and his continual shift between the Imaginary and the Symbolic onto the double agency of woman. In *Shiri* the women are destroyed, and in *JSA* men become self-destructive, leaving the women on the fringe and the men obsessed. Fueled by the genre codes of blockbuster films that conventionalize the narrative pleasures of male gaze and sadistic impulse, Korea's conflicting enrollment in the global capitalist system of the early twentieth century becomes the nodal point where other nations in Asia can also safely share a post-traumatic identity. The overlapping of history's erasure (through the evocation of the North Koreans as fetishistic entities that are detached from the real) and the masculine identity's recuperation in these films are not coincidental as the losses and pain in history and the constant threats against the changing social environment are fantastically rendered to be instances of disavowal and revival, a revival that has more particular resonance for the male gender.

Freud writes, "we are accustomed to say that every human being displays both male and female instinctual impulses, needs and attributes; but though anatomy, it is true, can point out the characteristic of maleness and femaleness, psychology cannot. For psychology the contrast between the sexes fades away into one between activity and passivity [that is, in describing the organization of the drives], in which we far too readily identify activity with maleness and passivity with femaleness, a view which is *by no means* universally confirmed" (my emphasis).[23] Being a man or a woman is a culturally defined term that exchanges evolving meanings and multiple functions over history. In Korean cinema of the last two decades of the twentieth century, the vicissitudes of masculinity follow the trajectory that shifts from a self-loathing pathetic being that desires to be controlled (masochism) to a self-sufficient subject that is capable destroying others (sadism). Meanwhile the female subject is fetishistically cast, fixed in an opposition that underpins not only the gender imbalance of power, but also Korean cinema's commercialization that has adopted a narrative convention akin to Hollywood's.

The crucial question remains unanswered: Where is the woman's place in Korean cinema? In a Korean narrative film, could the female subject identify and desire relations of power that do not invoke the unity and the totality of the diegesis without perpetually returning to the traumatic origin of masculine identity: the castration? In other words, could a story ever be conceived in cinema without "demanding" sadism?[24] As Barthes once stated, there may be a universal quality in a narrative where it simply assumes traits of "international, transhistorical, and transcultural . . . simply there, like life itself,"[25] delimiting the possibilities of narrative logic and pattern not only in Hollywood, but also in all commercial forms. Because there would be no desire without an object to desire, and no cinema without the desire to represent, the position of women in the male-dominated discourse (as a praxis of looking in cinema, language, and narrative) is bound to be irreducibly contradictory. Korean cinema has vied to recuperate a modern identity and also a story that complements and formulates this ideal. Yet the woman is once again posited at once as the object that stands only in relation to man's drive toward mastery of his time, environment, and being. In a medium borne out of fantasy, this kind of production of woman proves to be, without equivocation, only excessively prohibitive.

NOTES

Introduction: Hunting for the Whale

1 *Whale Hunting* was the fourth-ranked film in the box office of the 1980s, tallying 426,000 receipts in Seoul alone. (In Korea, until very recently, the box-office results from regions and cities other than Seoul could not be tallied since regional film distributors paid their fees in advance of a film's production and were not required to disclose their final accounting figures.) *Whale Hunting* spawned one sequel the following year and also established one of the most popular cultural tropes throughout the decade, with the theme song becoming a classic tune on airwaves. Theatrical musical productions based on the same plot also were produced during the 1990s.

2 The sex scene between Pyŏng-t'ae and Ch'un-ja is experimentally structured through black and white still frames, something that is familiar to contemporary audiences of Korean cinema as the style of Yi Myŏng-se, the director of *Nowhere to Hide* (*Injŏng sajŏng polgŏt ŏpta*, 1999). This is not coincidental; Yi Myŏng-se worked as an assistant director of Pae Ch'ang-ho on *Whale Hunting*.

3 Pyŏng-t'ae is a character that was originally created by the best-selling writer, Ch'oe In-ho. Pyŏng-t'ae's cinematic popularity dates back to 1976, when he was first characterized in *The March of Fools* (*Pabodŭl ŭi haengjin*), a film by movie critic and maverick director Ha Kil-jong. Pyŏng-t'ae was self-loathing in a comical way; a college student whose inability to verbalize his love to a woman tormented him. His reticence, albeit nihilistically cast, allegorized the period of military dictatorship that stretched throughout the 1980s, during which time dissenting intellectuals, students, and workers were forced to remain silent. Lacking eloquence, Pyŏng-t'ae was trapped in his misery and blamed himself for his cowardice, rather than externalizing his frustration. In 1987, Pae Chang-ho, the director of *Whale Hunting*, again gave the name Pyŏng-t'ae to the central protagonist of yet another road movie, *Hello! God* (*Ann-*

yŏnghaseyo hananim). Pyŏng-t'ae, this time handicapped with epileptic spasms and a verbal stammer, was an adult who had not yet grown up.

4   The relationship between a young intellectual and an unfortunate whore whose body is dirtied is nothing new in the context of Korean culture. Yi Kwang-su's nationalist novel written in 1917, *Mujŏng* (*The Heartless*), which was one of the first bestsellers of the twentieth-century, features a narrative whose protagonist Hyŏng-sik, a young English teacher of high aspirations, agonizes over his romantic commitment to a *kisaeng* (courtesan), a daughter of his teacher and a victim of rape.

5   Slavoj Žižek, *The Sublime Object of Ideology* (New York: Verso, 1989), 6.

6   See David E. James, "Im Kwon-Taek: Korean National Cinema and Buddhism," in *Im Kwon-Taek: The Makings of a Korean National Cinema*, eds. David E. James and Kyung Hyun Kim (Detroit: Wayne State University Press, 2001), 47–83.

7   Shim Hye-jin, the actress in the role of Yŏng-suk in *Black Republic*, has played virtually the same whore character in other films that are representative of the period: *White Badge*, *Out to the World*, and *Green Fish*. See the chapter on road movies for a more detailed analysis of Shim Hye-jin's screen persona in the 1990s.

8   Roy Armes, *Third World Film Making and the West* (Berkeley: University of California Press, 1987), 156.

9   The controversies surrounding Kim Ki-dŏk's work have become almost an annual festivity among Korean critics since his debut in 1996. *The Isle* (Sŏm, 2000) and *A Bad Guy* have especially irked feminist critics who have claimed that his films are "sexual terrors against women" (Chu Yu-shin). Many critics however have also supported his work, calling him "the only 'new' director in the thirty years of Korean film history" (Yu Un-sŏng). See "Na nŭn wae Kim Ki-dŏk ŭl chiji hanŭnga" [Why I support/object to Kim Ki-dŏk], *Ssine 21* [*Cine 21*] 18 (January 2002).

10 Susan Jeffords, *The Remasculinization of American Culture: Gender and the Vietnam War* (Bloomington: Indiana University Press, 1989).

11 The psychic desire to exert a strong and masculine identity in recent Chinese literature is a phenomenon that is specifically linked to what Xueping Zhong calls "yinsheng yangshuai" (the rise of the feminine and the decline of the masculine), which is a perception that was popularly accepted during the early 1980s in China. Xueping Zhong, *Masculinity Besieged? Issues of Modernity and Male Subjectivity in Chinese Literature of the Late Twentieth Century* (Durham: Duke University Press, 2000), 5.

12 *Shiri* was a blockbuster hit in Japan and Hong Kong as well. For a review of the film, see David Scott Diffrient, "Shiri," *Film Quarterly*, vol. 54, no. 3 (spring 2001): 40–46.

13 See chapter 9 for discussions of *Shiri* and *JSA*.

14 Max Horkheimer and Theodor W. Adorno, *Dialectic of Enlightenment* (New York: Continuum, 1994), 33.

15 Ibid., 36.

16 Sigmund Freud, *Beyond the Pleasure Principle*, trans. and ed. James Strachey (New York: Liveright, 1961), 34.

17 Ibid., 38.

18 Ibid., 46.

19 Ibid., 54.

20 The *objet petit a*, a crucial Lacanian term, indicates that both the lack and the surplus of the

other is constituted as an incessantly craved object of desire. In Slavoj Žižek's words, it is "the chimerical object of fantasy, the object causing our desire and at the same time—this is its paradox—posed *retroactively* by this desire . . ." (*The Sublime Object of Ideology*, 65). This retroactivity is only possible because of the reverse movement of the Lacanian signifying chain that vectors back through the *point de capiton* to the subject before the signifier has fully rendered its meaning or "a letter always reaches its destination" as Lacan euphemistically stated in his essay, "*The Purloined Letter*." This essay can be found in *The Seminar of Jacques Lacan: Book II, The Ego in Freud's Theory and in the Technique of Psychoanalysis 1954–1955*, ed. Jacques-Alain Miller (New York: W. W. Norton & Company, 1991). To read more on the graph of retroactivity, see Jacques Lacan, "Subversion of the Subject and Dialectic of Desire," in *Écrits: A Selection*, trans. Alan Sheridan (New York: W. W. Norton & Company, 1977), 292–324.

21 Laura Kipnis, "Adultery," *Critical Inquiry*, vol. 24, no. 2 (winter 1998): 291.

22 Kaja Silverman, *Male Subjectivity at the Margins* (New York: Routledge, 1992), 30.

23 See Seungsook Moon, "Begetting the Nation: The Androcentric Discourse of National History and Tradition in South Korea," in *Dangerous Women: Gender & Korean Nationalism*, ed. Elaine H. Kim and Chungmoo Choi (New York: Routledge, 1998), 33–66.

24 The subject of national ethics that focused on specific moments in history was formally administered by the Park Chung Hee regime through the creation of several institutions that mobilized research for these purposes. Seungsook Moon writes, "Admiral Yi [Sun-shin] was elevated to the position of a 'sacred hero' who saved the nation from total destruction and inspired many young men who inherited the spirit of *hwarang* (elite youth corps from the Silla period of seventh-century) to join *ŭibyŏng* (the righteous army)" (ibid., 43).

25 Though Korean cinema has financially rebounded from the embarrassing and miserable days of the 1980s when its most successful films were erotic films and formulaic melodramas, it has still not matched the commercial success of the Golden Age. During the late 1960s and the early 1970s, over 200 films were produced by the film industry. Theaters were the most popular family entertainment venue, drawing over 173 million audiences in 1969. In comparison, despite the population growth, in 2001 only about 82 million tickets were sold nationwide.

26 The "quality film" policy was perhaps the most significant reason behind the demise of the Golden Age of Korean Cinema in the 1970s. Together with the "quota quickies" that abused the quota system on foreign films, quality films ravaged the domestic industry. On the subject of "quality film" policy, see my "Korean Cinema and Im Kwon-Taek: an Overview," in *Im Kwon-Taek: the Making of a Korean National Cinema*, 26–28.

27 With the government encouraging films that heroically depict historical figures, the 1970s was a period when many narratives featured heroes sacrificing themselves to defend the nation. Some of them, including *The Great King Sejong* (*Sejong Daewang*, Ch'oe In-hyŏn, dir., 1978), were not exhibited for the public even though they were among the most expensive Korean films ever made. *The Great King Sejong* cost 500 million won (approximately U.S.$12 million) to produce, clearly the most expensive Korean film to have been made until most recently. See Lee Young-Il, *The History of Korean Cinema: Main Current of Korean Cinema* (Seoul, Korea: Motion Picture Promotion Corporation, 1988), 206–7.

28 The Golden Age of Korean Cinema that began immediately after the Korean War in the mid-1950s lasted roughly until the early 1970s. An amendment in the motion picture laws passed in 1973 was one of the main reasons for its precipitous and premature end. In order to better

control the film industry, the government, which then had just passed the Yushin constitution, gave a lifetime term of president to Park Chung Hee, and also stiffened the guidelines on
social and cultural freedom, forcibly merging the many existing production companies into
twelve.

29 Korean cinema had a long history of emasculated and inauspicious images of male characters
on screen. Na Un-gyu was quite possibly Korea's first legitimate movie star during the Japanese
colonial period. Na's emaciated and maddening persona unleashed the fury and frustration
that allegorized Korea's grief as a nation without its sovereignty. But he was hardly a muscular
masculine icon; his star image was instead generated from his short and toad-like look that
suited him in peasant roles.

30 I will later return to a more elaborate discussion of "post-trauma" and the ways in which it is
particularly expressed in films. Read the introduction to section I: "Genres of Post-Trauma"
and chapter 4: "Post-Trauma and Historical Remembrance in *A Single Spark* and *A Petal*."

31 Park Chung Hee was shot by Kim Chae-gyu, the director of his secret service agency, at a dinner party. Kim was ironically one of the only two men who could carry a firearm around Park.

32 Although there were a few signs of Park's political demise in the late 1970s, such as the labor
union strife and urban protests in Pusan and Masan, cities in the southeast that led popular
insurgence, because of his strong record in the postwar restructuring of the Korean economy,
it was not anticipated that Park would fall from power so suddenly.

33 I return to the discussion of Kwangju in chapter 4 while discussing *A Petal*, which cinematically
depicts Kwangju.

34 Bruce Cumings, "Introduction," in Lee Jae-eui, *Kwangju Diary: Beyond Death, Beyond the
Darkness of the Age*, trans. Kap Su Seol and Nick Mamatas (Los Angeles: UCLA Asian Pacific
Monograph Series, 1999), 25.

35 Kim Young Sam was voted into office in 1992 only because of the overwhelming votes (close
to 90 percent) for him in the Kyŏngsang Province, his home. In the next presidential election in 1997, Kim Dae Jung, whose popular base was in Chŏlla, won only because the votes
for him exceeded 90 percent in his home province. He won despite his failure to compete in
Kyŏngsang.

36 In a survey taken in 1979, more than half of the respondents replied that they considered themselves to be a part of the lower class. This statistic dramatically changed during the 1980s when
the middle class markedly grew. See "Kukmin pan isang i na nŭn haryu saenghwal" (More
than half the population responds "I have a low class life"), *Tong-a Ilbo* (December 7, 1979).
During the 1980s and the 1990s, the middle class exploded in Korea. In 1997, more than 65
percent of the survey respondents claimed to be members of the middle class (*Chungang Ilbo*
[Central Daily], September 16, 1998, p. 1).

37 The expansion and rising wages of the middle class sustained the consumerist boom throughout the 1980s. Middle-class income was 70 percent of the income of the upper class until the
early 1980s, when middle-class income grew quickly, as it was strengthened by the rise of sal-
aries and job security of the industrial working class in the mid- to late-1980s. Middle-class
wages rose to an all-time high, proportionally to that of the upper class, and became 75.8
percent of upper class income in 1992 (*Chungang Ilbo*, May 30, 1998).

38 The financial confidence of the middle class was confirmed by the monthly financing programs for television sets and automobiles that were heavily advertised in the newspapers. As
early as 1980, catchphrases like *mai k'a sidae* (my car generation) became popular. A Samsung

color television set could be purchased in 1980 for a monthly payment as low as 10,000 won, newspapers then advertised.

39   Laura C. Nelson, *Measured Excess* (New York: Columbia University Press, 2000), 22. The Summer Olympic Games held in Seoul in 1988 allowed Korea to further expose its local market to the rest of the globe and to celebrate a new culture of indulgences and excess. The orgiastic ceremonies visualizing and showcasing the "economic miracle" were broadcasted globally, generating envies and aggravating despairs of its neighboring nation with more recent historical misfortunes. Immediately after the Olympics, *Bingbai Hancheng* (*Military Humiliation in Seoul*), a lengthy book that covers Seoul, became a bestseller in China, prompting the political leaders in Beijing to seek its own Olympics. Now the spacious Olympic Park in Seoul is seldom used and the vast recreational grass area remains off limits to the public, who must only walk on the paved paths outside it. See Xudong Zhang, *Chinese Modernism in the Era of Reforms: Cultural Fever, Avant-Garde Fiction, and the New Chinese Cinema* (Durham: Duke University Press, 1997), 412.

40   Chun seems to have understood that "the more frustrated or blocked the aspirations to 'democracy' are, the more the market booms," because "if you cannot choose your political leaders, you can at least choose your own cloths." Like the case in Hong Kong, where the critic Ackbar Abbas wrote the passage above, if the sizeable middle class has the power to purchase Levi's jeans, own Hyundai sedans, eat at McDonald's, and watch Hollywood movies, the authorities in Korea assumed that they would not mind that they were dispossessed of their rights to vote. History attests that the middle class in Korea eventually did care as virtually the entire population protested Chun Doo Hwan's initial decision to deny constitutional amendments to allow direct election of the president in 1987. Ackbar Abbas, *Hong Kong: Culture and the Politics of Disappearance* (Minneapolis: University of Minnesota Press, 1997), 5.

41   It was through the representation of the female bodies victimized by patriarchic tradition that Im Kwon-Taek patented his allegories of Korea in his films made during the 1980s. For a more explicit analysis of Im Kwon-Taek's style and theme, see my essay, "Korean Cinema and Im Kwon-Taek: An Overview," in *Im Kwon-Taek: The Making of a Korean National Cinema*, 19–46.

42   Because of the North Korean *chuch'e* (self-reliance) ideology, which represented one of the most important principles for radical intellectuals in South Korea, and of the South Korean state that then abdicated any movement toward reconciliation between the two Koreas, South Korean leftist politics of the day were fused with nationalism. Some viewed the popular movement for democracy in South Korea as an anticolonial struggle. *Minjok* (nation) became a category that was as totalizing as, if not more than, *minjung* (people) under which leftist insurgence was mobilized. Although there have been arguments that cast minjok of the 1980s as a democratic, counter-hegemonic trope (see Henry H. Em's "Overcoming Korea's Division: Narrative Strategies in Recent South Korean Historiography," in *positions: east asia cultures critique*, vol. 1, no. 2 [fall 1993]: 450–85), it would be almost impossible to overlook the "totalizing" and "othering" processes that the minjung intellectuals have continually invoked in constructing and representing the "people." See Chungmoo Choi's critique of minjung intellectuals and ideology in her "Decolonization and Popular Memory: South Korea," in *positions: east asia cultures critique*, vol. 1, no. 1 (spring 1993): 77–102, particularly 97–99.

43   Quoted in Silverman's *Male Subjectivity at the Margins*, 54.

44   Fredric Jameson, *The Political Unconscious: Narrative as a Socially Symbolic Act* (Ithaca, N.Y.: Cornell University Press, 1981), 101.

45 Michel Foucault, "Language to Infinity," in *Language, Counter-Memory, Practice*, ed. Donald Bouchard (Ithaca, N.Y.: Cornell University Press, 1977), 56.

46 The film's narrative movement backwards in time is not entirely new in the history of feature films. Jane Campion's Australian film, *2 Friends* (1986), chronicles the year-long destruction of the friendship of two adolescent girls from the moment they are broken up at the film's end to where they are freeze-framed intimately at the height of their relationship. More recently, *Memento* (Christopher Nolan, dir., 2000) also employed a similar narrative strategy to travel backwards in time.

47 Helene Moglen, *The Trauma of Gender: A Feminist Theory of the English Novel* (Berkeley: University of California Press, 2001), 7.

48 What must be noted, however, is that these political films were not directly protesting the governmental position of history. By the time *White Badge* was made, more than a decade had passed since Park Chung Hee's death, and a number of Hollywood films about Vietnam that took a liberal-humanist view of the war — such as Michael Cimino's *Deer Hunter* (a film that is self-reflexively acknowledged in *White Badge*), Oliver Stone's *Platoon* and Francis Ford Coppola's *Apocalypse Now* — had been released in Korea. These developments had allowed the making of *White Badge*, a film critical of Park Chung Hee and his role in the Vietnam War, without much political controversy. Also, *Peppermint Candy* was made and first screened in 1999, the first year of Kim Dae Jung's presidency. Kim was a dissident politician from the Chŏlla Province who had been sentenced to death for his role in "inciting riots" in Kwangju.

Part I   Genres of Post-Trauma

1 Thomas Sobchack, "Genre Film: A Classical Experience," in *Film Genre Reader*, ed. Barry Keith Grant (Austin: University of Texas Press, 1986), 112.

1   At the Edge of a Metropolis in *A Fine, Windy Day* and *Green Fish*

1 During the 1970s, the Korean film industry suffered box-office setbacks. After the peak year, 1968, when the average Korean made 5.7 visits to the movie theaters a year, the movie-going pattern dramatically changed during the ensuing decade. In 1982, only 1.1 movie tickets per capita were sold. Because of the competition created by the widespread dissemination of television, the Yushin Constitution of the Park Chung Hee era that consolidated and censored the film industry, and the quota system that restricted foreign films, cinema could not sustain the public's interest. Only in the mid-1990s did the public's interest in cinema revive, making possible the Korean cinema's renaissance. See chapter 9 for a detailed account of Korean cinema's commercial revival.

2 See chapter 3 for a more elaborate discussion on the representation of *yanggongju* and virtuous mothers in Korean War films, especially pages 81–87.

3 Kaja Silverman, *Male Subjectivity at the Margins* (New York: Routledge, 1992), 53.

4 The public reason for Yi Chang-ho's hiatus during the latter part of the 1970s was his arrest for the charge of marijuana inhalation in 1976. Though he had emerged as the "hit" director in Korean cinema with his debut film, *Home of the Stars* (*Pyŏldŭl ŭi kohyang*) in 1974, he had suffered indefinite suspension of all public activity by the state. A small misdemeanor charge that should have only prompted a light fine or a warning by the court resulted in retiring Yi

Chang-ho for deliberate political reasons. This "marijuana" incident gave the government a convenient reason to ban Yi, a director of "social problem" films. Not unlike hundreds of other entertainers who were also prohibited from performing in public during the Park Chung Hee regime for dubious charges, Yi's ban was de facto politically motivated.

5 *A Fine, Windy Day* was theatrically released in 1988 with the promotional line, "Fine, Windy Days Are Back," a direct reference to the social unrest of the day.

6 The young critics of the film journal *Yŏnghwa ŏn'ŏ* (*Film Language*) voted *A Fine, Windy Day* as the best film of the 1990s (*Sŭk'ŭrin* [March 1990]: 235). *A Fine, Windy Day* was also the first film selected in the special series of articles on the Korean film classics in the film monthly, *Sŭk'ŭrin* (*Sŭk'ŭrin* [October 1988]: 312–19).

7 Only a week later, on December 12, 1979, Chun Doo Hwan led a coup d'état that reverted Korea back to military dictatorship.

8 Found guilty of mass murders during the Kwangju massacre—along with mutiny, treason, and corruption—the former president Chun Doo Hwan received a life-sentence in 1996. He was later pardoned by the president-elect Kim Dae Jung in 1998.

9 This demand to amend the censorship laws went unheeded when the rule of military dictatorship continued after Chun Doo Hwan led his military coup. The same censorship effectively continued for almost another fifteen years until the supreme court in Korea finally ruled such censorship "unconstitutional" on October 4, 1996.

10 *All That Heaven Allows* is one of the most important texts in film theory. In his 1972 article, "Tales of Sound and Fury: Observations on the Family Melodrama," Thomas Elsaesser focused on Sirk's films to illustrate how hysteria bubbling below the seemingly placid social surface gushes out into the open. The genre of melodrama characterized by a film text like *All That Heaven Allows* is—in Elsaesser's words—"fixed by the claustrophobic atmosphere of the bourgeois home and/or the small-town setting; its emotional pattern is that of panic and latent hysteria" (Thomas Elssaesser, "Tales of Sound and Fury: Observations on the Family Melodrama" in *Film Genre Reader*, ed. Barry Keith Grant [Austin: University of Texas Press, 1986], 300).

11 This was An Sŏng-gi's first lead role after making his comeback as an adult actor. Having started his career in the 1950s as a child actor, he starred in some of the most important films of the Golden Age, including *The Housemaid*. After concentrating on his education during the 1970s, he made his return in *A Fine, Windy Day*. For over two decades since then, he led the resurgence of Korean cinema. He starred in many Korean films that are representative of the films of the 1980s and the 1990s. Among the films featured in this book, he stars in no less than eight feature works. Other than *A Fine, Windy Day* and *The Housemaid*, he starred in *White Badge*, *Spring in My Hometown*, *The Taebaek Mountains*, *Chilsu and Mansu*, *To the Starry Island*, and *Age of Success*.

12 Roland Barthes, quoted in *The Cinema Book*, ed. Pam Cook (London: BFI, 1985), 52.

13 Chungmoo Choi, "The Magic and Violence of Modernization in Post-Colonial Korean Cinema," in *Post-Colonial Classics of Korean Cinema* catalog (Irvine: University of California, Irvine, 1998), 11.

14 Land speculation precipitated a sharp increase in the real estate and home prices throughout the 1970s and the 1980s. After redirecting its housing projects from a government-initiated one to private projects, the military government worked closely with the *chaebols* in urban development during this time period, allowing, for example, Hyundai Construction Company

to develop large-scale luxury apartments between 1975 and 1983 in Apkujŏngdong along the southern bank of the Han River. See Joochul Kim and Sang-Chul Choe, *Seoul: The Making of a Metropolis* (Chichester, U.K.: John Wiley & Sons, 1997), 196–97.

15 David Harvey asks: "How could a new world be created, after all, without destroying much that had gone before?" While such questions lent justification for many societies to modernize across ideological spectrums, Harvey notes that horror, tragedy, and pain also accompanied this process of development. See David Harvey, *The Condition of Postmodernity* (Cambridge, Mass.: Blackwell, 1990), 16.

16 Silverman, *Male Subjectivity at the Margins*, 7.

17 Ibid., 125.

18 See chapter 5 for a more descriptive analysis of the representation of male crisis in Park Kwang-su's films.

19 Murray Pomerance, "Introduction: Gender in Film at the End of the Twentieth Century," in *Ladies and Gentlemen, Boys and Girls: Gender in Film at the End of the Twentieth Century*, ed. Murray Pomerance (Albany: SUNY Press, 2001), 7.

20 Judith Butler, in *Gender Troubles*, writes: "that the gendered body is performative suggests that it has no ontological status apart from the various acts which constitute its reality" (Judith Butler, *Gender Trouble: Feminism and the Subversion of Identity* [New York: Routledge, 1999], 173). It is this reality that is fabricated, which is no different from fantasy and sustained through corporeal enactments and plays.

21 Yi Ch'ang-dong was an award-winning writer before making films. His collection of short stories, *Nokch'ŏn e nŭn ttong yi mant'a* (*Shit Covers Nokch'ŏn*) (Seoul, Korea: Munhak kwa chisŏng sa, 1992), criticized the society that was becoming increasingly affected by ideological dogma in the 1980s. Yi made his directorial debut, after having coscripted the two films directed by Park Kwang-su, *To the Starry Island* and *A Single Spark*.

22 One of the most popular films made during the colonial period, *The Passenger Boat without the Boatsman* (*Sagong ŏpnŭn narutpae*, Yi Kyu-hwan, dir., 1932), tells the agonizing story of Su-sam, a farmer who arrives in Seoul and works in a menial job first as a rickshaw puller. In the city, he falls prey to the lure of money, committing a theft to provide hospital fees for his pregnant wife. Once he is imprisoned, however, his wife takes another lover, a chauffeur of an automobile (registering a stark contrast with the premodern rickshaw Su-sam "drives"), and leaves him. With only his daughter, Su-sam returns to his rural hometown and finds work, this time transporting passengers across the river on a boat. Reconstructed only as a single father household, the family rediscovers peace. Yet, his happiness is fleeting because the Japanese government commissions a railroad company to provide a rail bridge over the river, posing a threat to the livelihoods of Su-sam and his daughter. To further complicate the matter, the Japanese construction engineer finds the daughter attractive and attempts to seduce her. With both his means of survival and his only remaining love in danger, the boatsman grabs a hatchet and attacks the engineer. The engineer is instantly killed. Consumed with madness, Su-sam resumes his attack on the rail-track. As he continues to fight an inanimate object against which he cannot win, he fails to see the oncoming train, and is also instantly killed. The issue critical here is not the personal loss or the violent temperament of an individual. The madness that drives him is deeply drenched in the collective national fear of colonial modernity that threatens not only to dismantle the things that were once considered to be immutable (the family and the community), but also to deny the prospects modern societies guarantee for

people in the colony, who ultimately cannot equally share an ontological experience as urban citizens.

23 In Yi Ch'ang-dong's second film, *Peppermint Candy*, the male lack is also physically inscribed through the constant limp of Yŏng-ho when in a crisis. See the Introduction for a discussion of this film.

24 Han Sŏk-kyu is quite possibly the first male star of the New Korean Cinema to break the mold of masochistic comedy that typified the Korean male stars for decades. Cast in serious romantic, dramatic, and action roles, he became the most visible box-office draw throughout the late 1990s when Korean cinema had a commercial renaissance. His filmography includes blockbuster hits: *Contact* (*Chŏpsok*, Chang Yun-hyŏn, dir., 1997), *Christmas in August* (*Palwŏl ŭi ch'ŭrisŭmasŭ*, Hŏ Chun-ho, dir., 1998), and *Shiri* (Kang Jae-gyu, dir., 1999). He has recently reprised his conventional persona in his comeback film, *The Double Agent* (*Ijung Kanch'ŏp*, Kim Hyŏn-jŏng, 2003). See chapter 9 for a more extended discussion of *Shiri*.

2 Nowhere to Run: Disenfranchised Men on the Road in *The Man with Three Coffins, Sopyonje*, and *Out to the World*

1 Even the celebrated North Korean films such as *Sea of Blood* (*P'ibada*, Chosŏn Yŏnghwa Ch'waryŏngso, dir., 1969) and *The Flower Girl (Kkot p'anŭn ch'ŏnyŏ*, Chosŏn Yŏnghwa Ch'waryŏngso, 1972) prominently feature the road as a site of suffering.

2 See the introduction for a more detailed discussion of *Whale Hunting*.

3 The same pattern can also be found in the American road movies. While the road movies in the United States often deconstructed and destabilized many of the formulaic mythologies developed by film genres, they also refigured masculinity. In other words, the road movies helped to recuperate a male subject that reeled from the threat of emasculation at a specific moment in history. Ina Rae Hark writes "the man behind the wheel or on the bike is generating that speed, steering those curves, and deciding which exit ramp to take that gives his journey its phallic frisson" (Ina Rae Hark, "Fear of Flying: Yuppie Critique and the Buddy-Road Movie in the 1980s," in *The Road Movie Book*, ed. Steven Cohan and Ina Rae Hark [New York: Routledge, 1997], 214).

4 The film uses an unorthodox casting strategy—not unlike the one utilized by the surrealist films of Luis Bunuel's *That Obscure Object of Desire* (1977)—where both Sun-sŏk's wife and the nurse is played by the same actress, Yi Po-hŭi. Yi Po-hŭi also has a third role in the film as an inexperienced prostitute who dies of a car accident the day after having a sexual relationship with Sun-sŏk.

5 The rendezvous is symptomatic of the dramatic three-day family reunion that the two Korean governments arranged in 1985, two years before the release of *The Man with Three Coffins*. It was the first and only family reunion meeting arranged by the two governments before it became an annual affair in 2000.

6 One cannot help but think that if the old man had lived thirteen more years, he would have had a chance to see his family through the family reunions that began in 2000, fifty years after the outbreak of the Korean War.

7 The two Koreas—despite the recent move toward reconciliation—have yet to sign a peace treaty. They are still technically at war, with only a cease-fire armistice accorded between the two.

8   It should be noted here that the South Korean government monopolized the channel through which any dialogue or contact could be made between the two nations. When North Korea enrolled in the AT&T network in 1995, technically allowing the South Korean civilians to telephone any party in North Korea equipped with a telephone, the South Korean state quickly responded. Only a day after the breaking news, it announced its "official position" concerning the opening of telephone lines between the United States and North Korea. The South Korean government stated that any of its citizens, including the ones with the permanent resident status of the United States, would need a special permission from the Secretary of the Reunification Ministry before communicating with North Korean residents through telephone or fax. Failing to report meant prosecution under the National Security Law, and those found guilty would be subjected to either a maximum sentence of three years or a maximum fine of 10 million won (an equivalent of then U.S.$12,000).

9   The two folktales prominently featured in the film are *Ch'unhyang-ga* and *Simch'ong-ga*.

10 The production company of *Sopyonje*, Taehŭng, had only expected the film to last a few weeks in the first-run theaters, anticipating to sell about 70,000–80,000 tickets. Yet, the film lasted over six months, breaking the box-office record for a local film, selling over one million tickets in Seoul alone. With the regional box-office receipts amounting to another one million, *Sopyonje* became the biggest Korean film hit in history. This record lasted six years until *Shiri* rewrote the history of Korean films in 1999, benefiting from a change of the distribution pattern of typically releasing a film in thirty-plus screens in Seoul alone. (*Sopyonje* only opened on one screen.)

11 In 1993 the Korean film industry, which reluctantly gave way to the demand of the United States to open its market in the late 1980s, saw already four American film companies in operation in Korea: UIP, Warner Brothers, Walt Disney, and 20th Century Fox. By that time, the boycott of American films that was mildly successful in the late 1980s could no longer be effective. Without protest, the Hollywood films dominated Korea's domestic market at an unprecedented pace. While *Sopyonje* received much attention in the popular media, *Cliffhanger* and *Jurassic Park* ended up selling millions of tickets more than *Sopyonje*.

12 While watching the film with my family members in a Korean theater, both of my parents, who lived in cities most of their lives, were exhilarated to find that the vast fields in Korea remain unspoiled by modernization and industrialization. In the book published to commemorate the success of *Sopyonje*, a travel guide has a meticulously drawn map that allows the reader to actually travel through the spots used as film locations.

13 Nick Browne, "Society and Subjectivity: On the Political Economy of Chinese Melodrama," in *The New Chinese Cinema: Forms, Identities, Politics*, ed. Nick Browne et al. (Cambridge, U.K.: Cambridge University Press, 1994), 41.

14 Chungmoo Choi, "The Politics of Gender, Aestheticism and Cultural Nationalism in *Sopyonje* and *Genealogy*," in *Im Kwon-Taek: the Making of a Korean National Cinema*, ed. David E. James and Kyung Hyun Kim (Detroit: Wayne State University Press, 2001), 107–33.

15 Whether or not a rape of Song-hwa takes place in the film has been one of the contentious points raised by scholars. Julian Stringer responds to Chungmoo Choi's claim that Yu-bong "rapes" Song-hwa by stating, "While acknowledging the force of Choi's argument[,] I am on occasion inclined to believe that Yu-bong does not in fact rape his adopted daughter: mistreat, abuse, and blind, yes, but not rape" (Julian Stringer, "*Sopyonje* and the Inner Domain of National Culture," in *Im Kwon-Taek: the Making of a Korean National Cinema*, 181).

16 Thomas Elsaesser, "Tales of Sound and Fury: Observations on the Family Melodrama," in *Film Genre Reader*, ed. Barry Keith Grant (Austin: University of Texas Press, 1986), 278–308.

17 Choi suggests that the return of Tong-ho can be compared to "the revolutionary son in many North Korean narratives [like *Sea of Blood* (1969) and *The Flower Girl* (1972)], who returns to complete the revolution and claim the credit for winning the struggle." She writes, "Tong-ho returns to authenticate Song-hwa's attempt to reestablish the preeminence of the national sound over the colonial music" (Choi, "The Politics of Gender, Aestheticism and Cultural Nationalism in *Sopyonje* and *The Genealogy*," in *Im Kwon-Taek: the Making of a Korean National Cinema*, 121). I have a slightly different interpretation of the ending. Choi's comparison of Tong-ho with some of the heroic returns of male sons to claim the victory of socialist insurgence in the classic films from North Korea after being missing during the entire narrative is not completely appropriate since North Korean films do not nostalgically yearn for a past tainted by unfulfilled, unrequited love. The socialist realist films invoke the colonial past not for the sake of lamentation, but for their celebration of anticolonial victory, however imagined this may be. In so doing, the constitution of the phallic subject as a revolutionary, historical, and symbolic subject ushers a post-traumatic, postcolonial identity. *Sopyonje*, on the other hand, remembers the past not through the declaration of a postcolonial era in which the Name of the Father has been issued and formulated as the central subjectivity; its present moment is one that is still complicated by loss, trauma, and denied love where a celebration can only take place by the acknowledgment of the phallus [the dead father, Yu-bong] as something that is lost, forever out of reach, at least in the physical realm. Choi is, however, right in pointing out that the heterosexual reunion at the end of *Sopyonje* can hardly be overlooked as it strongly suggests that the recuperation of national aesthetics is a sexualized matter only the return of a male subject can muster.

18 See chapter 5 for a more explicit discussion of films directed by Park Kwang-su.

19 As if to demonstrate that the road movies are only popular at times of socio-political crisis, the genre quickly fell out of public's favor after *Out to the World*. The only notable road movie made between 1994 and 2000 was *The Declaration of Geniuses* (*Ch'ŏnjae sŏnŏn*, 1998), Yi Chang-ho's sequel to *The Declaration of Fools*, a film that failed to attract the interest of the public and critics.

20 *Out to the World*'s director Yŏ Kyun-dong was himself a dissident intellectual during the 1980s. Yŏ participated in protest theaters and translated the philosophical books of Hegel and Lukács into Korean. *Out to the World* was not the first film Yŏ wanted to make. *Porno Man* was slated as his first film project before it was canned by the censors. That film would have explored men's innate desires and fantasies. *Out to the World* was both a critical and popular success, yielding the third largest box-office results among all Korean films released that year, 1994. The film even drew more critical raves and bigger crowds than the highly anticipated feature from Im Kwon-Taek, *The Taebaek Mountains* (*T'aebaek sanmaek*), which was also released the same year. Yŏ's second feature, *Porno Man*, was finally made in 1996, but it ironically flopped at the box office and was shunned by the critics.

21 The film playfully retained the real names of the actors, Mun Sŏng-gŭn, Yi Kyŏng-yŏng, and Shim Hye-jin for the fictional names in the film.

22 *Segyehwa* (globalization) has been a consistent political theme of the Kim Young-sam administration (1993–98). In his 1996 New Year speech, segyehwa was stressed as one of three tasks

of South Korea, which in Kim's words needed a new global orientation rather than insistence of old practices and values (*Tong-a Ilbo*, January 9, 1996, p. 1).

23 The military presidents, Chun Doo Hwan and Roh Tae Woo, who ordered thousands of civilians shot dead during the Kwangju massacre of 1980, had not yet been tried in the court.

24 The film is loosely based on the Chŏnju Prison Jailbreak Incident where the shooting of several refugees was captured on television, precipitating a debate on whether such cruel live footage was appropriate for television broadcast. The debate did not question the authority's decision to kill the refugees.

25 Michael Ryan and Douglas Kellner write, "Redford and Newman are the most important romantic couple of the [sixties] period" (*Camera Politica: the Politics and Ideology of Contemporary Hollywood Film* [Bloomington: Indiana University Press, 1990], 151).

26 Steven Cohan, *Masked Men: Masculinity and the Movies in the Fifties* (Bloomington: Indiana University Press, 1997).

27 The representation of homosexuality is still a very repressed subject in Korean cinema. Until 2002, there has been only one feature film that has openly engaged homosexuality by foregrounding gay characters at the center of narrative: *Broken Branches* (*Naeil ro hŭrŭnŭn kang*, Pak Chae-ho, dir., 1995). *The Pollen* (*Hwabun*, Ha Kil-jong, dir., 1974), *When Adam Awakens* (*Adam ŭi nŭnttŭl ttae*, Kim Ho-sŏn, dir., 1993), and *To You, from Me* (*Nŏ ege narŭl ponenda*, Chang Sŏn-u, dir., 1994) also feature gay characters, but they are all villains, with questionable moral sensibilities.

28 Rey Chow, *Woman and Chinese Modernity: the Politics of Reading Between West and East* (Minneapolis: University of Minnesota Press, 1991), 124.

29 This has been recounted from the point Fredric Jameson made of Taiwan, "a post-Third World country that can never really join the First World," in his analysis of *Terrorizer* directed by Edward Yang. See Fredric Jameson, *The Geopolitical Aesthetic: Cinema and Space in the World System* (Indianapolis: Indiana University Press, 1992), 145.

30 *Until Daybreak* (Hangyŏre Production, curated by Park Hye-jung for "The Revolution Will Be Televised: Social Movements in Asia" series, 1990) replays the real image of a student throwing himself off a roof, evidently in a suicide during a demonstration rally. This horrible scene is immediately superceded by a slow-motion shaman ritual, with a performer dancing around his dead body.

3 "Is This How the War Is Remembered?": Violent Sex and the Korean War in *Silver Stallion, Spring in My Hometown,* and *The Taebaek Mountains*

1 Cho, Chŏng-nae, "Land of Exile," in *Land of Exile: Contemporary Korean Fiction*, trans. and ed. Marshall R. Pihl, Bruce and Ju-Chan Fulton (New York: M. E. Sharpe, 1993), 212–13.

2 This province, located in Korea's southwest, is a traditional farming area; it was the site of fierce ideological contest during the war. It is also the homeland of both Cho Chŏng-nae and Im Kwon-Taek. See the Introduction for further description of Chŏlla Province.

3 After turning over his malnourished, six-year-old son to an orphanage, Mansŏk, decrepit and wretched, returns to his hometown, only to suffer an anonymous death.

4 Chungmoo Choi, "Nationalism and Construction of Gender in Korea," in *Dangerous Women: Gender and Korean Nationalism*, ed. Elaine H. Kim and Chungmoo Choi, (New York: Routledge, 1998), 17.

5   The only Korean War film that falls outside this conventional characterization comprising reputable men and shameful women is *Spring in My Hometown*, which depicts the father as a character who is complicit with the foreign colonizers. See pages 87–93.

6   *Seven Female Prisoners* focuses on a North Korean officer and his psychological dilemma before he defects to the South during the war. Although it is hardly a film that praises socialism or criticizes the South, the film's director, Yi Man-hŭi was prosecuted for not following the ideological mantra of the government, which firmly stipulated "no film will positively represent any member of the People's Army."

7   Yi Man-hŭi was eventually released, without being found guilty or innocent, and his sentence was suspended. The court took into consideration his rationale: Yi and his supporters insisted that his film is art, which deserves constitutional protection in accordance with the precepts of freedom of expression.

8   The diminished significance of Chŏlla Province in popular culture throughout the postwar period well into the 1980s reflects the unfair treatment the region has received politically and economically, despite its productive rice fields. Bruce Cumings writes, "The Chŏllas [of the southwest] had been left alone to feed rice to Japan in the colonial period, and they were left alone as the [Park Chung Hee] regime poured new investment into the southeast" (Bruce Cumings, *Korea's Place in the Sun: A Modern History* [New York: W. W. Norton & Company, 1997], 362).

9   The pilots in the Korean air force featured in *The Red Mufflers* (*Ppalgan mahura*, Shin Sang-ok, dir., 1964) are ill-equipped and inexperienced. Yet they are spiritually elated as they risk their lives, not only because the mission is strategically important—to destroy the enemy's bridge—but more importantly because it cannot be accomplished by the Americans, despite their technological superiority.

10 Cumings, *Korea's Place in the Sun*, 238.

11 For a more descriptive elaboration of Junghyo Ahn's novella *Silver Stallion*, see Hyun Sook Kim's excellent essay, "Yanggongju as an Allegory of the Nation: The Representation of Working-Class Women in Popular and Radical Texts," in *Dangerous Women: Gender and Korean Nationalism*, ed. Elaine H. Kim and Chungmoo Choi (New York: Routledge, 1998), 175–201.

12 Choi, "Nationalism and Construction of Gender in Korea," in *Dangerous Women*, 17.

13 Ibid, 25.

14 Here, I draw on the theory of Lacanian Imaginary/Symbolic where the child first learns to identify with the mother through the mirror that reflects the child's identity both separate from and together with her's (Imaginary), and the child later becomes aware—often traumatically—of the presence of the father (Symbolic). See Jacques Lacan, *Écrits: A Selection*, trans. Alan Sheridan (New York: W. W. Norton & Company, 1977). See especially "The mirror stage of formative of the function of the I" (pp. 1–7) and "The function and field of speech and language in psychoanalysis" (pp. 30–113) for descriptive explanations of the Imaginary/Symbolic.

15 The absence of the patriarchal authority is reaffirmed by the legendary general on a silver stallion who has failed to show up in the moment of national crisis.

16 At the time of intense demonstrations against Hollywood's demand to eliminate the Korean film industry's screen quota that puts a cap on the screening days of the Hollywood films during the winter of 1998–99, *Spring in My Hometown* was the only Korean film that provided an alternative to Hollywood filmmaking strategies. The popularly advertised demonstrations of

the local film stars marching in the streets of Seoul against the monopolistic practice of Hollywood helped this local film in receiving attention from many critics and intellectuals. Even the famous poet, Kim Chi-ha, wrote in one of his columns praising the film as an example of the remarkable achievement of local aesthetics.

17 Among the fifty films listed in the annual Top 10 box-office Korean films during the five-year period from 1994 to 1998, only four films foreground history as their meta-trope of narrative: *The Taebaek Mountains* (1994), *A Petal* (1996), *To the Starry Island* (1994), and *A Single Spark* (1995). The last two are made by the same director, Park Kwang-su.

18 Cumings, *Korea's Place in the Sun*, 304.

19 Quoted in Cumings, *Korea's Place in the Sun*, 303.

20 The red paint that cannot be rubbed off the father reminds us also of the witch-hunting label for the "commie" families in the village; it solicits viewers' sympathy.

21 Only once is her suffering communicated to the father in the film. When Yŏng-suk, now out of work, asks her father whether her boyfriend will ever come for a visit, the father tells her that he will soon. The father compliments him by adding that there aren't many like him. The exchange between the two reveals both the desperate status of Yŏng-suk, who remains deserted by her lover after being pregnant, and the powerlessness of the father, who ends up having to lie to his daughter that her boyfriend will soon come for a visit (though the two will never meet again).

22 The film was well received at the 1998 Cannes Film Festival. Although the film did not compete in the festival, it was listed as one of the most popular films featured at Cannes. It also won the best picture award at the 1998 Tokyo International Film Festival.

23 Bruce Cumings, in his superb research on the Korean War, has repeatedly asserted that the war had no single cause but rather many overlapping ones. See Bruce Cumings, *The Origins of the Korean War: Liberation and the Emergence of Separate Regimes* (Princeton: Princeton University Press, 1981).

24 *The Taebaek Mountains* was supposed to have been made in 1992, before the making of *Sopyonje*. However, it was canned after government officials told Im that it should be deferred until the inauguration of a civilian government. A director not noted for opposing the government, Im delayed production of *The Taebaek Mountains* until 1994, one year after Kim Young-sam, the first civilian president since 1961, came into power.

25 Approximately U.S.$2 million was spent on the production of *The Taebaek Mountains*.

26 This highly anticipated film did not do well at the box office, nor did it excite foreign critics; indeed, it was shunned at foreign film festivals. Its failure to generate positive reaction by foreign critics can probably be attributed to its uncritical use of melodramatic conventions.

27 A famous historical figure who had a brother across the ideological barrier is Park Chung Hee, the notorious right-wing military president of South Korea (1961–79). Park's older brother, a socialist, was killed in the Yŏsu-Sunch'ŏn Rebellion.

28 After the historic summit between Kim Dae Jung and Kim Jong-Il in June 2000, it was hoped that tensions between the two Koreas would ease.

29 The intrusion of Lim as a ruthless force, disrupting and reorganizing the local power structure, is framed in a melodramatic convention. Lim bickers constantly with the local police chief, whose obesity and comical gestures excessively underscore the ineffectiveness of the local tycoon.

30 There are two moments in the film where the women retaliate in self-defense against men who

approach them physically. In this scene, Chuksandaek bites off Lim's ear, and later Oesŏdaek bites Sang-gu's tongue when Sang-gu tries to rape her. In every public screening of *The Tae-baek Mountains* I have attended, these two scenes elicit audience laughter. Women biting men's body parts apparently releases the tension and horror projected when women are attacked by men. However, the laughter also consigns the film to genre conventions familiar to popular audiences rather than opening it up to realist conventions. Built-up suspense is released through comical elements. The symbolic significance of ear and tongue perhaps deserves some mention as well. When Chuksandaek bites Lim's ear, this underscores both their inability to communicate and the desperate measures of protest she must apply before she receives appropriate attention by the authorities. While the ear "receives" communication, the tongue emits words and rhetoric. Also, the tongue's metonymic signification as a sexual object allows Oesŏdaek's attack on Sang-gu to be read as a gesture to castrate him.

31 The film adaptation seems to have merged the two characters, Namyangdaek and Oesŏdaek, both of whom are raped by Sang-gu in the original novel. An even more intriguing development in the novel is that Namyangdaek is the wife of socialist Ha Tae-ch'i, who co-opts his own mistress elsewhere in the diegesis and further spreads the seeds of "unbelonging."

32 Gayatri Chakravorty Spivak, "Can the Subaltern Speak?" in *Colonial Discourse and Post-Colonial Theory: a Reader*, eds. Patrick Williams and Laura Chrisman (New York: Columbia University Press, 1994), 93.

4 Post-Trauma and Historical Remembrance in *A Single Spark* and *A Petal*

1 The two films remain theatrically unreleased in the United States. Several video distributors, including amazon.com, carry them on video. Unfortunately, these are Chinese-dubbed versions and are marketed without proper authorization.

2 The popularity of the television miniseries *Morae Sigye*, broadcast through Seoul Broadcasting System (SBS), was phenomenal. At the time of its broadcast, seven out of ten television sets in Korea were reportedly tuned to it. The miniseries focused on two men on different sides of the conflict: a law student who is drafted into the military and then deployed to Kwangju to quell the uprising and a conscientious gangster who participates in the protest for democracy.

3 Kirby Farrell's book *Post-Traumatic Culture: Injury and Interpretation in the Nineties* (Baltimore: Johns Hopkins University Press, 1998) defines "post-traumatic" symptoms as the psychological dislocation experienced particularly at the end of the two centuries: 1890s and 1990s.

4 Slavoj Žižek, *The Sublime Object of Ideology* (London: Verso, 1989), 73.

5 Thomas Elsaesser, "Primary Identification and the Historical Subject: Fassbinder and Germany," in *Narrative, Apparatus, Ideology*, ed. Philip Rosen (New York: Columbia University Press, 1986), 545.

6 One also recalls here the famous opening of another historical film: in *City of Sadness* (Hou Hsiao-hsien, dir., 1989), Emperor Hirohito announces Japan's surrender to the allies over the radio, while a baby is being born in Wen Ching's family.

7 Susan Hayward, *French National Cinema* (New York: Routledge, 1993), 5.

8 Thomas Elsaesser, *New German Cinema: A History* (New Brunswick, N.J.: Rutgers University Press, 1989), 3–4.

9   The recent commercial success of Korean films like *Shiri* (1999) and *Joint Security Area* (2000) across the markets in Asia has made cinema once again attractive investment items in the Korean financial quarter.

10 Ironically, Daewoo, a corporation that violently thwarted many labor-organizing efforts during the 1980s and early 1990s, was one of the major sponsors of *A Single Spark*.

11 Only Park Kwang-su produced his own films, *To the Starry Island* (*Kŭ sŏm e kagosipta*, 1993), *A Single Spark* (*Arŭmdaun ch'ŏngnyŏn, Chŏn T'ae-il*, 1996), and *Uprising* (*Yi Chae-su ŭi nan*, 1999). Jang, who still works as a contract director, is among the highest-paid directors in Korea, receiving more than $100,000 plus incentives per picture.

12 *A Single Spark* is so far the only film directed by Park that has had a commercial success. It sold over 300,000 receipts in Seoul alone.

13 The Seoul Film Collective (SFC) was one of the earliest film organizations to engage a new impulse aimed at alternative cinematic practice. The SFC was organized in 1982 primarily by student activists and had as members some of today's most distinguished feature filmmakers in Korea. With the publication of *Saeroun yŏnghwa rŭl uihayŏ* [*For a New Cinema*] (Seoul, Korea: Hakminsa) in 1983, the SFC proposed that discussion of cinema be engaged politically. It used some of the most popular theories of the Third Cinema developed in Latin America during the 1960s that attempted to secure a unique aesthetic foothold apart from the influences of Hollywood and European art cinema.

14 The protest for democracy in South Korea was most fierce during the summer of 1987. Once the South Korean government decided in April 1987 to deny the people the right to vote, hundreds of thousands of people poured into the streets in June of that year, making all urban streets "virtual battlefields." See Bruce Cumings, *Korea's Place in the Sun: a Modern History* (New York: W. W. Norton & Company, 1997), 387.

15 In the 1980s, An Sŏng-gi, the biggest star of Korean cinema during the last two decades of the twentieth century, played mostly characters who were mentally or physically handicapped. For instance, in *Whale Hunting* (*Korae sanyang*, 1984), An was the actor who played Wangch'o, the vagabond character. Before his role as an intellectual in Park's films, he played variants of the idiot savant.

16 See the discussion of his style in chapter 6.

17 Tony Rayns, "Sexual Outlaws," *Sight and Sound*, vol. 10, no. 2 (February 2000): 28.

18 Anton Kaes states, "Fassbinder leaves it deliberately ambiguous whether [Maria Braun] simply forgets or intentionally chooses not to remember" turning on the stove that emits the gas that kills her" (Anton Kaes, "History, Fiction, Memory: Fassbinder's *The Marriage of Maria Braun* (1979)," in *German Film and Literature: Adaptations and Transformations*, ed. Eric Rentschler [New York: Methuen, 1986], 285).

19 Many local critics criticized the film for failing to indict those responsible for the massacre. This response is not dissimilar to criticism of Oshima Nagisa's film about an actual incident in which a Korean, Ri Chin'u, was executed for raping and murdering a girl in Japan. For instance, Keiko McDonald claimed Oshima's *Death by Hanging* (1968) was too "belligerent." See Maureen Turim, *The Films of Oshima Nagisa: Images of a Japanese Iconoclast* (Berkeley: University of California Press, 1998), 65.

20 Many lives were indeed lost during the struggle for democracy. Not only were students and workers killed during demonstrations, rallies, and police tortures, but thousands of civilians were lost during the Kwangju massacre.

21 Kim Young-sam, like his predecessors, largely ruled by decrees. He consistently implemented his policies without seeking the approval of the National Assembly and thereby refused to relinquish power that has long been concentrated in the president.

22 Georg Lukács writes, "The fetishistic character of economic forms, the reification of all human relations, the constant expansion and extension of the division of labor which subjects the process of production to an abstract, rational analysis, without regard to the human potentialities and abilities of the immediate producers, all these things transform the phenomena of society and with them the way in which they are perceived" (*History and Class Consciousness* [Cambridge, Mass.: MIT Press, 1968], 6).

23 Ibid., 20.

24 Kaja Silverman, *Male Subjectivity at the Margins* (New York: Routledge, 1992), 55.

25 Kenneth Turan, "Days of 'Bread and Roses,'" *Los Angeles Times*, May 13, 2000, F16.

26 The biography of Chŏn T'ae-il, *Chŏn-T'ae-il P'yŏngjŏn*, did have a tremendous real-life impact on the public when it was published in the late 1970s. Although Kim Yŏng-su in the film is a fictitious character, the biography was supposedly ghost written by Cho Yŏng-nae, a human rights lawyer, an undercover intellectual like Kim himself.

27 Cumings, *Korea's Place in the Sun*, 371.

28 See chapter 5.

29 Here, I use the term "masked," following Steven Cohan's book *Masked Men: Masculinity and the Movies in the Fifties* (Bloomington: Indiana University Press, 1997), in which he characterizes the dominant traits of the male protagonists in Hollywood films of the 1950s as masquerading, unable to fully resist sexual anxieties and homoerotic impulses.

30 *The Night before the Strike*, produced by the film collective Changsankotmae, is perhaps the most celebrated film of Minjung cinema. Fully endorsed by the newly organized *Chŏnnohyŏp*, the national labor union confederation that preceded the current national labor organization *Minju noch'ong*, the film tells of the political awakening of workers in a steel factory.

31 *Sopyonje* (Im Kwon-Taek, dir., 1993), one of the biggest films in the postwar history of Korea, is an exception to this rule.

32 There were two previous attempts to represent the Kwangju massacre in feature films; neither *Oh! Dreamland* (*O! Kkŭm ŭi nara*, 1989) nor *The Song of Resurrection* (*Puhwal ŭi norae*, 1990) succeeded in passing the censors.

33 *Ssine 21* [*Cine 21*], April 30, 1996, 61.

34 For an analysis of female protagonists in melodramas directed by Im Kwon-Taek, see Eunsun Cho's essay, "The Female Body and Enunciation in *Adada* and *Surrogate Mother*," in *Im Kwon-Taek: the Making of a Korean National Cinema*, ed. David E. James and Kyung Hyun Kim, (Detroit: Wayne State University Press, 2002): 84–106.

35 The Chun Doo Hwan regime (1980–87), which was responsible for the massacre, never acknowledged that thousands of civilians were killed.

36 Nowhere has this reading even been suggested despite the numerous reviews and debates *A Petal* has stirred. The only place I saw Oedipus mentioned in conjunction with *A Petal* was in the back of Ch'oe Yun's collection of short stories, *Chŏgi sori opsi han chŏm kkotnip i chigo* [*Over There Silently Wilts a Petal*] (Seoul: Munhak kwa chisŏng, 1992), in which literary critic Kim Pyŏng-ik wrote a response to Ch'oe Yun's novella. In it, after quoting the segment in the original version of *A Petal* in which the numerous dead from the massacre are horribly depicted, he states:

[The girl], like us who remember the event, desires to mask her eyes from seeing the horrendous world. They must not be seen, must not exist, must be hidden, and deleted from our conscious. She therefore must draw a "black curtain" around her vision, and her conscious. Her black curtain is the same curtain drawn by Oedipus who plucked his own eyes after realizing his predestined sin. Kim Pyŏng-ik, "Kot'ong ŭi arŭmdaum hokŭn arŭmdaum ŭi kot'ong," [The Beauty of Pain, or the Pain of Beauty], in *Chŏgi sori opsi han chŏm kkotnip i chigo*, 308.

Although not specific in his interpretation of *A Petal*, Kim notes that in the novella, the state's violence overlaps with the private fears and anxieties of the little girl. I think this was the challenge Jang confronted all along. He had to visualize the site of the unforgivable, the unspeakable, and the unseen using the oedipal, given the impossible task of interpreting the uninterpretable.

37 During the 1970s and 1980s, forced conscription was frequently used by the state to discipline student demonstrators. Once drafted, the students often received intolerable treatment from the army, sometimes resulting in tragic deaths.

38 For an assessment of ghost films in the context of Asian cinema and how they are constituted as historical allegory, see Bliss Cua Lim, "Spectral Times: The Ghost Film as Historical Allegory," *positions: east asia cultures critique*, vol. 9, no. 2 (fall 2001): 287–329.

39 There are many rapes in Korean films, but no one has given the rapist a more notable look than Jang. For instance, in *The Road to the Racetrack* (1994), R returns home to Korea after completing his Ph.D. in France, only to find out that his partner, J, no longer wants him. Every time they meet, he attempts to rekindle the old relationship and tries, despite her refusals, to have intercourse with her. The sex is forced and her honor violated. Yet never is the fulfillment of romantic reunion signified through sex. In *To You, from Me*, Paji (Pants)—played by Chŏng Sŏn-gyŏng—is raped by a student activist whose sadistic impulses can be traced to his humiliated national identity, which can only be subservient to the United States. Yelling "down with U.S. imperialism," he violently forces his penis in Paji's anus despite her denial that she is not an imperialist. In *Timeless, Bottomless Bad Movie* (*Nappŭn yŏnghwa*, 1997), one of the most unforgettable sequences involves a rape. (This scene is excised from the theatrical version released in Korea.) Runaway teenaged boys, with whom the audience has developed an identification despite their violent tendencies, betray our trust by raping a defenseless girl. The festive mood, the disco music soundtrack, and their guilt-free faces during the rape are painful to watch. See pages 200–202.

40 In an exit poll conducted by a film magazine, viewers were asked what they considered the most memorable scene in the film. It was neither the documentary footage of the massacre nor the image of the violent rapes; instead, it was the haunting sequence in which the girl's mother is shot (*Ssine 21* [*Cine 21*], April 9, 1996, 45).

41 Jacques Lacan states that the mirror stage is when the child notes his own reflection with pleasure and fear, and finally realizes that his identity is separate from the mother. See Jacques Lacan, "The Mirror Stage as Formative of the Formation of the I as Revealed in Psychoanalytic Experience," in *Écrits: A Selection*, trans. Alan Sheridan (New York: W. W. Norton & Company, 1977), 1–7.

42 Sigmund Freud, "A Child Is Being Beaten," in *Sexuality and the Psychology of Love*, ed. Philip Rieff, (New York: Simon & Schuster, 1963), 97–122.

43 Gaylyn Studlar, "Masochism and the Perverse Pleasures of the Cinema," in *Movies and Methods*, vol. 2, ed. Bill Nichols, (Berkeley: University of California Press, 1985), 606.

44 Ibid., 606.

45 In an earlier scene, the girl was not able to separate herself from the tavern lady whom she met on the road.

46 René Girard has extensively elaborated on this issue of mimetism in Freudian psychoanalytic thought and the strong identification with the father that the child feels during the preoedipal stage. See René Girard, *Violence and the Sacred*, trans. Patrick Gregory (Baltimore: Johns Hopkins University Press, 1979), 169–92.

47 The haunting retelling of a political holocaust through personalized trauma that challenges the very practice of remembrance reminds us of *Hiroshima Mon Amour* (Alain Resnais, dir., 1959). In that film, based on a screenplay by Marguerite Duras, a French woman's romantic engagement with a Japanese man on her visit to Hiroshima to make a film about peace triggers memories of witnessing her German lover's death. (The resemblance between *Hiroshima Mon Amour* and *A Petal* is not coincidental, considering that Ch'oe Yun wrote her doctoral thesis on Marguerite Duras while studying in France.) The use of flashbacks, segmented plot lines, contestations of the real, and interweaving of personal trauma and historical holocaust all cover ground from which the two films operate. "Tu n'as vu rien à Hiroshima" (You have seen nothing in Hiroshima), a phrase that is repeated several times in the film's opening, is thematically structured in *A Petal* as well. She has seen Kwangju, but she cannot remember that she has. The girl's witnessing of the massacre is just as traumatic as the man's remembrance of Hiroshima—too provocative for her to recount. Yet we must also account for the differences between the two films. Later on in *Hiroshima Mon Amour*, Duras's character does remember her past, verbally articulates what has happened between her and her Nazi lover, and is able to come to terms with her history and therefore her identity. Her trip to make a film in Hiroshima results in her recovering peace of mind. *A Petal* offers no such comforting notions.

48 Wilhelm Reich, *The Mass Psychology of Fascism* (New York: Noonsday Press, 1970), xiii.

49 Michel Foucault, in Gilles Deleuze and Felix Guattari, *Anti Oedipus: Capitalism and Schizophrenia*, trans. Robert Hurley, Mark Seem, and Helen R. Lane (Minneapolis: University of Minnesota Press, 1983), xiii. For a summary of these theoretical developments on fascism, see the chapter, "The Fascist Longings in Our Midst," in Rey Chow, *Ethics After Idealism* (Bloomington: Indiana University Press, 1998), 14–32.

50 Rey Chow, *Primitive Passions: Visuality, Sexuality, Ethnography, and Contemporary Chinese Cinema* (New York: Columbia University Press, 1995), 104.

51 Ibid., 100.

52 Ibid., 106.

Part II New Korean Cinema Auteurs

1 Park Kwang-su was born in 1955, Jang in 1952, and Hong in 1960.

2 Na Un-gyu, at the age of 22, with only a couple of years of acting experience, wrote, directed, and starred in one of the most popular films Korea has ever produced, *Arirang* (1926). *Arirang* is widely known as Korea's first nationalist film.

3 In another book, I have addressed the reasons behind the dismantling of the Golden Age

during the Park Chung Hee administration (1961–79). Please refer to "Korean Cinema and Im Kwon-Taek: An Overview," in *Im Kwon-Taek: The Makings of a Korean National Cinema* (Detroit: Wayne State University Press, 2002): 19–46.

4 Though the screen quota policies survived throughout the 1980s and the 1990s, the mandate for theaters to screen Korean films for 126 days per year was almost ignored by theater owners. The amendment in the motion picture law that allowed foreign distribution companies like Disney (later Buena Vista), Warner Brothers, and Columbia Tristar to operate their businesses in Korea also threatened the local industry that had relied on profits from foreign film distribution with extinction.

5 Male Crisis in the Early Films of Park Kwang-su

1 Laura Mulvey, "Visual Pleasure and Narrative Cinema," in *Narrative, Apparatus, Ideology: A Film Theory Reader*, ed. Philip Rosen (New York: Columbia University Press, 1987), 205.

2 Rey Chow, *Primitive Passions: Visuality, Sexuality, Ethnography, and Contemporary Chinese Cinema* (New York: Columbia University Press, 1995), 118.

3 Slavoj Žižek, *The Sublime Object of Ideology* (London: Verso, 1989), 157.

4 Nowhere is this truer than in Im Kwon-Taek's most successful film, *Sopyonje* (*Sop'yonje*, 1993). For more on this film, see the special section on *Sopyonje* in *Im Kwon-Taek: The Makings of a Korean National Cinema*, ed. David E. James and Kyung Hyun Kim (Detroit: Wayne State University Press, 2001).

5 It is not coincidental that Park's first feature film was released in the year of the Seoul Olympics. Park told me that the film was deliberately submitted for censorship review on the opening day of the summer games because it would have been undesirable for the authorities to cause a scandal on a day when so much international media attention was focused on Korea.

6 Park Kwang-su is one of the founding members of two film collectives, Yallasŏng and Sŏul yŏnghwa chiptan (Seoul Film Collective), that are quite significant in the history of Korean films. Both formed in the early 1980s, they produced short political films and published books that introduced Third World filmmakers and manifestos. See page 292 n.13.

7 Huang, Ch'un-ming, "The Two Signpainters," in *The Drowning of an Old Cat, and Other Stories*, trans. Howard Goldblatt (Bloomington: Indiana University Pres, 1980), 185–216.

8 Vladimir Propp, *Morphology of the Folktale*, trans. Laurence Scott (Austin: University of Texas Press, 1968), 63.

9 Yuejin Wang, "*Red Sorghum*: Mixing Memory and Desire," in *Perspectives on Chinese Cinema*, ed. Chris Berry (London: BFI Publishing, 1991), 83.

10 Ibid., 99.

11 Xueping Zhong has written extensively on this point in *Masculinity Besieged?: Issues of Modernity and Male Subjectivity in Chinese Literature of the Late Twentieth Century* (Durham, N.C.: Duke University Press, 2000), 32–40.

12 Many French feminists, including Julia Kristeva and Luce Irigaray, share Lacan's willingness to explore human subjectivity and challenge the gender biases Freud institutionalized. Their adherence to Lacanian theories, including the Imaginary and the Symbolic as well as the primacy of language, is well known. Yet, it would be misleading if I were to state that they look at Lacan's work uncritically and consider it only as a utility to further their feminist agendas. For instance, Kristeva's concept of the "chora" as a maternal space (in the words of Elisa-

beth Grosz, "the 'raw material' of signification, the corporeal, libidinal matter that must be harnessed") that operates a-symbolically and thereby redefines the function of women by departing from the Lacanian Imaginary and Symbolic. See Elisabeth Grosz, *Jacques Lacan: A Feminist Introduction* (New York: Routledge, 1990), 151.

13 For books on the gender crisis in these European cinemas, see Marcia Kinder's *Blood Cinema: The Reconstruction of National Identity in Spain* (Berkeley: University of California Press, 1993) and Eric Rentschler, ed., *Film and Literature: Adaptations and Transformations* (New York: Routledge, 1986).

14 Yet there are differences between the lies of Man-su and Ch'il-su. Man-su lies to find jobs; his lies are a simple survival tactic. Ch'il-su lies to "win the girl" and resolve his psychic anxiety. In other words, Man-su lies for material reasons, and Ch'il-su for romantic ones. They thus complement each other and are bound more firmly together.

15 Many Korean construction companies were subcontracted to provide skilled labor in the Middle East oil refineries in the 1970s. Although working in the heat was insufferable, many workers volunteered to go because the wages overseas averaged two to three times more than those in Korea. At the peak of the Middle Eastern construction boom in the late 1970s, as many as three hundred thousand Korean workers were in the oil fields in the Gulf.

16 After announcing on April 13, 1987 that the constitution would not be amended to allow a popular election in Korea, President Chun Doo Hwan was forced to concede his position only two months later after an uprising erupted across the nation that demanded that he step down.

17 Žižek, *The Sublime Object of Ideology*, 134.

18 Žižek also considers the possibility of the symbolic death preceding the biological death in his discussion of Antigone. He says that, unlike the ghost of Hamlet's father who returns as a *frightful apparition*, Antigone's "exclusion from the symbolic community of the city, precedes her actual death and imbues her character with *sublime beauty*" (*The Sublime Object of Ideology*, 135 [my emphasis]).

19 Workers launched more than seven thousand strikes between the summer of 1987 and late 1989, and unionization swept practically every shop across the nation. See Walden Bello and Stephanie Rosenfeld, *Dragons in Distress: Asia's Miracle Economies in Crisis* (San Francisco: A Food First Book, 1990), 3.

20 The reorganization of space required for a society to acquire the marks of modernity is heavily endowed with a system of signs. The participation of television in the era of late capitalism, for instance, cannot be interpreted only in the context of its passive role as a promotion of a consumerist culture. It has been argued that by mobilizing desire and fantasy, images on television fetishize and reproduce desires to the point that the actual product could never satisfy one's needs. For this process to materialize, consumers would have to undergo "a profound shift in the structure of feeling," reconstituting their relation to the image. See David Harvey, *The Condition of Postmodernity: An Inquiry into the Origins of Cultural Change* (Cambridge: Blackwell, 1990), 39–65.

21 Socially, their subjectivity that already suffers from alienation is further troubled by the setting of Pan-p'o, one of the first sections of Kangnam District to be developed and distributed to those who reaped their financial benefits from the real estate boom in the 1970s and the 1980s. This rich commercial and residential section of the city, which features one of the first department stores built outside of the old downtown in the northern part of the city, as well as a new bus terminal, quickly emerged as the new center of Seoul during the military regimes

of the 1970s and the 1980s. In 1974, the Korean Housing Company, a government subsidiary, completed its first modern apartment project in Pan-p'o, south of the Han River, which accommodated nearly thirty-eight hundred families. Seoul was spatially rearranged so most of its population would move south. According to statistics, in 1966 the distribution of the population between north and south of the Han River was 82.2 and 17.8 percent, respectively. However, by the mid-1990s, most of Seoul's population lived in the south, completely reversing the traditional pattern. See Sang-Chuel Choe and Joochul Kim, *Seoul: The Making of a Metropolis* (Chichester, U.K.: John Wiley and Sons, 1997), 71.

22 Jacques Lacan, "Subversion of the Subject and Dialectic of Desire," in *Ecrits: A Selection*, trans. Alan Sheridan (New York: W. W. Norton & Company, 1977), 316.

23 Žižek, *The Sublime Object of Ideology*, 112–13.

24 Ibid., 113.

25 Although "Kim Ki-yŏng" is revealed to be not the real name of the film's protagonist, I will refer to him as "Ki-yŏng" throughout this chapter since this is the name that he is known by in the film.

26 Postscreening question-and-answer session with Park Kwang-su at California Art Institute (Valencia), February 13, 1998.

27 Although *King of the Children* was less popular on the festival circuit than some of the other films by the fifth generation filmmakers, it has received plenty of attention from academics. First analyzed by Tony Rayns in *King of the Children and the New Chinese Cinema*, it was also discussed by scholars Rey Chow and Xudong Zhang. See Rey Chow, "Male Narcissism and National Culture: Subjectivity in Chen Kaige's *King of the Children*," in *Primitive Passions*, 108–41; and Xudong Zhang, "A Critical Account of Chen Kaige's *King of the Children*," in *Chinese Modernism in the Era of Reforms: Cultural Fever, Avant-Garde Fiction, and the New Chinese Cinema* (Durham, N.C.: Duke University Press, 1997), 282–305.

28 Not coincidentally, *King of the Children* is one of the films that most influenced Park Kwang-su. See Park Kwang-su, "Naega chigŭm sarang hanŭn yŏnghwadŭl" (Movies I Love Now), in *K'ino*, no. 40 (May 1998): 45.

29 Chow, *Primitive Passions*, 127.

30 To read more on Park Chung-hun's star persona of the 1990s, see page 43.

31 Zhong, *Masculinity Besieged?* 137.

32 According to Thomas Elsaesser, melodrama is "iconographically fixed by the claustrophobic atmosphere of the bourgeois home and/or the small-town setting; its emotional pattern is that of panic and latent hysteria." Here, the "latent hysteria" that bubbles below the surface symptomizes the social repression in the claustrophobic setting of the family. See Thomas Elsaesser, "Tales of Sound and Fury," in *Film Genre Reader*, ed. Barry Keith Grant (Austin: University of Texas Press, 1986), 300.

33 In "Tales of Sound and Fury," Elsaesser considers *Written on the Wind* a quintessential melodrama of the 1950s.

34 In a shortsighted measure to revive the declining local economy, the Korean government recently approved the opening of a casino in Yŏngwŏl, a former mining town. This has stirred controversy in the congress where the effectiveness of this action was debated in October 2000.

35 At one point, Ki-yŏng tells his intellectual friend from Seoul who has come to persuade him to return that it was never the minjung, but the intellectuals, who were defeated.

36 In *A Single Spark* (*Arŭmdaun ch'ŏngnyŏn Chŏn T'ae-il*, 1996), Park figures a similar structure

that romantically binds a female worker and a male intellectual. The male intellectual awakens the female worker's consciousness to help her address the problems in her workplace.

37 Žižek, *The Sublime Object of Ideology*, 113.

38 Ibid., 131–49.

39 Freud wrote, "Psychoanalysis has revealed that the totem animal is in reality a substitute for the father; and this tallies with the contradictory fact that, though the killing of the animal is as a rule forbidden, yet its killing is a festive occasion—with the fact that it is killed and yet mourned" ("Totem and Taboo," in *Freud Reader*, ed. Peter Gay [New York: W. W. Norton & Company, 1989], 500).

6 Jang Sun-woo's Three "F" Words: Familism, Fetishism, and Fascism

1 The characters in *To You, from Me* are referred to by their job descriptions or by their nicknames. For example, the woman is referred to as "a woman who wears pants," the title of her award-winning poetry.

2 Gilles Deleuze, *Masochism: Coldness and Cruelty* (New York: Zone Books, 1989), 91.

3 Ibid., 92.

4 Seungsook Moon writes that the nationalist discourse produced by President Park Chung Hee (1961–79) was officially rendered from the spirit of Tan'gun, the spirit of hwarang, "state-protecting Buddhism," and Confucianism as the principal elements of Korean tradition and history. These components all putatively made up the Korean tradition to help Park establish its own legacy of militarist nationalism. See Seungsook Moon, "Begetting the Nation: The Androcentric Discourse of National History and Tradition in South Korea," in *Dangerous Women: Gender and Korean Nationalism*, ed. Elaine H. Kim and Chungmoo Choi (New York: Routledge, 1998), 33–66.

5 Foot fetishism is humorously depicted in Luis Bunuel's *El*, a film briefly discussed in the beginning of this chapter.

6 On Kim Ki-yŏng's films, see chapter 8.

7 Rey Chow—after arguing that fascism, rather than hatefulness and destructiveness, is about love and idealism—writes that fascism's effectiveness relies, like film, on "its foundation in projection" (19). Invoking Thomas Elsaesser who wrote, "Hitler appealed to the *Volk* but always by picturing the German nation, standing there, observed by 'the eye of the world,'" she argues that the specularization of private lives made fascism even more appealing to the masses and ensured its success (Rey Chow, *Ethics After Idealism: Theory-Culture-Ethnicity-Reading* [Bloomington: Indiana University Press, 1998], 20).

8 Deleuze, *Masochism*, 87.

9 See the earlier discussion of masochism and its invocation on another Korean film, *Out to the World*, in chapter 2.

10 Sigmund Freud, "A Child Is Being Beaten," *Sexuality and the Psychology of Love* (New York: Simon and Schuster, 1963), 97.

11 Fredric Jameson, *Fables of Aggression: Wyndham Lewis, the Modernist as Fascist* (Berkeley: University of California Press, 1979), 10.

12 As I have earlier stated, Deleuze has severed the tie that had been previously assumed of masochism: its close link to sadism. The unrestricted lust for self-destruction—especially when it comes to the male subject—does not necessarily dispense the desire to dominate or subjugate.

13 The novel, when it first came out in 1998, was immediately banned by the Korean authorities for its explicit sexual content, and it even led to the arrest and prosecution of its author, Chang Chŏng-il.

14 Deleuze, *Masochism*, 32.

15 Chow, *Ethics After Idealism*, 18.

16 One need look no further than Paul Schrader's 1985 film, *Mishima: A Life in Four Chapters*, for one of the most vivid cinematic depictions of fascism.

17 This is one of my favorite quotes from Louis Althusser that Fredric Jameson uses in explaining the concept of the "Real" that is neither an unknowable thing-in-itself, nor a truthful representation of consciousness. The quote appears in Jameson's *The Political Unconscious: the Narrative as a Socially Symbolic Act* (Ithaca, N.Y.: Cornell University Press, 1981), 29 and *Fables of Aggression*, 12.

18 Even *Hwaŏmgyŏng*, Jang's least controversial film made in the 1990s, features a boy—the embodiment of Buddha—constantly having sex with women on the road.

19 Gaylyn Studlar, "Masochism and the Perverse Pleasures of the Cinema," in *Movies and Methods*, vol. 2, ed. Bill Nichols (Berkeley,: University of California Press, 1985), 602–21.

20 Laura Mulvey, "Visual Pleasure and the Narrative Cinema," in *Narrative, Apparatus, Ideology: A Film Theory Reader*, ed. Philip Rosen (New York: Columbia University Press, 1987).

21 Bruce Cumings explains that Chun Doo Hwan's low popular support was due to his "lack of imagination and his slavish attempts to mimic Park Chung Hee's politics" (Bruce Cumings, *Korea's Place in the Sun: A Modern History* [New York: W. W. Norton & Company, 1997], 380).

22 See the Introduction, especially pages 18–19, for a more detailed analysis of Chun Doo Hwan's policy to encourage consumption and spending by the middle-class in the 1980s.

23 This was an extremely popular movement for democracy that was equally cultural as well as political. Jang himself was one of the active participants of this movement. He was particularly active in *madang gŭk* (mask theater) and wrote film criticism that argued for the creation of a new political cinema.

24 Slavoj Žižek, *The Sublime Object of Ideology* (London: Verso, 1990), 20.

25 For a short while, he worked in television and also in Yi Chang-ho's film production office.

26 Im, during the late 1950s and the early 1960s, was an assistant to Director Chang Chŏng-hwa, and Park worked under Yi Chang-ho during the mid 1980s.

27 Maureen Turim, *The Films of Oshima Nagisa: Images of a Japanese Iconoclast* (Berkeley: University of California Press, 1998), 258–59.

28 Marsha Kinder, *Blood Cinema: the Reconstruction of National Identity in Spain* (Berkeley: University of California Press, 1993), 286.

29 Hamid Naficy, *The Making of Exile Cultures: Iranian Television in Los Angeles* (Minneapolis: University of Minnesota Press, 1993), 127.

30 The word "postmodern" is quoted from the promotional line in the film's poster.

31 Fredric Jameson, *Postmodernism, or the Cultural Logic of Late Capitalism* (Durham, N.C.: Duke University Press, 1991).

32 The term, "the great divide" is derived from the title of the book by Andreas Huyssen, *After the Great Divide* (Bloomington: University of Indiana Press, 1986), in which he argues that the gap between high art and mass culture in the postmodern era has been reduced.

33 The fact that the award-winning story has been plagiarized from a Latin American novel can-

not be easily dismissed. References have been made between Korea's madang gŭk, a popular form of traditional theater that had been reformulated into protest theater during the minjung movement and Latin American "magical realism." See Chungmoo Choi, "Decolonization and Popular Memory: South Korea" in *positions: east asia cultures critique*, vol. 1, no. 1 (spring, 1993): 77–102.

34 As I have elsewhere enumerated, the representation of women during the 1980s and the 1990s was fixed on the rigid conventions of whores and mothers. See pages 6–8.

35 Chungmoo Choi, "Nationalism and Construction of Gender in Korea," in *Dangerous Women*, 23–24.

36 The highly popular novel was also adapted into a film in 1974 by Kim Su-yŏng.

37 Yi Sang-jin, "T'oji e nat'anan kajok munje wa mosŏngsŏng" (The Family Issue and Mother-hood in *T'oji*), in *Yŏsŏng munhak yŏnggu (Feminism and Korean Literature)*, no. 3 (Seoul, Korea: T'aehaksa, 2000), 156.

38 Kim Mi-hyŏn, *Han'guk yŏsŏng sosŏl kwa p'eminijŭm (Korean Women Novels and Feminism)* (Seoul: Shingu, 1996), 75.

39 Nancy Chodorow, *The Reproduction of Mothering: Psychoanalysis and the Sociology of Gender* (Berkeley: University of California Press, 1999), 194.

40 Freud, "Fetishism," in *Sexuality and the Psychology of Love*, ed. Philip Rieff (New York: Touchstone, 1997), 205.

41 Kaja Silverman, *Male Subjectivity at the Margins* (New York: Routledge, 1992), 35.

42 In Abigal Solomon-Godeau's essay, "The Legs of Countess," she examines the photographs of the countess de Castiglione in the mid-nineteenth century, which were commissioned by the countess herself, and the daguerreotypes of the era. Solomon-Godeau, even though an astute feminist, acknowledges that the photographs of the countess are "troubling" because she voluntarily obliged to a "scopic regime that inevitably undercuts her pretended authority as orchestrator of the look in these photographs." This attests to the ambiguities of the very question of reification that these erotic and subversive gestures and poses reenact. Solomon-Godeau, rather than providing a definitive solution to this question, instead ends the essay with the question: "In its broadest implications, the photographic legacy of the countess de Castiglione—image and object of desire—confronts us with the question of whose urgency is a function of whatever empowerment woman can thus far claim: whose desire." In a similar vein, the question of "whose desire?" can similarly be posed for Paji. See "The Legs of Countess," in *Fetishism as Cultural Discourse*, ed. Emily Apter and William Pietz (Ithaca, N.Y.: Cornell University Press, 1993), 306.

43 While discussing a South Korean film, *301/302*, Joan Kee argues that women's hysteria can be utilized as a powerful metaphor that can rupture the Korean patriarchal continuum. See Joan Kee, "Claiming Sites of Independence: Articulating Hysteria in Pak Ch'ŏl-su's *301/302* (1995)," in *positions: east asia cultures critique*, vol. 9, no. 2 (fall 2001): 449–66. Also *Gina Kim's Video Diary* (2002), a self-documented video diary piece, deals with anorexia in a provocative manner.

44 Žižek, *The Sublime Object of Ideology*, 71.

45 Included in the list of Jang's use of extratextual and noncinematic references are the theatrical conventions in *The Age of Success* and the animation sequence in *To You, from Me*.

46 Bill Nichols, *Blurred Boundaries: Questions of Meaning in Contemporary Culture* (Bloomington: Indiana University Press, 1994), 18.

47 Michael Renov, "Introduction: The Truth About Non-Fiction," in *Theorizing Documentary*, ed. Michael Renov (New York: Routledge, 1993), 7

48 In *Los Olvidados*, for instance, Jaivo is clearly the "bad boy," a villainous character who has implicated the film's protagonist, Pedro, as an accomplice in a murder. Making the matter more complicated, Jaivo sexually seduces Pedro's widowed mother, an angelic object of Pedro's desire, betraying his trust. Jaivo contaminates Pedro and gets him killed at the end.

49 Maureen Turim, *The Films of Oshima Nagisa: Images of a Japanese Iconoclast*, 251.

50 Providing here a synopsis of the film undermines *Bad Movie*'s narrative logic because it simplifies a film that otherwise resists linearity. I instead will be analytical, moving from one highlighted scene to another, treating the ruptures and contradictions between them as they visually appear.

51 The making of *Bad Movie* was documented by Yi Chŏng-ha, a writer who published his experiences of being part of the production team in his book, *Nappŭn yŏnghwa*.

52 Negative responses to *Bad Movie* flooded the press when it first came out.

53 July 1997 is well remembered as the month when quite possibly the fiercest social controversy took place in the cultural sector. After the underground circulation of the so-called *Ppalgan Mahura* that featured a self-taped pornographic affair among two high-school boys and a girl, the government issued on July 1st the youth protection law, a new credence that strictly prohibited the distribution of all print matter and public performance art on adult themes to anyone under the age of nineteen. State censorships on adult-themed publications and films were further reinforced although the new law had no direct bearing on the production of adult films and publications. In the same month, the most famous cartoonist in Korea, Yi Hyŏn-se, was arraigned by the state and his new series, *Ch'ŏnguk ŭi sinhwa* (*The Myth of Paradise*), banned from the market. In cinema, director Wong Kar-wai's visit to Seoul to celebrate the opening of his new film, *Happy Together*, on July 21 became scandalous because the government refused to give the film a rating, citing that its homosexual theme was inappropriate for all ages. The denial of the rating then, as today, means that the film cannot be publicly screened. The ban of *Happy Together* proved the standards of the censorship board to be extremely arbitrary because it had previously permitted the screenings of films that depict gay characters such as Ang Lee's *Wedding Banquet*, Stephen Frears's *My Beautiful Laundrette*, and Gus Van Sant's *My Own Private Idaho*. The refusal to give the film a rating in Korea—in a country that does not have a theater that can run a nonrated film—was essentially a ban. One of the most respected dailies in Korea, *Tong-a Ilbo*, also began a long editorial series on contemporary youth, holding them responsible for many of the social problems (*Hangyŏre*, July 25, 2000: 11).

54 Louis Althusser, "Ideology and Ideological State Apparatuses (Notes Towards an Investigation)," in *Lenin and Philosophy* (New York: Monthly Review Press, 1971), 165.

55 It must be noted that, unlike the youth leading the 1980s democratization movement who had to remain anonymous and underground because of the harsh government crackdown, one of the traits that distinguished the sinsedae of the 1990s was its visibility and conspicuity, outfitted with latest fashion designer threads and loud colors.

56 Mimesisŭ, ed., *Sinsedae: ne mŏt taero haera* (*Sinsedae, Do Whatever Pleases You*) (Seoul, Korea: Hyŏnsil munhwa yŏngu, 1993).

57 Dick Hebdige, *Subculture: the Meaning of Style* (London: Routledge, 1989), 105.

58 In actuality, Jang fired one of the principle cinematographers in *Bad Movie* for imitating the looks of Wong Kar-wai during the middle of the film shoot.

59 Hebdige, *Subculture*, 108.

60 Linda Williams, *Hard Core: Power, Pleasure, and the "Frenzy of the Visible"* (Berkeley: University of California Press, 1989), 115.

61 Famous actors including Song Kang-ho and Myŏng Kye-nam were to have participated in the central roles of the homeless. Yet, while filming, Jang Sun-woo realized that the real homeless were much better suited to the film than the actors pretending to be the homeless. Song's role was dramatically reduced, and he appears in the final version in one scene only as an extra. All of the scenes involving Myŏng were excised. According to Jang, the use of the nonprofessional actors, though heightening the reality of the film, made the filming incredibly difficult.

62 Michael Renov, "Video Confessions," in *Resolutions: Contemporary Video Practices*, ed. Michael Renov and Erika Suderburg (Minneapolis: University of Minnesota Press, 1996), 84.

7 Too Early/Too Late: Temporality and Repetition in Hong Sang-su's Films

1 *The Day a Pig Fell into the Well* was voted one of the five best films of the decade by *K'ino*, the monthly film magazine in Korea. See *K'ino*, no. 67 (September 2000): 125.

2 In its original Korean dialogue, the phrase is "sarang hago sip'ŏyo." I am slightly altering its literal translation, "I want to love you," because this would be closer to the colloquial phrasing in English.

3 J. Hillis Miller, *Speech Acts in Literature* (Stanford: Stanford University Press, 2001), 135.

4 There are many places in Derrida's work where he explains and makes the application of his term, *différance*. Gayatri Chakravorty Spivak in her "translator's preface" to *Of Grammatology* offers an excellent account of Derrida's *différance*. Readers who are interested in finding out more about this concept should refer to Gayatri Chakravorty Spivak, "Translator's Preface," in Jacques Derrida's *Of Grammatology* (Baltimore: The Johns Hopkins University Press, 1974), xliii.

5 The term, "forking-path," is derived from David Bordwell's *Planet Hong Kong: Popular Cinema and the Art of Entertainment* (Cambridge, Mass.: Harvard University Press, 2000). He writes, "The most intricate model of plotting depends on forking-path patterns, like those in Kieslowski's *Blind Chance* (1981) and Resnais's *Smoking/No Smoking* (1994). Here the plot presents one string of events, hops back to a nodal point, and traces out an alternative set of consequences" (268).

6 Spivak, "Translator's Preface," xi.

7 In 1994, *Sŏrŭn chanch'i nŭn kkŭnnatta* (*Age Thirty, Party is Over*) (Seoul, Korea: Ch'angjak kwa pip'yongsa) by Ch'oe Yŏng-mi, a former-activist-turned poet, became the best-selling book of poetry. It produced both *nostalgia* and *disillusionment* for the *undonggwŏn* (the activists), marking that the militant student and labor activism that swept the nation during the late 1980s and the early 1990s was already something of the past.

8 Jacques Derrida, *Limited Inc.*, trans. Samuel Weber and Jeffrey Mehlman (Evanston, Ill.: Northwestern University Press, 1988), 11.

9 One of the classic moments in the Italian Neo-Realism that has been cited by critics as its

"purest" example is the sequence in *Umberto D* (Vittorio De Sica, dir., 1951) depicting a maid getting out of bed to begin her morning chores. In this scene, the pregnant maid, the friend of Mr. Umberto D, finds a cat walking on the roof as she opens her eyes. She then crosses the hall, drowns the ants around the kitchen sink, and grinds coffee. This scene, hailed by critics, was claimed by Deleuze to "reveal itself in a visual and sound nakedness, crudeness and brutality" (Gilles Deleuze, *Cinéma*, vol. 2: *The Time-Image*, trans. Hugh Tomlinson and Robert Galeta [Minneapolis: University of Minnesota Press, 1989], 3). The stalling of the narrative movement at this particular instance, in lieu of the expression of power embodied in the trivialities of everyday routines, has also been made an exemplary case by Marsha Kinder in her study of the "subversive potential" of the pseudo-iterative. Kinder takes her cue from the literary discourse of Genette, who explored the use of imperfect tense ("I used to go to bed early") in modernist literature and its modification in film studies by Brian Henderson, and argues that the strength of "iteratives," which implicitly create the illusion of habitual action despite having appeared only once in the narrative, engenders a subversive kind of film practice. If narrative film and sadism, as Laura Mulvey has argued in her "Visual Pleasure and Narrative Cinema," are inseparable, then by forestalling the narrative movement, she insists, the iterative seeks to "subvert the sadistic drive of the oedipal plot, that key master narrative of Western patriarchal culture." See Marsha Kinder, "The Subversive Potential of the Pseudo-Iterative," *Film Quarterly*, vol. 43, no. 2 (winter 1989–90): 7. No imperfect past tense can be visually created in a film with the precision of literary language other than to suggest it through voice-over narration, but a singular event can be represented as if it is habitual using deep and resonant mise-en-scène. Because cinema, as argued by Henderson, "has no built-in tense system as language does," it can potentially be freed from temporal order, where the past, the present, and the future are arranged without them being clearly demarcated from each other, making "pseudo-iteratives" subversively float. See Brian Henderson, "Tense, Mood, and Voice in Film (Notes After Genette)," in *Film Quarterly: Forty Years—A Selection*, ed. Brian Henderson et al. (Berkeley: University of California Press, 1999), 57.

10 Mimicry is one of the themes that lays the foundation of Hong Sang-su's latest film: *Turning Gate* (*Saenghwal ŭi palgyŏn*, 2002).

11 Jacques Derrida, "Of Grammatology," in *Derrida Reader*, ed. Peggy Kamuf (New York: Columbia University Press, 1991), 47.

12 Derrida, *Limited Inc.*, 62.

13 This subplot involving "making a movie" pursued by Yŏng-su is as important as the obsessive refusal of the protagonist Francisco to relinquish his father's land in Bunuel's film, *El* (*This Strange Passion*, 1952). Both of their dreams will remain unfulfilled until the very end. For a descriptive analysis of *El*, see Marsha Kinder's *Blood Cinema* (Berkeley: University of California Press, 1993), 303–14.

14 I take my cue from Bill Nichols, who states in his introduction on documentary film that "[d]ocumentary film has a kinship with those other nonfictional systems that together make up what we may call the discourses of sobriety. . . . Discourses of sobriety are sobering because they regard their relation to the real as direct, immediate, transparent" (Bill Nichols, *Representing Reality* [Bloomington: Indiana University Press, 1991], 3–4).

15 To heighten the reality of acting, Hong Sang-su demands his actors to actually drink on the set before the shooting begins. Because many scenes in Hong Sang-su's films take place in

bars or restaurants where the characters become drunk, actors in Hong Sang-su spend a lot of time during production actually drunk.

16 Despite the insistence that Su-jŏng and Chae-hun had earlier claimed to possess faculties of "reliable memory," they constantly forget things. At one point in *Virgin Stripped Bare*, while they cuddle in bed Chae-hun calls Su-jŏng by the name of another woman whom he also sees. His momentary forgetting of Su-jŏng's name squanders his opportunity to "score in bed" once again.

17 Fredric Jameson, *The Geopolitical Aesthetic: Cinema and Space in the World System* (Bloomington: Indiana University Press, 1992), 116.

18 I thank Hwang Ho-dŏk, a Korean literary critic, for his insights on this particular scene.

19 For a discussion of Jang Sun-woo's representation of rape, see pages 174–95, 200–202.

20 Thousands of highly suggestively named lodgings, such as the Honeymoon Park Inn and Eros Motel, have sprouted up all across Korea; they cater to many couples engaged in illicit affairs.

21 At a boutique she denies to a shoe salesman about ever having visited his store when in fact she is knowledgeable of the display arrangements in the store.

22 Min-su has made his entrance earlier in the film as an extra who was seen contesting a fine with an officer in the same courthouse where Hyo-sŏp was sentenced before he is properly introduced.

23 Although Min-jae thinks that Min-su is a sympathetic person who really cares for her, the audience knows that he is not honest. He takes advantage of his position as the theater manager and informs the owner that she had slipped out of work. Min-su uses this ploy to create opportunities for him to help Min-jae with her work-related troubles.

24 Gilles Deleuze and Felix Guattari, *A Thousand Plateaus: Capitalism and Schizophrenia*, trans. Brian Massumi (Minneapolis: University of Minnesota Press, 1987), 474. Deleuze and Guattari explain the division of the two nomadic spaces between "the smooth and the striated."

25 For Žižek's fantasy and its relationship to reality or the Lacanian Real, read his elucidations of Freud's dream and Zhuang Zi's butterfly, which he reconstitutes as the fantasy that becomes an embodiment of reality, not a separate entity. See Slavoj Žižek, *The Sublime Object of Ideology* (London: Verso, 1989), 46.

26 Žižek, *The Sublime Object of Ideology*, 107.

Part III Fin-de-siècle Anxieties

1 *The Hollywood Reporter*, April 18–24, 2000, 1.

8 Lethal Work: Domestic Space and Gender Troubles in *Happy End* and *The Housemaid*

1 Trains have always been conceived as gigantic, metallic phalluses. From Sigmund Freud to Alfred Hitchcock, the use of trains as a sexual metaphor has been frequent and pervasive. Lynne Kirby, in *Parallel Tracks: the Railroad and the Silent Cinema* ([Durham, N.C.: Duke University Press, 1997], 77), writes, "[f]ilms like Alfred Hitchcock's *North by Northwest* (1959), in which a train entering a tunnel is meant to signify and parody sexual intercourse, epitomize this popular notion . . . . train as a specifically male object."

2 Kim Ki-yŏng had hardly affected the New Korean Cinema filmmakers who made their directorial debuts in the 1980s. Park Kwang-su and Jang Sun-woo, the most famous filmmakers
who represent the New Korean Cinema movement, were unfamiliar with Korean film history
and failed to recognize the importance of Kim's work. Although Park and Jang were among
the first generation of filmmakers who learned the trade of filmmaking through film collectives, they were not formally trained in filmmaking, and the history of Korean cinema was
then rarely taught in colleges. The new generation of young filmmakers who made their first
feature films in the 1990s, Chŏng Chi-u, Pak Ki-hyŏng (best known for *Whispering Corridors*
[*Yŏgo kwedam*], 1998), and Pak Ch'an-uk (best known for JSA: *Joint Security Area* [*Kongdong
kyŏngbi kuyŏk JSA*], 2000), however, had studied Korean film history. Also, many retrospective screenings and Korean film history classes featuring Kim Ki-yŏng films had given these
directors the opportunity to be profoundly affected by the man known as "Mr. Monster."

3 In 2002, there are four film weeklies, four monthlies, innumerable internet sites, and a handful
of entertainment dailies that cover cinema, most of them on an exclusive basis.

4 Korea is now second only to the United States in the number of domain names registered
each year, and it leads the world in online stock trading. Also, 15.3 million people out of a
population of 45 million have internet access at homes. See Mark Magnier, " 'PC Bang' Helps
S. Koreans Embrace Net," *Los Angeles Times*, July 19, 2000, A12.

5 Lynn Spigel, *Make Room for TV: Television and the Family Ideal in Postwar America* (Chicago:
University of Chicago Press, 1992), 97.

6 Along with *The Housemaid* and *The Stray Bullet* (Yu Hyŏn-mok, dir., 1960), *Madame Freedom*
is one of the most popular films programmed in Korean retrospectives in the film festivals
abroad. In the 1990s, when Korean films were showcased in various retrospectives around the
world — Paris, Hong Kong, Pusan, and Irvine, among others — *Madame Freedom* was included
in the programs' selection. It also remains one of the most hotly debated films in Korean film
scholarship.

7 Soyoung Kim, "Questions of Woman's Film: The Maid, Madame Freedom, and Women," in
Post-Colonial Classics of Korean Cinema catalog, ed. Chungmoo Choi (Irvine, Calif.: University of California, Irvine, 1998), 18–19.

8 Even in the Korean War films, women's promiscuity is highlighted as one of the most prominent cultural phenomena, provoking the male characters to violently react. See chapter 3 for
a more elaborate discussion of the Korean War films.

9 The economic situation in Korea was quite dire in 1998, plunging millions of people into
poverty. The "Miracle on the Han" economy that continued its phenomenal growth rate of
close to 10 percent during the 1990s collapsed to negative growth in 1998, virtually stalemating
the economy for the first time since the 1950s. See "Middle Class is Casualty of Asian Crisis,"
The Los Angleles Times, December 27, 1998, A9.

10 A fired bank employee has to be accounted as only a recent phenomenon, since employment
in a bank is one of the more socially stable and respected jobs in Korea. That Min-gi is a former
bank employee points to the fact that he is an educated man. Another hit film from the period,
Foul King (*Panch'ikwang*, Kim Chi-un, dir., 2000), also places the central protagonist in the
role of a banker as he tries to find relief from work pressures in the era of the new recession,
during which the bank demands its employees to play by the old and corrupt rules.

11 Anne Allison asserts that motherhood in Japan is explicitly elaborated by handsome and

scrumptious children's lunchboxes that symbolize and fetishize full-time, stay-at-home mothers. See Anne Allison, "Japanese Mothers and *Obentos*: The Lunch Box as Ideological State Apparatus," in *Permitted and Prohibited Desires: Mothers, Comics, and Censorship in Japan* (Boulder, Colo.: Westview Press, 1996), 81–104. Also, in one of the best-selling collections of short stories in Korea during the 1990s, *Punggŭm i ittŏn chari* (*The Place Where an Organ Used to Be*), Shin Kyŏng-suk creates a narrator—a woman who is having an affair with a married man—who recalls the childhood memory of her father's girlfriend. In this story, the father's lover replaces the mother, and she avoids the initially incredulous gaze of the brothers by packing generous and gorgeous lunchboxes (*dosirak*) that "resemble flowerbeds." The new "mother" impresses the narrator with her culinary skills, and earns the respect as an ideal mother, something that the "real" mother never garnered. It is not coincidental that Shin Kyŏng-suk also centrally figures a woman who is having an affair in the celebrated story. Many female writers who emerged in the literary scene during the 1990s, such as Ŭn Hŭi-gyŏng and Chŏn kyŏng-rin also frequently depict women having extramarital affairs. See Shin Kyŏng-suk, *P'unggŭm i ittŏn chari* (Seoul: Munhak kwa chisŏng sa, 1993), 26.

12 Nancy Chodorow, *The Reproduction of Mothering* (Berkeley: University of California Press, 1999), 14. Chodorow sarcastically critiques this questionable assumption that refuses to take into consideration that human behavior, including mothering, is "not instinctually determined but culturally mediated" (ibid.). Mary Ann Doane also writes, "In Western culture, there is something obvious about the maternal which has no counterpart in the paternal." See Mary Ann Doane, *The Desire to Desire: The Woman's Film of the 1940s* (Bloomington: Indiana University Press, 1987), 70.

13 *The Housemaid*, with its bold representation of sexuality and eroticism, was a huge hit when it first came out in 1960. But, because of the Korean cinema's slump during the 1970s and the 1980s and also Kim Ki-yŏng's fall to relative obscurity during this period, *The Housemaid* was largely forgotten, until its resurgence through retrospective screenings in film festivals during the 1990s.

14 The website can be found at http://www.knua.ac.kr/cinema/. The website, "The House of Kim Ki-young," is created by Kim Soyong and Chris Berry, and was cowritten with the graduate students in film studies at the Korean National University of the Arts.

15 See my article, "Korean Cinema and Im Kwon-Taek," in *Im Kwon-Taek: The Makings of a Korean National Cinema*, ed. David E. James and Kyung Hyun Kim (Detroit: Wayne State University Press, 2001).

16 Controversial when it first came out, *The Housemaid* continues to irk present-day audiences. After its screening in 1998 at the *Post-Colonial Classics of Korean Cinema* festival at Irvine, a couple of Korean American spectators furiously complained to me, then one of the festival programmers, about the film. They protested that *The Housemaid* should not have been programmed for it does not accurately represent Korean society.

17 This scene featured a mouth-to-mouth kissing shot, one of the first ever shown in a Korean film.

18 Kim Chin-gyu, the same actor who plays the father in *The Housemaid*, also is cast as Ch'ŏl-ho in *The Stray Bullet*.

19 Yuejin Wang, "*Red Sorghum*: Mixing Memory and Desire," in *Perspectives on Chinese Cinema*, ed. Chris Berry (London: British Film Institute, 1991), 86–87.

20 Soyoung Kim, "Questions of Women's Film," 17. Also, see "Interview with Kim Ki-young," in *Kim Ki-young: Cinema of Diabolical Desire and Death* catalog (Pusan: Pusan International Film Festival, 1997), 53.

21 Linda Williams, " 'Something Else Besides a Mother': *Stella Dallas* and the Maternal Melodrama," *Cinema Journal*, vol. 24, no. 1 (fall 1984): 2.

22 Originally published in " 'Something Else Besides a Mother'," 2–27, and reprinted in Christine Gledhill's anthology, *Home Is Where the Heart Is: Studies in Melodrama and the Woman's Film* (London: BFI, 1987), this essay is discussed at length in Linda Williams' new article, "Melodrama Revised," in *Refiguring American Film Genres: History and Theory*, ed. Nick Browne (Berkeley: University of California Press, 1998), 46.

23 See also Mary Ann Doane's chapter on *Stella Dallas* and the representation of the pathetic motherhood, "The Moving Image: Pathos and the Maternal," in *The Desire to Desire*, 70–95.

24 The scene that features the housemaid's stabbing of Cho is remarkably constructed, worthy of a scrupulous analysis here. Accompanied by a modernist music orchestra soundtrack and the diegetic sound effects of a thunderstorm in the background, the film creates the ambience of *film noir* style. The camera follows the maid in her usual dark attire clenching a knife in the kitchen and then walking up the staircase from a side angle. This is an unusual camera position that has never been featured before even though the same staircase has been photographed many times prior to this scene. Rather than the conventional long shot that had the staircase pictured either from the top or from below, the camera is placed on the side, with the handrail obstructing much of the view. We soon understand why. Following the maid as she moves with the camera in a full shot, we see her shadow reflected on the wall that is prominently featured through the banister; this escalates the drama. The sequence resumes in the piano room where the maid, in a slightly crouched position, enters and points her knife at Cho. Captured from the outside balcony in a swift tracking movement, the maid enters the room quickly from the right, bypasses Tong-sik, who stands in the front of the frame, and threatens Cho. The maid tells Miss Cho, who is shuddering with fear, to get off the piano. "You are the real bitch," announces the maid, and warns her that the next time she calls Tong-sik, "sŏnsaengnim" (mister), she will not stand pat. The camera settles briefly to a medium shot where the maid is pulled away from Cho by Tong-sik, framing Tong-sik and the maid together, separately from Cho. When Cho ignores the maid's warning, the camera moves into a closeup of the maid's face that transforms from an expression of anguish to one of rage. The next shot cuts to Cho's upper body in another closeup — neck to waist — with the knife thrusting from the lower part of the frame to the upper part. Once it strikes the target in the shoulder, the camera cuts to Cho's face. She screams and then slowly fades from the frame. During the crucial moment when the knife strikes, the drama is aurally enhanced by both Cho's scream and the sound of thunder. Visually, the shot of the knife piercing through Cho's shoulder is coordinated with artificial lightning to heighten the effect of lighting as it suddenly turns white, and then for several frames it becomes pitch black.

25 Kim Ki-yŏng's long involvement in theater before his filmmaking career (even though he was a dentist who had gone to medical school) gave him access to the conventions of avant-garde theater where the boundary between fiction and reality is deliberately obfuscated through the rejection of the imaginary border between performers and spectators. Such stylistic codes, including the actor's dramatic method acting and expressionist mise-en-scène and décor, remind us of Ufa's *The Cabinet of Dr. Caligari*, (Robert Wiene, dir., 1919). I raise this film as a

point of reference for *The Housemaid*, because they similarly insert a narrative frame to attain a dreamlike quality and also the projection of madness that cannot be clearly and safely confined to a gated space. *Dr. Caligari* ends with these words stated by the director of the mental asylum, "At last now I can understand the nature of his madness. He thinks I am that mystic Caligari. Now I see how he can be brought back to sanity again." The ambiguities of truth, the difficulty of determining who the mad man is between Francis, the young student, and the director, as well as the subsequent historical emergence of Adolf Hitler in Germany who reminded the world of the evil somnambulist have placed the film in the legendary rank. Of course, in the Korean film made in 1960, it may be an overstatement, not unlike the one Siegfried Kracauer made many decades ago, that the film's projection of ambiguity over the veracity of the extramarital affair of the father has a symbiotic relationship with the real dictator who soon came into power in Korea: Park Chung Hee. But the ambiguities between truth and fiction, and between madness and reason symptomize the historical reign of terror and intense modernization pursued by the Park administration (1961–79).

26   Jinsoo An, "Chungsanch'ŭng kajŏng ŭl yujihanŭn kŏtsŭn ŏlmana" (How Much It Takes to Maintain a Middle-Class family), *Cine 21*, no. 149 (April 20, 1998): 76–77.

27   Kathleen McHugh, *American Domesticity: From How-to Manual to Hollywood Melodrama* (New York: Oxford University Press, 1999), 131–32.

28   When I was living in Korea as a child in a middle-class home, only in the late 1970s were we able to move into a house that had a kitchen fully equipped with a kitchen sink and two faucets.

29   In the "Rat Man" case, Sigmund Freud diagnosed an obsessional young lawyer who seemed to lapse into sexual fantasies where rats were frequently his object of psychological fixation. Freud concluded that his identification of the rats was derived from a fear of syphilis deeply ingrained by the oedipal anxiety that stemmed from his father's licentious life. Noticing that his patient kept mispronouncing the word *installments* (Raten) so that it would sound just like another word, *rats* (Ratten), he also deciphered yet another meaning to "rats": money. The patient's identical pronunciation of the two words, "Raten" and "Ratten" alike, psychologically triggered his obsession over installment payments. The patient was familiar with the *installment* payments because he was negotiating with his own clients and creditors through those very financial arrangements. Although the word "rats" is a signifier, "chwi," differently enunciated from "installments" or "money" in Korean, there is a good chance that Kim Kiyŏng would have been impressed with the Freudian symbolism of the rat, prompting him to use it in *The Housemaid*. See Sigmund Freud, "Notes Upon a Case of Obsessional Neurosis ("Rat Man") and Process Notes for the Case History," in *Sigmund Freud Reader*, ed. Peter Gay (New York: W. W. Norton & Company, 1989), 331.

30   In 1985, Korea was the third largest manufacturer of pianos in the world, only behind Japan and the United States, and responsible for the production of 129,000 pianos. See Cyril Ehrlich, *The Piano: A History* (Oxford: Clarendon Press, 1990), 222.

31   James Parakilas in his book, *Piano Roles* (New Haven: Yale University Press, 1999), states that many of the famous impressionists, Paul Cezanne, Edouard Manet, Edgar Degas, Gustave Caillebotte, and Auguste Renoir used the image of "the woman at the piano" as an increasingly popular theme. He writes, "[t]hese illustrations attest to the centrality of piano lessons in feminine education, as well as to the cultural currency of the 'woman at the piano' motif" (p. 216). During my adolescence in Korea, one of the images that stuck with me is a Van Gogh

painting of a well-proportioned woman seated in front of an upright piano in a rural bourgeois home. Such an image was common and pervasive in Korea, emblematic of ideal femininity.

32 I thank Nancy Abelmann for pointing this out to me.

33 Leslie Regan Shade, "Women and Television," *Postmodern Culture (PMC)* 3, no. 3 (May 1993). See http://jefferson.village.virginia.edu/pmc/.

34 In *Shiri* (Kang Che-gyu, dir., 1999), the biggest hit film of the decade, Ch'oe Min-sik plays a villainous North Korean terrorist who conspires against his own leader in order to force a war between the North and the South. He continued to develop this screen persona, playing the maverick painter in the latest Im Kwon-Taek film, *Ch'wihwasŏn* (2002).

35 Chris Berry, "Introducing 'Mr. Monster': Kim Ki-young and the Critical Economy of the Globalized Art-House Cinema," in *Post-Colonial Classics of Korean Cinema* catalog, 42.

9 "Each Man Kills the Thing He Loves": Transgressive Agents, National Security, and Blockbuster Aesthetics in *Shiri* and *Joint Security Area*

1 During the postclimax interrogation, Agent Yu tells his authorities that the tragic division of the two Koreas had forced Yi Pang-hŭi to assume the identity of "Hydra, a beast from the Greek myth."

2 Barbara Creed, *The Monstrous-Feminine: Film, Feminism, Psychoanalysis* (London: Routledge, 1993), 7.

3 In the South Korean military post where Su-hyŏk works, there is a bulletin that officially states that "any communication — verbal, bodily, or by hand signal — with North Korean military personnel is strictly prohibited."

4 The theme song repeatedly used in the film is "ŏnŭ idŭngbyŏng ŭi norae" ("The Song of an Anonymous Private"), sung by Kim Kwang-sŏk, a folk singer who mysteriously committed suicide at the height of his young career. The song is an important melodramatic text, denoting the lamentation of youth and the separation anxiety of a man who is waiting for a train to take him to a military training camp. When Lieutenant Ch'oe breaks up the farewell party on the fated night, this song is also interrupted in the middle.

5 Julian Stringer, " 'Your Tender Smiles Give Me Strength': Paradigms of Masculinity in John Woo's *A Better Tomorrow* and *The Killer*," *Screen* 38:1 (spring 1997): 32.

6 The melodramatic longing for the Other in *Shiri* of course also exists, but only when the asexual Yi Pang-hŭi takes off her black "terrorist" attire and transforms into Yi Myŏng-hyŏn.

7 David Scott Diffrient, "Seoul as Cinematic Cityscape: Shiri and the Politico-Aesthetics of Invisibility," *Asian Cinema*, vol. 11, no. 2 (fall/winter 2000): 82.

8 René Girard, *Violence and the Sacred*, trans. Patrick Gregory (Baltimore: Johns Hopkins University Press, 1977), 48.

9 According to the figures distributed by the Korean Film Commission (KOFIC) in winter 2002, the promotion and advertising (P&A) fee comprised of one-third (33 percent) of the entire production cost of an average film. From 1997 to 2001 the P&A fee had increased 364.5 percent. KOFIC releases figures and statistics of the Korean film industry through its English-language quarterly, *Korean Film Observatory*. To request a copy, visit its website: www.kofic.co.kr.

10 Because distribution rights to the region outside Seoul are sold in advance and ticket sales are not computerized in the theaters outside the countryside, the nationwide box-office figures can only be estimated.

11　*Hangyŏre*, March 6, 1999, p. 19.

12　"Hwanran . . . oehwa suip opch'e saengjon momburim" (Currency Exchange Crisis Makes Foreign Film Import Businesses Desperate for Survival), *Chungang Ilbo*, December 24, 1997, p. 25.

13　The high demand for Korean films in the Asian market was precipitated by the popularity of Korean television programs in China and Southeast Asian nations slightly before Korean films became popular in these regions. In 1999, the export figures of Korean television programs reached well over U.S.$12 million, far more than the export figures of Korean movies that year (U.S.$5.73 million). The Asian market was responsible for the high demand for Korean programming, comprising more than 70 percent of the total sales revenue. For instance, a long series family melodrama, *Sarang i mwŏgilrae* (*Whatever Love Is*) was broadcast on CCTV, one of China's national channels, in 1997; it recorded a rating that was the third highest in the nation's history. The Korean stars of this television drama instantaneously became China's most appealing actors. Many of the dance-music pop stars of Korea are also popular idols in China and other Asian countries. "Hanguk norae wa yŏnghwa, Asia sijang ŭl hwipssŭlda" (Korean Music and Movies Sweep the Asian Market), *Wŏlgan Chosŏn* (*Monthly Chosun*), July 2000, internet version, http://monthly.chosun.com/.

14　Euphemistically termed after the computer chip megahertz speed, the "386-generation," referes to the people who are in their 30s, entered college during the 1980s, and were born in the 1960s.

15　In the special feature section of the DVD version of *Foul King* (*Panch'ikwang*, 2000), one of the most popular comedy films ever made, its director, Kim Chi-un, though he works within genre constraints, discusses the films of Tarkovsky, Cassavetes, and Bresson as the most inspirational foundation of his own work.

16　Yoo Chang-yup, "Money Pouring into Film Industry along with Concerns," *Korea Times*, January 18, 2001, 11.

17　The English-language remake rights of several blockbuster films like *My Wife Is a Gangster* (*Chop'ok manura*, Cho Chin-gyu, dir.) and *Hi, Dharma* (*Talma ya nolja*, Pak Ch'ol-gwan, dir., 2001) were sold to Hollywood studios in 2001 and in 2002. Warner Bros., MGM, and Dreamworks SKG have all paid sums of around U.S.$1.1 million for these rights.

18　Toby Miller et al., *Global Hollywood* (London: British Film Institute, 2001), 1.

19　Tony Rayns, "Cinephile Nation," *Sight and Sound*, vol. 9, no. 1 (January 1998): 24.

20　For instance, *Nabi* (Mun Sŭng-uk, dir., 2001), a winner of many awards in international film festivals, was given only a few days of courteous theatrical run. One of the most impressive films made in 2001, *Nakt'a(dŭl)* (*Camel[s]*), directed by Park Ki-yong, remains still unreleased at the time of this writing because it is a low-budget black-and-white movie.

21　David Bordwell, "The Art Cinema as a Mode of Film Practice," in *Film Theory and Criticism*, 5th ed., ed. Leo Braudy and Marshall Cohen (New York: Oxford University Press, 1999), 720.

22　This includes the sale of box-office receipts, video, DVD, and television copyrights, and overseas sales in the year 2002. See *Korean Film Observatory*, no. 7 (winter 2002/3): 12.

23　Freud, *Civilization and its Discontents* (New York: W. W. Norton & Company, 1989), 61–62, n. 7.

24　I am here quoting from Laura Mulvey's famous line in her essay, "Visual Pleasure and Narrative Cinema," where she states that "sadism demands a story, depends on making something happen, forcing a change in another person, a battle of will and strength, victory/defeat, all occurring in a linear time with a beginning and an end." This quote anchors an important discussion on narrative structure and gender in Teresa De Lauretis's *Alice Doesn't: Feminism, Semiotics, Cinema* (Bloomington: Indiana University Press, 1984), 103. It also appears in D. N. Rodowick's *The Difficulty of Difference: Psychoanalysis, Sexual Difference and Film Theory* (New York: Routledge, 1991), 5.

25 Roland Barthes, "Introduction to the Structural Analysis of Narratives," in *Image-Music-Text*, trans. Stephen Heath (New York: Hill and Wang, 1977), 79.

SELECT FILMOGRAPHY OF MAJOR DIRECTORS

OF THE NEW KOREAN CINEMA

Chang Chin (b. 1971)
> *The Happenings* (*Kimakhin sanaedŭl* 1998)
> *The Spy* (*Kanch'ŏp Li Ch'ŏljin*, 1999)
> *Guns and Talks* (*K'ilrŏdŭl ŭi suda*, 2001)

Chang Sŏn-u (Jang Sun-woo, b. 1952)
> *Seoul Jesus* (*Seoul Yesu*, co-dir. with Sŏnu Wan, 1986)
> *Age of Success* (*Sŏnggong shidae*, 1988)
> *Lovers in Woomuk-Baemi* (*Umukpaemi ŭi sarang*, 1989)
> *Road to the Racetracks* (*Kyŏngmajang kanŭn kil*, 1991)
> *Hwa-om-kyung* (*Hwaŏmgyŏng*, 1993)
> *To You, from Me* (*Nŏ ege narŭl ponenda*, 1994)
> *Cinema on the Road* (A feature documentary, 1995)
> *A Petal* (*Kkotnip*, 1996)
> *Timeless, Bottomless Bad Movie* (*Nappŭn yŏnghwa*, 1997)
> *Lies* (*Kŏjinmal*, 1999)
> *The Resurrection of the Little Match Girl* (*Sŏngnyang
> p'ali sonyŏ ŭi chaerim*, 2002)

Chŏng Chi-yŏng (b. 1946)
> *Mist Whispers Like a Woman* (*Angae nŭn yŏja ch'ŏrŏm
> soksakinda*, 1982)
> *Color of Memories* (*Ch'uŏk ŭi pit*, 1984)
> *Street Musician* (*Kŏri ŭi aksa*, 1987)

A Woman in Crisis (Wigi ŭi yŏja, 1987)
A Forest for Women to Hide In (Yŏja ka sumnŭn sup, 1988)
Sanbaeam (Sanbaeam, 1988)
The Southern Army (Nambugun, 1990)
Beyond the Mountain (Sansani pusŏjin irŭm iyŏ, 1991)
White Badge (Hayan chŏnjaeng, 1992)
The Life and Death of the Hollywood Kid (Hŏlriudŭ
    k'idŭ ŭi saengae, 1994)
Black Jack (Pŭlraek Chaek, 1997)
The Naked Being (Kka, 1998)

Hŏ Chin-ho (b. 1963)
Christmas in August (Palwŏl ŭi k'urisŭmasŭ, 1998)
One Fine Spring Day (Pom nal ŭn kanda, 2001)

Hong Sang-su (Hong Sangsoo, b. 1960)
The Day a Pig Fell into the Well (Tweji ga umul e ppajin nal,
    1996)
The Power of Kangwon Province (Kangwon do ŭi him, 1998)
Virgin Stripped Bare by Her Bachelors (O! Su-jŏng, 2000)
Turning Gate (Saenghwal ŭi palgyŏn, 2002)

Im Kwŏn-t'aek (Im Kwon-Taek, b. 1936) Since 1978
The Evergreen Tree (Sangnoksu, 1978)
The Little Adventurer (Chŏ p'ado wi e ŏmma ŏlgŭri, 1978)
The Genealogy (Chokpo, 1978)
Near Yet Far Away (Kakkapkkodo mŏngil, 1979)
Again Tomorrow (Naeil tto naeil, 1979)
The Divine Bow (Singung, 1979)
The Hidden Hero (Kippal ŏmnŭn kisu, 1979)
The Wealthy Woman (Pokppuin, 1980)
Pursuit of Death (Tchakk'o, 1980)
High School Tears (Usang ŭi nunmul, 1981)
Mandala (Mandara, 1981)
Abenko Green Beret (Abengo kosugundan, 1982)
The Polluted Ones (Oyŏmtoen chasiktŭl, 1982)
In the Bosom of a Butterfly (Nabip'um esŏ urŏtta, 1982)
Village in the Mist (Angae maŭl, 1982)
Daughter of the Flames (Pul ŭi ttal, 1983)
The Eternal Flow (Hŭrŭnŭn kangmul ŭl ŏtchi magŭrya, 1984)
Gilsottum (Kilsottŭm, 1985)
Ticket (Tik'et, 1986)
Surrogate Mother (Ssibaji, 1986)
Diary of King (Yŏnsan ilgi, 1987)
Adada (Adada, 1988)

Come, Come, Come Upward (*Ajeaje paraaje*, 1989)
The General's Son (*Changun ŭi adŭl*, 1990)
The General's Son 2 (*Changun ŭi adŭl 2*, 1991)
Fly High, Run Far: Kae Byok (*Kaebyŏk*, 1991)
The General's Son 3 (*Changun ŭi adŭl 3*, 1992)
Sopyonje (*Sŏp'yŏnje*, 1993)
The Taebaek Mountains (*T'aebaek sanmaek*, 1994)
Festival (*Ch'ukje*, 1996)
Chang, the Prostitute (*Nonŭn kyejip, Chang*, 1997)
Chunhyang (*Ch'unhyangdyŏn*, 2000)
Chihwaseon (*Ch'wihwasŏn*, 2002)

Im Sang-su (b. 1962)
Girls Night Out (*Ch'ŏnyŏ dŭl ŭi chŏnyŏk shiksa*, 1998)
Tears (*Nurmul*, 2000)
A Good Lawyer's Wife (*Param nan kajok*, 2003)

Im Sun-rye (b. 1960)
Three Friends (*Se Ch'ingu*, 1996)
Waikiki Brothers (*Waik'ik'i Pŭradŏsŭ*, 2001)

Kang Che-gyu (Kang Jae-gyu, b. 1962)
The Ginkgo Bed (*Ŭnhaeng namu ch'imdae*, 1996)
Shiri (*Swiri*, 1999)

Kang U-sŏk (b. 1960)
Sweet Brides (*Talk'omhan shinbudŭl*, 1988)
School Record Isn't Proportional to Happiness (*Haengbok ŭn sŏngjŏksun i anijanayo*, 1989)
I Stand Up Everyday (*Na nŭn nal mada irŏsŏnda*, 1990)
Who Has Seen the Dragon's Toenail? (*Nuga yong ŭi palt'ot ŭl poatnŭnga*, 1991)
Teenage Love Song (*Yŏlahop chŏlmang kkŭt e purŭnŭn hana ŭi sarang norae*, 1991)
Until Twenty (*Sŭmu sal kkajiman salgo sipp'ŏyo*, 1991)
Mr. Mamma (*Misŏt'ŏ Mamma*, 1992)
Two Cops (*T'u K'apsŭ*, 1993)
How to Top My Wife (*Manura chukigi*, 1994)
Two Cops 2 (*T'u K'apsŭ 2*, 1996)
Bedroom and Courtroom (*Saengkwabu Wijaryo Ch'ŏnggu sosong*, 1998)
Public Enemy (*Kongkong ŭi chŏk*, 2002)

Kim Chi-un (b. 1964)
The Quiet Family (*Choyonghan kajok*, 1998)

Foul King (*Panch'ikwang*, 2000)
A Tale of Two Sisters (*Changhwa wa Horgryŏn*, 2003)

Kim Hong-jun (b. 1956)
Ma Vie En Rose (*Changmi bit insaeng*, 1994)
Jungle Story (*Chŏnggŭl sŭt'ori*, 1996)

Kim Ki-dŏk (b. 1960)
Crocodile (*Akŏ*, 1996)
Wild Animals (*Yasaeng tongmul poho kuhyŏk*, 1997)
Birdcage Inn (*Paran taemun*, 1998)
The Isle (*Sŏm*, 2000)
Real Fiction (*Silje sanghwang*, 2000)
Address Unknown (Such'wiin pulmyŏng, 2001)
A Bad Guy (*Nappŭn namja*, 2002)
Coast Guard (*Haeansŏn*, 2002)
Spring, Summer, Fall, Winter . . . and Spring (*Pom, yŏrŭm, kyŏul. . . kŭrigo pom*, 2003)

Kim Ŭi-sŏk (b. 1957)
Marriage Story (*Kyŏlhon yiyagi*, 1992)
That Man, That Woman (*Kŭ yŏja Kŭ namja*, 1993)
Gun and Gut (*Ch'ongjapi*, 1995)
Holiday in Seoul (*Hollideyi in Seoul*, 1997)
The Great Chef (Pukgyŏng panjŏm, 1999)

Pae Ch'ang-ho (b. 1953)
People in a Slum (*Kkobang tongnae saram dŭl*, 1982)
The Iron Men (*Ch'ŏlin dŭl*, 1982)
The Flower of Equator (*Chŏkdo ŭi kkot*, 1983)
Whale Hunting (*Korae sanyang*, 1984)
So Warm Was That Winter (*Kŭ hae kyŏul ŭn ttattŭthaenne*, 1984)
Deep Blue Night (*Kipko p'urun pam*, 1984)
Whale Hunting 2 (*Korae sanyang 2*, 1985)
Hwang Jin-I (*Hwang Chin-yi*, 1986)
Our Sweet Days of Youth (*Kippŭn uri chŏlmŭn nal*, 1987)
Hello! God (*Annyŏnghaseyo hananim*, 1987)
Dream (*Kkum*, 1990)
The Stairway to Heaven (*Ch'ŏnguk ŭi kyedan*, 1991)
The Young Man (*Chŏlmŭn namja*, 1994)
Love Story (*Rŏbŭ sŭt'ori*, 1996)
My Heart (*Chŏng*, 1999)
The Last Witness (*Hŭksusŏn*, 2001)

Pae Yong-gyun (Bae Yong-kyun, b. 1951)
   Why Has Bodhi-Dharma Left for the East (*Talma ga tongjjok
   ŭro gan kkadalgŭn*, 1989)
   The People in White (*Kŏmŭna ttang e hŭina paeksŏng*, 1995)

Pak Ch'an-uk (b. 1963)
   The Moon Is What the Sun Dreams Of (*Tal ŭn . . . hae ga
   kkunŭn kkum*, 1992)
   A Gang of Trio (*Saminjo*, 1997)
   Joint Security Area (*Kongdong kyŏngbi kuyŏk JSA*, 2000)
   Sympathy for Mr. Vengeance (*Poksu nŭn na ŭi kŏt*, 2002)
   Old Boy (*Oldŭ poyi*, 2003)

Pak Ch'ŏl-su (b. 1948) Since 1995
   301.302 (1995)
   Farewell My Darling (*Haksaeng pugun shinwi*, 1996)
   Push! Push! (*Sanpuingwa*, 1997)
   Kazoku Cinema (*Kajok sinema*, 1998)
   Bongja (*Pongja*, 2000)

Pak Chong-wŏn (b. 1958)
   Kuro Arirang (1989)
   Our Twisted Hero (*Uri dŭl ŭi ilgŭrojin yŏngung*, 1992)
   Eternal Empire (*Yŏngwŏnhan cheguk*, 1995)
   Rainbow Trout (*Songŏ*, 1999)
   Paradise Villa (*P'aradaisŭ pilra*, 2001)

Pak Ki-hyŏng (b. 1967)
   Whispering Corridors (*Yŏgo kwedam*, 1998)
   Secret (*Pimil*, 2000)
   Acacia (*Ak'asia*, 2003)

Pak Ki-yong (b. 1960)
   Motel Cactus (*Mot'el sŏninjang*, 1997)
   Camel(s) (*Nakt'a[dŭl]*, 2001)

Pak Kwang-su (Park Kwang-su, b. 1955)
   Chilsu and Mansu (*Ch'il-su wa Man-su*, 1988)
   Black Republic (*Kŭ dŭl do uri ch'ŏrŏm*, 1990)
   Berlin Report (*Perŭlrin rip'ot'ŭ*, 1991)
   To the Starry Island (*Kŭsŏm e kagosipta*, 1993)
   A Single Spark (*Arŭmdaun ch'ŏngnyŏn Chŏn T'ae-il*, 1996)
   Uprising (*Yi Chae-su ŭi nan*, 1999)

Pong Chun-ho (b. 1969)

Barking Dogs Never Bite (*Pŭlrandasŭ ŭi kae*, 2000)

Memories of Murder (*Salin ŭi ch'uŏk*, 2003)

Pyŏn Yŏng-ju (b. 1966)

Murmuring (*Najŭn moksori*, A feature documentary, 1995)

Habitual Sadness (*Najŭn moksori 2*, A feature documentary, 1997)

My Own Breathing (*Sumgyŏl*, A feature documentary, 2000)

Ardor (*Milae*, 2002)

Yi Ch'ang-dong (Lee Chang-dong, b. 1954)

Green Fish (*Ch'orok mulgogi*, 1997)

Peppermint Candy (*Pakha sat'ang*, 1999)

Oasis (*Oasisŭ*, 2002)

Yi Chae-yong (b. 1965)

An Affair (*Chŏngsa*, 1998)

Asako in Ruby Shoes (*Sunaebo*, 2000)

Untold Scandal (*Sŭk'aendal*, 2003)

Yi Chang-ho (b. 1945)

Home of the Stars (*Pyŏldŭl ŭi kohyang*, 1974)

It Rained Yesterday (*Ŏje naerin pi*, 1974)

You Too Became a Star (*Nŏ tto han pyŏl i twaeŏ*, 1975)

Yes, Goodbye Today (*Kŭrae kŭrae onŭl ŭn annyŏng*, 1976)

A Fine, Windy Day (*Param purŏ chŭn nal*, 1980)

They Shot the Sun (*Kŭ dŭl ŭn t'aeyang ŭl ssoatta*, 1981)

People in Dark (*Ŏdum ŭi chasikdŭl*, 1981)

Come Low Down unto Us (*Najŭndero imhasosŏ*, 1982)

Pine Bough (*Ilsongjŏng p'urŭn sol ŭn*, 1983)

Declaration of Fools (*Pabo sŏnŏn*, 1983)

Widow's Dance (*Kwabu ch'um*, 1983)

Between the Knees (*Murŭp kwa murŭp sai*, 1984)

Oudong (*Ŏudong*, 1985)

Alien Baseball Team (*Yi Chang-ho ŭi oeingudan*, 1986)

The Man with Three Coffins (*Nagŭne nŭn kil esŏdo shwiji annŭnda*, 1987)

Y Story: Personal Experience (*Wai ŭi ch'ehŏm*, 1987)

Miss Rhino and Mr. Wagon (*Missŭ K'oppŭlso Misŭt'ŏ K'orando*, 1989)

Myungja Akiko Sonya (*Myŏngja Akkiko Sonya*, 1992)

Declaration of Geniuses (*Ch'ŏnjae sŏnŏn*, 1995)

Yi Chŏng-hyang (b. 1964)

Art Museum by the Zoo (Misulgwan yŏp dongmulwŏn, 1998)

The Way Home (Chip ŭro . . ., 2002)

Yi Hyŏn-sŭng (b. 1961)

The Blue in You (Kŭ dae an ŭi pŭlru, 1992)

Sunset into the Neon Lights (Neon sok ŭro noŭl chida, 1995)

Il Mare (Siwŏlae, 2000)

Yi Myŏng-se (b. 1957)

Gagman (Kegŭmaen, 1988)

My Love, My Bride (Na ŭi sarang, na ŭi shinbu, 1990)

First Love (Ch'ŏt sarang, 1993)

Affliction of Man (Namja nŭn koerowŏ, 1995)

Their Last Love Affair (Chidok han sarang, 1996)

Nowhere to Hide (Injŏng sajŏng polgŏt ŏpta, 1999)

Yŏ Kyun-dong (b. 1958)

Out to the World (Sesang pakküro, 1994)

Porno Man (Maen, 1995)

Filmmaking (Chukinŭn iyagi, 1997)

La Belle (Miin, 2000)

INDEX

Cumings, Bruce, 81, 88, 289 n.8, 290 n.23, 300 n.21
Curtiz, Michael, 159

Daewoo, 109, 292 n.10
Day a Pig Fell into the Well, The (Tweji ga umul e ppajin nal), 13, 14, 21–22, 203–6, 208, 210, 223–30, 236–27
De Sica, Vittorio, 303 n.9
Death, 200; accidental, 56, 176–77, 285 n.4; casualties of war, 97, 100–106, 290 n.27; of a child, 229, 242–43, 244, 250; in history, 16, 17, 107, 110, 280 n.31; murder, 41, 42, 48, 77–78, 159, 177, 221, 228–29, 232, 233, 236, 239–40, 244, 250, 263, 292 n.19, 302 n.48; narration of, 115, 118–19; of natural cause, 40, 56; possibility of, 14; protest against state, 113, 117–19, 150–51, 288 n.30; sacrificial, 16, 111, 113; sexual pleasure and, 12–13, 176, 205, 224, 269; shooting by the authorities, 65, 69, 75–76, 97, 99, 123, 141, 288 n.24, 294 n.40; suicide, 13, 23, 111, 113, 117–19, 141, 150–51, 159, 229–30, 244, 258, 268–69, 310 n.4; trauma and, 44, 75–76, 113, 117, 246, 275; wish, 55; of women; 54, 56, 63, 102, 106, 123, 223, 228–30, 232, 233, 239–40, 257, 278. *See also* Masculinity: and death
Declaration of Fools (Pabo sŏnŏn), 54, 141
Declaration of Geniuses (Ch'ŏnjae sŏnon), 287 n.19
Deleuze, Gilles, 72, 164, 299 n.12, 304 n.9
Derrida, Jacques, 208, 209, 213
Diary of the Korean-Japanese War, The (Nan-jung Ilgi), 16
Différance, 206, 209, 213, 303 n.4
Diffrient, David Scott, 267
Disease and disorder: epileptic spasm, 278 n.3; Innate Immunodeficiency Syndrome, 260; mental insanity, 21, 121, 127, 284 n.22, 308 n.25; polio, 247; syphilis, 251, 309 n.29; venereal disease, 205; verbal stammer, 34, 39–40, 278 n.3
Divorce, 237
Doane, Mary Anne, 307 n.12
Documentary, 187, 190, 192, 199–200, 294 n.40, 303 n.61, 304 n.14
Dominant fiction, 16, 19, 33
Duras, Marguerite, 295 n.47

Easy Rider, 53
Ego, 50, 136, 142, 155, 159, 163, 210, 211
El, 162, 299 n.5, 304 n.13
Elevators, 223, 247, 249–50
Elsaesser, Thomas, 108, 283 n.10, 298 nn.32–33, 299 n.7

Family, 20, 28, 48, 55, 60–66, 78, 80, 85, 87–92, 95, 97–106, 108, 115, 124, 138, 141, 143–44, 165–69, 176–77, 234, 235–37, 241–46; dead father and, 61, 64, 65, 147, 287, 297 n.18; fragmentation of, 2, 28, 40, 52–66, 68, 71, 77–78, 89, 97–98, 100–106, 121, 143–46, 229; home and, 2, 5, 27, 52–53, 58–59, 60, 64–65, 77–78, 84, 87, 89, 98–99, 101–3, 161, 246–47, 288 n.3; patriarchy, 22, 31, 33, 41, 46–48, 63–66, 78, 80, 82–92, 103–5, 115, 119, 123, 139, 150–52, 164, 175, 182, 246, 261, 266, 289 n.15, 290 n.21, 301 n.43, 309 n.25; reunion, 7, 57–59, 62, 145–46, 285 nn.5–6, 287 n.17. *See also* Adultery; Divorce; Patricide; Women: domesticity and; as mothers
Fantasy, 1, 5, 9, 11, 26, 42, 70, 75, 123–24, 136, 143, 144, 147–48, 166–67, 174, 179, 224, 228, 229, 240, 268–69, 276, 305 n.25
Farrell, Kirby, 291 n.3
Fascism, 108, 111, 120, 126–27, 165–69, 176, 295 nn.47, 49, 299 n.7, 300 n.16, 308 n.25
Fassbinder, Rainer Werner, 109, 126, 292 n.18
Fetish, 38, 59, 60, 62–64, 84, 86, 118, 136, 142, 147, 163, 165–69, 172, 179, 183–84, 196, 243, 247–48, 254, 269, 299 n.5
Film criticism, 35, 61, 120, 133, 236, 242, 278 n.9, 283 n.6, 302 n.52, 303 n.1
Film festivals, 8, 19, 27, 135, 177, 231, 240, 273–74, 290 nn.22, 26, 306 n.6, 307 n.13
Film style, 58, 61, 62, 70, 91, 118–19, 155, 156, 169–71, 187–89, 198–202, 209, 220, 229–30, 240–41, 246, 256, 267, 277 n.2, 308 n.24
Fine, Windy Day, A (Param purŏ choun nal), 6, 11, 20, 29, 34–43, 45, 48, 141, 283 n.11
Flower Girl, The (Kkot p'anŭn ch'ŏnyŏ), 285 n.1, 287 n.17
Flower of Hell (Chiokhwa), 32
Folktales, 286 n.9
Forman, Milos, 230
Forrest Gump, 120
Foucault, Michel, 196
Foul King (Panch'ikwang), 306 n.10, 311 n.15

Kyung Hyun Kim is Associate Professor of East Asian Languages
and Literatures at the University of California, Irvine.

Library of Congress Cataloging-in-Publication Data
Kim, Kyung Hyun
The remasculinization of Korean cinema / Kyung Hyun Kim.
p. cm. — (Asia-Pacific)
Includes bibliographical references and index.
ISBN 0-8223-3278-7 (cloth : alk. paper) —
ISBN 0-8223-3267-1 (pbk. : alk. paper)
1. Motion pictures — Korea (South).   2. Men in motion pictures.
3. Masculinity in motion pictures.   I. Title.   II. Series
PN1993.5.K6 K524   2004
791.43'6521'09519 — dc22

2003016644